Library of Ancient Inscriptions

# BABYLONIAN AND ASSYRIAN LAWS, CONTRACTS AND LETTERS

BY

C. H. W. JOHNS, M.A.

LECTURER IN QUEENS' COLLEGE, CAMBRIDGE, AND
KING'S COLLEGE, LONDON

THE LAWBOOK EXCHANGE, LTD.
UNION, NEW JERSEY
1999

ISBN 1-58477-022-8

*Printed in the United States of America*
*On Acid-Free Paper*

**The Lawbook Exchange, Ltd.**
965 Jefferson Avenue
Union, New Jersey 07083-8605

*Please see catalogue at rear of this volume*
*or our website* www.lawbookexchange.com
*for a selection of our other reprints.*

**Library of Congress Cataloging-in-Publication Data**

Johns, C.H.W. (Claude Hermann Walter), 1857-1920.
Babylonian and Assyrian laws, contracts, and letters / by C.H.W. Johns.
p. cm.
Originally published : Edinburgh : T. & T. Clark, 1904. (Library of ancient inscriptions ; 6).
Includes bibliographical references and index.
ISBN 1-58477-022-8 (cloth : alk. paper)
1. Law, Assyro-Babylonian. 2. Assyro-Babylonian letters.
3. Civilization, Assyro-Babylonian—Sources. I. Title.
II. Series: Library of ancient inscriptions ; 6.
KL1606.5.J64 1999
340.5'35—dc21 99-32862
CIP

Library of Ancient Inscriptions

# BABYLONIAN AND ASSYRIAN LAWS, CONTRACTS AND LETTERS

# THE LIBRARY OF ANCIENT INSCRIPTIONS

PREPARED BY

Leading Scholars in America and Europe

UNDER THE GENERAL EDITORSHIP OF

CHARLES FOSTER KENT, PH.D.

WOOLSEY PROFESSOR OF BIBLICAL LITERATURE IN YALE UNIVERSITY

AND

FRANK KNIGHT SANDERS, PH.D., D.D.

PROFESSOR OF BIBLICAL HISTORY AND ARCHÆOLOGY IN YALE UNIVERSITY

ARRANGEMENT OF VOLUMES

I. **History of the Discovery and Decipherment of the Ancient Inscriptions**

PART I. Semitic Inscriptions. By Professor CHARLES FOSTER KENT, Ph.D.

PART II. Egyptian Inscriptions. By Dr. GEORGE A. REISNER, Director of the Hearst Archæological Expedition in Egypt.

II. **Old and New Babylonian Historical Inscriptions**

By Professor CHRISTOPHER JOHNSTON, Ph.D., of Johns Hopkins University.

III. **Assyrian Historical Inscriptions**

By Professor MORRIS JASTROW, Jr., Ph.D., of the University of Pennsylvania.

IV. **Inscriptions of Palestine, Syria, and Arabia**

By Professor CHARLES CUTLER TORREY, Ph.D., D.D., of Yale University.

V. **Egyptian Historical and Biographical Inscriptions**

By Professor W. MAX MÜLLER, Ph.D., of the Reformed Episcopal Church Seminary, Philadelphia.

VI. **Babylonian and Assyrian Laws, Contracts, and Letters** (*Now Ready*)

By the Reverend C. H. W. JOHNS, M.A., of Cambridge University.

VII. **Egyptian Tales, Proverbs, Poems, and Belles Lettres**

By Professor G. MASPERO, D.C.L., Directeur de la Service de l'Antiquité in Egypt.

VIII. **Babylonian and Assyrian Epics, Penitential Psalms, Proverbs, and Religious Texts**

By Professor FRIEDRICH DELITZSCH, Ph.D., of Berlin University.

IX. **Egyptian Religious, Magical, Medical, and Scientific Texts; Legal and Business Documents.**

By FRANCIS LLEWELLYN GRIFFITH, M.A., F.S.A., of Oxford University.

Library of Ancient Inscriptions

# BABYLONIAN AND ASSYRIAN LAWS, CONTRACTS AND LETTERS

BY

C. H. W. JOHNS, M.A.
LECTURER IN QUEENS' COLLEGE, CAMBRIDGE, AND
KING'S COLLEGE, LONDON

EDINBURGH
T. & T. CLARK
1904

Printed by the Trow Directory, Printing and Bookbinding Company
New York, U. S. A.

TO

MY MOTHER

IN MEMORY OF LOVING HELP

# PREFACE

The social institutions, manners, and customs of an ancient people must always be of deep interest for all those to whom nothing is indifferent that is human. But even for modern thinkers, engrossed in the practical problems of our advanced civilization, the records of antiquity have a direct value. We are better able to deal with the complicated questions of the day if we are acquainted with the simpler issues of the past. We may not set them aside as too remote to have any influence upon us. Not long ago men looked to Greece and Rome for political models. We can hardly estimate the influence which that following of antiquity has had upon our own social life.

But there is a deeper influence even than Greek politics and Roman law, still powerfully at work among us, which we owe to a more remote past. We should probably resent the idea that we were not dominated by Christian principles. So far as they are distinct from Greek and Roman ideals, most of them have their roots in Jewish thought. When a careful investigation is made, it will probably be found that the most distinctive Christian principles in our times are those which were taken over from Jewish life, since the Old Testament still more widely appeals to us than the New. But those Jewish ideas regarding society have been inherited in turn from the far more ancient Babylonian civilization. It is startling to find how much that we have thought distinctively our own has really come down to us from that great people who ruled the land of the two streams. We need not be ashamed of anything we can trace back so far. It is from no savage ancestors that it descends to us. It bears the "hall mark," not only of extreme antiquity but of sterling worth.

The people, who were so highly educated, so deeply religious, so humane and intelligent, who developed such just laws, and such permanent institutions, are not unprofitable acquaintances. A right-thinking citizen of a modern city would probably feel more at home in ancient Babylon than in mediæval Europe. When we have won our way through the difficulties of the language and the writing to the real meaning of their purpose and come into touch with the men who wrote and spoke, we greet brothers. Rarely in the history of antiquity can we find so much of which we heartily approve, so little to condemn. The primitive virtues, which we flatter ourselves that we have retained, are far more in evidence than those primitive vices which we know are not extinct among us. The average Babylonian strikes us as a just, good man, no wild savage, but a law-abiding citizen, a faithful husband, good father, kind son, firm friend, industrious trader, or careful man of business. We know from other sources that he was no contemptible warrior, no mean architect or engineer. He might be an excellent artist, modelling in clay, carving rocks, and painting walls. His engraving of seals was superb. His literary work was of high order. His scientific attainments were considerable.

When we find so much to approve we may naturally ask the reason. Some may say it is because right was always right everywhere. Others will try to trace our inheritance of thought. At any rate, we may accord our praise to those who seized so early in the history of the race upon views which have proved to be of the greatest and most permanent value. Perhaps nowhere else than in the archives of the old Assyrian and Babylonian temples could we find such an instructive exhibition of the development of the art of expressing facts and ideas in written language. The historical inscriptions, indeed, exhibit a variety of incidents, but have a painful monotony of subject and a conventional grandeur of style. In the contracts we find men struggling for exactness of statement and clearness of diction. In the letters we have untrammelled directness of address, without regard to models of expression. In the one case we have a scrupulous following of precedent, in the other freedom from rule or custom. One result is that while we are nearly always sure what the contract said and intended, we often are completely unable to see why the given phrases were used for their particular purpose. Every phrase is technical and legal, to a degree that often defies translation. On the other hand, the letters are often as colloquial in style as the contracts are formal. Hence they swarm with words and phrases for which no parallel can be found. Unless the purpose of the letter is otherwise clear, these words and phrases may be quite unintelligible. Any side issue may be introduced, or even a totally irrelevant topic. While the point of these disconnected sentences may have been perfectly clear to the recipient of the message, we cannot possibly understand them, unless we have an intimate acquaintance with the private life and personal relations of the two correspondents.

Hence, quite apart from the difficulties of copying such ancient inscriptions, often defaced, originally ill-written, and complicated by the personal tastes of individual scribes for odd spellings, rare words, or stock phrases; besides the difficulties of a grammar and vocabulary only partly made out; the very nature of both contracts and letters implies special obscurities. But the peculiarities of these obscurities are such as to excite curiosity and stimulate research.

The wholesome character of the subject-matter, the absence of all possibility of a revision in party interests, the probable straightforward honesty of the purpose, act like a tonic to the ordinary student of history. Nowhere can he find more reliable material for his purpose, if only he can understand it. The history he may reconstruct will be that of real men, whose character and circumstances have not yet been misrepresented. He will find the human nature singularly like what he may observe about him, once he has seen through superficial manners and customs.

One important point cannot be too strongly insisted upon. Numerous as our documents are, they do not form a continuous series. One collection is chiefly composed of temple archives, another comes from a family deed-chest, where only such documents were preserved as were of value to the persons who collected them. At one period we may have a great number of documents relating to one sort of transaction. In the next period we may have hardly any reference to similar transactions, but very complete evidence regarding other matters. We may assume that, in such a conservative country as Assyria or Babylonia, things went on for ages in much the same way. Conclusions rightly drawn for early times are probably true for the later periods also. As far as we can test this assumption, it holds good. We may even assume that the converse is true, but that is more doubtful.

Thus, we find that the practice of taking a pledge as security for debt is fully established for later times and we may therefore hesitate to deny its existence in early periods, although we have no direct evidence on the point. This absence of evidence may be due to the nature of the early collections. It may be an accident. It may also be due to the fact that the tablet acknowledging a loan was usually broken up on the return of the sum. But it might also be the fact that pledges were not usual in early times. Such was, indeed, formerly the conclusion drawn from the absence of documents referring to pledges; but Dr. B. Meissner pointed out that the legal phrase-books bore witness to the existence of the custom. The discovery of the Code of Ḫammurabi has shown that the practice not only existed, but was regulated by statute in his time. Hence the argument from silence is once more shown to be fallacious.

On the other hand, it is well to avoid a dogmatic statement of the existence of a practice before the date at which we have direct evidence of it: thus, it has been stated that the tithe was paid in Babylonia "from time immemorial." The only direct evidence comes from the time of Nebuchadrezzar II. and later. In view of such an early antiquity as that, the use of the phrase "time immemorial" was perhaps once justified. But we are now equipped with documentary evidence concerning customs two or three thousand years earlier. Until we can discover some direct evidence there of tithe, we must content ourselves with saying that it was regularly paid under the Second Empire of Babylonia. We may be firmly convinced that a custom so widespread did not spring into being all at once. But the tithe may have been a composition for earlier dues, and as such may have been introduced from Chaldea by Nabopolassar. It may therefore not have been of native Babylonian growth.

In this and many similar cases it is well not to go beyond the evidence.

To some extent the plan of this work must necessarily be different from that of the rest of the series. When a historical inscription is once well translated its chief bearings can be made out and it is its own interpreter to a large extent. But the object in a contract is to legally bind certain parties to a course of action, and there its translation ends. We do not find much interest now in the obligations of these parties, save in so far as they illustrate the progress of civilization. It is the conclusion we are to draw which gives the interest. When we have reached that, a thousand more contracts of the same type add nothing to that point. We may use them to make a study of proper names, or to correct our notions of chronology by their dates, or to draw up genealogies, or even to elaborate statistics of occurrences of particular forms of words, of prices, and the like; or try to reconstruct the topography of a town; but from the point of view of a student of law and history, a thousand are little better than one.

As a rule, however, we rarely find a fresh example of an old type without some small deviation, which is worth recording. But to translate it, for the sake of that small difference, would fill a book with examples, so similar as to be wearisome in their monotony. The only way then is to select some bold example, translate it as a fair average specimen, and then collect in an introduction and notes the most interesting additional items of information to be gathered from others of the type. Hence most of the types here selected have involved the reading and study of scores of texts, though but one is given in translation. Other points of great interest arise, as for example, the obligations to public service, which are not the direct subject of any one text. Hence, no single example can be selected for translation. The data of many texts must be collected, and only a sentence here and there can be utilized for translation. Hence, while other volumes of the series are properly translations, with brief introductions and a few notes, this must consist of copious introductions and many notes with a few translations.

Of course, all technical, philological and historical discussions must be avoided. Those who wish to find further examples, illustrating the points given, will be referred to the sources and commentaries which give almost endless repetitions of the same type. As a rule, a fresh example, which has not been translated before, will be used here. In some cases, however, where the most typical examples have already been used, they are reproduced.

The more important and new details are substantiated by references in foot-notes. When several references could be given, it has been the rule to give only one. For fuller information the literature of the subject may be consulted. But where the Assyrian or Babylonian words are given, the reader will consult the lexicons first. There are many admirable glossaries attached to the editions of texts, which for students are a valuable supplement to the lexicons. All philological discussions are, of course, excluded. As a rule, doubtful interpretations will be ignored or at least queried. It is, on the other hand, impossible to give detailed proofs of what is certain to the writer, when it disagrees with recognized authorities. Nor is it desirable to puzzle the reader with alternative views, when there is no opportunity for him to judge of their merits.

Every attempt will be made to discard non-essentials. Thus, in order to insure that there should be no mistake as to the persons intended, the ancient scribe usually gave not only the name, but the father's name, and often added the name of his tribe, or his occupation. For example, "Ardi-Ishtar, son of Ashur-bânî, the son of Gaḫal," might be the scribe's careful specification of one party to some transaction. But unless some other party is a relation and the transaction explicitly concerns what could take place between relations, the whole line gives us no information of value for illustrating the subject for which it is quoted. Indeed, in most cases, the name itself is of no interest. It is true that the names have a value of their own; but that is aside from the purpose of this book. The examples are selected to illustrate legal points, not for the sake of the names. And indeed, the few interesting names so given would be insufficient to serve any useful purpose; they might even be misused, for no permanent results can be obtained by picking up here and there a name, with some fanciful likeness to Abraham, or Jacob, unless a complete list of similar names be available to check and control the readings.

Hence, as a rule, the name of a party is condensed into a single letter, chosen usually in order to suggest the part played by the person in the transaction. Thus S stands for the seller, B for the buyer, J for the judge, C for the creditor, L for the lender, D for the debtor or borrower, and so on. These abbreviations may be used without any detriment to the argument, as the context usually defines the relation and there is no need to remember what they mean. This seems preferable, for the most part, to the Continental system of using A-A-G for the above name.

As a further abbreviation, all lists of witnesses are excluded. The date is usually suppressed, for, unless we are following a series of transactions between the same parties, nothing more than the epoch is of importance. As the material is arranged by epochs, there can be no question in this regard. If any evolution of process or any reference to former transactions is involved, so that the date is important, it is given.

A collection of legal documents may be studied in a variety of ways.

Perhaps the least productive plan is to ransack them for illustrations of a theory, or a particular point. When the theory is already well known, as in the case of Roman or mediæval law, such a procedure is justifiable, but when the theory has to be made out, it is wellnigh inexcusable. Some valuable monographs have followed this method, but they can hardly expect to give permanent results. For comparative purposes our material is so new, and so little worked, that it is sheer waste of time to seek for parallels elsewhere until everything is clearly made out to which parallels are to be sought. The whole bulk of material must be read through and classified. Until this is done, some important point may easily be overlooked.

The first attempts at classification will be provisional. A certain amount of overlapping is sure to occur. For example, slave sales obviously form a provisional group. But slaves were sold along with lands or houses. Shall these sales be taken into the group? The sales of lands may be another group. To which group shall we assign the sale of a piece of land and the slaves attached to it? To answer that question we may examine the sales of slaves and the sales of lands to see if either group has peculiarities, the recurrence of which in a sale of land and slaves might decide. But we soon find that a slave was sold exactly like a piece of land or any chattel. The only exception is that certain guarantees are expected with the slave, which differ from those demanded with a piece of land. On the whole, then, the chief group will be "sales," with subdivisions according to the class of property used. Hence we cannot assume that there was already present to legal consciousness a difference between real and personal property, or in any other sense that a slave was a person. He was a chattel.

The classification which will be adopted is not one that will suit modern legal ideas. It depends on the form of document alone. If two documents have the same type of formula, they will be grouped together. A future revision will, no doubt, assign to many of these a place in modern schemes. But it is very easy to be premature in assigning an ancient document to modern categories.

The groups will be subdivided according to subject-matter. The order of the groups will be determined by the greater or less complexity of the documents. It is best to take those first which can be easily made out. The experience gained in discussing them will be of great service in dealing with more complicated cases. The reader must not, however, suppose that no obscurities will remain. Subsequent investigation will lead to redistribution. Each such revision will, however, bring us nearer to sound results.

One of the most interesting and instructive methods of dealing with a large collection of documents is to group together the transactions, distributed over a number of years, of one man, or of a single family. This method has often been adopted and makes most fascinating reading.

Thus, M. V. Revillout, in the appendix to M. E. Revillout's lectures entitled *Les obligations en droit egyptien*, under the title of *Une famille des commerçants*, discussed the interrelations of a large number of tablets published by Strassmaier. These had a special connection, being found, and practically kept, together. They are concerned chiefly with the business transactions of three persons and their descendants. The three men do not seem to have been related, but to have become partners. The first transaction in which they are concerned is an equitable division of property which they had held in common. They and their descendants lived side by side in Larsa and gradually extended their possessions on every side. They were neighbors to two wealthy landowners from whom and from whose descendants they gradually acquired lands and houses. Especially did two brothers, sons of one of the original three, buy up, piece by piece, almost all the property of these two neighboring families. Further, in acquiring a piece of land, they seem to have come into possession of the deeds of sale, or leases, of that plot, which had been executed by previous owners. Thus, we can, in some cases, follow the history of a plot of land during several reigns.

Such a collection of documents probably did not come

from the public archives, but from the muniment-chest of a private family, or of a firm of traders. That duplicates of some of these tablets should have been found in other collections, points either to the collections having been purchased from native dealers, who put together tablets from all sources, or to the duplicates having been deposited in public archives, as a kind of registration of title.

In Assyrian times the transactions of the great Rîmâni-Adadi, the chief charioteer and agent of Ashurbânipal, who for some thirteen years appears almost yearly, as buyer or seller, lender or borrower, on some forty tablets, may serve as a further example,[1] or we may note how Baḫiânu appears, chiefly as a corn lender, year after year, for thirty-three years, on some twenty-four tablets.[2]

For the Second Empire of Babylonia, Professor J. Kohler and Dr. F. E. Peiser have given some fine examples of this method. Thus, for the bankruptcy of Nabû-aplu-iddin,[3] they show that the creditors distrained upon the bankrupt's property and found a buyer for most of it in a great Neriglissar, afterwards King of Babylon. The first creditor was paid in full, another received about half of the amount due to him, a third about the same, while a fourth obtained less than a quarter of what was owed him. They also follow out the fortunes of the great banking firm of Egibi[4] for fully a century. The sketch, of course, is not complete, and can only be made so by a prolonged search through thousands of documents in different museums; but it is intensely interesting and written with wonderful insight and legal knowledge. Another example is the family, or guild, of the priests of Gula.[5] This is less fully made out but most valuable, as far as it goes. In both cases a genealogy is given extending over many generations.

[1] A. D. D., iii., p. 83. [2] A. D. D., vi., 218. [3] A. B. R., iii., pp. 24 ff. [4] A. B. R., iv., pp. 21 ff. [5] A. B. R., iv., pp. 41 ff.

Later still, the Babylonian Expedition of the University of Pennsylvania, in the ninth volume of Cuneiform Texts, gives a collection of the business documents of one firm, "Murashu Sons, of Nippur," in the reign of Artaxerxes I. Here we have to do with a family deed-chest, a collection of documents found together and fortunately kept together.

But this method, attractive though it is, cannot be followed here. The reader is best led on from the known to the unknown. Those things must be taken first which must be understood in order to appreciate what is placed later. We consider first the law and the law-courts. The reader can thus follow the references to procedure which occur in the other sections. The rights of the State, the family, and the private individual come next. Then we learn of the classes of property and the various ways of disposing of it. After that is taken up a variety of disconnected topics, whose order is mainly indifferent. Some overlapping of divisions is sure to occur in any order. This system has been found, after many permutations, to present the least inconvenience.

While it is hoped that this volume will give a fairly complete account of what is really known and also point out some things that are reasonably conjectured to be true, it is fully recognized that much remains to be done. Indeed, it may serve by its omissions to redirect attention to openings for future fruitful work.

# CONTENTS

## CONTENTS



## BABYLONIAN AND ASSYRIAN LETTERS



## APPENDIX.

# LIST OF ABBREVIATIONS

A. B. R. *Aus dem babylonischen Rechtsleben.* Professor J. Kohler and Dr. F. E. Peiser. Leipzig, 1890–.

A. D. B. *Assyrian Doomsday Book.* Vol. XVII of *Assyriologische Bibliothek.* Leipzig, 1901.

A. D. D. *Assyrian Deeds and Documents.* In three vols Cambridge, 1898–.

A. J. S. L. *American Journal of Semitic Languages and Literatures.* Chicago.

A. O. F. *Altorientalische Forschungen.* Dr. H. Winckler. Leipzig, 1893–.

B. A. L. *Babylonian and Assyrian Life.* Professor A. H. Sayce. New York, 1901. (Semitic Series.)

B. A. S. *Beiträge zur Assyriologie.* Professors Delitzsch and Haupt. Leipzig, 1890–.

B. E. P. *The Babylonian Expedition of the University of Pennsylvania.* Series A. Cuneiform Texts. 1898–.

B. V. *Babylonische Verträge.* Dr. F. E. Peiser. Berlin, 1890.

C. Ṭ. *Cuneiform Texts from Babylonian Tablets, etc., in the British Museum.* London, 1896–.

D. E. P. *Délégation en Perse, Memoires.* Pub. by French Ministry of Instruction. Professor V. Scheil. 1900–.

E. B. H. *Early Babylonian History.* Dr. H. Radau. New York, 1900.

H. A. B. L. *Assyrian and Babylonian Letters.* Professor R. F. Harper. Chicago, 1892–.

H. W. B. *Assyrisches Handwörterbuch.* Professor Delitzsch. Leipzig, 1894.

I R., II R., III R., IV R., V R. *The Cuneiform Inscriptions of Western Asia.* H. C. Rawlinson. London, 1861, 1866, 1870, 1880–4.

K. A. S. *Keilinschriftliche Aktenstücke.* Dr. F. E. Peiser. Berlin, 1889.

K. B. *Keilinschriftliche Bibliothek.* Professor Eb. Schrader. Berlin, 1889–.

K. L. Ḫ. *The Letters and Inscriptions of Ḫammurabi.* Three vols. L. W. King, M.A. London, 1898–.

K. P. See A. B. R.

L. H. See K. L. Ḫ.

H. A. P. *Beiträge zum altbabylonischen Privatrecht.* Dr. Br. Meissner. Leipzig, 1893.

P. S. B. A. *Proceedings of the Society of Biblical Archæology.* London, 1872–.

*Rev. Ass.* *Revue d'Assyriologie.* Professors J. Oppert and E. Ledrain. Paris, 1884–.

Z. A. *Zeitschrift für Assyriologie.* Professor C. Bezold. Leipzig, 1886–.

Z. K. F. *Zeitschrift für Keilschriftforschung.* Professor C. Bezold. Leipzig, 1884–.

*Camb., Cyr., Dar., Ev. Mer., Nbd., Nbk., Nerig.*, denote the volumes of *Babylonische Texte; Inschriften von Cambyses, Cyrus, Darius, Evil Merodach, Nabonidus, Nebuchodonosor, Neriglissar*, pub. by Pater J. N. Strassmaier. Leipzig, 1887–.

H denotes the text published in H. A. B. L.

K denotes a text from Kouyunjik, now in the British Museum.

S denotes a text at Constantinople, from Sippara.

V. A. Th. denotes a text in the Berlin Museum.

B, $B^1$, $B^2$ denote texts of the collections "from Warka," Bu. 88-5-12, and Bu. 91-5-9.

# SOURCES AND BIBLIOGRAPHY

# SOURCES AND BIBLIOGRAPHY

THE chief sources from which is derived our knowledge of Babylonian and Assyrian law are the contemporary inscriptions of the people themselves. These are not supplemented to any appreciable extent by the traditions of classical authors. So far as they make any references to the subject, their opinions have to be revised by the immeasurably greater knowledge that we now possess, and seem to be mostly based upon "travellers' tales" and misapprehensions. Character of the available material

These inscriptions are now preserved in great numbers in European and American museums, and have only been partly published. The bibliography is very extensive. For the earlier attempts to read and explain these documents the reader may refer to Professor C. Bezold's *Kurzgefässter Überblick über die babylonisch-assyrische Litteratur*,[1] which gives a fairly complete account up to 1887. Of course, many books and memoirs there mentioned have now only a historical interest for the story of decipherment and explanation. These, however, may be studied with the greatest profit after having first become acquainted with the more recent works.

The division which is adopted in this work, "law, contracts, and letters," is only conventional. The three groups have much that is common and mutually supplement one another. Previous publications have often treated them Division of subject

[1] Pages 147–62.

more or less together, both as inscriptions and as minor sources of history. Hence it is not possible to draw up separate lists of books treating each division of the subject. Only those books or articles will be referred to which are most valuable for the student. Many of them give excellent bibliographies of their special subject.

Laws and contracts

The contemporary sources include actual codes of law, or fragments of them, legal phrase-books, and legal instruments of all sorts. From the last-mentioned source almost all that is known of ancient Babylonian law has been derived. The historical and religious inscriptions contribute very little. The consequence is that, except from the recently discovered Code of Ḫammurabi scarcely anything is known of the law in respect to crimes. Contracts and binding agreements are found in great profusion; but there is nothing to show how theft or murder was treated. Marriage-contracts tell us how adultery was punished. Agreements or legal decisions show how inheritance was assigned. Consequently our treatment of law and contracts must regard them as inseparable, except that we may place first the fragments of actual codes which exist.

Letters

The letters are much more distinct. Each is a separate study, except in so far as it can be grouped with others of the same period in attempts to disentangle the historical events to which they refer. The deductions as to life and manners are no less valuable than those made from legal documents. In both wording and subject-matter they often illustrate legal affairs and even directly treat of them.

Chronologically treated

A first duty will be carefully to distinguish epochs. Great social and political changes must have left some mark upon the institutions we are to study. As far as possible, the material has been arranged for each subject chronologically.

The longest and by far the most important ancient code

hitherto discovered is that of Ḫammurabi (*circa* 2250 B.C.). The source for this is a block of black diorite about 2.25 metres high, tapering from 1.90 to 1.65 metres in circumference. It was found by De Morgan at Susa, the ancient Persepolis, in December, 1901, and January, 1902, in fragments, which were easily rejoined. The text was published by the French Ministry of Instruction from "squeezes" by the process of photogravure, in the fourth volume of the *Mémoires de la Délégation en Perse.* It was there admirably transcribed and translated by Professor V. Scheil. In all, the monument now preserves forty-four columns with some three thousand six hundred lines. There were five columns more, which were once intentionally erased and the stone repolished, probably by the order of some monarch of Susa, who meant to put his own name and titles there. There have been found other monuments in the French explorations at Susa, where the Elamite monarch has erased the inscription of a Babylonian king and inserted his own. This method of blotting out the name of a king was a favorite device in the ancient East and is frequently protested against and cursed in the inscription set up in Babylonia. This particular inscription did not fail to call down similar imprecations, which perhaps the Elamite could not read. But he stayed his hand, and we do not even know his name, for he wrote nothing on the vacant space.

The Code of Ḫammurabi

It seems probable that the stone, or at any rate its original, if it be a copy, was set up at Sippara; for the text speaks of *Êbarra šuati,* "this Ebarra," which was the temple of Shamash at Sippara. At the head of the obverse is a very interesting picture of Ḫammurabi receiving his laws from the seated sun-god Shamash. Some seven hundred lines are devoted to the king's titles and glory; to enumerating the gods he reverenced, and the cities over which he ruled; to invoking blessings on those who preserved his monument and respected his inscription, with the usual curses on those who did the opposite.[1] These belong to the region of history and religion and do not concern us here. We may note, however, that the king expected that anyone injured or oppressed would come to his monument and be able there to read for himself what were the rights of his case.

Later copies

The whole of this inscription is not entirely new matter. The scribes of Ashurbânipal somewhere found a copy, or copies, of this inscription and made it into a series of tablets. Probably their originals were Babylonian tablets, for we know that in Babylonia the Code had been made into a series which bore the name of *Nînu ilu ṣîrum*, from the opening words of the stele. But, judging from the colophon of the Assyrian series, the scribes knew that the inscription came from a stele bearing the "image" of Ḫammurabi. A number of fragments belonging to such copies by later scribes were already published, by Dr. B. Meissner[2] and Dr. F. E. Peiser.[3] These were further commented upon by Professor Fr. Delitzsch,[4] who actually gave them the name "Code Hammurabi." Some of these fragments enable us to restore one or two sections of the lost five columns.

These fragments are now easily set in order and will doubtless lead to the discovery of many others, the meaning of which has not yet been recognized. They exhibit some variants of interest, showing that they were not made directly from this particular monument. Even at Susa another fragment was found of a duplicate stele. Hence we may hope to recover the whole text before long.

Bibliography of this Code

The publication of the Code naturally excited great interest among scholars. It appeared in October, 1902, and,

[1] Cf. Appendix.
[2] B. A. S., III., pp. 473–523.
[3] Jurisprudentiæ, pp. 5–35.
[4] B. A. S., IV., pp. 78–87.

during the next month, Dr. H. Winckler issued a German translation of the Code under the title, *Die Gesetze Hammurabis Königs von Babylon um 2250 v. Chr. Das Älteste Gesetzbuch der Welt*, being *Heft 4* of the fourth *Jahrgang* of *Der alte Orient*. This marked an advance in some points on Scheil's rendering, but is not entirely satisfactory. The present writer read a paper in October, 1902, before the Cambridge Theological Society, an abridged report of which appeared in the January *Journal*. He further published a baldly literal translation in February, 1903, entitled, *The Oldest Code of Laws in the World*.[1] In the *Journal des Savants* for October and November, 1902, M. Dareste gave a luminous account of the subject-matter of the Code, especially valuable for its comparisons with the other most ancient law-codes. This of course was based on Scheil's renderings. In the *Orientalistische Litteratur-Zeitung* for January, 1903, Dr. H. Winckler, reviewing the fourth volume of the *Mémoires*, gave a useful account of the Code comparing it with some of the previously published fragments.

Mosaic parallels

The comparison with the Mosaic Code was sure to attract notice, especially as Professor F. Delitzsch had called the attention of the public to it, in his lecture entitled *Babel und Bibel*, even before more of the Code was known than the fragments from Nineveh. Dr. J. Jeremias has published a small book called *Moses und Hammurabi*, in which he deals with the relations pretty thoroughly. Professor C. F. Kent has also examined them in his article entitled *The Recently Discovered Civil Code of Hammurabi*, in *The Biblical World* for March, 1903. Some remarks on the subject are to be found in the *New York Independent*, December 11, 18, 1902, and January 8, 15, 22, 1903, accompanying a translation. All the above follow Winckler's renderings.

[1] T. and T. Clark, Edinburgh.

The translation here given makes use of the above works, but must be regarded as independent. It is impracticable to detail and justify the changes made. The renderings can hardly be regarded as final, where actual contracts do not occur to illustrate the Code; but there is very little doubt that we know the tenor of these laws with substantial accuracy.

Professor V. Scheil divided the text of the Code into sections according to subject-matter. But there are no marks of a division on the monument and Scheil's division is not adhered to in this work. For convenience of reference, however, his original section-numbers are given in connection with each law or sub-section of a law.

The legal phrase-books

Among the treasures preserved in the library of Ashurbânipal and in the archives of the Babylonian temples were a number of tablets and fragments of tablets which recorded the efforts made by Semitic scribes to render Sumerian words and phrases into Semitic. A large number of these are concerned with legal subjects. A fairly complete list of those now in the Kouyunjik Collections of the British Museum will be found in the fifth volume of Dr. Bezold's catalogue, page 2032. The greater part of them have been published either in the British Museum *Inscriptions of Western Asia*, in Dr. P. Haupt's *Keilschrifttexten*, Vol. I. of the *Assyriologische Bibliothek*, or in Dr. F. Hommel's *Sumerische Lesestücke*. In the latter will be found references to other publications. Dr. B. Meissner further published a number of later Babylonian editions of the same or allied series.[1]

Their plan

The plan of the series to which most of these tablets belong is well seen in Dr. Delitzsch's *Assyrische Lesestücke*, fourth edition, pp. 112–14. The name by which the series is usually known, to which most of these tablets

[1] Z. A., VII., p. 16 ff.

belong, is the Semitic rendering of the first Sumerian phrase given there, *ana ittišu*, "to his side." The sections into which the series is divided each deal with some simple idea and its expression in Sumerian. But the principle of arrangement is not very clear. We may take one section for example. "With him, with them, with me, with us, with thee, with you," are given in two columns, the first being the Sumerian for these phrases, the second the Semitic rendering. Owing to the form of treatment some of these texts have been called "paradigms."

Sumerian family laws

But the scribes also gave some fairly long and connected prose extracts in Sumerian with their Semitic renderings. What these were extracted from is still a question. Some of the clauses are known to have been employed in the contracts. But some of these even may well have been extracts from a code of laws. The name of "Sumerian Family Laws" has been given to certain sections.[1] Others seem to have been extracted from a Sumerian work on agriculture, with which Hesiod's *Works and Days* has been compared. But at present we are not in possession of the complete works from which these extracts are taken.

Such as they are, they have a value beyond that of enabling us to read Sumerian documents. They often afford evidence of customs and information which we get nowhere else.[2] The information given by them will be utilized in the subsequent portions of this work. Their translation here would serve no purpose, since they are very disconnected, but an example may be of interest. One section reads, "He fastens the buckets, suspends the pole, and draws up the water." This is a vivid picture of the work-

[1] Page 115 of Delitzsch's edition.

[2] Dr. B. Meissner has made excellent use of them in his *Altbabylonische Privatrecht*.

ing of a watering-machine, from which we learn its nature as we could not from its name only.[1]

Legal documents

Legal documents constitute by far the larger portion of the inscriptions which have come down to us from every period of Babylonian and Assyrian history. In the library of Ashurbânipal alone they are exceeded by the letters and even more by the works dealing with astrology and omens. In some periods, however, we have only a few inscriptions from monuments, or bricks.

Real character of the contract tablets

To some extent the term "contracts," which has commonly been applied to them, is misleading. The use of the term certainly was due to a fundamental misunderstanding, they being once considered as contracts to furnish goods. They were even thought to be promises to pay, which passed from hand to hand, like our checks, and so formed a species of "clay money." These views were both partially true, but do not cover the whole ground.

They were binding legal agreements, sealed and witnessed. They were binding only on the parties named in them. They were drawn up by professional scribes who wrote the whole of the document, even the names of the witnesses. Hence it is inaccurate to speak of them as "signed" by anyone but the scribe, who often added his name at the end of the list of witnesses. The parties and witnesses did impress their own seals at one period, but later one seal, or two at most, served for all. It is not clear whose seal was then used. But the document usually declares it to be the seal of the party resigning possession.

Their external form

As to external form, most of those which may be called "deeds" consist of small pillow-shaped, or rectangular, cakes of clay. In many cases these were enclosed in an envelope, also of clay, powdered clay being inserted to pre-

[1] H. W. B., p. 218a.

vent the envelope adhering. Both the inner and outer parts were generally baked hard; but there are many examples where the clay was only dried in the sun. The envelope was inscribed with a duplicate of the text. Often the envelope is more liberally sealed than the inner tablet. This sealing, done with a cylinder-seal, running on an axle, was repeated so often as to render its design difficult to make out, and to add greatly to the difficulty of reading the text. When the envelope has been preserved unbroken, the interior is usually perfect, except where the envelope may have adhered to it. Such double tablets are often referred to as "case tablets." The existence of two copies of the same deed has been of great value for decipherment. One copy often has some variant in spelling, or phrasing, or some additional piece of information, that is of great assistance. The envelope was rather fragile and in many cases has been lost, either in ancient times, or broken open by the native finders, in the hope of discovering gold or jewels within. But in any case, the envelope, so long as it lasted, was a great protection; and there are few tablets better preserved than this class of document.

In Assyrian times, few "case" tablets are preserved, they seem to have gone out of fashion except for money-loans and the like. But it may be merely an accident that so few envelopes are preserved. In the case of letters, where the same plan of enclosing the letter in an envelope was followed, hardly any envelopes have been found, because they had to be broken open to read the letter. The owner of a deed may have had occasion to do the same, but here there was less excuse, as the envelope was inscribed with the full text.

In early times, another method of sealing was adopted. A small clay cone was sealed and the seal attached to the document by a reed, which ran through both. The seal thus hung down, as in the case of many old parchment deeds in Europe.

How kept

The deeds were often preserved in private houses, usually in some room or hiding-place below ground. In the case of the tablets from Tell Sifr, which were found by Loftus *in situ*, three unbaked bricks were set in the form of a capital U. The largest tablet was laid upon this foundation and the next two in size at right angles to it. The rest were piled on these and on the bricks and the whole surrounded by reed matting. They were covered by three unbaked bricks. This accounts for their fine preservation.

Others were stored in pots made of unbaked clay. The pots, as a rule, have crumbled away, but they kept out the earth around. Sometimes this broke in and crushed the tablets. In some cases they were laid on shelves round a small room; but in others they seem to have been kept in an upper story, and so were injured, when the floor fell through.

The parties possessing copies

It seems certain that as a rule all deeds were executed in duplicate, each party receiving a copy. The scribe often appears to have kept another. At one time copies were also deposited in the public archives, most probably the city temple or the governor's palace. There are indications that copies of deeds executed in the provinces were sent to the capital. Whether this was in pursuit of a general policy of centralization or only accidental in the few cases known to us is not quite clear. In many instances we actually possess duplicates, sometimes three copies of the same deed.

Scope of legal documents

These documents are exceedingly varied in contents. The most common are deeds relating to the sale or lease of houses, fields, buildings, gardens, and the like; the sale or hire of slaves and laborers; loans of money, corn, dates, wool, and the like; partnerships formed or dissolved; adoption, marriage, inheritance, or divorce. But almost any alienation, exchange, or deposit of property was made the subject of a deed. Further, all legal decisions were embodied in a document, which was sealed by the judge and given to both parties to the suit. These were often really deeds by which the parties bound themselves to accept and abide by the decisions. Some are bonds or acknowledgments of debt. A great many closely allied documents are lists of money or goods which had been given to certain persons. They were evidence of legal possession and doubtless a check on demand for repayment.

General works on the subject

The bibliography of the subject is best dealt with under each general division; but reference must be made to works dealing with the subject as a whole. Professor J. Oppert's *Documents Juridiques* was the first successful attempt to deal with contracts in general and laid the foundation of all subsequent work. Dr. F. E. Peiser and Professor J. Kohler's *Aus Babylonischen Rechtsleben* deals with the later Babylonian documents as far as they throw light upon social life and custom. Professor Sayce's *Babylonians and Assyrians* makes large use of the data given by the contracts. Dr. T. G. Pinches's *The Old Testament in the Light of the Monuments of Assyria and Babylonia* also gives a very full account of what may be gleaned from them. The present writer's *Assyrian Deeds and Documents* makes an attempt to treat one branch fully. This work can only present the most essential facts. The whole amount of material is so vast, so much is yet unpublished, so many side-issues arise, all worth investigating, that it can only serve to introduce the reader to a fascinating and wide field of study.

Different epochs represented

The material with which we have to deal, for the most part, falls very naturally into epochs. The early

Babylonian documents, though very numerous, are mostly of the nature of memoranda and include few letters or contracts. The documents of the First Dynasty of Babylon are extremely rich in examples of both contracts and letters. Then the Tell Amarna letters form a distinct group. The Ninevite contracts and letters of the Sargonid Dynasty are well marked as separate from the foregoing. Lastly, those of the New Babylonian Empire are a group by themselves. A few scattered examples survive which form intermediate groups, usually too small to be very characteristic, and certainly insufficient to justify or support any theory of the intermediate stages of development.

Local features

It must be observed that to a great extent these groups are not only separated by wide intervals of time—several centuries as a rule—but that they are locally distinct. The first comes from Telloh, the larger part of the second from Sippara, the third from Egypt (or Syria), the fourth from Assyria, the last from Babylonia. Whether the documents of Sippara in the third period showed as great divergence from those of the second period as the Tell Amarna letters do, or whether each group is fairly characteristic of its age in all localities using the cuneiform script, are questions which can only be answered when the other documents of that period are available for comparison.

Characteristics of each group

The documents of each group have marked characteristics in form of script, in orthography, in language. So great are the differences that a slight acquaintance with these characteristics will suffice to fix the epoch of a given document. For the most part, however, these characteristics are not such as can appear in translation. They will be pointed out as far as possible in the opening sections dealing with each group. The aim will be to select characteristic specimens of each group for translation and to append a summary of what can be obtained by a study of the group.

The thousands of documents dealt with under these groups would, if translated, require a library of volumes. In the case of the contracts the repetition of scores of examples of the same sort would be wearisome. In the case of the letters, the translation alone would be almost as obscure as the original, without copious comment on the relationships, customs, and events referred to. In both cases it must be noted that many of the most interesting examples are incomplete and unavailable as specimens. The object of this work is to show what are the most important laws or legal documents of each period and to point out the chief subjects of information to be gained from them. For the letters no such summary of information can be given, partly because they are so many and varied, partly because so few are yet available.

First period: the early Babylonian

The first epoch is to be considered as one period only because its contribution to the subject is as yet small and chronologically precedes the first great group. It ranges from the earliest beginnings of history to somewhere about B.C. 2300. The dates are largely conjectural, but for the most part the sequence of the events is known. It is the period covered by Dr. H. Radau's *Early Babylonian History.*

Some very ancient documents fall under this period. The early tablets which show the nearest approach to the original picture-writing[1] are transfers of property. As a rule, however, such votive inscriptions do not come under the head of contracts. One of the earliest of our monuments, the Stele of Manistusu, King of Kish, records the sale of land. Another very early monument of similar style[2] deals with the sale of plots of land. Others will be found in the *Mémoires de la Délégation en Perse.*

[1] Such as that published by Professor G. Barton, in the *American Oriental Society's Journal*, 1902, pp. 19–28.

[2] First published by Professor H. V. Hilprecht, in *Old Babylonian Inscriptions*, I., plates vi., vii., viii.; again with additions and corrections by Professor V. Scheil, *Receuil de Travaux*, XXII., p. 29–36.

But by far the greatest number of inscriptions belong to the finds of Telloh, made by De Sarzec in his explorations for the French Government. His greatest find, some thirty thousand tablets which were in the archives there, was dispersed by the Arabs, and has found its way into various museums. They have been sold in Europe, as coming from different localities. It is certain that other finds of the same period and same general character have been made elsewhere, so that it is often difficult now to determine their place of discovery.

A very large number of these tablets, from the collection of T. Simon, now in the Berlin museums, were copied and edited by G. Reisner, as *Tempelurkunden aus Telloh.*[1] The admirable abstracts of the contents there given[2] will furnish all the information that anyone but a specialist will need. They consist of lists of all sorts of natural products, harvests from fields, seed and other expenses allowed for cultivating fields, lists of the fields with their cultivators, numerous receipts for loans or grants, accounts of sheep and cattle, stipends or allowances for certain people; but only one, number 125, is doubtfully said to concern a sale of some slaves.

Dr. H. Radau, in his *Early Babylonian History*, gives the texts of a large number of similar tablets.[3] He also classified, transliterated, and tentatively translated most of them. The kind of information to be obtained is well brought out in his notes and comments.[4] They contain receipts, accounts of all sorts, lists of animals, skins, wool, oil, wine, grain, pitch, and honey; but none relate to the usual subjects treated in contract-tablets.

---

[1] *Heft XVI.* of the *Mittheilungen aus den Orientalischen Sammlungen, Berlin, 1901.*

[2] Pages vii–xviii and 1–58.

[3] From the *E. A. Hoffman Collection of Babylonian Clay Tablets in the General Theological Seminary, New York.*

[4] Pages 322–29.

M. Thureau-Dangin edited and discussed a number of tablets of the same character in the *Revue d'Assyriologie*.[1] Especially valuable is his memoir, *L'accomptabilité agricole en Chaldée*,[2] where many interesting facts are collected and published.

The second period: the First Dynasty of Babylon

A very large number of texts of this period were published by Mr. L. W. King, in *Cuneiform Texts from Babylonian Tablets, etc., in the British Museum*.[3] These have been discussed in a few instances by various writers in scientific journals. In the short descriptions prefixed to these editions mention is made of "contracts," but it is difficult to see to which the term could be properly applied.

A number of extracts from early "contracts" are given by Professor V. Scheil in the recent files of the *Receuil de Travaux*. According to the descriptions given, many of them are legal instruments. Besides advances of grain and receipts for the same,[4] or sales of land,[5] we have a legal decision concerning a marriage.[6] Of several of these only a few lines are given and the description of others is misleading. They are mostly preserved at Constantinople. Some are purely Sumerian, others Semitic. The same remarks apply to this author's publications in his *Une Saison de fouilles à Sippar*. Valuable as are the portions available, they chiefly make us long for more.

A very large number of tablets belonging to the second period are now in Europe and America. They seem to have been purchased from dealers, either in the East or West; and may be presumed to have been discovered by the natives. No reliable information can therefore be had

[1] IV., pp. 69–86; V., page 3.
[2] III., pp. 118–46.
[3] Parts I., III., V., VII., IX., X.
[4] XVIII., p. 73, XIX., pp. 54 ff., Nos. 1, 3, 11, 17, 20, 46, 48, 56, 330.
[5] XVII., p. 30, XIX., p. 58, No. 335.
[6] XXII., p. 153 f.

as to their origin. Various places are mentioned: Sippara, Abu Habba, Senkereh, Telloh, Warka, have all been stated to be the place of discovery. There seems no good reason why tablets of this period should not be found anywhere in Babylonia. But on examination it is found that collections said to be from widely different places contain duplicates; while the same collection contains tablets dated at different cities and with dates a thousand years apart. It is conceivable that the records of important transactions, especially the transfers of land, were deposited by order in the archives at the capital, wherever that was for the time being. We may imagine that the archives at Sippara or Larsa were afterwards transferred to Babylon, for safety, or in pursuance of a policy of centralization. Certain it is that a large number of the texts imply a devotion to Shamash as chief deity, while others ascribe the pre-eminence to Marduk or Sin. But this fact is quite consistent with the archives having been discovered in either Babylon or Sippara.

**Present location of the tablets: London**

On the other hand, it is not unlikely that the apparent centralization is of purely modern production. The dealers put together tablets from all sources and ascribe the collection to the place of origin which best suits their fancy. As a consequence, scarcely any collection contains a homogeneous series belonging either to one period or source. This is the more deplorable because so few are competent to date a tablet by the style of writing upon it, and internal indications are often lacking.

In the British Museum we have the following collections:

I. A number of "case" tablets brought from Tell Sifr by Loftus in 1850. Owing to a misleading statement in Layard's *Nineveh and Babylon*, p. 496, these have generally been taken to be from Warka, the ancient Erech. But the account given on pages 270–72 of Loftus, *Travels and Re-*

*searches in Chaldea and Susiana*, leaves no doubt of the place and date of their discovery. These are usually denoted by B.

II. A number of tablets now in the Kouyunjik Collections. It is certain that these do not come from Nineveh, and in the British Museum Catalogue they are usually ascribed to Warka, but with an implied doubt. One or two are dated at Erech. The D. T. Collection also contains many tablets, said to be "not from Kouyunjik."

III. The collection 81–7–1 contains some forty at least, comprising the accounts of the temple of Ninib, from the time of Ammiditana and Ammizaduga.

IV. The collection 82–7–14 also has a few tablets of this period.

V. The collection 82–9–18 has at least one contract.

VI. The collection Bu. 88–5–18, purchased by Dr. E. A. W. Budge in the East, consists of some seven hundred tablets. They are said to come from Sippara; and date from B.C. 2300 to the time of Darius. These will be denoted by $B^1$.

VII. The collection Bu. 91–5–9, also purchased by Dr. E. A. W. Budge in the East, consists of some three thousand tablets. These will be denoted by $B^2$.

The purchases for the British Museum also include a large number of other tablets of this period. They are now numbered consecutively, thus Bu. 91–5–9, 606 is known as Brit. Mus. No. 92,679. This renders it difficult to further particularize the contents of the collections; or to know whether a given tablet belongs to one of the above collections.

In the Museum of the Louvre at Paris are a few tablets belonging to this epoch. Seven of them are published in M. Heuzey's *Découvertes en Chaldée.*[1] Paris

[1] Pl. 41.

Berlin

At the Berlin Museum is a collection known by the name of Homsy.

The tablets are marked V. A. Th., but this mark includes other tablets widely separated in date and found at different sites.

Philadelphia

At the University of Pennsylvania collections known as J. S., Kh., and H. contain tablets of this period. Professor R. F. Harper, writing in *Hebraica*,[1] gives some account of these collections; from which it appears that the J. S. collection contains tablets of Ḫammurabi, Samsuiluna, and Ammiditana; while the Kh. collection has tablets of Ḫammurabi, Samsuiluna, Ammiditana, and Ammizaduga. He announced the discovery of the name of Abêshu on contemporary documents,[2] belonging to that reign. The two collections contain over a thousand tablets. The H collection has six hundred and thirty-two tablets, many of this epoch.

Constantinople

In the Imperial Ottoman Museum at Constantinople are a large number of tablets of this period. They are denoted by N, the Nippur collection found by the American explorers there; S, the Sippar collection from the explorations conducted by Pater V. Scheil at Abu Habba; the T or Telloh collection from the explorations of De Sarzec.

A few tablets are owned by Sir Henry Peek, Bart.

A few tablets exist in the Fitzwilliam Museum at Cambridge, the gift of Mr. Bosanquet.

The Rev. J. G. Ward possesses a tablet, published by Dr. T. G. Pinches in *P. S. B. A.*, XXI., pp. 158–63, of the time of Mana-balte-el, which seems to be of this period.

A number of other tablets of the period are known to be in different museums or in the hands of private individuals.

Publications

The historical value of the events used in dating these tablets was recognized by G. Smith, who published the

---

[1] V., pp. 74–76; and VI., pp. 59, 60.

[2] J. S., 41, 42, 43, 142, and Kh. 19, 198.

dates of a number of the Loftus tablets, in the fourth volume of the *Cuneiform Inscriptions of Western Asia*, p. 36.

The earliest publication of the texts was by Pater J. N. Strassmaier in the *Verhandlungen des V Internationalen Orientalistischen Congresses zu Berlin*, 1881. In the *Beilage* he gave the lithographed text of one hundred and nine tablets under the title of *Die altbabylonischen Verträge aus Warka.* He made many important observations upon their character and style, and gave a valuable list of words and names. As was to be expected from a first attempt, both his readings of the texts and his transcriptions from them leave room for some improvement. He arranged his texts according to the reigns of the kings mentioned.

This edition formed the subject of M. V. Revillout's article, *Une Famille commerçant de Warka*, and of numerous articles by other scholars in the journals. Dr. B. Meissner seems to have collated a number of these texts for his *Beiträge zum altbabylonischen Privatrecht.*

In 1888, Dr. T. G. Pinches published *Inscribed Babylonian Tablets in the possession of Sir Henry Peek, Bart.* It was followed by other parts and by *Babylonian and Assyrian Cylinder-seals and Signets in the possession of Sir Henry Peek, Bart.*, in 1890. These are most valuable for their full treatment—photographs of the originals, drawings, and descriptions of the seals, transliterations, translations, and comments, giving a better idea of what these documents are like than can be obtained without actually handling the originals. Dr. Pinches in his introduction assigns their discovery to the ruins of Sippara. The texts published by him only include three from our period, Nos. 1, 13, 14; but nowhere will a beginner find more assistance in his studies of this class of tablet.

In 1893 Dr. B. Meissner published his invaluable *Bei-*

*träge zum altbabylonischen Privatrecht,* Vol. XI. of Delitzsch and Haupt's *Assyriologische Bibliothek.* This gave a full transliteration and translation of one hundred and eleven texts published in autography. Full notes and comments were added giving practically all that could then be said on the subject. His introduction summarized the information, to be extracted from his texts, bearing on the social institutions of Babylonia. By arranging the texts in classes according to their purport and contents he was able to elucidate each text by comparison with similar documents and so to gain a very clear idea of the meaning of separate clauses, even when the exact shade of meaning of individual words remained obscure. Any advance which the interpretation of these documents may make must be based on his researches and follow his methods. He gave a useful glossary, but no list of proper names.

In the fourth volume of Schrader's *Keilinscriftliche Bibliothek,* 1896, Dr. F. E. Peiser adopted the plan of arranging the then known contract-texts in chronological order. He gave, in transliteration and translation, the texts of thirty-one tablets of this period. Of these many had been previously published by Strassmaier and Meissner, but Dr. Peiser's renderings and short notes are of great value.

In 1896 began the grand series of publications, *Cuneiform Texts from Babylonian Tablets, etc., in the British Museum, printed by order of the Trustees,* which has been continued to the present date. Volumes II., IV., VI., and VIII. contain copies by Dr. T. G. Pinches of no fewer than three hundred and ninety-five texts from the B[1] and B[2] Collections. They also contain a number of letters and other texts, some of a date as late as Xerxes, but from the same two collections.

In the *Journal of the Royal Asiatic Society,* 1897[1] and

[1] Page 589 f.

1899,[1] Dr. T. G. Pinches gives transliterations, translations, and comments upon fifteen of these texts.

A word of notice must be given to the excellent Guides published by the trustees of the British Museum. The *Guide to the Kouyunjik Gallery*, with four autotype plates, 1885, and the *Guide to the Nimroud Central Saloon* are now superseded by the *Guide to the Babylonian and Assyrian Antiquities* with thirty-four plates, photographic reproductions of the originals, 1900. On pages 104–13 will be found a most useful account of the class of tablet and short descriptions of ninety-four exhibited case tablets. Most of these tablets have been published by Strassmaier or in *Cuneiform Texts*, but are now indicated by their new registration numbers.

It will be evident from the above remarks that only a small proportion of the material in our museums has yet been published. It is greatly to be desired that every existing tablet should be published, as in no other way can we hope to solve many important problems. Not only the chronology but much of the actual history can be recovered from these tablets, while the names of the witnesses and parties to the transactions will settle the order of the years which are still doubtful. It is from these deeds that the greater part of this work will be constructed. They form the groundwork, while later documents fill in details.

**The chronological system**

The years were given names. Thus the second year of Ḫammurabi is called "the year in which Ḫammurabi the king established the heart of the land in righteousness." The year often received its name from the capture of some city. Are we to suppose that these events actually occurred on the first day of the year? If not, by what name was the year called up to the occurrence of the event in question? There is evidence that some years passed by

[1] Page 103 f.

two names, one of which was probably conferred after the year had begun. An examination of all dated tablets would doubtless result in fixing the time of the year at which the new year-name came into use. This can only be achieved by the custodians of our great collections. But, speaking generally, it seems obvious that names were often given to the years which attached to them a memory of the previous rather than a record for the current year. When in after years scribes drew up lists of the dates of a reign, they may well have made mistakes as to the exact year in which an event took place and have also credited a king with too long a reign, by counting as separate years two dates which were really the alternatives for one and the same year. In this way we may perhaps account for the discrepancies between the Chronicle and the King Lists.

Key to the order of events in a reign

The tablets often mention the name of the reigning king as well as the year-name; thus we read as a date, "the year when Samsuiluna was king," followed by "the year in which the canal of Samsuiluna named Ḫegallu was dug," which was the year-name of Samsuiluna's fourth year. Also the parties often swore an oath to observe their contract by the name of one or more gods and of the reigning king. Hence, very often, when the date is not preserved at all, we know what reign was concerned. On the other hand, in some reigns we have dated tablets from almost every year. If all the tablets were published, the witnesses and other parties would enable us to fix the sequence of the years. As these year-names each give a prominent event for the year we could thus reconstruct a skeleton history of the reign. Indeed, the present writer had already determined the order of several years, in more than one reign, from consideration of the persons named in each. Of course, no assurance could thus be had that some intermediate years were not omitted in such a scheme, since there is no certainty that we know the name-dates for each year of a reign. The order of the kings themselves and the lengths of their reigns were already known from the King List published by Dr. T. G. Pinches.[1]

The chronicle of the king

It seemed probable that the scribes of those days would have made lists of the year-names, in order to know how much time had elapsed since a given event had occurred. Hence great was the excitement and delight when in *C. T. VI.* was published a tablet which once contained a list of year-names from Sumuabu to Ammizaduga. This was followed by the publication in Mr. L. H. King's *Letters of Ḫammurabi* of a duplicate, which served to restore and complete the list down to the tenth year of Ammizaduga's reign. Mr. King further added the year-names actually used on the dated tablets then published; thus showing how the year-names of the list were quoted and either abbreviated or expanded. He very appropriately called this the *Chronicle of the Kings of Babylon.* In the meantime Professor A. H. Sayce had given a translation of the first published list.[2] In the fourth volume of the *Beiträge zur semitischen Sprachwissenschaft*,[3] Dr. E. Lindl has given a full discussion of the first published list. He further adds a small list of the same character giving the year-names in order for part of the reigns of Ḫammurabi and Samsuiluna.[4] Dr. Lindl used the published dates of the contracts to complete and restore the first list. Thus a great deal of excellent work has been done on these lists. None of them are complete for the whole dynasty, nor even for the part which they originally covered, and the known dated documents do not serve to fully restore them. But

---

[1] P. S. B. A., 1884, pp. 193–204.
[2] P. S. B. A., XXI., pp. 11–17, January, 1899.
[3] Pages 338–409. [4] Pages 342–43.

so far as they go, they must take the precedence of the King List, being almost contemporary documents.

Other kings mentioned

Besides the kings of the First Dynasty of Babylon the collections above referred to designate several other persons as kings. Thus the B collection of the British Museum names Nûr-Adadi, Sin-idinnam, and Rim-Sin as kings. The texts enable us to fix all these as kings of Larsa. Hence evidently the Tell Sifr, where these tablets were found, was in the territory of Larsa. The whole question is well discussed by Dr. Lindl.[1] The date on the tablet B. 34a refers to the setting-up of a throne for Shamash by Nûr-Adadi. The date on B. 35 refers to the completion of a temple in Eridu by Sin-idinnam, King of Larsa. It is scarcely conceivable that these refer to other than the Nûr-Adadi, who set up the kingdom of Larsa in the south of Babylonia about the same time as Sumuabi founded the dynasty of Babylon. Sin-idinnam, his son, succeeded him as King of Larsa and claimed to be King of Shumer and Akkad. Elam, however, under Kudurnanhundi I., invaded the south, defeated Sin-idinnam and set up Rim-Sin as King of Larsa. It seems that Rim-Sin reigned thirty-seven years, partly as vassal of Ḫammurabi, from the seventeenth year of Sin-mubalit until the thirty-first of Ḫammurabi. Whether Sin-idinnam was then restored to his throne as vassal of Ḫammurabi, or whether Rim-Sin was succeeded by a second Sin-idinnam, or whether the restoration of Sin-idinnam, after a temporary expulsion of Rim-Sin, took place within the thirty-seven years of the latter's reign, is not yet clear.

Era of Isin

Of great interest is the fact of the use of an era in the south of Babylonia. A large number of tablets are dated by the years after the capture of Isin. Thus tablets are dated in the 1st, 2nd, 3rd, 4th, 5th, 6th, 7th, 8th, 13th, 18th,

[1] B. A. S., IV., pp. 382 ff.

22nd, 23rd, 26th, 27th, 28th, and 30th years after the capture of Isin. Most of them are related to the kingdom ruled by Rim-Sin, which clearly included Tell Sifr, Nippur, Eridu, as well as Larsa.[1] The first year of this era was probably the seventeenth year of Sin-mubalit.

Various historical identifications

A king Immeru is mentioned,[2] usually alone, but once with Sumu-lâ-ilu;[3] where the form of the oath, "by Shamash and Immerum, by Marduk and Sumu-lâ-ilu," suggests that while Sumu-lâ-ilu was king of Babylon, the Marduk city, Immeru was king of a Shamash city. As he comes first, he was probably king of Sippara, where Shamash was the city god, and whence the collections, $B^1$, $B^2$, and V. A. Th., seem, on other grounds, to have come. That it was needful to name Sumu-lâ-ilu also points to that king being overlord of Sippara at the time.

The king Ilu-ma-ilu, named[4] in the oaths, associated with Shamash, may well be a vassal king of Sippara, though Professor Delitzsch[5] suggests that he may be the first king of the second dynasty of Babylon, whose name appears in the King list B as Ilu-ma(ilu).

The king Mana-balte-el, on the Rev. J. G. Ward's tablet, seems to belong to the First, or Second, Dynasty, perhaps as a vassal king, but may have preceded them by some short period.

The king Bungunu-ilu, mentioned by King,[6] was associated with Sumu-lâ-ilu. Probably he was vassal king of Sippara before Immeru.

The third epoch: the Kassite kings

A number of extracts from the legal documents of the third period have been given by Father V. Scheil in the *Re-*

[1] See Lindl, B. A. S., IV., pp. 384–85.

[2] $B^1$ 58, 346. $B^2$ 318, 2439a, 2527, V. A. Th. 863.

[3] $B^2$ 318.

[4] $B^2$ 380, 2378.

[5] B. A. S., IV., p. 363, foot-note.

[6] L. H., III., p. 220, note 16.

*ceuil de Travaux.*[1] The full text is rarely given and there is consequently nothing for use here. They come from Nippur and are at Constantinople. The Semitic language is used largely, but a few Sumerian phrases remain. All the names of persons except those of the kings are pure Babylonian. The determinative of personality before proper names is common, but not before a king's name. The tablets are dated by regnal years, no longer by year-names. The kings have a determinative of divinity before their names. The money in use is either gold or bronze, silver is hardly named, while in other epochs it is almost always used. Gold was now legal tender, as silver was afterwards.

The many extremely fine charters of this period are of great value for the questions concerning land tenure. Descriptions and figures of some of them will be found in the Guide.[2] The text of several was published by Dr. C. W. Belser,[3] under the title *Babylonische Kudurru-inschriften.* Some of these are transliterated and translated in Schrader's *Keilschriftliche Bibliothek,*[4] where references to the literature will be found. In many cases these charters or boundary-stones are the only monumental evidence for their period. They therefore figure largely in the histories.

Some of the best examples are found in the second volume of the *Mémoires de la Délégation en Perse,* beautifully reproduced by photogravure, admirably transliterated and translated by Professor V. Scheil. Some fine examples are also to be found in *Cuneiform Texts from Babylonian Tablets, etc., in the British Museum.*[5]

---

[1] Vol. XIX., pp. 56 ff., Nos. 70, 133, 147, 266, 572.

[2] Pages 85–89. [3] B. A. S., II., pp. 111–205.

[4] III.[1], p. 154 f., 164 f.; IV., p. 56 f.

[5] The so-called *Caillou de Michaux* was published I. R. 70, and discussed by Oppert, *Doc. Jur.*, pp. 87 ff., and Boissier, *Recherches sur quelques contrats babyloniens* K. B., IV., pp. 78 ff. A fine charter from the time of Merodach-baladan I. was published IV. R. 38, discussed by Oppert, *Doc. Jur.*, pp. 129 ff., and K. B. IV., pp. 60 ff. Another of the same date was published, K. B. IV., pp. 164 ff.

Of the time of Marduk-shum-iddin, B.C. 853–833, we have a black boundary-stone, published by Dr. F. E. Peiser, in *Keilschriftliche Acten-stücke*, No. 1. It is dated in the twenty-eighth year of the reign of Nabû-aplu-iddina, *circa* B.C. 858, and the eleventh year of Marduk-shum-iddina, *circa* B.C. 842. It rehearses the contents of two or more deeds by which a certain Kidinu came into possession of property in the city of Dilbat.

**The Cappadocian tablets**

The Cappadocian tablets are still somewhat of a problem. The first notice of them was given by Dr. T. G. Pinches.[1] According to the dealer's account one acquired by the British Museum had come from Cappadocia. The script was then quite unfamiliar and it was thought that they were written in a language neither Semitic nor Akkadian. Various attempts, which are best forgotten, were made to transcribe and translate them under complete misapprehension of the readings of the characters. But in 1891 Golénischeff published twenty-four tablets of the same stamp, which he had acquired at Kaisarieh. His copies were splendidly done for one who could make out very little meaning. But he showed that many words were Assyrian and read many names. Professor Delitzsch[2] made a most valuable study of them, and laid the foundation for their thorough understanding. Professor P. Jensen[3] added greatly to our knowledge of their reading and interpretation. Dr. F. E. Peiser then[4] gave a transcription and translation of nine texts of contracts.

They are now recognized to be purely Semitic. They must have been written in some place where Assyrian influence was all-powerful. There are many names compounded of Ashur. They are dated by eponyms as in Assyria. The

[1] P. S. B. A., November 1, 1881.
[2] *Abhand. d. phil. hist. Classes der K. Sachs. Ges. d. Wiss. 1893, No. IV.*
[3] Z. A., IX., pp. 62–81.
[4] K. B., IV., pp. 50–56.

discovery of many more of them at Boghaz Keui, Kara Eyuk, and elsewhere published by Professor V. Scheil in the *Mémoires de la Mission en Cappadoce par Ernest Chantre*, and commented on by M. Boissier,[1] make it certain that they are from this region.

If subject to Assyria, their date may be before the earliest eponyms whose date is known from the Canon lists. They may be contemporary with the very earliest kings of Assyria. But it is not impossible that the eponyms referred to were local only and not Assyrian in origin Dr. Peiser put them after the First Dynasty of Babylon, but before the Third Dynasty.

They are full of unusual forms of words and have a phraseology of their own. They cannot as yet be translated with any confidence. In general they are very similar to the contracts, money-loans, and letters of the First Dynasty of Babylon. As far as they can be understood, they offer no new features of interest. The obscure phrases and words give rise to many speculations which will be found in the above-mentioned works. These are of great interest, but need further data for elucidation. They are too questionable to be profitably embodied here.

The Elamite contracts

The Elamite contract-tablets were found at Susa and are published by Professor V. Scheil in Tome IV. of the *Mémoires de la Délégation en Perse*.[2]

In external form they closely resemble the Babylonian documents of a similar nature. They are drawn up in practically the same way. But there is a blunt directness about them which recalls the usages of the First Dynasty of Babylon, rather than Assyria, or the Second Babylonian Empire. Hence we have little to indicate date. Until we are better acquainted with the Elamite script at various periods we cannot hope to date them.

---

[1] P. S. B. A., XXII., p. 106 f. [2] Pages 169–94.

They have many peculiar words and phrases. Some may be Elamite, or that form of Semitic which obtained in Elam, but the rest of the language is ordinary Babylonian. It is possible that some characters had a value in Elam not known in Babylonia, or ideographic values not yet recognized. But, as a rule, the general sense is fairly clear.

The fourth epoch: Assyria

The legal documents of Assyria are in many respects a separate group. They are sometimes said to have come from the library of Ashurbânipal, which Mr. H. Rassam claims to have discovered at Kouyunjik in 1852–54. But it seems far more probable that, as large numbers were already found by Layard in 1849–51, we have rather to do with the contents of some archives. The absence of any large number of temple-accounts seems to exclude the probability that they were connected with a temple; but the fact that nearly every tablet has for one principal party some officer of the king, lends great probability to the view that the transactions were really made on behalf of the king; or—to be more exact—of the palace in Nineveh. The exceptions may be accounted for as really deeds concerned with former sales; or mortgages of property, finally bought in for the king. The conjecture is raised to a moral certainty by the contents of such a collection as Knudtzon's *Gebete an den Sonnengott*, found together with them; which consisted of copies of the requests and inquiries made of the Sun-god oracle regarding the troubles and difficulties of the king and royal family, domestic as well as public, in the reigns of Esarhaddon and Ashurbânipal. The letters too, found in the same collection, are the letters received by the king from his officers in all parts of his realm. The lists are connected with expenses of his household. Such votive tablets as are preserved are concerned with offerings of the royal family, or such high officers as probably were permanent inmates of the palace. We have, in fact, the contents of the muniment chests of the Sargonid kings of Assyria. That the royal library was mixed up with these documents may be due to the contents of an upper chamber falling, when its floor was burnt out; but the mixing may have been done by the discoverers.

In a very real sense these come from a record office, but are confined to royal rather than state documents; though a few duplicates of charters occur. Hence we look in vain for many classes of documents, such as are common in the archives of temples or private families. We have no marriage settlements, no adoptions, no partnerships.

Can we believe that such transactions were less common in Nineveh than fifteen centuries before in Sippara, or Larsa, or Babylon; or later in Babylon, Sippara, or Nippur? There cannot be a shadow of doubt that such documents exist in shoals somewhere in the ruins of Nineveh and will one day be found. Hence we must regard it as extremely improbable that the ordinary citizens of Nineveh contributed the records of their transactions to the Kouyunjik Collections now in the British Museum. They either kept them in their own houses or in some temple archives. As will be seen later, a few have already been found; but it is extremely difficult to locate them exactly. It is quite certain that a few of the tablets in the British Museum were found at other localities, such as Sherif Khan, Ashur, Kalah, Erech, Larsa, and Babylon.

For the most part these appear to have been placed in one collection by the discoverers, and only internal evidence can now decide where they were found. But the great bulk of the Kouyunjik Collections, as far as contracts, legal documents, and kindred tablets are concerned, are the result of explorations conducted on the site of the ancient Nineveh, by Layard and Rassam. They probably came from palace archives, and as a result possess a special character of their own.

Aramaic dockets

Aramaic dockets very early attracted the attention of Assyriologists. The presence of short inscriptions in Aramaic on a few contract-tablets naturally raised hopes, in the early days of decipherment, of finding some check upon the reading of cuneiform. So far as these went they were by no means inconsistent with the readings of the cuneiform. But they were too few, too disconnected, and in themselves too uncertain, to be of great value. Indeed, for many of them, it is the cuneiform that now gives the key to their possible sense. The whole of these Aramaic inscriptions have now been published by Dr. J. H. Stevenson in his *Assyrian and Babylonian Contracts with Aramaic Reference Notes*, where references to the literature will be found.

The collections of tablets

In connection with these Aramaic legends a number of the texts of Assyrian contracts were published in the *Corpus Inscriptionum Semiticarum, Pars Secunda, Tomus I.* A number more were published in Vol. III. of the *Cuneiform Inscriptions of Western Asia*, by Sir H. C. Rawlinson. A few others were published in various journals; and by Oppert in his epoch-making treatise on the juristic literature, *Documents Juridiques;* by Peiser, in Vol. IV. of Schrader's *Keilinschriftliche Bibliothek;* and by Strassmaier in his *Alphabetisches Verzeichnis.* The whole of the texts of the Assyrian contracts from the Kouyunjik Collections in the British Museum are now published in *Assyrian Deeds and Documents recording the Transfer of Property, etc.* (three volumes published).[1] A bibliography will be found there, on page ix of the preface to Vol. I.

Their peculiar style

The very remarkable style which most of these tablets show is so unlike the contemporary documents in Babylonia that we may expect that transactions between private

[1] Deighton, Bell & Co., Cambridge, England.

citizens in Assyria at this time were quite different. A few such documents exist. Professor V. Scheil, in the *Receuil de Travaux*,[1] published the text of four which are quite unlike any of the Kouyunjik examples.

The plan of arrangement in the volume

In *Assyrian Deeds and Documents* the same plan of arrangement was followed, to some extent, as in this work. Being all of one epoch and showing no signs of any development the tablets were grouped, provisionally, according to subjects. The arrangement in each group was to place first the best specimens of the group and then the injured and fragmentary specimens, which thus received illustration, and in some cases, could be restored. It would, however, be an error to regard the Assyrian documents as the intermediate link between the old and new Babylonian documents, though they belong chronologically to an interval which precedes the latter immediately. The Assyrian scribe used a formula that was closer to the Old Babylonian than to the contemporary Babylonian. It had an independent development, looking rather to the royal charters as models than to the private document. In fact, the closest parallels of all are to be found on the Babylonian boundary-stones and charters. When, therefore, in our chronologically arranged sketch of a given subject, reference is made to Assyrian usage, next to that of the First Dynasty of Babylon, it will be understood that only the nature of the transaction is akin; and that, as a rule, the verbal treatment of it is quite distinct.

Contemporary Babylonian documents

A few contemporary documents have reached us from the cities of Babylonia. They have little or no affinity with the immediately preceding groups, but carry on the local development from the second epoch. They come from many sites and are published in a variety of journals. A tentative list of them will be found in the Appendix.

[1] Vol. XX., pp. 202 ff.

They refer to transactions in the reigns of Shalmaneser IV., Sargon II., Merodach-baladan II., Sennacherib, Esarhaddon, Shamash-shum-ukin, Kandalanu, Ashur-etil-ilâni, and Sin-shar-ishkun. In style they belong to the next epoch.

**Fifth epoch: the second Babylonian empire**

The second Babylonian empire, commencing with Nabopolassar and extending to the end of the independent existence of a Babylonian empire, is represented by thousands of tablets in our museums. A small part of these has been published. Pater J. N. Strassmaier has given some one thousand six hundred in his *Babylonische Texte.* Dr. Peiser published many more in his *Keilinschriftliche Acten-stücke* and *Babylonische Verträge.* The Rev. B. T. A. Evetts, Dr. Moldenke, Dr. Pinches and others have published many more. A detailed list will be found in the Appendix.

**Persian Empire, and later**

In the times of the Persian kings very many documents were drawn up very similar to these. The series is quite unbroken, down through Macedonian rule, the Arsacid period, to as late as B.C. 82. The list will be found in the Appendix.

Of the whole period we may say that the variety and quantity of written evidence are amazing. Every sort of transaction that could be made the subject of a deed or memorandum was written down. They come from most of the chief cities in Babylonia.

**Classification**

The classification of this material is no easy task. As in the case of the Bibliography, so here, the first and apparently the only attempt has been made by Dr. C. Bezold in his invaluable *Kurzgefässter Überblick.*

The view taken there depended upon Professor Oppert's estimate of the nature of the documents and that again was often founded on imperfect copies of the text. A great advance has since been made in understanding the contents of the texts then published, and the number published has enormously increased.

The publications, where accompanied by translations, have generally given some classification. Dr. Peiser, in the fourth volume of Schrader's *Keilinschriftliche Bibliothek*, gives most suggestive indexes.[1] Dr. Tallqvist, in his *Sprache der Contrakte Nabunâ'id's* gives a very valuable classification.[2] Dr. Meissner classified his texts in *Altbabylonische Privatrecht*.

A number of monographs have been written collecting the different texts from many sources bearing on one subject, thus acting as a kind of classification. A complete work on the subject is still needed.

Monographs

Of great importance are Dr. F. E. Peiser's *Jurisprudentiæ Babylonicæ quæ supersunt, Cöthen*, 1890 (Inaug. Diss.); Dr. B. Meissner's *De Servitute babylonico-assyriaca*, Leipzig, 1882 (Inaug. Diss.); and Dr. V. Marx, *Die Stellung der Frauen in Babylonien* (*Nebuchadnezzar to Darius* B.C. *604–485*) published in the *Beiträge zur Assyriologie*, Vol. IV., pp. 1–77. These should certainly be read by any serious student of the times. To reproduce their contents would occupy too much space.

On the whole subject of social life, as illustrated by these contracts, there is a valuable study by Dr. F. E. Peiser, called *Skizze der Babylonischen Gesellschaft*.[3] Professor Sayce's *Babylonians and Assyrians* in the *Semitic Series*, 1900, is an excellent account, though in some respects not sufficiently critical. But in all such preliminary work it is easy to feel sure of conclusions which have to be revised with fuller knowledge. Time will doubtless show this to be true of what is said in the present work. But wherever doubt is felt by the writer, it will be indicated.

---

[1] Pages xi–xx. [2] Pages xi–xviii.
[3] In the *Mitteilungen der Vorderasiatischen Gesellschaft*, 1896, No. 3.

# LAWS AND CONTRACTS

# I

## THE EARLIEST BABYLONIAN LAWS

WE are still completely in the dark as to the rise of law in Babylonia. As far back as we can trace the history or its written monuments, there is no time of which we can say, "As yet there was no law." Our chief object to-day is to discover what the law was. For the most part, and until lately, we were compelled almost entirely to infer this from such contracts as were drawn up between parties and sworn to, witnessed, and sealed. Among them were a large number of legal decisions which recorded the ruling of some judicial functionary on points of law submitted to him. These and the hints given by the legal phrase-books had allowed us to attain considerable knowledge of what was legal and right in ancient Babylonia or Assyria.

Nature of the oldest Babylonian laws

But the question remained, Was it "right" or "law"? Were there enactments by authority, making clear what was right, and in some cases creating right, where there was none before? There was much to suggest the existence of enacted law, even of a code of laws, and the word "law" had been freely applied. But there was no known ascription of any law to a definite legislator. There was no word for "law," only the terms "judgments," "right," and "wrong." It was significant that the parties to a suit always seemed to have agreed on what was right between man and man, and then to have sworn by their gods to observe the "right."

Data hitherto uncertain

Evidence that there were very ancient codes

We definitely know of one great code of laws, that of Ḫammurabi, and we are greatly strengthened in the view that there were laws, and even codes, centuries before him. The way in which contracts quote the phrases of his code is exactly parallel to the way in which far earlier contracts quote phrases which are evidently extracts, in the phrase-books, from some connected work. Hence we are warranted in thinking that these extracts come from a Sumerian code of laws. We do not yet know to whom we should ascribe its compilation.

Codes antecedent to that of Ḫammurabi

For the Code of Ḫammurabi is also a compilation. He did not invent his laws. Phrases found in them appear in contracts before his time. Doubtless he did enact some fresh laws. But he built for the most part on other men's foundations. The decisions already passed by the judges had made men ready to accept as "right" what was now made "law." But the question is only carried back a stage further. Did not those judges decide according to law? In some cases we know they did, for we have the law before them. When we try to penetrate further into the background of history we can only surmise. Documents fail us to prove whether judges first made or administered the law. But we have now a very high antiquity for laws recognized and obeyed as right.

Sumerian laws found in the phrase-books

That laws were already enacted in the pre-Semitic or Sumerian days we may regard as certain. The legal phrase-books drawn up by later scribes, especially those known as forming the series called *ana ittišu*, give as specimens certain laws. These were evidently given by the scribes as examples of connected prose in Sumerian, accompanied by a rendering into Semitic. Their object was primarily grammatical, or at any rate educational; but they are most valuable because they contain specimens of the Sumerian legislation. Owing to their limited scope they were at first regarded as family laws. But there can be little doubt that they really are extracts from something like a code of laws. We are as yet quite ignorant of the date of their first promulgation, place of origin, and legislator. The seventh tablet of the series *ana ittišu*, Col. III. l. 22 to Col. IV. l. 22, gives the seven following laws:

I. If a son has said to his father, "You are not my father," he may brand him, lay fetters upon him, and sell him. **Repudiation of father by son**

It may be doubted whether this applies to any but adopted sons. "You shall not be my father" is a possible rendering. But the phrase may only refer to rebellious conduct. The word rendered "brand" has often been taken to mean "shave." The cutting short of the hair was a mark of degradation. The Semitic Babylonians wore their hair long, while slaves, and perhaps also Sumerians as a race, are represented as hairless. However that may be, the same word is used of "branding" cattle and it implies cutting or incision. It may mean a tattooed mark. The word rendered "fetter" seems also to be used of a branded body-mark. The whole law means that the rebellious son is to be degraded to the status of a slave and treated as such.

II. If a son has said to his mother, "You are not my mother," one shall brand his forehead, drive him out of the city, and make him go out of the house. **Repudiation of mother by son**

Here the same ambiguity about branding is found. Some take the word rendered "forehead" to mean the hair of the head. His head would then be shaved. "To go out from the house" means "to be cut off from kith and kin." But here the son retains his freedom, only he is an exile and homeless. In this case it is not the mother who exacts the penalty. The verb is plural and may be taken impersonally. The family or the city magistrates are probably the ones to execute the law.

Disinheritance of son by father

III. If a father has said to his son, "You are not my son," he shall leave house and yard.

Here the father has power to repudiate a son, who must go. The word for "leave" is literally "take himself up," "go up out of." The word "yard" is simply "inclosure" and may mean the city walls, as a symbol of shelter.

Disinheritance of son by mother

IV. If a mother has said to her son, "You are not my son," he shall leave house and property.

Here we expect, by analogy with Laws I. and II., that this penalty is rather less than that in III. The "property" means "house furniture." The son must leave home and can take no house furniture with him. He has no claim to inherit anything. But he need not leave the city. Hence it seems likely that III. denied him the right of city shelter.

Repudiation of husband by wife

V. If a wife hates her husband and has said, "You are not my husband," one shall throw her into the river.

Repudiation of wife by husband

VI. If a husband has said to his wife, "You are not my wife," he shall pay half a mina of silver.

The contrast in the penalties is startling. Note the impersonal form of V. The executioners here are the family, or city, not the husband. Publicity is therefore implied. It is not a private quarrel, but a refusal of conjugal rights. In the second case the man divorces, or puts away, his wife, but pays a heavy fine.

Responsibility of employer

VII. If a man has hired a slave and he dies, is lost, has fled, has been incapacitated, or has fallen sick, he shall measure out 10 *ḳa* of corn *per diem* as his wages.

Here the Sumerian text differs from the Semitic. In the former the employer is said to "cause" the slave to suffer these detriments, in the latter he is said to come by them. The verb rendered "lost" is used in that sense in the later Code of Ḫammurabi. What is the exact sense of the verb rendered "has been incapacitated" is not clear. Professor

Hommel[1] renders *durchbrennen*, Delitzsch[2] renders *weichen, entweichen, oder zu arbeit aufhören.* But it is clear that the employer is to pay a daily fine for injury done to the slave, or for loss to his owner, caused or connived at by him. The slave's refusal to work could not be made the ground for fining him. If anyone paid for that it would be the owner. The employer pays for his work, but is bound to keep him safe and treat him reasonably well and return him in good condition to his owner. In later times the owner often took the risk of death and flight, but then he probably charged more hire. At any rate it is clear that the owner is not named in this law.

It is not profitable to discuss these mere fragments of a code. The most interesting thing is their existence. We may one day recover the Code in full. These are not retranslations into Sumerian, by learned scribes, of late laws. For exactly these words and phrases occur in the contracts of the First Dynasty of Babylon, before and after the Code of Ḫammurabi, which deals with the same cases, but in different words. In fact, this Sumerian Code is quoted, as the later Code was quoted, in documents which embody the sworn agreement of the parties to observe the section of the Code applying to their case. This is indeed the characteristic of the early contracts: after indicating the particulars of the case, an oath is added to the effect that the parties will abide by the law concerning it. Even where no reference is made to a law, it is because either no law had been promulgated on the point, or because the law was understood too well to need mention. Later this law-abiding spirit was less in evidence and the contract became a private undertaking to carry out mutual engagements. But even then it was assumed that a law existed which would hold the parties to the terms of an engagement voluntarily contracted.

---

[1] *Sumerische Lesestücke*, p. 112.

[2] *H. W. B.*, p. 542.

# II

## THE CODE OF ḪAMMURABI

Witchcraft and the ordeal by water

§ 1. If a man has accused another of laying a *nêrtu* (death spell?) upon him, but has not proved it, he shall be put to death.

§ 2. If a man has accused another of laying a *kišpu* (spell) upon him, but has not proved it, the accused shall go to the sacred river, he shall plunge into the sacred river, and if the sacred river shall conquer him, he that accused him shall take possession of his house. If the sacred river shall show his innocence and he is saved, his accuser shall be put to death. He that plunged into the sacred river shall appropriate the house of him that accused him.

False witness in capital suit

§ 3. If a man has borne false witness in a trial, or has not established the statement that he has made, if that case be a capital trial, that man shall be put to death.

In civil case

§ 4. If he has borne false witness in a civil law case, he shall pay the damages in that suit.

Judgment once given not to be altered

§ 5. If a judge has given a verdict, rendered a decision, granted a written judgment, and afterward has altered his judgment, that judge shall be prosecuted for altering the judgment he gave and shall pay twelvefold the penalty laid down in that judgment. Further, he shall be publicly expelled from his judgment-seat and shall not return nor take his seat with the judges at a trial.

Burglary and acceptance of stolen goods

§ 6. If a man has stolen goods from a temple, or house, he shall be put to death; and he that has received the stolen property from him shall be put to death.

Dealings with irresponsible persons

§ 7. If a man has bought or received on deposit from a minor or a slave, either silver, gold, male or female slave, ox, ass, or sheep, or anything else, except by consent of elders, or power of attorney, he shall be put to death for theft.

Theft

§ 8. If a patrician has stolen ox, sheep, ass, pig, or ship, whether from a temple, or a house, he shall pay thirtyfold. If he be a plebeian, he shall return tenfold. If the thief cannot pay, he shall be put to death.

§ 9. If a man has lost property and some of it be detected in the possession of another, and the holder has said, "A man sold it to me, I bought it in the presence of witnesses"; and if the claimant has said, "I can bring witnesses who know it to be property lost by me"; then the alleged buyer on his part shall produce the man who sold it to him and the witnesses before whom he bought it; the claimant shall on his part produce the witnesses who know it to be his lost property. The judge shall examine their pleas. The witnesses to the sale and the witnesses who identify the lost property shall state on oath what they know. Such a seller is the thief and shall be put to death. The owner of the lost property shall recover his lost property. The buyer shall recoup himself from the seller's estate.

**Procedure in case of the discovery of lost property**

§ 10. If the alleged buyer on his part has not produced the seller or the witnesses before whom the sale took place, but the owner of the lost property on his part has produced the witnesses who identify it as his, then the [pretended] buyer is the thief; he shall be put to death. The owner of the lost property shall take his lost property.

§ 11. If, on the other hand, the claimant of the lost property has not brought the witnesses that know his lost property, he has been guilty of slander, he has stirred up strife, he shall be put to death.

§ 12. If the seller has in the meantime died, the buyer shall take from his estate fivefold the value sued for.

§ 13. If a man has not his witnesses at hand, the judge shall set him a fixed time not exceeding six months, and if within six months he has not produced his witnesses, the man has lied; he shall bear the penalty of the suit.

**Judgment by default**

§ 14. If a man has stolen a child, he shall be put to death.

**Kidnapping**

§ 15. If a man has induced either a male or female slave from the house of a patrician, or plebeian, to leave the city, he shall be put to death.

**Abduction of slave**

§ 16. If a man has harbored in his house a male or female slave from a patrician's or plebeian's house, and has not caused the fugitive to leave on the demand of the officer over the slaves condemned to public forced labor, that householder shall be put to death.

**Harboring a fugitive slave**

The capture of a fugitive slave

§ 17. If a man has caught either a male or female runaway slave in the open field and has brought him back to his owner, the owner of the slave shall give him two shekels of silver.

§ 18. If such a slave will not name his owner, his captor shall bring him to the palace, where he shall be examined as to his past and returned to his owner.

§ 19. If the captor has secreted that slave in his house and afterward that slave has been caught in his possession, he shall be put to death.

§ 20. If the slave has fled from the hands of his captor, the latter shall swear to the owner of the slave and he shall be free from blame.

Burglary

§ 21. If a man has broken into a house he shall be killed before the breach and buried there.

Highway robbery

§ 22. If a man has committed highway robbery and has been caught, that man shall be put to death.

§ 23. If the highwayman has not been caught, the man that has been robbed shall state on oath what he has lost and the city or district governor in whose territory or district the robbery took place shall restore to him what he has lost.

§ 24. If a life [has been lost], the city or district governor shall pay one mina of silver to the deceased's relatives.

Theft at a fire

§ 25. If a fire has broken out in a man's house and one who has come to put it out has coveted the property of the householder and appropriated any of it, that man shall be cast into the self-same fire.

Duties and privileges of an officer over the levy

§ 26. If a levy-master, or warrant-officer, who has been detailed on the king's service, has not gone, or has hired a substitute in his place, that levy-master, or warrant-officer, shall be put to death and the hired substitute shall take his office.

§ 27. If a levy-master, or warrant-officer, has been assigned to garrison duty, and in his absence his field and garden have been given to another who has carried on his duty, when the absentee has returned and regained his city, his field and garden shall be given back to him and he shall resume his duty.

Rights and duties of his son

§ 28. If a levy-master, or warrant-officer, has been assigned to garrison duty, and has a son able to carry on his official duty, the field and garden shall be given to him and he shall carry on his father's duty.

§ 29. If the son be a child and is not able to carry on his father's duty, one-third of the field and garden shall be given to his mother to educate him.

§ 30. If such an official has neglected the care of his field, garden, or house, and let them go to waste, and if another has taken his field, garden, or house, in his absence, and carried on the duty for three years, if the absentee has returned and would cultivate his field, garden, or house, it shall not be given him; he who has taken it and carried on the duty connected with it shall continue to do so.

Penalty for neglect of his benefice

§ 31. If for one year only he has let things go to waste and he has returned, his field, garden, and house shall be given him, and he himself shall carry on his duty.

§ 32. If such an official has been assigned to the king's service (and captured by the enemy) and has been ransomed by a merchant and helped to regain his city, if he has had means in his house to pay his ransom, he himself shall do so. If he has not had means of his own, he shall be ransomed by the temple treasury. If there has not been means in the temple treasury of his city, the state will ransom him. His field, garden, or house shall not be given for his ransom.

His ransom, if captured

§ 33. If either a governor or a prefect has appropriated to his own use the corvée, or has accepted and sent on the king's service a hired substitute in his place, that governor, or prefect, shall be put to death.

Duties of district governors

§ 34. If either a governor, or a prefect, has appropriated the property of a levy-master, has hired him out, has robbed him by high-handedness at a trial, has taken the salary which the king gave to him, that governor, or prefect, shall be put to death.

Governors not to oppress subordinates

§ 35. If a man has bought from a levy-master the sheep, or oxen, which the king gave him, he shall lose his money.

The benefice of a levy-master, warrant-officer, or tributary inalienable

§ 36. The field, garden, or house, of a levy-master, warrant-officer, or tributary shall not be sold.

§ 37. If a man has bought field, garden, or house, of a levy-master, a warrant-officer, or tributary, his title-deed shall be destroyed and he shall lose his money. He shall return the field, garden, or house to its owner.

§ 38. A levy-master, warrant-officer, or tributary, shall not bequeath anything from the field, garden, or house of his benefice to his wife or daughter, nor shall he give it for his debt.

Not to be bequeathed to his family

§ 39. From the field, garden, or house which he has bought and acquired, he shall make bequests to his wife, or daughter, or shall assign for his debt.

The obligation resting upon a buyer of real estate

§ 40. A votary, merchant, or resident alien may sell his field, garden, or house, and the buyer shall discharge the public service connected with the field, garden, or house that he has bought.

A benefice not to be exchanged

§ 41. If a man has given property in exchange for the field, garden, or house, of a levy-master, warrant-officer, or tributary, such an official shall return to his field, garden, or house, and he shall appropriate the property given in exchange.

Responsibilities of land-tenants

§ 42. If a man has hired a field to cultivate and has caused no corn to grow on the field, he shall be held responsible for not doing the work on the field and shall pay an average rent.

§ 43. If he has not cultivated the field and has left it alone, he shall give to the owner of the field an average rent, and the field which he has neglected he shall break up with mattocks and plough it, and shall return it to the owner of the field.

The rent of unbroken land

§ 44. If a man has taken a piece of virgin soil to open up, on a three years' lease, but has left it alone, has not opened up the land, in the fourth year he shall break it up, hoe it, and plough it, and shall return it to the owner of the field, and shall measure out ten *GUR* of corn for each *GAN* of land.

Loss of crop by storm apportioned between landlord and tenant

§ 45. If a man has let his field to a farmer and has received his rent for the field but afterward the field has been flooded by rain, or a storm has carried off the crop, the loss shall be the farmer's.

§ 46. If he has not received the rent of his field, whether he let it for a half, or for a third, of the crop, the farmer and the owner of the field shall share the corn that is left in the field, according to their agreement.

Landlord cannot restrain a satisfactory tenant from subletting

§ 47. If a tenant farmer, because he did not start farming in the early part of the year, has sublet the field, the owner of the field shall not object; his field has been cultivated; at harvest-time he shall take rent, according to his agreement.

Abatement of debt on account of storm, flood, or drought

§ 48. If a man has incurred a debt and a storm has flooded his field or carried away the crop, or the corn has not grown because of drought, in that year he shall not pay his creditor. Further, he shall post-date his bond and shall not pay interest for that year.

Rights in a crop pledged for debt

§ 49. If a man has received money from a merchant and has given to the merchant a field, planted with corn, or sesame, and has said to him, "Cultivate the field and reap and take the corn, or sesame, that shall be grown"; if the bailiff has reared corn, or sesame, in the field, at harvest-time the owner of the field shall take what corn, or sesame, has been grown in the field and shall pay corn to the merchant for his money that he took of him and its interest, and for the maintenance of the bailiff.

§ 50. If the field he gave was [already] cultivated, or the sesame was grown up, the owner of the field shall take the corn, or sesame, that has been grown in the field, and shall return the money and its interest to the merchant.

§ 51. If he has not money enough, he shall give to the merchant sesame, or corn, according to its market price, for the money which he took from the merchant and its interest, according to the king's standard.

§ 52. If the bailiff has not reared corn or sesame in the field the debtor's obligation shall not be lessened.

Riparian responsibilities

§§ 53, 54. If a man has neglected to strengthen his dike and has not kept his dike strong, and a breach has broken out in his dike, and the waters have flooded the meadow, the man in whose dike the breach has broken out shall restore the corn he has caused to be lost. [54]. If he be not able to restore the corn, he and his goods shall be sold, and the owners of the meadow whose corn the water has carried away shall share the money.

Penalty for neglect to shut off water

§ 55. If a man has opened his runnel for watering and has left it open, and the water has flooded his neighbor's field, he shall pay him an average crop.

§ 56. If a man has let out the waters and they flood the young plants in his neighbor's field, he shall measure out ten *GUR* of corn for each *GAN* of land.

Damage done to growing crop by sheep

§ 57. If a shepherd has not agreed with the owner of the field to allow his sheep to eat off the green crop and without consent of the owner has let his sheep feed off it, the owner of the field shall harvest his crop, but the shepherd who without consent of the owner of the field caused his sheep to eat it shall give to the owner of the field, over and above his crop, twenty *GUR* of corn for each *GAN* of land.

§ 58. If, after the sheep have come up out of the meadows and have passed into the common fold at the city gate, a shepherd has placed his sheep in a field and caused his sheep to feed in the field, the shepherd shall keep the field he has grazed, and, at harvest-time, he shall measure out to the owner sixty *GUR* of corn for each *GAN* of land.

Cutting down a tree without permission

§ 59. If a man without the consent of the owner has cut down a tree in an orchard, he shall weigh out half a mina of silver.

Rent of a garden-plot

§§ 60, 61. If a man has given a field to a gardener to plant a garden and the gardener has planted the garden, he shall train the garden four years; in the fifth year the owner of the garden and the gardener shall share the garden equally, the owner of the garden shall gather his share and take it. [61]. If the gardener, in planting the garden, has not planted all, but has left a bare patch, he shall reckon the bare patch in his share.

§ 62. If he has not planted the field which was given him as a garden; then, if it was arable land, the gardener shall measure out to the owner of the field an average rent for the years that were neglected, and shall perform the stipulated work on the field (*i.e.*, make it into a garden), and return it to the owner of the field.

§ 63. If the land was uncultivated, he shall do the stipulated work on the field, and return to the owner of the field and shall measure out for each year ten *GUR* of corn for each *GAN*.

Garden rented on shares

§ 64. If a man has given his garden to a gardener to farm, the gardener, as long as he holds the garden, shall give the owner of the garden two-thirds of the produce of the garden and shall take one-third himself.

§ 65. If the gardener has not tilled the garden and has diminished the yield, the gardener shall pay an average rent.

Here came the five erased columns, of which the three following sections are restored from copies in Ashurbâni-pal's library:

Obligations of owner to gather a date-crop assigned for debt

§ X. [If a man has borrowed money of a merchant and has given a date grove] to the merchant and has said to him, "Take the dates that are in my grove for your money"; that merchant shall not consent, the owner of the grove shall take the dates that are in the grove and shall answer to the merchant for the money and its interest, according to the tenor of his agreement, and the owner of the grove shall take the surplus of the dates that are in the grove.

Eviction of house-tenant

§ Y. [If a man has let a house] and the tenant has paid to the owner of the house the full rent for a term of years, and if the owner of the house has ordered the tenant to leave before his time is up, the owner of the house, because he has ordered his tenant to leave before his time is up, [shall repay a proportionate amount] from what the tenant has paid him.

§ Z. [If a man has borrowed money of a merchant] and has not corn or money wherewith [to pay], but has goods; whatever is in his hands, he shall give to the merchant, before the elders. The merchant shall not object; he shall receive it. Acceptance of goods in payment of debt, in default of money or corn

After the loss of about thirty-five sections the Code resumes:

§ 100. [If an agent has received money of a merchant, he shall write down the amount] and [what is to be] the interest of the money, and when his time is up, he shall settle with his merchant. Responsibility of a travelling salesman

§ 101. If he has not had success on his travels, he shall return double what he received to the merchant.

§§ 102, 103. If the merchant has given money, as a speculation, to the agent, who during his travels has met with misfortune, he shall return the full sum to the merchant. [103]. If, on his travels, an enemy has forced him to give up some of the goods he was carrying, the agent shall specify the amount on oath and shall be acquitted. Robbery, substantiated by oath, a valid excuse

§ 104. If a merchant has given to an agent corn, wool, oil, or any sort of goods, to traffic with, the agent shall write down the money value, and shall return that to the merchant. The agent shall then take a sealed receipt for the money that he has given to the merchant. Responsibility to be indicated by legal receipts

§ 105. If the agent forgets and has not taken a sealed receipt for the money he gave to the merchant, money that has not been acknowledged by receipt shall not be put down in the accounts.

§ 106. If an agent has taken money of a merchant, and his principal suspects him, that principal shall prosecute his agent, put him on oath before the elders, as to the money taken; the agent shall pay to the merchant threefold what he misappropriated. Punishment of fraud of an agent

§ 107. If the principal has overcharged the agent and the agent has [really] returned to his principal whatever his principal gave him, and if the principal has disputed what the agent has given him, that agent shall put his principal on oath before the elders, and the merchant, because he has defrauded the agent, shall pay to the agent sixfold what he misappropriated. Fraud practised by principal

Fraud in ordinary drink-traffic

§ 108. If the mistress of a beer-shop has not received corn as the price of beer or has demanded silver on an excessive scale, and has made the measure of beer less than the measure of corn, that beer-seller shall be prosecuted and drowned.

Connivance at unlawful assemblages

§ 109. If the mistress of a beer-shop has assembled seditious slanderers in her house and those seditious persons have not been captured and have not been haled to the palace, that beer-seller shall be put to death.

Drink-traffic forbidden to votaries

§ 110. If a votary, who is not living in the convent, open a beer-shop, or enter a beer-shop for drink, that woman shall be put to death.

Rate of payment with produce

§ 111. If the mistress of a beer-shop has given sixty *ḲA* of *sakani* beer in the time of thirst, at harvest, she shall take fifty *ḲA* of corn.

Carrier's liability for misappropriation of goods

§ 112. If a man staying abroad has given silver, gold, precious stones, or portable goods to another man to transport, and if that man has not delivered the consignment, where he has carried it, but has appropriated it, the owner of the consignment shall prosecute him, and the carrier shall give to the owner of the consignment five-fold whatever was intrusted to him.

Unauthorized seizure of goods denied a creditor

§ 113. If a man has a debt of corn, or money, due from another and without the consent of the owner of the corn has taken corn from the granary, or barn, the owner of the corn shall prosecute him for taking the corn from the granary, or barn, without his consent, and the man shall return all the corn he took, and further lose whatever it was that he had lent.

Punishment of vexatious distraint

§ 114. If a man has no debt of corn or money due from a man on whom he has levied a distraint, for each such distraint he shall pay one-third of a mina of silver.

Creditor responsible for fair treatment of a man held as security for debt

§ 115. If a man has corn or money due from another man and has levied a distraint and the hostage has died a natural death in the house of the creditor, he cannot be held responsible.

§ 116. If the hostage has died of blows or want in the house of the creditor, the owner of the hostage shall prosecute his creditor, and if the deceased were free born, the creditor's son shall be put to death; if a slave, the creditor shall pay one-third of a mina of silver, Further, he shall lose whatever it was that he lent.

Limitations on the holding of such hostages

§ 117. If a man owes a debt, and he has given his wife, his son, or his daughter [as hostage] for the money, or has handed someone over to work it off, the hostage shall do the work of the creditor's house; but in the fourth year he shall set them free.

§ 118. If a debtor has handed over a male or female slave to work off a debt, and the creditor proceeds to sell same, no one can complain.

§ 119. If a man owes a debt, and he has assigned a maid who has borne him children for the money, the owner of the maid shall repay the money which the merchant gave him and shall ransom his maid.

Responsibility of owners of warehouses

§ 120. If a man has deposited his corn for safe keeping in another's house and it has suffered damage in the granary, or if the owner of the house has opened the store and taken the corn, or has disputed the amount of the corn that was stored in his house, the owner of the corn shall declare on oath the amount of his corn, and the owner of the house shall return him double.

Rate of payment for storage of corn

§ 121. If a man has stored corn in another man's house he shall give, on each *GUR* of corn, five *ḲA* of corn, yearly, as the rent for storage.

Receipt for deposit of valuables

§ 122. If a man has given another gold, silver, or any goods whatever, on deposit, all that he gives shall he show to witnesses, and take a bond and so give on deposit.

§ 123. If he has given on deposit without witnesses and bonds, and has been defrauded where he made his deposit, he has no claim to prosecute.

Responsibility of bankers

§ 124. If a man has given on deposit to another, before witnesses, gold, silver, or any goods whatever, and his claim has been contested, he shall prosecute that man, and [the man] shall return double what he disputed.

Their own losses no excuse

§ 125. If a man has given anything whatever on deposit, and, where he has made his deposit, something of his has been lost together with something belonging to the owner of the house, either by house-breaking or a rebellion, the owner of the house who is in default shall make good all that has been given him on deposit, which he has lost, and shall return it to the owner of the goods. The owner of the house shall look after what he has lost and recover it from the thief.

Depreciation of property

§ 126. If a man has said that something of his is lost, which is not lost, or has alleged a depreciation, though nothing of his is lost, he shall estimate the depreciation on oath, and he shall pay double whatever he has claimed.

Slander of votary or married woman

§ 127. If a man has caused the finger to be pointed at a votary, or a man's wife, and has not justified himself, that man shall be brought before the judges, and have his forehead branded.

Marriage-bonds

§ 128. If a man has taken a wife and has not executed a marriage-contract, that woman is not a wife.

Punishment of flagrant adultery

§ 129. If a man's wife be caught lying with another, they shall be strangled and cast into the water. If the wife's husband would save his wife, the king can save his servant.

Rape of a betrothed virgin

§ 130. If a man has ravished another's betrothed wife, who is a virgin, while still living in her father's house, and has been caught in the act, that man shall be put to death; the woman shall go free.

Suspicion of adultery cleared by oath

§ 131. If a man's wife has been accused by her husband, and has not been caught lying with another, she shall swear her innocence, and return to her house.

Ordeal of water permissible to accused wife

§ 132. If a man's wife has the finger pointed at her on account of another, but has not been caught lying with him, for her husband's sake she shall plunge into the sacred river.

Rights and duties of the wives of those who have been taken captive in war

§ 133. If a man has been taken captive, and there was maintenance in his house, but his wife has left her house and entered into another man's house; because that woman has not preserved her body, and has entered into the house of another, that woman shall be prosecuted and shall be drowned.

§ 134. If a man has been taken captive, but there was not maintenance in his house, and his wife has entered into the house of another, that woman has no blame.

§ 135. If a man has been taken captive, but there was no maintenance in his house for his wife, and she has entered into the house of another, and has borne him children, if in the future her [first] husband shall return and regain his city, that woman shall return to her first husband, but the children shall follow their own father.

Right of a deserted wife to remarry

§ 136. If a man has left his city and fled, and, after he has gone, his wife has entered into the house of another; if the man return and seize his wife, the wife of the fugitive shall not return to her husband, because he hated his city and fled.

Rights of a divorced woman who has borne children

§ 137. If a man has determined to divorce a concubine who has borne him children, or a votary who has granted him children, he shall return to that woman her marriage-portion, and shall give her the usufruct of field, garden, and goods, to bring up her children. After her children have grown up, out of whatever is given to her children, they shall give her one son's share, and the husband of her choice shall marry her.

§ 138. If a man has divorced his wife, who has not borne him children, he shall pay over to her as much money as was given for her bride-price and the marriage-portion which she brought from her father's house, and so shall divorce her. Rights of a divorced woman who is childless

§ 139. If there was no bride-price, he shall give her one mina of silver, as a price of divorce.

§ 140. If he be a plebeian, he shall give her one-third of a mina of silver.

§ 141. If a man's wife, living in her husband's house, has persisted in going out, has acted the fool, has wasted her house, has belittled her husband, he shall prosecute her. If her husband has said, "I divorce her," she shall go her way; he shall give her nothing as her price of divorce. If her husband has said, "I will not divorce her," he may take another woman to wife; the wife shall live as a slave in her husband's house. Status of a worthless wife

§ 142. If a woman has hated her husband and has said, "You shall not possess me," her past shall be inquired into, as to what she lacks. If she has been discreet, and has no vice, and her husband has gone out, and has greatly belittled her, that woman has no blame, she shall take her marriage-portion and go off to her father's house. Status of a wife who repudiates her husband

§ 143. If she has not been discreet, has gone out, ruined her house, belittled her husband, she shall be drowned.

§ 144. If a man has married a votary, and that votary has given a maid to her husband, and so caused him to have children, and, if that man is inclined to marry a concubine, that man shall not be allowed to do so, he shall not marry a concubine. Marriage with a votary

§ 145. If a man has married a votary, and she has not granted him children, and he is determined to marry a concubine, that man shall marry the concubine, and bring her into his house, but the concubine shall not place herself on an equality with the votary.

§ 146. If a man has married a votary, and she has given a maid to her husband, and the maid has borne children, and if afterward that maid has placed herself on an equality with her mistress, because she has borne children, her mistress shall not sell her, she shall place a slave-mark upon her, and reckon her with the slave-girls. A votary's rights against a maid assigned to her husband

§ 147. If she has not borne children, her mistress shall sell her.

Status of a wife afflicted with a disease

§ 148. If a man has married a wife and a disease has seized her, if he is determined to marry a second wife, he shall marry her. He shall not divorce the wife whom the disease has seized. In the home they made together she shall dwell, and he shall maintain her as long as she lives.

§ 149. If that woman was not pleased to stay in her husband's house, he shall pay over to her the marriage-portion which she brought from her father's house, and she shall go away.

Wife's right to property deeded to her by her husband

§ 150. If a man has presented field, garden, house, or goods to his wife, has granted her a deed of gift, her children, after her husband's death, shall not dispute her right; the mother shall leave it after her death to that one of her children whom she loves best. She shall not leave it to her kindred.

Marital responsibility for ante-nuptial debts

§ 151. If a woman, who is living in a man's house, has persuaded her husband to bind himself, and grant her a deed to the effect that she shall not be held for debt by a creditor of her husband's; if that man had a debt upon him before he married that woman, his creditor shall not take his wife for it. Also, if that woman had a debt upon her before she entered that man's house, her creditor shall not take her husband for it.

§ 152. From the time that that woman entered into the man's house they together shall be liable for all debts subsequently incurred.

Connivance at husband's murder by a wife

§ 153. If a man's wife, for the sake of another, has caused her husband to be killed, that woman shall be impaled.

Incest with own daughter

§ 154. If a man has committed incest with his daughter, that man shall be banished from the city.

Incest with daughter-in-law

§ 155. If a man has betrothed a maiden to his son and his son has known her, and afterward the man has lain in her bosom, and been caught, that man shall be strangled and she shall be cast into the water.

§ 156. If a man has betrothed a maiden to his son, and his son has not known her, and that man has lain in her bosom, he shall pay her half a mina of silver, and shall pay over to her whatever she brought from her father's house, and the husband of her choice shall marry her.

Incest with mother

§ 157. If a man, after his father's death, has lain in the bosom of his mother, they shall both of them be burnt together.

Incest with step-mother

§ 158. If a man, after his father's death, be caught in the bosom of his step-mother, who has borne children, that man shall be cut off from his father's house.

§ 159. If a man, who has presented a gift to the house of his prospective father-in-law and has given the bride-price, has afterward looked upon another woman and has said to his father-in-law, "I will not marry your daughter"; the father of the girl shall keep whatever he has brought as a present. Penalty for breach of promise

§ 160. If a man has presented a gift to the house of his prospective father-in-law, and has given the bride-price, but the father of the girl has said, "I will not give you my daughter," the father shall return double all that was presented him. Rights of a rejected suitor

§ 161. If a man has brought a gift to the house of his prospective father-in-law, and has given the bride-price, but his comrade has slandered him and his father-in-law has said to the suitor, "You shall not marry my daughter," [the father] shall return double all that was presented him. Further, the comrade shall not marry the girl. Slandering rival not to profit by his calumny

§ 162. If a man has married a wife, and she has borne him children, and that woman has gone to her fate, her father shall lay no claim to her marriage-portion. Her marriage-portion is her children's only. Disposal of a wife's marriage-portion

§ 163. If a man has married a wife, and she has not borne him children, and that woman has gone to her fate; if his father-in-law has returned to him the bride-price, which that man brought into the house of his father-in-law, her husband shall have no claim on the marriage-portion of that woman. Her marriage-portion indeed belongs to her father's house.

§ 164. If the father-in-law has not returned the bride-price, the husband shall deduct the amount of her bride-price from her marriage-portion, and shall return her marriage-portion to her father's house.

§ 165. If a man has presented field, garden, or house to his son, the first in his eyes, and has written him a deed of gift; after the father has gone to his fate, when the brothers share, he shall keep the present his father gave him, and over and above shall share equally with them in the goods of his father's estate. Effect upon the inheritance of a father's gift to a favorite son

§ 166. If a man has taken wives for the other sons he had, but has not taken a wife for his young son, after the father has gone to his fate, when the brothers share, they shall set aside from the goods of their father's estate money, as a bride-price, for their young brother, who has not married a wife, over and above his share, and they shall cause him to take a wife. Reservation of a bride-price for a young unmarried brother

Inheritance of children in case of two fruitful marriages

§ 167. If a man has taken a wife, and she has borne him children and that woman has gone to her fate, and he has taken a second wife, and she also has borne children; after the father has gone to his fate, the sons shall not share according to mothers, but each family shall take the marriage-portion of its mother, and all shall share the goods of their father's estate equally.

Disinheritance of a son

§ 168. If a man has determined to disinherit his son and has declared before the judge, "I cut off my son," the judge shall inquire into the son's past, and, if the son has not committed a grave misdemeanor such as should cut him off from sonship, the father shall disinherit his son.

§ 169. If he has committed a grave crime against his father, which cuts off from sonship, for the first offence he shall pardon him. If he has committed a grave crime a second time, the father shall cut off his son from sonship.

Status of children by a slave-woman

§ 170. If a man has had children borne to him by his wife, and also by a maid, if the father in his lifetime has said, "My sons," to the children whom his maid bore him, and has reckoned them with the sons of his wife; then after the father has gone to his fate, the children of the wife and of the maid shall share equally. The children of the wife shall apportion the shares and make their own selections.

§ 171. And if the father, in his lifetime, has not said, "My sons," to the children whom the maid bore him, after the father has gone to his fate, the children of the maid shall not share with the children of the wife in the goods of their father's house. The maid and her children, however, shall obtain their freedom. The children of the wife have no claim for service on the children of the maid.

The rights of a widow in personal property

The wife shall take her marriage-portion, and any gift that her husband has given her and for which he has written a deed of gift and she shall dwell in her husband's house; as long as she lives, she shall enjoy it, she shall not sell it. After her death it is indeed her children's.

§ 172. If her husband has not given her a gift, her marriage-portion shall be given her in full, and, from the goods of her husband's estate, she shall take a share equal to that of one son.

Her rights in the home

If her children have persecuted her in order to have her leave the house, and the judge has inquired into her past, and laid the blame on the children, that woman shall not leave her husband's house. If that woman has determined to leave, she shall relinquish to her children the gift her husband gave her, she shall take the marriage-portion of her father's estate, and the husband of her choice may marry her.

§ 173. If that woman, where she has gone, has borne children to her later husband, after that woman has died, the children of both marriages shall share her marriage-portion. Dower rights of her children by second marriage

§ 174. If she has not borne children to her later husband, the children of her first husband shall take her marriage-portion.

§ 175. If either a slave of a patrician, or of a plebeian, has married the daughter of a free man, and she has borne children, the owner of the slave shall have no claim for service on the children of a free woman. And if a slave, either of a patrician or of a plebeian, has married a free woman and when he married her she entered the slave's house with a marriage-portion from her father's estate, be he slave of a patrician or of a plebeian, and from the time that they started to keep house, they have acquired property; after the slave, whether of a patrician or of a plebeian, has gone to his fate, the free woman shall take her marriage-portion, and whatever her husband and she acquired, since they started house-keeping. She shall divide it into two portions. The master of the slave shall take one half, the other half the free woman shall take for her children. Property rights of the children of slave-father and free mother

§ 176. If the free woman had no marriage-portion, whatever her husband and she acquired since they started house-keeping he shall divide into two portions. The owner of the slave shall take one half, the other half the free woman shall take for her children.

§ 177. If a widow, whose children are young, has determined to marry again, she shall not marry without consent of the judge. When she is allowed to remarry, the judge shall inquire as to what remains of the property of her former husband, and shall intrust the property of her former husband to that woman and her second husband. He shall give them an inventory. They shall watch over the property, and bring up the children. Not a utensil shall they sell. A buyer of any utensil belonging to the widow's children shall lose his money and shall return the article to its owners. Property rights of the young children of a widow who remarries

§ 178. If a female votary, or vowed woman, has had given her by her father a portion, as for marriage, and he has written her a deed, and in the deed which he has written her he has not written that she may leave it as she pleases, and has not granted her all her The property rights of a votary desire; after her father has gone to his fate, her brothers shall take her field, or garden, and, according to the value of her share, shall give her corn, oil, and wool, and shall content her heart. If they do not give her corn, oil, and wool, according to the value of her share, and do not satisfy her, she shall let her field and garden to a farmer, whom she chooses, and the farmer shall support her. The field, garden, or whatever her father gave her, she shall enjoy, as long as she lives. She shall not sell it, nor mortgage it. The reversion of her inheritance indeed belongs to her brothers.

Her right to convey property

§ 179. If a female votary, or vowed woman, has had a portion given her by her father, and he has written her a deed, and in the deed that he has written her has [declared] that she may give it as she pleases, and has granted her all her desire; after her father has gone to his fate, she shall leave it as she pleases; her brothers shall make no claim against her.

Her right of inheritance

§ 180. If the father has not given a portion to his daughter, who is a female votary, or vowed woman; after her father has gone to his fate, she shall share in the property of her father's house, like any other child. As long as she lives, she shall enjoy her share; after her, it indeed belongs to her brothers.

Her proportion of her father's property

§ 181. If a father has vowed his daughter to a god, as a temple maid, or a virgin, and has given her no portion; after the father has gone to his fate, she shall share in the property of her father's estate, taking one-third of a child's share. She shall enjoy her share, as long as she lives. After her, it belongs to her brothers.

Additional privileges of votary of Marduk of Babylon

§ 182. If a father has not given a portion, as for marriage, to his daughter, a votary of Marduk of Babylon, and has not written her a deed; after her father has gone to his fate, she shall share with her brothers from the goods of her father's estate, taking one-third of a child's share. She shall not be subject to duty. The votary of Marduk shall leave it after her to whom she pleases.

Rights of a daughter by a concubine, if provided for by father on marriage

§ 183. If a father has given a portion, as for marriage, to his daughter by a concubine, and has given her to a husband, and has written her a deed; after her father has gone to his fate, she shall not share in the goods of her father's house.

If not so provided for by father

§ 184. If a man has not given a portion, as for marriage, to his daughter by a concubine, and has not given her to a husband; after her father has gone to his fate, her brothers shall present her with a marriage-portion, according to the wealth of her father's estate, and shall give her to a husband.

§ 185. If a man has taken a young child, a natural son of his, to be his son, and has brought him up, no one shall make a claim against that foster child. Adoption of natural son

§ 186. If a man has taken a young child to be his son, and after he has taken him, the child discover his own parents, he shall return to his father's house. Adoption of child of living parents

§ 187. The son of a royal favorite, of one that stands in the palace, or the son of a votary shall not be reclaimed.

§§ 188, 189. If a craftsman has taken a child to bring up and has taught him his handicraft, he shall not be reclaimed. If he has not taught him his handicraft that foster child shall return to his father's house. Responsibilities of a craftsman to his adopted child

§ 190. If a man has brought up the child, whom he has taken to be his son, but has not reckoned him with his sons, that foster child shall return to his father's house. Rights of inheritance of an adopted son

§ 191. If a man has brought up the child, whom he took to be his son, and then sets up a home, and after he has acquired children, decides to disinherit the foster child, that son shall not go his way [penniless]; the father that brought him up shall give him one-third of a son's share in his goods and he shall depart. He shall not give him field, garden, or house. Obligations on discarding an adopted son

§ 192. If the son of a palace favorite or the son of a vowed woman has said to the father that brought him up, "You are not my father," or to the mother that brought him up, "You are not my mother," his tongue shall be cut out. Punishment for the repudiation of adoptive parents

§ 193. If the son of a palace favorite or the son of a vowed woman has come to know his father's house and has hated his father that brought him up, or his mother that brought him up, and shall go off to his father's house, his eyes shall be torn out.

§ 194. If a man has given his son to a wet-nurse to suckle, and that son has died in the hands of the nurse, and the nurse, without consent of the child's father or mother, has nursed another child, they shall prosecute her; because she has nursed another child, without consent of the father or mother, her breasts shall be cut off. Penalty for substituting one infant for another

§ 195. If a son has struck his father, his hands shall be cut off. Assault on a father

Graded penalties for assault and battery

§ 196. If a man has knocked out the eye of a patrician, his eye shall be knocked out.

§ 197. If he has broken the limb of a patrician, his limb shall be broken.

§ 198. If he has knocked out the eye of a plebeian or has broken the limb of a plebeian, he shall pay one mina of silver.

§ 199. If he has knocked out the eye of a patrician's servant, or broken the limb of a patrician's servant, he shall pay half his value.

§ 200. If a patrician has knocked out the tooth of a man that is his equal, his tooth shall be knocked out.

§ 201. If he has knocked out the tooth of a plebeian, he shall pay one-third of a mina of silver.

Brutal assault

§ 202. If a man has smitten the privates of a man, higher in rank than he, he shall be scourged with sixty blows of an ox-hide scourge, in the assembly.

§ 203. If a man has smitten the privates of a patrician of his own rank, he shall pay one mina of silver.

§ 204. If a plebeian has smitten the privates of a plebeian, he shall pay ten shekels of silver.

§ 205. If the slave of anyone has smitten the privates of a free-born man, his ear shall be cut off.

Fatal assault

§ 206. If a man has struck another in a quarrel, and caused him a permanent injury, that man shall swear, "I struck him without malice," and shall pay the doctor.

§ 207. If he has died of his blows, [the man] shall swear [similarly], and pay one-half a mina of silver; or,

§ 208. If [the deceased] was a plebeian, he shall pay one-third of a mina of silver.

Assaults upon pregnant women

§ 209. If a man has struck a free woman with child, and has caused her to miscarry, he shall pay ten shekels for her miscarriage.

§ 210. If that woman die, his daughter shall be killed.

§ 211. If it be the daughter of a plebeian, that has miscarried through his blows, he shall pay five shekels of silver.

§ 212. If that woman die, he shall pay half a mina of silver.

§ 213. If he has struck a man's maid and caused her to miscarry, he shall pay two shekels of silver.

§ 214. If that woman die, he shall pay one-third of a mina of silver.

§ 215. If a surgeon has operated with the bronze lancet on a patrician for a serious injury, and has cured him, or has removed with a bronze lancet a cataract for a patrician, and has cured his eye, he shall take ten shekels of silver. Gradation of surgeon's fees

§ 216. If it be plebeian, he shall take five shekels of silver.

§ 217. If it be a man's slave, the owner of the slave shall give two shekels of silver to the surgeon.

§ 218. If a surgeon has operated with the bronze lancet on a patrician for a serious injury, and has caused his death, or has removed a cataract for a patrician, with the bronze lancet, and has made him lose his eye, his hands shall be cut off. Penalties for unskilful operations

§ 219. If the surgeon has treated a serious injury of a plebeian's slave, with the bronze lancet, and has caused his death, he shall render slave for slave.

§ 220. If he has removed a cataract with the bronze lancet, and made the slave lose his eye, he shall pay half his value.

§ 221. If a surgeon has cured the limb of a patrician, or has doctored a diseased bowel, the patient shall pay five shekels of silver to the surgeon. Cure of limb or bowel

§ 222. If he be a plebeian, he shall pay three shekels of silver.

§ 223. If he be a man's slave, the owner of the slave shall give two shekels of silver to the doctor.

§ 224. If a veterinary surgeon has treated an ox, or an ass, for a severe injury, and cured it, the owner of the ox, or the ass, shall pay the surgeon one-sixth of a shekel of silver, as his fee. Fees for the treatment of the diseases of animals

§ 225. If he has treated an ox, or an ass, for a severe injury, and caused it to die, he shall pay one-quarter of its value to the owner of the ox, or the ass.

§ 226. If a brander has cut out a mark on a slave, without the consent of his owner, that brander shall have his hands cut off. Brander's liabilities

§ 227. If someone has deceived the brander, and induced him to cut out a mark on a slave, that man shall be put to death and buried in his house; the brander shall swear, "I did not mark him knowingly," and shall go free.

§ 228. If a builder has built a house for a man, and finished it, he shall pay him a fee of two shekels of silver, for each *SAR* built on. Builder's fee and liabilities for bad workmanship

§ 229. If a builder has built a house for a man, and has not made his work sound, and the house he built has fallen, and caused the death of its owner, that builder shall be put to death.

§ 230. If it is the owner's son that is killed, the builder's son shall be put to death.

§ 231. If it is the slave of the owner that is killed, the builder shall give slave for slave to the owner of the house.

§ 232. If he has caused the loss of goods, he shall render back whatever he has destroyed. Moreover, because he did not make sound the house he built, and it fell, at his own cost he shall rebuild the house that fell.

§ 233. If a builder has built a house for a man, and has not keyed his work, and the wall has fallen, that builder shall make that wall firm at his own expense.

Boatmen's fees and liabilities

§ 234. If a boatman has built a boat of sixty *GUR* for a man, he shall pay him a fee of two shekels of silver.

§ 235. If a boatman has built a boat for a man, and has not made his work sound, and in that same year that boat is sent on a voyage and suffers damage, the boatman shall rebuild that boat, and, at his own expense, shall make it strong, or shall give a strong boat to the owner.

Hire of boats

§ 236. If a man has let his boat to a boatman, and the boatman has been careless and the boat has been sunk or lost, the boatman shall restore a boat to the owner.

Responsibility of boatmen carrying goods

§ 237. If a man has hired a boat and boatman, and loaded it with corn, wool, oil, or dates, or whatever it be, and the boatman has been careless, and sunk the boat, or lost what is in it, the boatman shall restore the boat which he sank, and whatever he lost that was in it.

§ 238. If a boatman has sunk a man's boat, and has floated it again, he shall pay half its value in silver.

§ 239. If a man has hired a boatman, he shall pay him six *GUR* of corn yearly.

Law of collision

§ 240. If a boat, on its course, has run into a boat at anchor, and sunk it, the owner of the boat that was sunk shall estimate on oath whatever was lost in his boat, and the owner of the moving vessel, which sank the boat at anchor, shall make good his boat and what was lost in it.

Working ox not to be distrained

§ 241. If a man has levied a distraint on a working ox, he shall pay one-third of a mina of silver.

Hire of oxen and cows

§ 242. If a man has hired a working ox for one year, its hire is four *GUR* of corn.

§ 243. As the hire of a milch cow one shall give three *GUR* of corn to its owner.

Liability for loss of ox or ass by accident

§ 244. If a man has hired an ox, or an ass, and a lion has killed it in the open field, the loss falls on its owner.

Compensation for loss of ox by ill-treatment

§ 245. If a man has hired an ox and has caused its death, by carelessness, or blows, he shall restore ox for ox, to the owner of the ox.

§ 246. If a man has hired an ox, and has broken its leg, or cut its neck (?), he shall restore ox for ox, to the owner of the ox.

§ 247. If a man has hired an ox, and knocked out its eye, he shall pay to the owner of the ox half its value.

Responsibility for unavoidable accidents to a hired ox

§ 248. If a man has hired an ox, and has broken its horn, cut off its tail, or torn its muzzle, he shall pay one-quarter of its value.

§ 249. If a man has hired an ox, and God has struck it, and it has died, the man that hired the ox shall make affidavit and go free.

Death by goring, accidental

§ 250. If a bull has gone wild and gored a man, and caused his death, there can be no suit against the owner.

Responsibility for a vicious ox

§ 251. If a man's ox be a gorer, and has revealed its evil propensity as a gorer, and he has not blunted its horn, or shut up the ox, and then that ox has gored a free man, and caused his death, the owner shall pay half a mina of silver.

§ 252. If it be a slave that has been killed, he shall pay one-third of a mina of silver.

Responsibility of a tenant farmer

§ 253. If a man has set another over his field, hired him, allotted him tools, and intrusted him with oxen for cultivating the field and provided harnesses for them, and if that man has appropriated the seed or provender, and they have been found in his possession, his hands shall be cut off.

§ 254. If he has taken the provender or rations and has enfeebled the oxen, he shall make it good from the corn he has hoed.

§ 255. If he has let out the man's oxen for hire, or stolen the seed-corn, or has not produced a crop, that man shall be prosecuted, and he shall pay sixty *GUR* of corn for each *GAN*.

§ 256. If he is not able to pay his compensation, he shall be torn in pieces on that field by the oxen.

Wages of laborers

§ 257. If a man has hired a field-laborer, he shall pay him eight *GUR* of corn yearly.

§ 258. If anyone has hired an ox-herd he shall pay him six *GUR* of corn yearly.

Theft of agricultural instruments

§ 259. If a man has stolen a watering-machine from the meadow, he shall pay five shekels of silver to the owner of the watering-machine.

§ 260. If a man has stolen a *shadduf*, or a plough, he shall pay three shekels of silver.

Wages of herdsmen

§ 261. If a man has hired a herdsman, to pasture oxen, or sheep, he shall pay him eight *GUR* of corn yearly.

Their liability

§ 262. If a man has intrusted ox or ass to . . . [Passage mutilated.]

§ 263. If he has lost the ox, or ass, given to him, he shall restore ox for ox, and ass for ass to its owner.

§ 264. If a herdsman, who has had oxen or sheep given to him to pasture, has received his wages for the business, and been satisfied, then diminish the herd or lessen the offspring, he shall give increase and produce according to the nature of his agreements.

§ 265. If a herdsman, to whom oxen or sheep have been given, has defaulted, has altered the price, or sold them, he shall be prosecuted, and shall restore oxen, or sheep, tenfold, to their owner.

§ 266. If lightning has struck a fold, or a lion has made a slaughter, the herdsman shall purge himself by oath, and the owner of the fold shall bear the loss of the fold.

§ 267. If the herdsman has been careless, and a loss has occurred in the fold, the herdsman shall make good the loss in the fold; he shall repay the oxen, or sheep, to their owner.

Hire of animals for threshing

§ 268. If a man has hired an ox, for threshing, its hire is twenty *ḲA* of corn.

§ 269. If he has hired an ass, for threshing, its hire is ten *ḲA* of corn.

§ 270. If he has hired a young animal, for threshing, its hire is one *ḲA* of corn.

Hire of wagon, oxen, and driver

§ 271. If a man has hired oxen, a wagon, and its driver, he shall pay one hundred and sixty *ḲA* of corn daily.

§ 272. If a man has hired the wagon alone, he shall pay forty *ḲA* of corn daily.

Graded wages of day-laborers

§ 273. If a man has hired a laborer from the beginning of the year to the fifth month, he shall pay six *ŠE* of silver daily; from the sixth month to the close of the year, he shall pay five *ŠE* of silver daily.

§ 274. If a man has hired an artisan, he shall pay as his daily wages, to a . . . five *ŠE* of silver, to a potter five *ŠE* of silver, to a tailor five *ŠE* of silver, to a stone-cutter . . . *ŠE* of silver, to a . . . *ŠE* of silver, to a . . . *ŠE* of silver, to a carpenter four *ŠE* of silver, to a rope-maker four *ŠE* of silver, to a . . . *ŠE* of silver, to a builder . . . *ŠE* of silver.

Wages of artisans

§ 275. If a man has hired a boat, its hire is three *ŠE* of silver daily.

Hires of various boats

§ 276. If he has hired a fast boat he shall pay two and a half *ŠE* daily.

§ 277. If a man has hired a ship of sixty *GUR* he shall pay one-sixth of a shekel of silver daily for its hire.

§ 278. If a man has bought a male or female slave and the slave has not fulfilled his month, but the *bennu* disease has fallen upon him, he shall return the slave to the seller and the buyer shall take back the money he paid.

Compensation for defect discovered in a slave after sale

§ 279. If a man has bought a male or female slave and a claim has been raised, the seller shall answer the claim.

§ 280. If a man, in a foreign land, has bought a male, or female, slave of another, and if when he has come home the owner of the male or female slave has recognized his slave, and if the slave be a native of the land, he shall grant him his liberty without money.

Manumission of native slaves taken captive and bought back by travelling merchant

§ 281. If the slave was a native of another country, the buyer shall declare on oath the amount of money he paid, and the owner of the slave shall repay the merchant what he paid and keep his slave.

Of foreign slaves

§ 282. If a slave has said to his master, "You are not my master," he shall be brought to account as his slave, and his master shall cut off his ear.

Punishment for repudiating a master

This is not the place to write a commentary on the Code, but there are a few necessary cautions. One of the first is that most clauses are permissive rather than positive. The verb "shall" is not an imperative, but a future. Doubtless in case of heinous crimes the death-penalty had to be inflicted. But there was always a trial, and proof was demanded on oath. In many cases the "shall" is only permissive, as when the Code says a widow "shall" marry again. There is no proof that the jury decided only facts and found the prisoner guilty or not, leaving the judge no

General character of the Hammurabi Code

option but to inflict the extreme penalty. The judge, on the contrary, seems to have had much legislative power. When this view is taken, the Code appears no more severe than those of the Middle Ages, or even of recent times, when a man was hanged for sheep-stealing. There are many humanitarian clauses and much protection is given the weak and the helpless. One of the best proofs of its inherent excellence is that it helped to build up an empire, which lasted many centuries and was regarded with reverence almost to the end.

## III

### LATER BABYLONIAN LAW

VERY little is yet known regarding later Babylonian law. Dr. F. E. Peiser published in the *Sitzungsberichte der Königliche Akademie der Wissenschaften zu Berlin* (1889, pp. 823 ff.) a very interesting fragmentarily preserved text (82–7–14, 988, in the British Museum), which contains either a collection of abstracts of cases which have been decided, or precedents, or else an extract from some code later than that of Ḫammurabi. Dr. Peiser thought that the date was the second year of Ashurbânipal, king of Babylon. This seems rather unlikely, but may, of course, be true. Bibliography

In his inaugural dissertation, Dr. Peiser, under the title of *Jurisprudentiae Babylonicae quae supersunt,* commented upon and illustrated the above text by numerous examples of cases, actually occurring during the period of the second empire. But the whole collection of fragments of law with which he had to deal was too small to do more than show what may be hoped for as the result of future discoveries.

As specimens of these laws we may take the following:

**Law A.** [Col. II. 4–14.]

The man who has sealed a tablet, by the name of another, in favor of an owner of a field, or has sealed a bond, and has not caused to be executed a deed giving him power of attorney, or has not taken a duplicate of such a tablet [cannot take possession]; the man, in whose name the tablet, or bond, is written, shall take that field, or house. Agent not able to recover without power of attorney

If a man acted as buyer, or lender, for another, he incurred liabilities, for which he could not indemnify himself, unless he had secured from his principal a deed empowering him so to act. But, if without such power of attorney, A had acted for B, and bought a house, or field, of C, and had the conveyance made out to B, of course paying C; or had lent money to C, in the name of B; and the transaction had been completed, by sealing the deed of sale or bond; then B was the owner of the field, or house, or the creditor for the loan. A could not plead that he was the real owner, even if he had not been able to recover the purchase-money or loan from B, in whose name he had made it. B, whose name appeared in the deed or in the bond, was the rightful owner.

**Law B.** [Col. II. 15–23.]

Responsibility of one who sells

The man, who has sold a female slave and has had an objection made concerning her, shall take her back. The seller shall give to the buyer the price named in the deed of sale, to its exact amount, and shall pay half a shekel of silver for each of the children born to her.

How long after sale objection could be raised is not stated. In early times a month was allowed for fever to develop; in Assyrian contracts a hundred days were allowed for fever or seizure. But a *sartu*, or "vice," could be pleaded, at any time, as ground for returning the slave. Here it is clear that time was allowed for a slave to bear one or more children, before the repudiation lost effect. It is noteworthy that the seller had to buy back such children. The maid may have been bought to bear her master children, and if these were not sound, the master had ground for complaint and could not be held responsible for them. Also it was objectionable to separate mother and children. The price named is trifling. Compare § 278 of the Code, where, however, no mention is made of the children of a maid.

The next law is unintelligible at present, owing to the *lacunae*, and doubtful readings of the text, which, moreover, is only given in transcription. It appears to concern a woman and her interests in a field or plantation and the trees in it, and its produce.

Law C. [Col. III. 3–15.]

A man has given his daughter to a freeborn man and the father has fixed something in a deed and given to his son, and the first-named has fixed a marriage-portion for his daughter and they have mutually executed deeds of settlement. They shall not alter their deeds. The father shall give in full the settlement (*nuṣurru*), which he had promised his son by deed, to the father-in-law, and deliver it.

Permanent settlements at marriage between father of bride and the bridegroom

The father here named appears to be the father of the bridegroom. He must make a settlement on his son, as well as the father of the bride on his daughter. The point of the law seems to be that these settlements on the part of the parents to the young couple are irrevocable. No subsequent engagements entered into can affect them. This settlement by the bridegroom's father on his son, which he has to pay over to the bride's father, evidently takes the place of the *terḫatu*, or "bride-price" of the Code. The obligation of a father to find his son the means for a bride-price appears in the Code, § 166; but there is no section which answers directly to this law. The marriage-portion is now *nudunnu*, in the Code it was *šeriktu*, while *nudunnu* was the husband's gift to the wife.

Law D. [Col. III. 16–22.]

When the father [of the bridegroom] has had his wife taken away by fate, has taken to himself a second wife, and she has borne him sons, the sons of the second wife shall take a third of his property remaining.

Inheritance rights of children of second marriage

This appears as part of the same section as Law C, and is enacted again in Law K, page 69. It is not easy to see why it is here, except to make plain that settlements on marriages of the sons of the first family are a first charge on the father's property. The second family takes a third, not of all the father once had, but of what is left after these gifts by deed have been taken out. The married sons of the first family are not disinherited by virtue of these gifts, but take among them two-thirds of what is left. This is against the Code, § 167.

Law E. [Col. III. 23–31.]

Procedure in case the father-in-law is unable to carry out his promise of dowry

A man who has promised a marriage-portion to his daughter, or has written her a deed of gift, and afterward his means have diminished, shall give to his daughter a marriage-portion according to his means that are left. Father-in-law and son-in-law shall not quarrel one with the other.

Dr. Peiser has shown that the marriage-portion was often held back a long time. Suits were brought to recover it from fathers-in-law. There is no corresponding section in the Code.

Law F. [Col. III. 32–37.]

Marriage-portion of childless wife

A man has given a marriage-portion to his daughter and she has neither son nor daughter and fate has carried her off; her marriage-portion returns to her father's house.

Exactly as in the Code, § 163.

The first seven lines of Col. IV. are too fragmentary to give a connected sense, but are still concerned with the marriage-portion.

Law G. [Col. IV. 8–24.]

Rights of inheritance of a childless widow

A wife, whose marriage-portion her husband has received, who has no son or daughter, and fate has carried off her husband, shall be given from her husband's property the marriage-portion, whatever that was. If her husband has made her a gift, she shall receive the gift of her husband with her marriage-portion and take it away. If she had no marriage-portion, the judge shall estimate the property of her husband and, according to her husband's means, shall grant her something.

It is noteworthy that in the above laws the old usage is reversed. Now the *nudunnu* is the marriage-portion, given with the bride, and the *šeriktu* is the husband's assignment to the wife. With this alteration the law agrees with the Code, § 171. But there she has a family.

**Law H.** [Col. IV. 25–45.]

A man has married a wife and she has borne him children; after that man has been carried off by fate, and that woman has set her face to enter the house of another, she shall take the marriage-portion which she brought from her father's house, and whatever her husband presented her as a gift, and shall marry the husband of her choice. As long as she lives, she shall enjoy food and drink from them. If there be children of this husband, they and the children of the former husband shall share her marriage-portion. The sisters . . .

**The rights of a widow with children in case of remarriage**

This is practically the same as Code, § 170, but it is differently arranged and the phrases differ markedly. Note that the sisters were separately treated.

**Law K.** [Col. V. 33–46.]

A man has married a wife and she has borne him children, and fate has carried off his wife; he has married a second wife and she has borne him children; after the father has gone to his fate, the children of the former wife shall take two-thirds of the goods of their father's house, the children of the second wife shall take one-third. Their sisters who are dwelling in their father's house . . .

**Division of the estate of a man twice married**

This must be contrasted with § 167 of the Code. There all sons share equally. Here the first family take two-thirds. The sisters were also treated separately. It is clear that we have to do with a code which preserves many features of the early times, but has many new features of its own. It is greatly to be desired that further portions should be published.

## IV

## THE SOCIAL ORGANIZATION OF THE ANCIENT BABYLONIAN STATE

The three great classes of the population: the gentry, the common men, and the slaves

THE State appears in the light of the Ḫammurabi Code to have been composed of three great classes, the *amêlu*, the *muškênu*, and the *ardu*. To the first class belonged the king and the chief officers of state, and also the landed proprietors. Their liabilities for fines and punishments were higher. Also in their case the old law of "eye for eye, tooth for tooth" still held; while others came under a scale of compensations and damages. This may point to a racial difference. The ancient laws of Arabia may have been carried with them by Ḫammurabi's tribal followers, while the older subject-residents accepted the more commercial system of fines. The old pride of the Arab tribesman may have forbidden his taking money as payment for his damaged eye, or tooth. But the *muškênu* was more "humble," as his name denotes, and may well have formed the bulk of the subject-population. He was a free man, not a beggar. He was not without considerable means, as we see from the sections referring to theft from him. He had slaves,[1] and seems to have been liable to conscription. His fees to a doctor or surgeon were less than those paid by an *amêlu*. He paid less to his wife for a divorce,[2] and could assault another poor man more cheaply than could an *amêlu*. There can be no doubt that the *amêlu* was the

[1] § 15. [2] § 140.

"gentleman" or "nobleman," and the *muškênu* a common man, or poor man. But the exact force of the terms is uncertain.

In process of time *amêlu* came to be used, like our "sir," and even "esquire," of those who had no special qualifications for the title. Like the "gentleman's gentleman" of the servant's hall, he was only a respectable person. So, even in the Code, *amêlu* usually means no more than "man." It already appears as a mere determinative of personality in the titles of laborers and artisans,[1] when it cannot stamp them as landed proprietors. But it may mark them as members of the guilds of craftsmen and recall the respect due to such. If, however, we press this, we must admit a guild of day laborers.

There is no suggestion of any legal disability on the part of a *muškênu;* he is merely a person of less consideration. Whether or not his ranks were recruited from the children of slaves by free parents is not clear, but it is very probable that they were.

The slave was at his master's command and, like a child in his father's house, to some extent a chattel. He could be pledged for debt, as could a wife or child. He was subject to the levy,[2] and his lot was so far unpleasant that we hear much of runaway slaves. It was penal to harbor a slave, or to keep one caught as a fugitive.[3] Any injury done to him was paid for, and his master received the damages.[4] But he was free to marry a free woman and the children were free. So a slave-girl was free on her master's death, if she had borne him children; and the children were also free. He was subject to mutilation for assaulting a free man, or repudiating his master.[5] But his master had to pay for his cure, if sick.[6] He was not free to contract, except by deed and bond.[7] Yet he and his free wife

---

[1] §§ 273, 274. [2] § 16. [3] §§ 16, 17, 19. [4] § 199.
[5] §§ 205, 282. [6] §§ 218, 223. [7] § 6.

could acquire property, half of which would fall to his wife and children on his death.

The levy-master and the warrant-officer

The Code reveals the existence of a class of men, who were indeed known from the letters of Ḫammurabi and the contemporary contracts, but whose functions are not easy to fix. They were the *rîd ṣâbî* and the *bâ'iru*. By their etymology these titles seemed to mean "slave-driver," and "catcher." But the Code sets them in a clearer light. They were closely connected, if not identical, officials. They had charge of the levy, the local quota for the army, or for public works. Hence "levy-master" and "warrant-officer" are suggestive renderings. For the former official, "taskmaster," the one over the gang of forced laborers and reminiscent of the old time press-gang officers, is a fair translation. "Field cornet" would perhaps suit the military side. For some aspects of their office the ancient "reeve" may be compared. Whether the "catcher" actually was a local policeman, whose chief duty was to apprehend criminals and reluctant conscripts, is not yet clear. The same name is used of "fishermen," who were "catchers" in another sense, and of hunters. A really satisfactory rendering is impossible, as we have now no officials whose duties actually correspond to theirs.

Their compensation

Each of these officials held what may be called a benefice, or perhaps a feoff. It consisted of land, house, and garden, certain sheep and cattle as stock, and a salary. It was directly ascribed to the king as benefactor. We may compare the Norman lords settled in England by the Conqueror, or the Roman soldier-colonists. The men may well have been the followers of the first founder of the dynasty. In a very similar way the Chaldean conqueror, Merodach-baladan II., long after, settled his Chaldean troops in Babylonia. We may regard these men as retainers of the king, and probably as originally foreigners. The benefice was held by them for personal service. They were to go "on the king's errand" when ordered. It was a penal offence to send a substitute.[1] The errand might take them away from home and detain them a very long time. In such enforced absence the official might delegate his son to take his place and carry on his duty.[2] This implies that there was a local duty besides the personal service. Further, this needed a grown man to discharge it.[3] The *locum tenens* enjoyed the benefice,[4] with a reserve of one-third for the wife to bring up the children of the absent official. An official by neglecting the care of his benefice ran the risk of forfeiture.[5] This came about by his absence giving the *locum tenens* opportunity to acquire a prescriptive right, which he might do in three years, if he showed himself a more worthy holder. But this was only if the absentee had been neglectful, and a one-year tenancy conferred no such right.[6]

**The risks of public service**

The service on which the official might be engaged was evidently military and had risks. It is not certain whether the *dannatu*[7] is really a "fortress," or a "defeat." The word has both meanings. It does not really matter. Either way the official is captured by the enemy of the king. He was bound to pay for his own ransom, if he had the means; or if not, his town must ransom him and, failing that, the state. But he could not raise money on his benefice. Moreover, while it could descend to his son, it was inalienable. No diminution by bequest to his female relatives, no sale of part of it, no mortgage on it, nor even its exchange for other like estate, was allowed.

Further, the official and his benefice were protected. He could not be hired out by his superior officers, nor in any way plundered or oppressed. He held tax free, subject only to his feudal duty.

In some cases the tributary there is associated with these

---

[1] § 26. [2] § 28. [3] § 29. [4] § 29. [5] § 30. [6] § 31. [7] § 32.

The tributary

two officials. No duty is set down for him, beyond that implied in his name of paying a tribute. It is not clear that all land was held on one or the other scheme, but it is so in parts of the East still. Some land is held by personal service, some on payment of a tax. This tax later became the tithe. The personal service was later compounded for by furnishing a soldier or two for the army. The liability to serve in the levy continued to be borne by slaves and the lower classes.

All land subject to royal taxation

That all land did owe either personal service, or tax, is probably to be deduced from § 40, where we read that though a levy-master, warrant-officer, or tributary could alienate nothing of their holdings, other land-owners could do so. But they did so subject to the buyer taking over the duty, or service, of the land so transferred. One of the classes here named, the votary, appears subject to service elsewhere. The votary of Marduk is expressly exempt from this service.[1] The merchant, who represents another class, appears very often to have been a foreigner, only temporarily resident in the country.

The votaries

The votary was already known to us from the contracts, but there was little to fix her functions. As seen in the Code, she was a highly favored person. Vowed to God, usually to Shamash at Sippara, or Marduk at Babylon, there seems little to connect her with the prostitute-votaries of Ishtar at Erech. She ordinarily lived in the convent, or "bride-house" of Shamash. She was given a portion, exactly like a bride, on taking her vow and becoming the "bride" of Shamash. But her property did not go to the convent. At her father's death, with her consent, her estate might be administered by her brothers, or she could farm it out. At any rate, she was provided for during her lifetime. But at her death, unless her father had specially given her power to bequeath it, her property went

[1] § 183.

back to her family. She was not, however, doomed to spend all her days in the convent. She could leave it and even marry. But she was expected to maintain a high standard of respectability. For her to open a beer-shop or even enter one for drink was punished by burning. She remained a virgin, even if married. She could have no children and must provide her husband with a maid, if he wished to have a family. But she was carefully guarded from any reproach as childless. She ranks as a married woman, even if unmarried, and is protected from slander. Many noble ladies, and even kings' daughters, were votaries.[1]

The merchant continually appears. Some passages suggest that he was a state official. But this is really pressing too far the interest which the state took in him. He was, doubtless, like the Jew of the Middle Ages, a valuable asset to the king. He seems to have been the usual money-lender, so much so that in many places "merchant" and "creditor" are interchangeable. A man is usually said to borrow of "his merchant," as we say "of his banker." Doubtless, the king also borrowed from him. It is certain that the Code was very lenient to him. But the merchant also did business in the way of ordinary trade. As a capitalist he sent out his travellers and agents with goods far and wide, even into domains where the king's authority did not reach. Much of the Code is occupied with regulating the relations between the merchant and his agent. The agency was that form of *commenda* which is so characteristic of the East at the present. The agent takes stock or money of his principal, signs for it, agrees to pay so much profit, and goes off to seek a market, making what profit he can. There is much to suggest that the merchant was not usually a Babylonian. In later times, the Arameans were the chief merchants, and travelled all over Mesopotamia, Palestine, Syria, and into Asia Minor.

The merchant

[1] For fuller information and references, see A. J. S. L., XIX., pp. 98 ff.

## V

## JUDGES, LAW-COURTS, AND LEGAL PROCESSES

Antiquity of the judicial organization

PARTLY because specific references to judges and legal processes are not necessarily to be expected in historical inscriptions, and partly because we do not really know which are the earliest monuments of the race, it is impossible to decide when law-courts first came into existence. It is generally admitted, however, that the stele of Manistusu is one of the earliest known monuments. There we read of Galzu, a judge. There also we find many of the officials, who later acted as judges upon occasion. Hence it may fairly be said that judges were to be found in ancient Babylonia from time immemorial. They must have decided what was right when there was no written law to which to appeal. With the judges were associated as assessors the elders of the city. This was so marked a feature, that in some cases we read, that after hearing the complaint the judge "assembled the city" to hear the case. In Babylonia the maxim, *littera scripta manet*, was so well understood that hardly anything of importance was done without committing it to writing. Hence we are as well informed about domestic affairs in Babylonia as about those of Europe in the Middle Ages.

Sources of our knowledge of early legal procedure

It seems best to consider legal usages first, because they are essential to the understanding of all others. When we have a simple contract between two parties we do not at once see where the reference to the law comes in. But the contract was not valid unless sealed and witnessed. The sealing was accompanied by an oath. The oath probably had to be made in court. The witnesses seem often to have been a body of men who could only be found at the court. Even when there is least trace of the law and the judge, the case is similar to others where the judge appears explicitly. It is also worthy of remark that, partly owing to our possession of the Code and partly owing to the fuller nature of the legal decisions, we know far more of this subject, as of many others, in the early periods than in the later. Hence the discussion of early legal usage is unusually full. When the evidence from later times merely supports this, it will not be noticed. Only divergences are worthy of record. As a rule, the procedure changes very little for many centuries.

Judges not often mentioned

1. **Judges.** The references to judges are less numerous than one would expect in the Code. But it seems probable that the sentences there laid down had to be pronounced by the judge, if not carried out by him. We are, however, still in complete ignorance as to the machinery of police administration. We may argue from analogy in other countries and ages, but this is not a theoretical treatise on comparative sociology. We must content ourselves with direct evidence.

Their varied duties

Some sections deal explicitly with the duties of a judge. Thus,[1] if a judge had given a judgment, decided the case, and embodied it in a legal decision, he was subjected to severe penalties for afterwards revoking his decision. If he had inflicted a penalty, he had now to repay it twelvefold to him from whom it was exacted. Further he was to be publicly deposed from his office, expelled from his seat of judgment, *kussû daianûtišu*, and no longer be permitted to sit with the judges. It is, of course, assumed that when

[1] § 5.

he was called to account he could not justify his former judgment, or else could not justify the change. But, as the law reads, it seems simply calculated to render a judgment, once pronounced, irrevocable,—at any rate, for that judge. Probably its revocation, in the case of injustice, was provided for by the right of appeal.

He had to consider the words of the witnesses, *amâtišunu amâru*, literally, "to see their words," perhaps implying that the depositions were written, but there are instances where *amâru* simply means "to consider."[1]

In a criminal case, where a man had to produce witnesses to save his life from a death-sentence, the judge might grant him six months' grace in which to produce his witnesses.[2] In later times we have many examples of such a stay of process that evidence might be produced.[3]

Special directions to judges

Special directions are also given to a judge as to his procedure, when a father was minded to disinherit his son; or, when a widow with a young family wished to marry again.[4] A slanderer was summoned before the judge,[5] a son could not be cut off without referring the case to a judge,[6] the children who wished to turn their widowed mother out of her house had to appear before a judge.[7]

Position, rank, and qualifications

For the most part judges constituted a distinct profession, but it must not be understood that they had no other means of livelihood. Indeed, there is no hint anywhere that they received any remuneration for their services. But it was a high honor and by no means subsidiary to another office. Among those who officiated as judges we find most of the higher officials. Doubtless the king himself acted as judge on occasions, and probably no great official of the realm was wholly free from the call to act in a judicial capacity. But, as a rule, the judge is simply noted as "judge." That the priests were judges is quite unproved.

[1] § 9. [2] § 13. [3] § 169. [4] § 177. [5] § 127. [6] § 168. [7] § 172.

The judges were men of great importance and high rank, but there is nothing to show that they were priests. An age qualification is more likely.

Method of appointment

The judge was a professional man. We often find a man, bearing the title "judge," acting as party to a suit, or witness to a deed, when he is certainly not acting in his judicial capacity. To a certain extent he was a territorial officer, had his own district for jurisdiction, and was jealous of cases being taken elsewhere. How the ranks of the judges were filled we do not know, but there is a hint of royal appointment in the phrase, "the king's judges." On the other hand, there is clear evidence of the office being hereditary. Thus, Ibik-Anunîtum had no less than three sons, Idin-Ishtar, Marduk-mushallim, and Nannar-idinnam, all judges. Whether a right to the office descended in the female line is not quite clear, but we find a lady, Ishtar-ummu, among the judges, on occasion. She was also the scribe.[1]

The chief-justice

Though many high officials acted as judges, and so doing are named before the simple "judge," there is no evidence of the existence of any "chief judge." The order of names appears to be that of seniority alone. This may be due to the nature of our documents. The phrase-books name a "chief judge" for Sumerian times. In the later Assyrian period the chief-justice was called *sartênu*, evidently because he fixed the *sartu*, or fine, on the condemned party. Then also many high officials acted as judges.[2]

The scribes

2. **Scribes.**—The scribe exercised his craft as a profession. One often meets with a scribe, *tupšarru*, acting in a private capacity, as party to a suit, or as witness. He retains the title even when the deed is drawn up by another writer. The class was very numerous. Almost every document is drawn up by a fresh scribe, so far as the scribe's name is

[1] B² 327. [2] A. D. D. § 567.

recorded, for he often omits his title. Generally he is the last of the witnesses, but not always so.

Their duties

He wrote the whole of the document, including the names of the witnesses. There is no evidence that anyone else ever wrote a word on the document. As a rule, even when the names of the fathers of the witnesses are given, the scribe is content to write only his title after his name. Hence we have no evidence whether the office was hereditary or not.

Female scribes

Women certainly were scribes. Out of a total of ninety names of scribes known, at least ten were women. Here a difficulty arises from the way in which women's names occur. At this period proper names are usually written without the determinative which marks sex. Nor do the names decide, for both men and women bore the same name. Thus Taribatum is the name of two men and also of two women. Only when the title *tupšarru* is given, is the feminine determinative prefixed to that. We have, however, ten clear examples.

In the later times the scribe usually was a man, but female scribes are known.[1] The Aramaic scribe is often named, also the Egyptian. The scribe usually "held" the agreement, which probably means that the parties were willing to leave it in his safe-keeping.

The scribe not a judge

The scribe was not a judge. It may be true that he sometimes acted as judge or became one, but then the higher office overshadowed the lower. He was no longer scribe but judge. A judge may sometimes have written down his legal decision and so acted as scribe, but we have no evidence of such a case. The judge seems never to have dispensed with the services of the scribe.

The scribe was not a priest. There is no evidence whatever that either priests were all scribes, or could all write,

[1] A. D. D., 827, 2.

or that scribes were necessarily priests. As a matter of fact, the same man may have acted both as scribe and priest. But the offices are distinct and no one man ever bears both titles. That in later times the *amêlu* RID, whose title can be read *šangû*, usually acts as scribe is due to the peculiar nature of the documents. These concern transactions in which the property of the temple, or of its officials, was in question, and one of the college of priests attached to that temple was charged with the duty of notary where temple interests were concerned. One might as well say that every clerk in the Middle Ages was a priest, because all the deeds of the monastery with which we were dealing were drawn up by Brother A, whose name was entered in some monastery list of the brethren as a priest. Whether the scribes were clerics, and always attached to some temple, in minor orders, is not clear. On the whole, the evidence is against this conclusion.

The scribe not a priest

3. **Witnesses.**—The word used to designate a witness is *šîbu*, which denotes those who are "gray-headed," but it is not certain that it can have no other meaning. It may mean those who were "present." In actual use we can distinguish three classes of persons to whom the term "witness" can be applied.

The witnesses

First we have the elders, the *šîbu*, of a city.[1] Possibly the Kar-sippar, by which some men swore, or in presence of which a contract was drawn up, were these elders of Sippar. They formed the *puḫru*, or "assembly," in whose presence a man was scourged,[2] from which a prevaricating judge was expelled.[3] They may have been nominated, or at least approved, by the king; for we read of *šîbê šarri*. They were not exclusively men, for we have *šîbê û šîbatu*.[4] The recurrence of the same names, at the same dates, indicates that a body of official witnesses were held in readi-

The elders of a city

[1] M. A. P., 80, B[1] 199, B[2] 2458. [2] § 202. [3] § 5. [4] B[2] 2182.

ness to act on such occasions. Many of them were temple officials, or members of the guild of Shamash votaries.

Their jury duties

Sometimes they are associated with the judges in such a way as to show that they were assessors.[1] They included judges sometimes, at any rate "this witness" is attached to a list of names which included a *nâgiru* of Babylon, a judge, and other high officials.[2] In the time of Nûr-Adadi they sent a case before the king.[3] They actually gave judgment.[4] We may regard them as a jury, especially a grand jury, qualified by their own knowledge to understand the rights of the case and to judge of evidence. The judge gave the sentence.

Trial witnesses

Secondly, we may distinguish the witnesses examined on oath. It is not clear that these were called by the same name. In the Code we read of *šîbi mûdi*, "the witnesses that know," who seem to resemble very closely the Greek *Histores*. These, of course, were usually not on the jury. They testified, and were chosen by the parties to the suit. But the judge might examine persons who, in his opinion, would know. He selected and sent for them, directing the parties whom to produce. He might even adjourn the case for the production of witnesses.[5]

Witnesses to deeds

Thirdly, we may distinguish the witnesses to a document. Very often we can discern that these had an interest in the case. They might be relatives of the parties, neighbors of the estate in question, officials whose rights were concerned. In later times they received the special name of *mukinnu*, "the establishers." They may be presumed to have known at least the general purport of the deed which they witnessed. When the deed was called in question, they would be cited to state what they knew. In the case of legal decisions, both judges and jury occur as witnesses in this sense. Hence, in a great many cases the distinctions drawn

---

[1] M. A. P., 80. [2] $B^2$ 824, 838. [3] B 34. [4] $B^1$ 99. [5] § 13.

above do not hold. Whether the term *šibu* was ever applied to the third class is doubtful. Their names are usually preceded by the sign which means "before," however it was read.

4. **Cases of dispute settled out of court.**—When parties disagreed, they might discuss their difference between themselves and arrive at an agreement. Then they procured a scribe, who embodied the agreement in a binding compact, *duppu lâ ragâmi.* This took the form of a contract, the parties mutually undertaking not to withdraw from the agreement, re-open the dispute, or bring legal action, one against the other. To give sanction to this agreement, they swore by the gods and the king. Witnesses were called upon to be cognizant of and attest the contract; and their names were added to the contract. To authenticate their names both parties and witnesses often impressed their seals or, in default of seals, made a nail-mark. The date was then added. Each party seems to have taken a copy of the agreement and the scribe held a third, or deposited it in the archives. Such cases may be said to have been settled "out of court." At any rate they contain no reference to a judge, or court. But it is possible that the administration of the oath was a judicial, or perhaps a sacerdotal function. Further, the witnesses may have been drawn from a body of men held in readiness at court to perform that function. It is certain in some cases, that agreements arrived at independently were taken to a judge for confirmation,[1] and the Code expressly directs some cases to be taken to a judge. But it is probable that many cases were settled by mutual agreement.

Settlements out of court

When the intervention of a judge was deemed essential, one of the parties "complained." The word really means to "cry out," "protest"; but it is used in the freest way as

Recourse to a judge

[1] B[1] 38, B[2] 838.

equivalent to bringing the action. There is no evidence that anyone then submitted to wrong "under protest." Whether the people were naturally litigious, or simply because access to the courts was so easy, a protest usually involved a suit.

The advocate

The plea was made by the principals to the suit. There is no mention of an advocate, or solicitor. But the verb generally used of the plea *ragâmu*, gives rise to *targumânu*, the original of the modern dragoman. He usually appears in later texts as the "interpreter," but may originally have been the "advocate." At any rate, in the bilingual days he might well have combined the offices. Another verb common at this period, *pakâru*, gave rise to *pâkirânu*, later the usual word for "plaintiff," or "claimant."

The plaintiff in the reports

Here may be noted a peculiarity of the scribe's conception of the case. It will be found that, as he puts the case, the plaintiff generally loses. This is because the scribe will not prejudge the case by saying who was right. He writes "A claimed the property of B." In actual fact it may have been that B laid claim to what he proved was his. But that excludes the scribe from saying that B claimed the property of A, because it never was A's. Hence, writing after the event, he ascribes the property to the rightful owner from the start of his document, and regards the wrongful holder as laying claim to it. Hence, we must not assume that the parties were not both claimants. In fact, both parties agreed, as a rule, so far as to submit their case to a judge. This is clear from the statements which follow the statement of the cause of dispute. Both parties "went to the judges," or rather quaintly, "they captured a judge." The preliminary discussion between the parties resulted in agreement to submit the case to a judge. Both were willing to abide by the decision. Once, it is true, the plaintiff is said to have caught the defendant;[1] but there is no evi-

[1] M. A. P., 79.

dence of unwillingness to submit. So too, when the parties are said to "receive a judge," they evidently both sought him.

Summons before the judge

Sometimes affairs did not go so smoothly. One party had to act and bring the other before the judges[1] or "caused them to come before the judge."

There are indications that the judges sometimes had to summon a party before them, or as the scribe puts it, "bring him before the other party." This is also expressed by the judges "sending up" a party.[2]

Appeals

There is considerable evidence that cases might be sent before the judges by a higher party, the king himself. These cases were probably on the suit of a plaintiff. In the letters of the First Dynasty we have examples of the king sending to the local judges his own decision on the case, which they had to carry out; or in other cases he simply sent the case for trial.[3]

Various places for holding a court

The parties, having found a judge and obtained a day for hearing, "entered," or "went down to," the great temple of Shamash, at Sippara, called Ebabbarim.[4] There, as we know, Ḫammurabi set up one of the copies of the Code. The case was heard sometimes at the "old gate."[5] At Babylon, the parties were taken to the temple of Merodach, Esagila.[6] At Larsa, the "gate" of *NIN-MAR-KI*, or the temple of Sin, might be chosen.[7] The temple of Ishhara is also named.[8]

Legal procedure

5. **Procedure.**—We have only scattered hints regarding legal procedure. The Code says that the judges "saw the pleas."[9] The scribe uses the same expression.[10] As a rule, he records the plaintiff's statement of claim first. Then he records a counter-statement. There is a strong

---

[1] M. A. P., 100, B[1] 294. [2] B[2] 272.
[3] King, *Letters of Ḫammurabi*, p xxxix f. [4] B[2] 360. [5] B[1] 711.
[6] M. A. P., 100. [7] B 57, 73. [8] B[2] 279. [9] § 9. [10] B[2] 2444 A.

suggestion that he quotes from written documents. The judges read these, or heard the verbal statements.

The deity the theoretical source of all judicial authority

As part of the legal process, the object in dispute, or, at any rate, the deeds relating to it, were brought into court, and resigned into the hands of the god.[1] He was to discern the rightful owner and restore the object to him. Hence the decision was "the judgment of Shamash in the house of Shamash,[2] the judgment of the house of Shamash."[3] So the defendant was said "to make his account before Shamash."[4] In bringing a suit the parties "sought the altar of Shamash."[5] In case of loss or damage, the claimant recounted it "before god."

Summoning witnesses

In confirmation of the statements alleged witnesses might be called for, who were put on oath before god and the king. They were supposed to know the object claimed and whose it was,[6] or to know that a transaction had taken place.[7]

Bribing witnesses

Tampering with witnesses, or with a jury, was penalized by the Code.[8] The judges might refuse to accept the witness,[9] and then might decide the case on the sworn deposition of the plaintiff.

Different kinds of testimony

Documentary evidence might be demanded. The judges might decide to take the evidence of their own senses and go to see an estate or a house in dispute.[10] Or they might determine that it was a case for the accused to purge himself, which he did by oath.[11]

Rendering the decision

Having thus informed themselves of the rights of the case the judges proceeded to pronounce a decision, "they caused them to receive judgment." This phrase nearly always occurs in the legal decisions. The decision might be called "the judgment of the particular judge," for example, *dîn Išarlim*, "Israel's judgment."[12] The sentence

---

[1] M. A. P., 79, 105. [2] B² 2463. [3] B² 327. [4] B² 301.
[5] B² 272. [6] §§ 122, 123. [7] § 13. [8] §§ 3, 4.
[9] B¹ 160. [10] B² 2182. [11] B² 2181. [12] B² 2474.

is sometimes stated in the words of the judges themselves, introduced by *ikbu*, "they said."[1] Thus we read "the tablet which A granted to B is good, they said."[2]

The collection of damages

If one party was in the wrong, the judges laid the wrong on him,"[3] or "put him in the wrong."[4] When the suit was to recover a debt, or find compensation, the judges might name a sum which they paid over to the proper person.[5] This was damages, not a fine.

Breaking a contract-tablet

A ceremony which often took place on the annulment of a former agreement, or cancelling of a deed was the breaking of the tablet embodying the former contract. The same ceremony took place on repayment of a debt, or on dissolution of a partnership, apparently without recourse to judges. This was ordered by the Code in case of purchases of property which it was illegal to sell or buy, such as the benefice of a reeve or runner.[6] So when an adopted child had failed to carry out the bond to nourish and care for the adoptive parent, the deed of adoption was formally broken by the judges.[7]

For later times we have little evidence. What there is was collected by Kohler-Peiser,[8] and agrees in general with the above.

The legal decision

6. **The decision.**—In these ways the judges "quieted the strife," "composed the complaint."[9] It was the standard conception of a legal decision that it should be irrevocable. The Code enacts the deprivation and deposition of a judge for revoking his judgment.[10] The legal decisions lay down the stipulation that the losing party shall not "turn back," shall not "complain." These phrases nearly always occur, as they do also in contracts. To insure compliance with the decision the judges again exacted an oath. Whether both parties swore, or only the losers, is not clear. The state-

---

[1] B² 2458. [2] B² 2516. [3] B² 387. [4] B² 2182. [5] B² 2458.
[6] § 37. [7] B² 586, 2177 A. [8] A. B. R. *passim*. [9] B² 327. [10] § 5.

ment usually is "they swore," without mention of the persons who did so.

Documentary form

The decision, being complete, was embodied in a document drawn up by the scribe, regularly witnessed, often by the judges, and sealed. Thus it was that the judges granted him an irrevocable tablet.[1] These irrevocable tablets, practically imperishable also, have now come after thousands of years, to tell their tale.

Administration of oaths

7. **Administration of the oath.**—The ceremony of swearing to the truth of evidence, or the terms of a compact, is continually mentioned. The exact form of words used in taking the oath is not certain; but in actual suits, in the law-court procedure, the judges administered an oath to both parties and witnesses. In the Code oaths were admitted for purgation of alleged crime,[2] as evidence of loss, deposit, injury;[3] and the reception of a sworn deposition is recorded.[4] References to oaths continually occur in the contracts.

Form of the oath

The judges "gave them to the oath before Shamash and Adad,"[5] or, more briefly, "gave him to the oath of god."[6] The name of the god by whom men swore is usually given. As might be expected, the god who figured most prominently in the Code was Shamash, the chief deity of Sippara, often associated with his consort, Aia, or Malkatu. Sometimes the oath was "by the king."[7] Often one or more gods and the king are named together. When Babylon became supreme it was usual to swear by Marduk and the local gods as well. The significance of these oaths for historical purposes is great, both as indicating political relationships, and as often affording by the name of the king the only clew to the date of the document. Mr. King, in his

---

[1] $B^2$ 387. [2] § 20, 131, 227, 266.
[3] §§ 23, 103, 120, 126, 206, 240, 249. [4] § 9.
[5] $B^1$ 160. [6] $B^1$ 188. [7] $B^1$ 295.

edition of the Chronicle,[1] and Dr. Lindl,[2] have made skilful use of these oaths in determining chronology.

The place where it was administered

The administration of the oath took place before the censer of Shamash[3] or at the shrine, *Šašaru*, of Shamash,[4] in Sippara; or before the emblematic dragon sculptured on the doors of the Marduk temple at Babylon.[5] Other places are named which we are not yet able to identify. A kind of magical conjuration appears sometimes to have been employed,[6] which is not yet understood.

Its purport

The purport of the oath was, not to give false evidence, or, in the case of contracts, not to alter the stipulated agreements. It is often followed by the words, "whoever shall alter or dispute the words of this tablet," evidently a quotation of the words of the oath; but the consequence of so doing is not given. Either it was too well known, or too awful, for the scribe to write it down.

Its gradual decrease in importance

In Assyrian times the oath did not play such an important part. Still, it was in use occasionally. The oath is generally found in documents of the grand style, such as royal charters. Oaths also are of interest for the pantheon of Assyria.[7] A common way of expressing the same thing was to call on a god to be judge of the case, as for example, "Shamash be judge," or "Shamash be advocate," that is, "take up the case." So the king's son, or crown prince, is invoked to be the advocate. An appeal was also made to the decision of the king. The gods, "Ashur, Sin, Shamash, Bêl, and Nabû, the gods of Assyria, shall require it at his hands" is another way of putting the case. These examples illustrate the meaning of the older oaths. There do not seem to be any cases of the witnesses being put on oath.

But the oath lingered on into very late Babylonian times,

---

[1] *Letters of Ḫammurabi*, pp. 212–54. [2] B. A. S., iv., p. 338 f. [3] $B^1$ 199.
[4] $B^2$ 2178 A. [5] $B^2$ 2182. [6] $B^1$ 199. [7] A. D. D., § 604.

Its preservation as an antique form

when we have some very full forms. If anyone shall change or alter the agreement, "may Marduk and Zarpanit decree his destruction."[1] In Persian times we find a curse on the same breach of faith in the terms, "whosoever shall attempt to alter this agreement, may Anu, Bêl, and Ea curse him with a bitter curse, may Nabû, the scribe of Esagila, put a period to his future."[2] It is curious thus to note a recrudescence of old forms in these later times. Was it merely an antiquarian fashion or had the Persians earlier come under strong Babylonian influence and preserved the old forms which had died out in their native home? The Elamite contracts suggest exactly the same question. In them it seems evident that Elam, once under Babylonian influence, adopted and preserved, under native rulers, forms of which we have no trace in Babylonia, but which clearly came from that country. Assyria is another case in point. She kept forms which we know date back before the time of her independence and which had disappeared from the contemporary Babylonian documents. In the later Babylonian times we still find the parties and the witnesses in a law-court put to the oath.[3]

Penalties for perjury

8. **Penalties.**—An unsuccessful suitor was not allowed to get off merely with the loss of his suit. He had been put on his oath and been unable to justify himself, or the word that he had spoken. According to the Code, if the suit was a capital suit, this was punished with death.[4] But even if the case was less serious, it was slander to have brought a false accusation, and the penalty for slander was branding.[5] This penalty was inflicted on an unsuccessful suitor for possession of a house sold by his father.[6] Another form of penalty for unsuccessful litigation was that the suitor should not only lose his case but actually be condemned

---

[1] Nbk., 368. [2] Cyr., 277. [3] Cyr., 312, A. B. R., II., pp. 16, 73.
[4] § 3. [5] § 127. [6] B² 2190.

to pay the penalty which he, if successful, would have brought on the other party.[1] That this is what was really intended by the clauses is shown by the case of Belilitum, who as late as B.C. 555,[2] having brought a suit to recover a debt which she alleged was not paid, was convicted of perjury by the production of the receipt, and by the evidence of her own children, and not only lost her case, but was condemned to pay the sum for which she had sued to him from whom she sought to obtain it. This was of course a form of retaliation.

Forfeits

In Assyrian times the parties usually bound themselves not to litigate, nor attempt to disturb the settlement made between them, under heavy forfeits to the treasury of a god, often tenfold the value of the object in dispute, and sometimes prohibitive in amount. Such sums as two talents of silver, or two talents of gold, controvert the idea that these forfeits were looked upon as possible deposits by a claimant desiring to reopen the case. They were terrific penalties intended to deter any attempt at litigation.

Nature of the forfeits

The forfeit sometimes took the form of white horses, or foals (?), which were dedicated to a divinity. Very interesting is the mention of the dedication of the eldest child to a god, or goddess. This is worded as if the dedication was to be by fire. The additional mention of incense or cedarwood, as accompanying the offering, renders it probable that it was really meant that the litigant should be punished by the sacrifice of his child as a "burnt offering" to the god. But this only makes it clearer that such penalties were simply meant to be deterrent. We have no proof that such an offering ever took place. It was a memory of bygone horrors, but not less interesting as showing what had once been possible. A more natural and extremely common penalty was the payment of a tenfold value to the dis-

[1] §§ 4, 13. [2] Nbd., 13.

turbed owner. In later times this was twelvefold. This was an example of the multiple restitution so common in the Code.

The ordeal

Something very like an ordeal was occasionally imposed. The very fragmentary condition of the texts which give it adds to its obscurity. But it appears to have consisted in the litigant being compelled to eat a mina weight of some magically concocted food and to drink the contents of an inscribed bowl. What the result was expected to be is not stated. One fragmentary text appears to name the ingredients of the magic potion. All that can be made out points to an ordeal, somewhat similar to that inflicted upon a suspected wife in Numbers v. 12–31.

9. **Penalties for wrong-doing.**—We are chiefly indebted to the Code for our knowledge of the penalties which the judge and his assessors might inflict.

The death-penalty

Foremost we may place the death-penalty. This was inflicted by the Code for witchcraft, for theft, for corruption of justice, for rape, for causing death by assault, for neglect of duties by certain officials, for allowing a seditious assembly, for causing death by bad building, and for varieties of these crimes. It is curious that no mention is made of murder pure and simple. But this is only accidental. It is evidently assumed. For the Code brings several cases of murder under this penalty. Procuring the death of a husband is punished by it; even a fatal assault, as that on a pregnant woman who dies of miscarriage as the result. The need of an oath to establish lack of malice in giving a blow in a quarrel which led to death tends to show that murder was punished by death, and that it was regarded as death intentionally caused. An explicit statement was clearly not needed. We do not yet know how this sentence was carried out. Usually the Code only says "he shall be killed"; by whom, or how, is not stated. For special cases the manner is described.

Death by drowning was inflicted on a beer-seller for selling beer too cheaply; on a woman for adultery, for being a bad wife, for incest, or for desertion of her husband's house. In every case the victim was a woman. When men were drowned they shared a woman's fate. In two cases, adultery and incest, we read of the criminals being bound. In the latter, § 155, it seems that the man was "bound" and the woman drowned. In the former, § 129, both were "bound" and both drowned. It is hardly likely that "bound" can mean merely tied up, or imprisoned, in the case of the man who committed incest. I would suggest that in both cases it means "strangled." The alternative would be that the confusion in § 155 is due to the scribe. Drowning

Death by fire is directly ordered for a votary who opens or enters a beer-shop, for a man and his mother in incest, and indirectly for a thief at a fire. Burning

Impalement on a stake is ordered for a wife procuring her husband's death. Impalement

Indirectly the death-penalty would often be the consequence of an appeal to the ordeal by water, in §§ 2, 132. Ordeal by water

The various sorts of mutilation named are of two types: (1) retaliation for bodily disfigurement, (2) symbolical of the offence itself. Thus eye for eye, tooth for tooth, limb for limb, are pure retaliations. But the hands cut off mark the sin of the hands in striking a father, in unlawful surgery, or in branding. The eye torn out was the punishing of unlawful curiosity. The ear cut off marked the sin of the organ of hearing and obedience. The tongue was cut out for the ingratitude evidenced in speech. Mutilations

Scourging is the only other form of corporal punishment. It was done with an ox-hide scourge, or thong, and sixty strokes were ordered to be publicly inflicted for a gross assault on a superior. Scourging

Banishment

Banishment from the city was the penalty for incest.[1]

Simple restitution

Restitution may, perhaps, hardly be regarded as a penalty. Thus a man who was found in possession of lost property had to restore it. In case of loss caused by neglect or ill-treatment of hired property, or of goods deposited or intrusted, or by want of care in treating diseased limbs, restitution, goods for goods, ox for ox, ass for ass, *et cetera*, was ordered.[2]

Multiple restitution

But restitution of many times the damage inflicted is a distinct penalty. The Code orders threefold for cheating a principal,[3] fivefold for loss or theft of goods by carrier,[4] sixfold for defrauding an agent,[5] tenfold for theft by a poor man, or for careless loss by shepherd or herdsman,[6] twelvefold for a false sentence by a judge,[7] thirtyfold for theft on the part of a gentleman.

Retaliation

The infliction of the same loss on a criminal that he caused another is seen in the cases of mutilation, eye for eye, limb for limb, tooth for tooth,[8] but also in the penalty of son for son, daughter for daughter, slave for slave;[9] and in the rule that a vexatious suitor shall pay the penalty which his suit was calculated to bring on the defendant.

Vicarious punishment

This retaliation is the explanation of what seems to be vicarious punishment, where a man suffers in the person of his son, or daughter, for the loss he has caused to the son or daughter of another.[10]

Loss of claim

Another penalty was the voidance of a claim. If a man took the law into his own hands to repay his debt, he lost all claim to recover it through the courts. When the purchase was illegal and void, as that of an officer's benefice or of a ward's property, the purchaser had to return his purchase and lose what he had paid for it.

---

[1] § 154. [2] §§ 9, 10, 12, 125, 219, 231, 232, 245, 246, 263.
[3] § 106. [4] § 112. [5] § 107. [6] §§ 8, 265. [7] § 5.
[8] §§ 196, 197, 200. [9] §§ 116, 210, 219, 230, 231. [10] §§ 116, 210, 230.

Cases where no claim is allowed

In certain cases no suit was allowed to gain standing. Contributory negligence,[1] the natural death of hostage for debt,[2] the accidental goring of a man by a wild bull,[3] are excluded from litigation. Such events cancel all further claim or are expressly said to have no remedy. There is no case for prosecution.

Compensation

Compensation for loss caused by crime, or neglect, is ordered on a scale fixed by the Code. Where a tenant takes a field on produce-rent his neglect to cultivate caused a loss to the landlord. He was thus bound to pay an average yield, or a crop like his neighbor's, or that of the next field.[4] In later times, the vagueness of this rule, which might give rise to dispute, was avoided by stating in the lease the average rent to be expected. For certain classes of land, where no comparison with the next field could be instituted, a fixed rate was set down.[5] Compensation for premature ejectment was ordered.[6]

---

[1] § 123. [2] § 115. [3] § 250. [4] § 42. [5] § 44. [6] § Y.

# VI

## LEGAL DECISIONS

Meaning of the term

By a legal decision we understand a "judgment" pronounced by some judicial authority upon a case submitted. It is not easy to say whether the Babylonians had a separate name for this sort of transaction; but it had some peculiarities by which it can be easily recognized. It usually opens with the words, *duppu ana*, "tablet on," followed by the statement of the object in dispute. This is very often abbreviated to a simple *ana*, "on," or *aššum* = *ana šum*, "concerning," or *eli* with the same sense.

These usages explain the curious tablet[1] where we have a long series of sections each containing names associated with other names by the word *aššum*. Thus we read:[2]

"Nishînishu, daughter of Rîsh-Sin, *aššum* Shamash-ellatsu, son of Itti-Sin-dinim."

Technical terms used

It is not clear whether Shamash-ellatsu was the adversary of Nishînishu, or the subject of her suit. But we clearly have here a "trial list" of seventeen cases. Whether they were all decided in one day, month, or year, or whether they were reserved for the royal audience, we have no means of telling. It is merely a list. The object in dispute, "two *sar* of land," is occasionally given; or the court is named "the temple of Shamash," or "at the gate of Shamash." The whole text is too fragmentary to be translated, but we may

[1] $B^2$ 316. [2] Rev. 1–4.

note that some lady or other is always a party to the suit. If we could find the tablets referring to the decisions intended and they should turn out to be of different years, this list might prove of value for chronology.

Their arrangement

Legal decisions relate to all manner of subjects and consequently are difficult to arrange. Dr. Meissner adopted the excellent plan of appending them to the groups concerned with the class of property dealt with under them. Thus a legal decision concerned with the sale of a house would be grouped with the house sales. But this does not suit all cases, and both in formula and subject the legal decisions are really distinct. Most legal decisions add nothing to our knowledge of the law, merely recording that "A sued B and lost the day and is now bound over not to renew the litigation." A large number go only a little further, thus:[1]

Suit concerning inheritance

Ribatum, daughter of Salâ, was sued by the sons of Erib-Sin, Shumma-ilu and Mâr-erṣitim, concerning what Salâ, her father, and Mullubtim, her mother, had left her. They took judges who restored to her one-half *GAN* of land, her property. Shumma-ilu and Mâr-erṣitim, sons of Erib-Sin, shall not renounce this agreement nor dispute it. They swore by Shamash, Malkat, Marduk, and Samsu-iluna the king. Four judges appear as witnesses. Dated the 10th of Elul, in the second year of Samsu-iluna.

Here it is not stated what was the ground on which the parties disagreed, nor that they laid claim to more than one-half *GAN* of land. They lost the case. That is all we know in many other cases. Often we do not know the object in dispute. Other cases are quite full and often very instructive. Thus:[2]

Suit for paternal power over daughter

About the maid Adkallim, whom Aiatîa had left to her daughter Ḫulaltum. Ḫulaltum had taken care of her mother Aiatîa; while Sin-nâṣir, the husband of Aiatîa, who was in Buzu for twenty years,

[1] B[a] 511. [2] B[c] 2474.

had left Aiatîa to her fate, loved her not. Now after Aiatîa was dead, Sin-nâṣir laid claim on whatever Aiatîa had, and on Ḫulaltum for the maid Adkallim. Isharlim, the *rabiânu* of Sippar, with the Kar-Sippar, assigned sentence; they laid the blame on him. He shall not renounce the agreement, nor dispute it. They swore by Shamash, Marduk, and Ḫammurabi the king. The judgment of Isharlim. Four witnesses. Dated in Elul, the 9th year of Ḫammurabi.

This was a bad case of desertion. The husband, Sin-nâṣir, deserted his wife for twenty years, but on her death came back and claimed her property. This he was not allowed to do, by the Code.[1] In his absence, Ḫulaltum had cared for Aiatîa, either as his real, or only adopted, daughter. In either case, Aiatîa had left Ḫulaltum a slave-girl, Adkallim, whom Sin-nâṣir now claimed. His claim was disallowed.

The decisions which we now possess give little further information as to the legal procedure, but a series of abstracts will illustrate the legal points which they raise.

Suit on partnership

Ṣilli-Ishtar and Amêl-ili, sons of Ilu-eriba, were sued by Eribam-Sin, son of Ubar-Sin, concerning a house, etc., which they bought of Sin-mubaliṭ and his brothers. They say that they bought with money which Ṣilli-Ishtar received from his mother and which formed no part of that which they had in common with plaintiff as partners. Deposition accepted Ḫammurabi 34.[2]

Suit for incomes

The sons of Zâzîa sue Sin-imgurâni and Sin-uzilli for rights in a house next the temple of Ningirsu, five days' income in the temple of Sin, sixteen days' income in the shrine of Bêlit, and eight days' income in the shrine of Gula. Claim not made out. Era of Isin 6.[3]

No claim on property

Idin-Adadi and Mattatum have no claim on property which Ḫishatum has or shall inherit. Rim-Sin (?).[4]

Partnership

Adadi-idinnam and Ardi-Martu agree on dissolution of partnership. Zabum 1.[5]

---

[1] § 136.
[2] M. A. P., 39.
[3] M. A. P., 41.
[4] M. A. P., 44.
[5] M. A. P., 79.

Brothers of Ur-ilishu agree not to proceed against Sala-ilu and Ur-ilishu concerning property left by latter. Apil-Sin (?).[1] Inheritance

Family of Urra-gâmil sue Erib-Sin for account of his partnership with and his indebtedness to Urra-gâmil deceased. Erib-Sin settles. N. D.[2] Partnership

Sin-ellâtsu gave a ring to Ramê-Ishḫara. The children of Sin-ellâtsu agree not to sue her for it. Ḫammurabi (?).[3] Gift

Private settlement of claims to property. N. D.[4] Settlement "out of court"

In the above cases there is no explicit mention of judges. The next group are cases before judges where fact of suit, subject and result are given, but not the pleas presented.

Imgur-Sin and Ilu-eriba sue Iatratum concerning a house which she bought of their father. Nonsuited. Before judges of Babylon and Sippara.[5] Property bought

Ṣilli-Ishtar and Eribam-Sin entered into partnership. On dissolution of their partnership they chose judges, paid in their common stock and shared equally. The shares are scheduled in the deed of settlement. Ḫammurabi 34.[6] Partnership

Pala-Shamash and Apil-itishu dispute concerning a division of property. They obtain judges and city witnesses. The whole house and income is shared equally and each agrees to waive further claim. Ḫammurabi (?).[7] Inheritance

The two sons of Ḳû-Ishtar disagreed as to their shares. Nidnat-Sin, the *rab* Martu, makes equitable division. Ḫammurabi 33.[8] Inheritance

Apil-ilishu and Pala-Shamash dispute the latter's right to a house, ship, servants, money, and property in his possession. The city elders from Ḫuda and Shibabi gave judgment and confirmed the title of Pala-Shamash.[9] Property

The sons of Nûr-Shamash sue Bêlitum for the property left her. Before judges. Nonsuited. Sumu-lâ-ilu.[10] Inheritance

Shunu-ma-ili and Mâr-erṣitim sue Ribatum concerning her right to the legacy of Salâ and Mullubtim. The judges assign her an income, *ḫibiltu*. Samsu-iluna 2.[11] Income

Marduk-mubaliṭ and Sin-idinnam sue Shâd-Malkat concerning her house in Bît Gagim. Judges confirm her title. Apil-Sin.[12] Property

---

[1] M. A. P., 111. [2] B² 301. [3] B² 2465. [4] B² 2473.
[5] M. A. P., 40. [6] M. A. P., 78. [7] M. A. P., 80. [8] M. A. P., 110.
[9] B 199. [10] B² 327. [11] B² 511. [12] B² 586.

Incomes

Ḫuzalum and Pî-Malkat, children of Nabi-Shamash implead Shidi-lamazatanḫu of Gagim concerning various rights to incomes and rations in the temple of Shamash. The judges assign shares to each. Samsu-iluna (?).[1]

Property

Aliḳu and Sumu-ramê sue Shakumâtim about a house they sold him. Nonsuited. N. D.[2]

Property

Shamash-bêl-ili repudiates a sale of land to the Lady Mannashi. He is nonsuited. Ḫammurabi 15.[3]

Property

Family of Ardi-rabish against Erib-Sin on account of property left them by Ardi-rabish. Nonsuited. Sin-mubalit 20.[4]

Property

Ḫamaziru sues Manutum for house and property but is nonsuited. Sumu-lâ-ilu.[5]

Vexatious prosecution

Kasha-Upi bought a house of Itti-itishu and his sons, Bêlshunu and Ilushu-bânî. Amêl-Ninshuna, son of Bêlshunu, brought a suit about the house. Judges condemn him to be branded on the forehead and confirm Kasha-Upi's title. Sin-mubalit.[6]

Land

Nishinishu sues Ana-erishti-Malkat for three *SAR* of land before the king's judges. Nonsuited. Samsu-iluna 2.[7]

Land

Malkat-kuzub-mâtim sues Ani-talime for restitution of a field, before the judges of Babylon and Sippara. The witnesses sustain her claim, which is granted. Samsu-iluna 3.[8]

Family dispute

The family of Izidaria sue the family of Azalîa about the property of Izidaria deceased. Their title is confirmed. Zabum 12.[9]

House

Shamash-bêl-ili sues Nidnusha concerning a house bought by him of her. The judges grant him two shekels of silver. Ḫammurabi 1.[10]

Land

Shî-lamazi sues her brothers for a field and wins her case.[11]

Change of venue

Before Lushtamar, *nâgiru* of Babylon, Adadi-idinnam and Ibku-Ishtar, judges, Zariku was put to the oath and replied to Erib-Sin. He was told that as his domicile was at Sippara, he must not make his appeal to the judges of Babylon. So his case was dismissed. Ḫammurabi 28.[12] The record is defective.

Cases before judges where the plea and its result can be made out with some certainty are as follows:

A dispute about the title to land

Ardi-Sin, son of Eṭiru, sued the sons of Shamash-nâṣir who had sold a plot of land, two and a half *GAN* in area, to Ibni-Adadi the

[1] B[2] 2175 A. [2] B[2] 2177 A. [3] B[2] 2178 A. [4] B[2] 2181.
[5] B[2] 2186. [6] B[2] 2190. [7] B[2] 2444 A. [8] B[2] 2458.
[9] B[2] 2463. [10] B[2] 2502. [11] B[2] 2193. [12] B[2] 824.

merchant. He claimed the land as ancestral domain, *bît abišu*, and denied that he had ever alienated it. The sons of Ibni-Adadi, now in possession, produced the deed of sale, *duppu šimâti*, which Eṭiru and Sin-nâdin-shûmi, his brother, had executed to Shamash-nâṣir and his son. The judges assigned a small portion of the land, about a sixth, to Ardi-Sin, but make up the rest, apparently, from another quarter. Ammizaduga (?).[1]

A title now invalidated by a revolution

Mâr-Martu bought the garden of Sin-mâgir. Ilubânî disputed the legality, *ṣimdattu*, of the sale. Before the judges at the gate of Nin-marki he deposed that he was the adopted son of Sin-mâgir, which adoption had never been revoked. In the time of Rim-Sin the house and garden had been awarded to Ilubânî and then Sin-mubaliṭ had brought a suit against Ilubânî, which was regularly heard before judges and witnesses from Nin-marki. They had awarded the house and garden to Ilubânî. Sin-mubaliṭ was now bound over to dispute the title no more. Ḫammurabi.[2]

Here it seems that on the deposition of Rim-Sin by Ḫammurabi, Sin-mubaliṭ, excluded by his bond from disputing Ilubânî's title, sold his claim to Mâr-Martu, who attempted to enter into possession. Possibly it was thought that the new rulers would reverse the old decision.

Right of a widow on remarriage to her husband's property or gifts

The sons of Namiatum sue their mother, Iashuḫatum, about her share of their father's property. She appears before the judges of Babylon and puts in an inventory to show that she has taken nothing from the family possessions. Then the sons of Namiatum renounce further claim on the ground of family possession to the property of Idin-Adadi, Iashuḫatum and their descendants. Samsu-iluna 2.[3]

It seems that, after the death of Namiatum, Iashuḫatum married again. The children of the first marriage bring an action to secure judgment that she shall not take with her any property of their father's. She had, as we know, a right to take with her her marriage-portion, but not her husband's gifts to her.

---

[1] M. A. P., 42. [2] M. A. P., 43. [3] M. A. P., 100.

Rent

Amêl-Ninsaḫ sues Garudu for the rent of a field. The debtor not paying was ejected. Apil-Sin.[1]

Income

Shûmi-erṣitim sues for right to a sheep and some corn, the *naptânu* of a god. Judges grant him half share. Ḫammurabi 9.[2]

Deposit

Judges summon Ibik-iltum before Elali-bânî to account for corn. He purges himself on oath. N. D.[3]

Adoption

Amat-Shamash claims to be the adopted daughter of Shamash-gâmil and his wife Ummi-Araḫtum. Her witnesses proving unsatisfactory, her claim was disallowed on the oath of Ummi-Araḫtum that they had never adopted her. Ḫammurabi (?).[4]

Loss of hired ass

Ilushu-abushu hired a pack-ass, *imer bilti*, of Ardi-Sin and Ṣilli-Ishtar and lost it. The judges awarded them sixteen shekels of silver as compensation. Apil-Sin 5.[5]

Inheritance

Babilîtum sued Erish-Saggil, Ubar-Nabium, and Marduk-nâṣir for a share of her family possessions, *bît abiša*. The judges assigned her a share. Samsu-iluna 5.[6]

Forged will

Nidnusha and Shamash-abilu sue the daughter of Sin-eribam about property which she claimed to have inherited. They charge her with having forged the will of Amti-Shamash in her favor. The judges went to Gagim, where the property was, and examined witnesses who proved that Amti-Shamash had left the property to the daughter of Sin-eribam. The judges therefore confirmed her title. N. D.[7]

Legacy

Mâr-erṣitim left a female slave Damiḳtum to Erib-Sin. His wife Mazabatum and his brother Ibni-Shamash dispute this legacy. The judges inspect a document by which Erib-Sin, on the suit of Mâr-erṣitim, had granted Damiḳtum to Mazabatum and Ibni-Shamash. The judges return Damiḳtum to Mazabatum. Ḫammurabi (?).[8]

Legal practice of Assyrian times

In Assyrian times we have comparatively few legal decisions. The judges who appear are the *sartênu*, or chief-justice; the *ḫazânu*, the chief civil magistrate of a city, the parallel of the ancient *rabiânu;* the *sukallu*, or chamberlain; and one or two others, besides the simple *daiânu*, or judge. Some of these are not judicial officers, but act in that capacity.

---

[1] B[1] 40. [2] B[1] 188. [3] B[1] 295. [4] B[1] 160.
[5] B[1] 711. [6] B[2] 272. [7] B[2] 2182. [8] B[2] 2516.

Usually the judge is said to lay the blame on the guilty party, *arnam eli A emêdu;* or to lay the penalty upon one, *sartu eli A emêdu.* The sentence itself was a *dienu*, or "judgment." As in former times, the legal decisions refer to all manner of cases, and here more than anywhere else a mere translation does not convey much meaning to the reader.

Thus:[1] a scribe A prosecuted a farmer B for the theft of a bull. They came before Nabû-zêr-kênish-lîshir, the deputy *ḫazânu* of Nineveh. Restitution, bull for bull, was imposed on the defendant, who meantime was held for the fine. "On the day that he shall have made good the value of the bull he shall go free." Dated the 12th of Elul. Eponymy of Mushallim-Ashur. Twelve witnesses.

Theft of a bull

Again:[2] A stole four slaves of B, who summoned him before the *sukallu.* The judge laid on him a fine of two hundred and ten minas of copper. B then deposited a pledge with A, either himself, or a slave, to perform work equivalent to the amount of the debt. If B, or any representative of his, pays the money, the pledge is void. "Whoever shall withdraw from this agreement, Ashur and Shamash shall be his judges, he shall pay ten minas of silver and ten minas of gold, he shall pay it in the treasury of Bêlit." Dated the 10th of Adar, B.C. 678. Eleven witnesses.

Theft of four slaves

Here is another case, relating to a breach of trust:[3]

Damages for loss by agent

The decision of the chief-justice, which he laid on Ḫanî. Three hundred sheep, with their belongings, property of the king's son were lost, or killed by the shepherds. Each shepherd was condemned to pay two talents of bronze as his fine. Ḫanî, and his people, and his fields, were taken as security for the payment for the three hundred sheep, and the fines due from the shepherds. "Whoever shall demand him, his *šaknu*, his *rab kiṣir*, or any representative of his, shall pay for three hundred sheep and the fines for the shepherds and then Ḫanî shall be released." Dated 27th of Sebat, B.C. 679. Four witnesses.

The defendant had been intrusted with three hundred sheep, which he had to return in full, with a proper in-

[1] A. D. D., No. 160. [2] A. D. D., No. 161. [3] A. D. D., No. 164.

crease of lambs. But, evidently in the disorders which arose on the death of Sennacherib, Ḫanî had lost or made away with them. If he had intrusted them to shepherds, either the shepherds had killed them, or, as some take it, Ḫanî had killed the shepherds. In the former case he owed two talents of bronze as fine from each shepherd, in the latter he had to pay the same amount for each. Either way, he was held responsible for the value of three hundred sheep and two talents of bronze for each shepherd. He and all he had were seized for the liability. It is interesting to note that his district governor, or the colonel of the regiment to which he belonged, was thought likely to liberate him; but some other representative might do so. The lost property belonged to the king's son. This may have been Esarhaddon, or one of Sennacherib's other sons. But, at any rate, it is clear that Esarhaddon was putting his household in order.

Additional cases

The other examples known to us do not add to our legal knowledge. The subjects are chiefly misappropriations of property and there is little variety.

Later Babylonian decisions

The later Babylonian tablets throw some light upon legal procedure in Babylon. The greater detail exhibited by them is due largely to the fact that for this period we have so many private documents. The greater portion of the material for this part of the subject has been worked over by Professor J. Kohler and Dr. F. E. Peiser, in their valuable treatise *Aus Babylonische Rechtsleben.* Little can be added beyond additional examples and illustration.

Method of procedure

The judges acted as a college and not separately. There might be present at a case a chief judge and several judges assisting. Other cases were decided before a single judge. The *šibûtu* continue to act as a jury. They were the elders of the city, competent to decide the rights of the case. But the exact form of the organization is not yet quite clear.

The process began with the charge. The plaintiff preferred this himself, or by a messenger. His plea was heard and his proofs considered. Then the court caused the accused to come before them and answer the charge.

The possible complications

The process admitted of a third person intervening. Thus, A had pledged a plot of land to B for thirty-two shekels. Then he sold the property to C. C, dying, left the property to D, who wished to take possession from B, who continued to hold it in pledge. B goes to the judges and complains against D. A, being yet alive, intervenes and probably has to pay B. But the tablet being defective, we are not able to follow the case further. Only we see the sort of right which each had.

Dispute for the possession of a sum of money

Another case is where two parties dispute as to the possession of a sum which is actually in the hands of a banker. The banker accordingly undertakes to produce the sum and its interest in court, and to pay it over to the successful party in the suit. The decision was written down and the notary of the court gave a copy to the plaintiff, if not also to the defendant, and kept one copy for the archives. The plaintiff thus obtained a guarantee against the defendant. But how it was enforced we have no evidence.

Suit regarding loan on mortgage

The kind of points in dispute and decided are, as before, exceedingly varied. The decisions for the most part illustrate other subjects rather than the processes in court; but a few examples may be of interest: A made an advance of forty-four shekels to B, who pledged a house for it. This state of affairs continued until both were dead. Their sons inherited. A's son demanded forty-four shekels of B's son, who refused to pay. Both came before the judges. B's son pleaded that the money was never loaned or else repaid long ago. The judges demanded evidence. Either the contract or a receipt must be produced. The claimant was able to present the contract, but no receipt was produced. So the judges assigned the claimant a plot of land belonging to the defendant as satisfaction for the proved debt. Here we have the tablet witnessed by the chief judge, the judges, and the notary.[1] What is curious is that the claimant was not content to keep the pledge. But it is probable that the debt was secured on a house which the creditor did not take into his possession. It is also surprising that the judges did not order the house to be handed over to the claimant. That may have been avoided, because of the family rights over the house. The debtor might thus have been rendered houseless, or have lost "his father's house." The widow may still have been an inmate. A great part of the document is taken up with the specification of the land handed over to the claimant. Hence a complete translation is not given.

Regarding possession of a slave

A common type of case was a vindication of right to some sort of property. Thus[2] A had sold B a slave, but C came forward and said: "He is my slave who fled from me," and took an oath by Bêl and Nabû, that he knew where that slave was living with A. The judges decide that C shall go where the slave is, and when he has proved that he is with A, the slave shall return to C.

Acknowledgment of a debt

We have an acknowledgment before the court and a promise to pay the debt. This promise was usually made on oath, or guarantees were given. Here is an involved case. A is father of B's mother. B's father is long dead. The property of A, his grandfather, has now come into B's hands. He finds an old bond for an advance from A to C and D. The latter D is also dead but had a son E, who inherited. Hence B now sues C and E for the money. The bond is shown to C, who remembers and acknowledges the debt and he now undertakes to bring his fellow-debtor E and discharge the debt.

---

[1] Nbn. 1128. [2] Dar. 53.

Settlement out of court

Men did not always stand their trial, but sometimes settled the case by an agreement out of court.[1] A and his wife sued B for some slaves, people of their house. B dreads the trial and does not appear. The wife was B's mother, evidently remarried. B brings the slaves whom he still has and offers four minas as payment for one who has died in his house. The offer is accepted and parties agree to be quit.

A private settlement

The decision of a dispute was not always referred to professional judges. A very interesting example occurs,[2] when the eldest member of the family and *kinatti aplišu*, "the family of his son," act as judges. The plaintiff is an old lady, who had been married, and had a daughter married. These facts are not rehearsed in the tablet itself, which concerns a division of property, but are collected from a number of tablets, spread over some sixty years. The way in which information is thus collected is an instructive example of the manner in which the different documents illustrate and explain one another.[3]

Agreements to appear in court

Connected with legal decisions are the undertakings to appear before the court, of which we have several examples. Thus,[4] A undertakes to bring B to Babylon and answer the complaint of C. Or again, a certain gardener spoke to A before an official of the *mâr banûtu*. This official was subpœnaed, as we should say, and swore by Bêl, Nabû, and Darius, that on the 8th of Sebat, two days hence, he would come and take up the case.[5]

Production of witnesses

The production of witnesses is the subject of not a few undertakings. Thus,[6] by a fixed date, five days hence, A shall bring B to be questioned about some asses belonging to the royal household. Again,[7] N swears to come, six days hence, and bring another, on account of the witness about A. He further undertakes to establish the partnership.

---

[1] Dar. 260. [2] Dar. 410. [3] A. B. P., ii., pp. 70 ff.
[4] Dar. 159. [5] Dar. 229. [6] Dar. 299. [7] Dar. 176.

What was the exact cause of quarrel was not stated. These agreements to abide by the testimony of a named witness may have been entered into without reference to judges, but the oath may have been administered before the court. Thus,[1] two parties agree to waive their dispute and abide by witness produced. This they do before the *atû* official of the gate of the temple. Again,[2] A is to bring witnesses on the second of Ab, to the door of the *tikkalu's* house, and prove when and to whom he gave certain garments. If this be proved, that B had received them, B will restore the said garments to A; if not, B is free. Further, if B does not appear on that day, he shall be bound to restore the garments. Several other examples illustrate the point.[3]

Production of bond

A common method was, as has already been shown, to produce the bond or other document, establishing the claim. If, for some reason, the document was not producible, the oath of the scribe who wrote it might be admitted.[4] The witnesses whose names appear on the document do not seem to have been summoned. But in one case,[5] when two Persians had sold two slave-girls, also Persians, to a Babylonian; a third Persian, who had been witness to the sale, was called on to swear, "I know that the money was paid," and he sealed the document.

[1] Nbk. 52. [2] Nbk. 183. [3] A. B. P., i., pp. 31 ff.
[4] A. B. P., ii., p. 67. [5] Camb. 384.

## VII

### PUBLIC RIGHTS

The mixed population of Babylonia

THE early inhabitants of Babylonia are usually regarded as a non-Semitic race, whom we term Sumerians. Upon them was superimposed a layer of Semitic peoples. The first dynasty of Babylon is now often called Arabian. But the evidence of a previous admixture of peoples is not lacking. The subsequent history bears witness to many invasions by Kassites, Elamites, and nomad tribes, some Semitic, some probably not. Later came Persians and Medes, not to speak of Greeks and Parthians.

Position and rights of resident aliens

The foreign wars brought slaves from all the surrounding countries, even as far away as Egypt. We cannot here enter into any discussion of the foreign elements in the population; but it is important to note what the attitude of the Babylonians was to the foreigners resident in their midst. The evidence on the whole is very slight. It may be said, that as a rule, resident aliens became citizens and were under no disabilities. One section of the Code, if we correctly understand it, allows an alien to purchase an estate, provided he bears the liabilities to the state[1] which lay upon it. The "merchant" was probably usually an alien, and only temporarily resident. In the contracts of the Ḫammurabi period, with the exception of the frequent West-Semitic names, we have little trace of aliens. When the Kassites came we may expect the conquering race to

[1] § 40.

have had full rights. In Assyria there is no trace of disability. Egyptians, Elamites, Armenians, Jews, Arameans, contract exactly like natives. In later Babylonian times we find the same freedom. Of course Persians, and, later, Greeks, were under no disabilities. Hence there is very little at any time to chronicle under this head.

We have marriages between Persians and Egyptians, with witnesses, Babylonian, Persian, Aramean, and Egyptian.[1] Medes rent a Babylonian's house, and live there.[2] A Persian buys of a Babylonian.[3] A Persian father gives Babylonian names to his children.[4] A vivid picture of the mixed nationality in the time of Artaxerxes II. is given in the "Business Documents of Murashû Sons," and the list of proper names attached to Professor Hilprecht's edition sufficiently illustrates the point.

Tax on landed property

Ownership of land carried its liabilities of tax or service. These were carefully guarded and it was the mark of an oppressor to exceed the normal demand. That, however, seems to have been regularly and continually paid. A very good illustration of public rights over land, or the relation between the state and the private owner, is afforded by the construction, in the reign of Cyrus, of a canal of Shamash by the priest of Sippara. It was to pass through certain lands and the consent of the owners had to be obtained. The magistrates and honorables of the city A, through which it would pass, and the peoples of the neighboring fields were assembled. They were asked to swear, as Susians, subjects of the King of Susa, that they would raise no difficulty. Then the priest took on himself the cost of the work on the canal, but stipulated that when it was completed, the neighbors should keep it in repair. Also he forbade the construction of any rival canal.[5] Riparians

---

1 Dar. 201.
2 Dar. 57.
3 Dar. 410.
4 Dar. 509.
5 Cyr. 231, 232.

were responsible for the care of the canal as shown in the Code.[1]

State liabilities

The state undertook some duties. In the Code we note that the palace would, failing other means, redeem an official from captivity.[2]

District liabilities

There were certain local liabilities of a public nature. Thus the Code shows that the magistrate and his district were held responsible for highway robbery or brigandage in their midst.[3] It may be assumed that the funds to meet such liabilities were furnished by the city temple, for we note that if an official were captured, and his private means were not sufficient for his ransom, his city temple had to furnish the money.[4]

General system of taxation

The whole question of taxation is full of difficulties. There were certain persons who paid tribute, that is, some proportionate part of their produce, others did personal service. There is frequent mention of dues of various sorts, at ferries, market-places and the like. Demands were made on the stock or crops of the farmers. But we are not yet in a position even to sketch the system of taxation.

---

[1] § 53. [2] § 32. [3] § 24. [4] § 40.

# VIII

## CRIMINAL LAW

Reason for the lack of information regarding criminal law

CASES concerned with criminal law were naturally not embodied in contracts. Some cases doubtless may be inferred from the legal decisions, but these are only where the penalty had already been commuted from death or punishment to payment or restitution. They are better taken as examples of civil law. But this distinction is not the cause of their rarity or absence. When a man had to be put to death, scourged, or exiled, there was no need for a written bond. Hence the only references which we have outside the Code and the phrase-books, are the penalties set down in marriage-contracts for conjugal infidelity, or for breach of contract voluntarily agreed to by the parties to it.

Blood-vengeance commuted for a gift

We have one case from Assyrian times of the assignment of a slave-girl, as composition for manslaughter. Atarkâmu, a scribe, had caused the death of Samaku, whose son Shamash-ukîn-aḫi had the right to exact vengeance. Whether as the result of a legal decision or not, Atarkâmu hands over a slave-girl to Shamash-ukîn-aḫi and they agree to be at peace. The name of Ashurbânipal occurs in a position which strongly suggests that the king himself sat in judgment upon the case. The tablet is so fragmentary that little else can be made out, but it seems to have been stipulated that the slave should be handed over "at the grave."[1]

[1] A. D. D., No. 321.

In later Babylonian times we have a reference to imprisonment arising out of a case of guarantee.[1] The priest of Shamash at Sippara had put A in prison in fetters; B, a fellow-official of his of the same standing, bails him out, giving guarantee to the priests and *šibûtu* that A shall not go away, or if he does, that B will do his work. Imprisonment

A case of assault and forcible entry into a house occurs.[2] But the tablet is so defective that we cannot make out the rights of the case. The superintendent of the city Shaḫrin, in the eighth year of Cyrus complained to the priest of Shamash at Sippara, to the following effect: He had taken into his house, as a prisoner, a certain man A. He pleads that he is uncle to the priest and chief magistrate of the city. Why then has the priest raised his hand over him? Further, seven men, who are armed, have burst in his door and entered his house and taken a mina of gold. Whether this was a rescue by relatives of the prisoner, or by order of the priest, does not appear. As a result of this complaint, the elders of the city were assembled and depositions made. Beyond the plea on the part of the house-breakers that someone had paid them to break in the door, and that the prisoner A was someone's pledge, we get no further information. Assault

A case of procuration of desertion, forbidden by the Code[3] under pain of death, was condoned by the injured party.[4] A caused a maid of B's to leave her master's house. B received her back, pardoned A, and took no money of him. Tempting a slave to desert

Adultery was punished in the Code by drowning.[5] The Code in this and similar cases of sexual irregularity is explicit that the case must be flagrant. Suspicion was not enough.[6] But conduct leading to scandal had to be atoned Adultery and its punishment

---

[1] Cyr. 281. [2] Cyr. 328, 329. [3] § 15.
[4] Dar. 207. [5] § 129. [6] § 132.

for by submission to the ordeal. The Code did not take a higher ground than public opinion. The private contracts name death as punishment for adultery. Usually it is drowning, but being thrown from a high place, temple, tower, or pillar is named. In the later contracts death was still the penalty for a wife's adultery, but the penalty had ceased to be drowning only. The adulteress might be put to the sword.[1]

A woman's procuring her husband's death, for love of another, was punished by impalement.[2]

The punishment of incest

Incest on the part of a man with his own daughter involved his banishment.[3] Incest with a daughter-in-law, if she was his son's full wife, was apparently punished by his being drowned. The Code is obscure here and we are not sure whether she was drowned also.[4] If the girl was not yet fully married, the case was treated as one of ordinary seduction, and the culprit was fined half a mina.[5]

If a man committed incest with his own mother, both were burned.[6] If a man had intercourse with his foster-mother, or step-mother, who had borne children to his father, he was disinherited.[7]

[1] Z. A., iii., p. 78. [2] § 153. [3] § 154.
[4] § 155. [5] § 156. [6] § 157. [7] § 158.

## IX

## THE FAMILY ORGANIZATION

The sources of information

MARRIAGE is the bond which unites the different members of the family. The married pair, their children, slaves, and adjuncts, one side or the other, constitute the family unit. The Sumerian laws presuppose marriage; but, so far as known, merely attached penalties to repudiation of the wedded ties. The Code is very full and explicit and forms the basis of all our knowledge. The contemporary documents extend it in some particulars. In Assyrian times we know little or nothing about the laws concerning marriage. In later Babylonian times very little is known until the Persian period, when we have many illustrations. But what we know, or can gather from scattered hints, makes it clear that the state of things represented in the Code remained practically unchanged for the whole period.

The marriage-contract and its obligations

The Code is explicit that a woman was not a wife without "bonds."[1] This was a marriage-contract; of which the essentials were that the names of the parties and their lineage were given, the proper consents obtained and the declaration of the man that he has taken so-and-so to wife inserted. As a rule, stringent penalties are set down for a repudiation of the marriage-tie. In these bonds a man might be required to insert the clause that his wife was not to be held responsible for any debts he might have incurred before marriage. The Code enacts that such a clause shall be held to act both ways; if it is inserted, then the man shall

[1] § 128.

not be liable for his wife's debts before marriage.[1] But, if no such bond existed, the wedded pair were one body as far as liability for debt was concerned, by whichever it had been contracted and, in spite of such a bond, both were liable together for all debts contracted after marriage.

Family relations

The family relationship was of primary importance. Whatever may be said about traces of matriarchy in Babylonia, we have no legal documents which recognize the institution. The father is the head of the family and possesses full power over his wife and family. But the woman is not in that degraded condition in which marriage by capture, or purchase, left her. She was a man's inferior in some respects, but his helper and an honorable wife.

Ancient *gentes*

Not only was the family, which consisted of the wedded pair and their dependants, a unit, but there was also a connection with ancestors and posterity which enlarged the family to a clan or *gens*. In this sense it often appears. The family thus constituted had definite rights over its members. It was very important to a man to be sure of his family connection. We may note the importance attached at all epochs to a man's genealogy as distinguishing his individuality. His family identified him. There was a very large number of well-marked and distinguished families, which took their names from a remote ancestor. So far as our evidence goes, these ancestors were by no means mythical, but actually lived in the time of the first dynasty of Babylon. To all appearances they date back "to the Conquest." Unfortunately no attempt has yet been made to work out the family histories. But men of such families were the *mâr bânê*, or "sons of ancestors," and had special privileges, which continually emerge into notice. We may compare the hundred families of China and the patricians of many nations. There were other families of scarcely less antiquity

---

[1] § 157.

and consideration. They do not name their ancestor, but refer to him as a tradesman. They were sons of "the baker," of "the measurer," *et cetera*, with which we may compare our proper names Baker and Lemesurier. There was a court of ancestry, *bît mâr bânûti*, which investigated questions arising from claims to belong to such families and which doubtless preserved in its archives the genealogical lists of these exclusive families. They must have registered the birth of all fresh members and all adoptions; for men were adopted freely into such families.

**Guilds of working-men**

It is not clear whether all members of a family which traced descent, real or putative, from a trade-father, actually carried on that trade. If so, we should have examples of a workmen's guild. Certainly many men who carried on a trade were "sons" of the trade-father, but apparently not all. The Code notes the adoption of a child by an artisan who teaches him his trade. In certain cities the trades had their quarters. We read of the "city of the goldsmiths" in Nineveh.

**Their rivals**

It may well be that these guilds were close corporations at first and continued so to be in the less crowded trades, but rivals outside the guild also came to be tolerated. The slaves were artisans in great numbers and their increase may have led to the decay of the old artisan guilds of free workers.

**Public registration of family events**

The importance of descent was not a sentimental matter only. The laws of inheritance involved a careful distinction between proper heirs and a variety of claimants. Hence it seems likely that there was a registration of births, deaths, and marriages, at least covering the patrician families. We have such examples as a man claiming to be of same father as another, claiming brotherhood. The other repudiates the claim.[1] The tablet is too fragmentary for us

---

[1] Nbn. 69.

to follow the arguments. The slave Bariki-ilu claimed to be a *mâr bânû* and his claim was heard before the court of the *mâr bânê*.[1]

Entailed family property

Further, as the wife's marriage-portion, if she died childless, went back to the "house of her father," and as a man who died without issue had to leave his property to his "father's house," and as many had only a life-interest in their property, while the family usually had a right of preemption in the case of proposed sales, we see that the family always had a strong hold over property. Not only was it for the man's interest to be registered as of a certain family, but it was also for the family's interest to register all its members.

Responsibilities of family to its individual members

There are suggestions that the family assumed certain responsibilities over the man; for in Assyria it appears that the family might come forward and liberate a man from his debt. A free man, who had been sold as a slave to Ashnunnak, and who escaped to Babylon, after five years, being claimed as a slave by the levy-masters there, chose to serve his father's house. His brothers swore by Marduk and Ammiditana the king, making an irrevocable declaration that as long as he lived he should take up the duties of his father's house with his brothers.[2] In the later Babylonian times, the head of the family, though only a distant relation, was called upon to act as judge in a dispute concerning the disposition of property.

---

[1] Z. A., iii., p. 87 f. [2] B[2] 419.

# X

## COURTSHIP AND MARRIAGE

Amount of the bride-price

The suitor came with presents to the parents of the girl. Most writers see in this a survival of the purchase of the bride. The name of this gift, *terḫatu*, is undoubtedly connected with the name of the bride, *marḫitu*. This present, or bride-price, differed greatly with the circumstances of the parties. Both money and slaves were given, but a simple sum of money was more common. In cases where the bride was rich or highly placed the amount seems less. A very usual amount was ten shekels, but we have examples from one shekel up to three minas.[1] The Code assessed it at one mina of silver for a patrician and a third of a mina for a plebeian.[2]

Its disposal

Without this bride-price the young man could not take a wife. Hence it was expressly secured to him by the Code, if his father died before he was of age to marry, and reserved as a first charge on the father's estate. There is some evidence that a woman might make this present to her future husband. But that may have been because he was too poor to make it himself and she found him the means. As a rule, the parents gave this money to the bride. But we are not in a position to say whether they did so at once, on the consummation of the marriage, or on the birth of a child. The suggestion that it was her *Morgengabe* remains without support. Certain it is that it was not returned

[1] S. 34. [2] § 139.

always. In the contracts it seems to be given to the bridegroom with the bride. On a wife dying without children, the husband was bound to return her marriage-portion to her family. But if the bride-price which he had given for her had not been returned to him, he could deduct its value. On a divorce, he was bound to let his wife have not only her marriage-portion, but the bride-price paid back to him. If there had been none, he must give her a fixed sum instead of it.

Its presentation

From the phrase-books we may gather that there was a sort of ceremony about presenting the bride-price to the father: it was placed on a salver and brought in before the parents.[1] This was probably a part of the ceremony of betrothal.

If the father rejected the suitor, he was bound to return the bride-price offered.[2] A curious section of the Code enacts that if the suitor's comrade intrigued to break off the match, he was excluded from marrying the girl himself.[3]

Penalty for breach of promise

If, after he had brought in the bride-price to his prospective father-in-law, the suitor took a fancy to another girl, he might withdraw from the suit. But he then forfeited what he had offered. If this really was the result of having taken a dislike to a plain girl, we may suppose that such a maiden might accumulate several bride-prices and so acquire some wealth. This may explain Herodotus's idea that the handsome girls made a dowry for the plain ones. But there is not a shred of evidence for their doing so in the way he suggests. A girl was a virgin when she was married.[4]

Preliminaries of marriage

Of interest in the later Babylonian texts is the fact that the preliminaries of the marriage are more fully illustrated. Thus we read of the wedding of the daughter of Neriglissar:[5] Nabû-shum-ukîn, the *êrib bîti* of Nabû, judge of Êzida,

[1] V. R., 24, 48. [2] § 160. [3] § 161. [4] § 156. [5] Nergl. 1.

spoke to the King Neriglissar, saying thus: "Give to me Gigîtum, your young daughter, to wife." The tablet has only preserved a few lines, from which we cannot be sure that the marriage took place. The tablet was called a duplicate of Êzida, showing that it was preserved in the Nabû temple at Borsippa.

The following case is one of the clearest:[1]

Negotiation of a father for his son

Nabû-nâdin-aḫi, son of Bêl-aḫê-iddin, grandson of Ardi-Nêrgal, spoke thus to Shûm-ukîn, son of Mushallimu, saying: "Give me thy daughter, Ina-Esaggil-banat, the maiden, to wife, for Uballitsu-Gula, my son." Shûm-ukîn listened to him and gave his maiden daughter, Ina-Esaggil-banat to Uballitsu-Gula, his son. He gave also one mina of silver, three female slaves named, and house furniture, with Ina-Esaggil-banat, his daughter, as a marriage-portion to Nabû-nâdin-aḫi. Nanâ-kishirat, the maid of Shûm-ukîn in lieu of two-thirds of a mina of silver, her full price, Shûm-ukîn gave to Nabû-nâdin-aḫi out of the one mina of silver for her marriage-portion. The deficiency, one-third of a mina of silver, Shûm-ukîn will give Nabû-nâdin-aḫi, and then her marriage-portion is paid. Each took a writing.

Here the father negotiates for his son. There is no evidence of any bride-price being paid. But the examples of this kind of document are too few for us to establish any fixed conclusions. In the following case something very like it appears.[2]

Negotiation with a mother for her daughter

Dâgil-ilâni, son of Zambubu, spoke thus to Ḫammâ, daughter of Nêrgal-iddin, son of Babûtu, saying: "Give me thy daughter, Latubashinni, she shall be my wife." Ḫammâ listened to him and gave him her daughter, Latubashinni, to wife; and Dâgil-ilâni, in the joy of his heart, gave to Ḫammâ for Latubashinni, her daughter, Ana-eli-bêli-âmur, a maid, for half a mina of silver and a mina and a half of silver to boot. The day that Dâgil-ilâni shall take a second wife, Dâgil-ilâni shall give Latubashinni a mina of silver and she shall go back where she was before. With the cognisance of Shûm-iddin, son of Ina-êšhi-eter, son of Sin-damaku.

---

[1] Nbn. 243. [2] Nbk. 101.

Here the man himself negotiates. The mother gives the bride. Whether he really buys her is hard to say. The mother may have adopted the girl to care for her old age, as was often done. The bridegroom may have compensated the mother with means to adopt another daughter. What *locus standi* Shûm-iddin had is not clear. He may have been the real father of the bride and so had to be satisfied that she was fairly treated by the change in her position. Or his consent to the bridegroom's alliance may have been needed. The penalty set down for divorce is not high and the bride was probably poor; we see she was portionless. In other cases it was as high as six minas of silver.[1] Occasionally the deed of marriage also named a penalty for adultery on the part of the wife.

Rôle of the contracting parties

Women were given in marriage. The suitor for her hand did not perhaps see her until marriage, but this is not likely, since he is contemplated by the Code as capable of having cast his eyes upon another, and so desiring to retreat from his suit. At any rate, he brought presents to her father, who accepted or rejected him. There is no hint that the woman had any choice. The result of this power over the child's marriage was that conditions might be imposed on the marriage. The bride might be required to do service to an existing wife, or to the bridegroom's mother. Further, the disposal of property was not entirely free after marriage. It depended upon what the father had laid down in the marriage-settlement on his daughter. It was strictly limited to the woman's children, and if there were none it went back to her father's house.

Giving away the bride

In early times, the father usually gives the bride. But in a great many cases this duty fell on the mother. How this came about we do not usually know. The father being dead, or the girl illegitimate, seem the best explanations, as a rule.

[1] Cyr. 183, B. A. S., iv., p. 7.

In the absence of father and mother, the brother as head of the family assumed the duty. The examples of this are common enough.[1]

For later times also the examples are numerous of the power of agnates to give in marriage. It may perhaps be deduced that the children, in these cases, were young.[2]

Widows free to dispose of themselves

Women once married, were free to marry again of their own choice, whether divorced, separated, or widowed. A betrothed girl, or bride, if her marriage were not yet consummated, being seduced by her father-in-law, in whose house she had gone to live, was also free to marry. But it does not seem that women who were yet virgins could choose their own husbands. Even princesses were given in marriage.

Consent of bridegroom's father or guardian requisite for a legal marriage

The man was not altogether free to marry. The Code contemplates a boy left by the death of his father too young to marry. The brothers, when they divided the father's property, were bound to set aside for him, in addition to his share of his father's property, a sum for a bride-price, and take him a wife. It seems probable that men married while still young and living at home. For the Code contemplates the bride being brought to live in her father-in-law's house.[3]

In later Babylonian times, at any rate, the son could not marry without his father's consent. This we learn from a suit in high life, in the time of Cyrus.[4] A high official of the king's, A, brought a suit against B, who was "over the house," before the nobles and the king's judges. A accused B and C, an official of his house, of having given a tablet of marriage-contract of D, a sister of C's, to A's son without A's consent. Put to the oath, B swore that he did not seal the tablet. Then D was questioned. Then C acknowledged that he had drawn up and sealed with B's seal the

[1] See pages 162, 163

[2] B. A. S., iv., pp. 14–22.

[3] §§ 155, 156.

[4] Cyr. 312.

marriage-contract of D to A's son. The judges ordered D to return to her brother's house. The tablet was to be broken whenever found. If afterward D should be seen with A's son, she was to bear the sign of a concubine.

The court of registration

From other examples the conclusion is inevitable that if a woman desired to be a full and proper wife she had to obtain the consent of her bridegroom's father. Thus we read :[1] "The day that the woman A is seen with B he shall bring her to the wedding-house. If she does not say to the master of the wedding-house: Send for C, the father of B, then she shall wear the sign of a concubine." Her mother was present at the sealing of this agreement. From this we may deduce that weddings took place at a definite spot, called the "wedding-house." The name was literally "house of the males," or "of the named ones," and also house of the *mâr bânê*, or "sons of ancestors." It is clear that this was a registration court where all who had pretensions to ancestry, or were people of position, were enrolled. One whose name was found there was a man "with a name," also a "son of an ancestor." He was probably registered there at birth, marriage, and death. The master of that house was a registrar and evidently could marry people. It was expected in this case that the woman, if she wished to be properly married, would send for the bridegroom's father, whose consent was necessary. Another name for the house was *bît pirṣatum*, the meaning of which is obscure. But as Ishtar was *bêlit parṣê*, the "lady of the *parṣê*," we may connect it also with weddings.

The bride's dowry

We have seen that the *terḫatu*, or present made to the parents by the suitor before marriage, was usually handed over to the bride on her going to her husband's house. There is frequent reference to this essential preliminary. It had to be carefully laid aside for the young man by his

---

[1] Cyr. 307.

mother or brethren, if he had not married in his father's lifetime, and was secured to him by law, apart from and above what might come to him as a share of his father's property. Otherwise he would suffer loss in having to find it out of his own pocket, when his married brothers had been provided with the means during their father's lifetime. Usually it was an amount of silver, one shekel up to three minas. In later Babylonian times there is little evidence of the parents receiving gifts. We now and then find it so. Thus a man gave a slave and a mina and a half of silver for his wife to her mother,[1] but it is not clear whether or not this was to buy her.

**Her marriage-portion**

A far more valuable endowment of the bride was her marriage-portion. If her father was not alive to give it to her, the duty fell on his heirs, and she had a right to it over and above her daughter's share of his property. Thus we find that the brothers, on giving their sister a share, contract to further endow her if she marries.[2]

**Her trousseau**

We have one or two lists that show what might be expected as a trousseau by a Babylonian bride. One which illustrates the Code[3] extremely well, narrates first what had been given a notary and *NU-BAR* of Marduk by her father on her taking her vow and entering the temple of Anunitum. This was his "grant" to her and was known by the same name as the marriage-portion of a bride. It included half a shekel of gold for a nose-ring (?), two shekels of silver as a finger-ring, another ring of silver of one shekel, one *malumsa*, three cloaks, three turbans, one small seal worth five minas, two jewels of unknown character, one bed, five chairs, five different sorts of things apparently made of reeds, the concubine Suratum, her step-mother. Unfortunately many of these renderings are still quite conjectural. It is interesting to note that the father left to his

[1] Nbk. 101. [2] Page 163. [3] § 182.

daughter his concubine, who was probably a slave, and possibly really the girl's mother. But now this girl is about to marry and her own mother, Shubultum, at any rate, her father's full wife, together with her brothers and sisters, give her all this property and cause it to enter her husband's house. They had a reversionary right to her property, since as a votary she could not alienate it from her family.[1] So now they waive their right, as it will after her marriage pass to her children, if she has any.[2] So they are said to "give" her what her father had already "granted" her. Further, they return to her husband the *terḫatu*, of one-third of a mina of silver, which he had presented to them.[3] The marriage-portion could not be reclaimed by the wife's family at her death if she had children. If she had none, it went back to her family.[4]

Nature of the marriage-portion

Another long list, also a "grant" to a votary, is found in two documents which contain apparently a complaint of oppression made to the king. Neither is sufficiently complete to be decisive as to the purpose of the letters or reports which are written in the first person. But they are duplicates as far as they preserve the list and in many other long phrases. Here is the list:

> Four . . . of gold, two rings . . . each of them one . . . two dishes, carved with *karakku* birds, one dish carved as a lion, whose head is of *AB* wood, and its border of *KU* wood, one chair of *KU* wood, three chairs (of different makes) of *AB* wood, one oil-pot, *šalla*, one oil-pot containing two hundred *ḲA* of Carchemish work, one mixing-pot of copper, one *dupru kanku* containing thirty *ḲA*, two *kundulu* of copper, one . . . two . . . , one for . . .

Although this list is full of words of which the meaning is obscure as yet, one can see the main drift of it, jewelry, household furniture, pots and pans, and whatever went to

[1] § 178. [2] § 180. [3] B[1] 10. [4] §§ 162, 163.

the domestic equipment of the house. It is of interest to note that already Carchemish was celebrated for its wares.[1]

With these lists may be compared the Tell-el-Amarna lists given in transcription, with a few hints at translation, by Dr. Winckler.[2] They are lists of presents sent by a king of Egypt to a king of Babylon; by Dushratta, King of Mitanni, to Nimuria, King of Egypt, as the marriage-portion of his daughter, Taduḫipa, and another list of her dowry. The greater part of the names of these articles defy translation.

During the Fourth Dynasty of Babylon, the celebrated Michaux Stone[3] records the gift of lands by a father to his daughter on her marriage. From Kassite times we have a list similar to the above, but not easily translatable. The supposed examples of dowry in Assyrian times are not really such. But in the later Babylonian era the marriage-portion was still given by the father. It bears, however, the name *nudunnu*, once reserved for the husband's free gift to his wife. The *nudunnu*, in one case, is ten minas of silver, four maid-servants, house-furniture, and the like.[4] It might include sheep and oxen.[5] See also the later Babylonian laws about the marriage-portion.[6] A long list might be made out from these sources of the house-furniture,[7] but as before we do not know what half of the terms mean.

Later usage

There are many examples of receipts given for the marriage-portion received in full.[8] Sometimes it was merely promised. It was not always paid promptly. Law C made a note of this. The father might have promised a portion, and even given a deed of gift for it to his daughter. But if his means have diminished he cannot be held to a literal fulfilment of the promise. He may do what he can. The

Payment of the marriage-portion

---

[1] B[1] 19, B[1] 163.
[2] K. B., v., pp. 390–404.
[3] K. B., iv., pp. 78 ff.
[4] Camb. 193.
[5] Nergl. 25.
[6] Page 69.
[7] B. A. S., iv., p. 13 f.
[8] B. V., 19, 100, 122.

law adds significantly that "father-in-law and son-in-law shall not oppress one another." We find that actions were frequently brought to obtain a marriage-portion. We have an instance where the payment was withheld for nine years.[1]

Wife's pin-money

A husband might make a settlement on his wife. In the time of the Code this was called a *nudunnu*. It had to be by deed of gift. It might cover income-producing estate as well as personal property. But it was hers only for life. She could leave it as she chose among her children of the marriage, but not to members of her own family.[2] We may regard it as pin-money. Her husband's heirs could not disturb her possession of it as long as she lived. But she forfeited it, if she married again.[3]

The period of betrothal

The betrothed maiden did not at once leave her father's house. This we learn from the Code, which enacts a penalty on one who should seduce a betrothed maiden living in her father's house.[4] It seems that on both sides betrothal took place in early life and that the arrangements were in the hands of the parents. A father was expected to take a wife for his son.

The wedding-ceremony

Neither the Code nor any contracts throw light upon the marriage-ceremony, but a tablet published by Dr. Pinches in the Proceedings of the Victoria Institute, 1892–93, reprinted as "*Notes on some recent discoveries in the realm of Assyriology*," contains certain suggestions.[5] It is very fragmentary and in the form of an interlinear translation from the Sumerian. It is not always clear who are the actors referred to, but we may perhaps take it that the officiating ministers, priests, or elders, first placed their hands and feet against the hands and feet of the bridegroom, then the bride laid her head on his shoulder and he was made to say to her: "I am the son of nobles, silver and gold shall fill

---

[1] Cyr. 143, Camb. 23. [2] § 171. [3] § 172.
[4] § 130. [5] Pages 35 ff.

your lap, you shall be my wife, I will be your husband. Like the fruit of a garden I will give you offspring." Then there is a wide gap. But in the next column we seem to have a further part of the wedding-ritual. The officiating ministers ceremoniously bound sandals on the feet of the newly wedded pair, gave them a leather girdle (? or strap) and fastened to it a pouch or purse of silver and gold. The further ceremony included placing them somewhere in the desert. Then turning their faces to the sunset and addressing the man, the minister says: "I swear by the great gods and you may go." He bids him not to put off the garment of Ea, nor something belonging to Marduk of Eridu. Then comes a wide gap, but the fourth column seems to read "until you have settled in the house, until you have reached the city, eat no food and drink no water, taste not the waters of the sea, sweet waters, bitter waters, the waters of the Tigris, the waters of the Euphrates, waters of the well, nor waters of the river, to fly up to heaven direct not your wings, to burrow in the earth set not your dwelling. As a hero, the son of his god, let him be pure."

The passage is very difficult and much of the rendering is conjectural, but the point of the address seems to be that the young man was to go straight home, live with his wife, and be good, as a true child of God. The first column seems to be an enumeration of men who are cursed with misfortunes, for example, "one whom his mother brought forth with weeping," and perhaps forms part of a prayer that the bridegroom may not ever be like such men. We must hope some day to find a fuller text and so to determine the connection of the various columns. But it is difficult to imagine what else the text can be than part of a wedding-ceremony.

The first home

The young couple did not always set up a house of their own; they often went to live with the bridegroom's father.

This is shown by the penalty fixed by the Code for the seduction of a daughter-in-law by a father-in-law. The daughter-in-law was living in his house.[1]

Monogamy prevalent in early days

In the earlier days monogamy prevailed. A man ordinarily had one wife. Polygamy, however, was not unknown. For a variety of reasons men did sometimes have two wives, but these cases were treated as exceptions. A man might also have a concubine or a slave-girl to bear him children. These did not bear legitimate children. He might adopt them, but was not bound to do so. If a man married twice, the children of both marriages shared equally in his possessions; but they did not put their mothers' marriage-portions into a common fund and divide that equally. The children of the first wife divided among themselves their own mother's marriage-portion, and the children of the second marriage did likewise.[2]

Polygamy in later times

In Assyrian times there is clear evidence that among the slaves and serfs, at least, polygamy was fairly common.[3] In the later Babylonian era polygamy also existed. Wives might be sisters.[4] We read of a "second wife."[5] But taking a second wife was held to be a slight upon the first, in whose marriage-contract the clause was inserted that in such a case the husband must pay her a mina of silver and allow her to go back to her father's house. In that case the man was hardly bigamous. It was a case of divorce, and perhaps a legal ceremony before judges was also necessary.

Concubinage

A man might form a connection with a woman other than his wife. A concubine was a free woman, but had not the status of a wife; nevertheless she might bring with her a marriage-portion, over which she had the same rights as

---

[1] § 156. [2] § 167.

[3] See on these points *Assyrian Deeds and Documents*, iii., p. 385 f.; *Assyrian Doomsday Book*, p. 25 f.

[4] Camb. 193. [5] Nbk. 101.

a legal wife.[1] She was taken into the same house as the wife, but she might not rival her. A man's excuse for taking a concubine was that his wife was childless. He was not allowed to take a concubine, even if his wife was childless, if she gave him a maid to bear him children. Only when the wife was herself childless and would not allow him a maid, was he allowed to bring a concubine into his house. This second wife was married to him. She often seems to have been bound to serve the first wife and treat her as her mistress. But she had the same rights as a wife. If she were put away, the husband had to return her marriage-portion, if she had any. She had the usufruct of house, field, and goods. She was not deprived of her children, but had the custody and education of them. When they entered into possession of their father's property, she shared with them, taking the same share as a child. Then she was free to marry again.[2] It seems that in any case, the children of a concubine were full children and with the same standing as the children of the first wife. The father might dower his daughter for a concubine; she then had no claim to share with her brothers and sisters at his death.[3] But, if her father had given her no marriage-portion, her brothers must give her one at the division of his property.[4]

The case was different with the maid—a slave who by her mistress's consent bore children to her master. She was still a slave and if she rivalled her mistress, or was impertinent to her, she could be put back again among the slaves; perhaps even branded. But, if she had borne children, she was not to be sold as a slave. At the death of her master she was free. Her children by him were free in any case. If her master were so minded, he might make them full sons by verbal acknowledgment. It was enough to say, "my sons." But that he had done so probably had to

The maid as the wife of her master

---

[1] § 137. [2] § 137. § [3] 183. [4] § 184.

be proved by a witness. A family unacknowledged by the father would on his death have only a mother. In such a family the mother was the obvious ruler. We must be on our guard against mistaking her position, or that of the concubine above, for examples of matriarchy. If she was pledged for debt, she could not be sold, she must be bought back.

Marriages and inheritance among slaves

That a slave usually was married to a slave-girl with his master's consent and even by his direction is quite the rule. Masters even went so far as to buy a slave-girl to be wife to a slave. There is no reason to think that the master did not respect the slave's matrimonial rights. But the slave's wife was not always owned by the slave's master. Sometimes she was owned by a different master, or was free. There was no especial disgrace attaching to becoming the wife of a slave. A free woman might not only marry a slave, but bring with her a marriage-portion, as if she had married in her own rank. The man had no ancestral property, he was "a son of no one." Hence when he died all the property to be divided consisted of what the married couple had acquired together, and the wife's marriage-portion. To the latter she had full and unquestioned right. The master was his slave's heir. So the property which the pair had acquired during their married life was divided into two equal portions. The master took one half, the wife the other for herself and her children. The children were all free. When both father and mother were slaves, so were the children. There was no property then for the slave-children to inherit.[1]

Data from the contracts

Some further evidence from the contracts is worth noting here. Documents relating to marriage are not very common and may have owed their presence in the archives to some peculiarity in their form. Some are perhaps rather a

[1] § 176.

memorandum that the proper formalities have been complied with. Thus[1] we read that "A has taken to wife B, the daughter of C, from C and D his wife, and has paid ten shekels as *terḫatu* to C, her father." The rest is lost. If it only laid down the penalties for infidelity on either side, this was quite normal.

Whenever the mother alone appears, as giving her daughter in marriage, we may suspect that the father was dead, or the mother divorced. When the mother is a votary, we know that such a person was not entitled to have a daughter at all, and hence we are not surprised that the *terḫatu* offered for the girl is small, five shekels[2] or even one shekel.[3] So the penalty laid upon the man for divorcing such a wife is only ten shekels.[4] On the other hand if she was unfaithful she was to be drowned.[5]

**Fatherless girls**

Very singular are the cases in which a votary marries. We know from the Code that this sometimes took place; but the votary seems to have been expected, though married, to keep her vow of virginity. In one case we read that a woman first devotes her daughter, *ullilši*, then marries her, and declares at the same time that she is vowed, *ellit*, and that no one has any claim on her.[6]

**The marriage of votaries**

In some cases a sister had the power to give her sister in marriage, with the declaration that no one has any claim on her.[7] We may imagine the sisters orphans, without brothers. The name of their father is, however, given; and his sons and daughters are mentioned. It seems to be closely parallel to the case of the marriage of a king's daughter[8] where a sister also gives a sister in marriage. Here Elmeshu, daughter of the king Ammiditana, is given in marriage by Zirtum, also daughter of king Ammiditana, on the order of her brother, Shumum-libshi. The bride-

**Power of agnates**

**Marriage of a king's daughter**

---

[1] M. A. P., 88. [2] B[1] 617. [3] M. A. P., 92. [4] M. A. P., 90.
[5] M. A. P., 90. [6] B[2] 366. [7] B[2] 394. [8] B[1] 193.

groom was Ibku-Anunitum, son of Shamash-limir and Taram-shullim, his wife. The parents paid for their son only four shekels as *terḫatu*, which Shumum-libshi and Zirtum received. If the bridegroom repudiated his bride, he had to pay half a mina. It is not clear what penalty the bride had to pay if she repudiated her husband. This is dated in the reign of Ammiditana; but in which year of his reign does not appear, as the traces of the year-name do not agree with any in the Chronicle. It must then have fallen somewhere between the seventh and the twenty-second years. Hence the father of the princess was alive at the time. Why had he no hand in the marriage? The history of the reign is not very well known. Perhaps he was away from home. His son and successor, Ammizaduga, whom we may imagine to have been the eldest son, does not appear in the case. Perhaps he also was away. But it is remarkable that the king never does directly take part in any contract. That is probably due to his sacred character. The young princess was not treated with overmuch consideration, judging by the smallness of her dowry.

Marriage of two sisters to one man

We have a very singular case in the marriage of two sisters to one man. This has already been translated and commented upon by Meissner,[1] Pinches,[2] and Sayce.[3] It is, however, too important to omit here. There are two tablets concerned with it.[4] The first is the contract between the husband and his wives. We may render it thus:

Ardi-Shamash took to wife Taram-Saggil and Iltâni, daughters of Sin-abushu. If Taram-Saggil and Iltâni say to Ardi-Shamash, their husband, "You are not my husband," one shall throw them down from the *AN-ZAG-GAR-KI;* and if Ardi-Shamash shall say to Taram-Saggil and Iltâni his wives, "You are not my wives," he shall leave house and furniture. Further, Iltâni shall obey the orders of Taram-Saggil, shall carry her chair to the temple of her god. The

---

[1] A. P., 89.
[2] J. R. A. S. 97, pp. 407 ff.
[3] B. A. L., p. 27 f.
[4] $B^1$ 21 and $B^2$ 2176 A.

provisions of Taram-Saggil shall Iltâni prepare, her well-being she shall care for, her seal she shall not appropriate (?).

Then follow ten witnesses, but no date.

The second document seems to be drawn up rather from the point of view of the sisters. We may render it thus:

Iltâni, the sister of Taram-Saggil, Ardi-Shamash, son of Shamash-ennam, took to wife, from Uttatum, their father. Iltâni shall prepare the provisions of her sister, shall care for her well-being, shall carry her chair to the temple of Marduk. The children which she has borne, or shall bear, shall be their children. [If Taram-Saggil] shall say to Iltâni, her sister, "you are not my sister" [the penalty is lost]. [If Iltâni shall say to Taram-Saggil her sister], "You are not my sister," one shall brand her, and sell her. If Ardi-Shamash shall say to his wife, "You are not my wife," he shall pay one mina of silver; and if they say to Ardi-Shamash their husband, "You are not our husband," one shall tie them up and throw them into the river.

Here there are eleven witnesses, but again no date.

Meissner deduces from the mention of children that Taram-Saggil was already married. The exact relation between the sisters is not clear. In one case they seem to be daughters of Uttatum, in the other of Sin-abushu. Or it may be that Iltâni alone was daughter of Sin-abushu. If so, perhaps Uttatum had adopted her. Sayce clearly thinks so. But they might be daughters of the same mother by different fathers, one of whom is mentioned in one case, the other in the other. Or they might really be children of Sin-abushu, if their mother afterwards married Uttatum, who was thus their step-father. It is clear that Iltâni was to wait on her sister, and, if she repudiated her, was to be treated as a slave. This is exactly parallel to the status of the slave-maid, whom a wife or votary in the Code[1] provided for her husband. Perhaps Taram-Saggil had become a chronic invalid. A comparison of the two

[1] § 146.

texts is interesting in other respects. The penalties differ curiously. If Ardi-Shamash repudiates his wives, in one case, he loses house and furniture; in the other case, he pays one mina. Was one the penalty for repudiating Taram-Saggil, the other for repudiating Iltâni? But if they repudiate him, the penalties are different in the two documents, unless indeed the *AN-ZAG-GAR-KI* be an ideogram for the "steep place" from which they were to be thrown into the water.

Marriage with attached conditions

Marriages are not infrequent which impose conditions upon the husband and wife with relation to outside parties. Thus a mother gives her daughter in marriage to a man, on condition that she shall continue to support her mother as long as she lives. In this case, if the husband put away his wife, he was to pay one mina of silver; while, if she hated her husband, she was to be thrown from a pillar, *dimtu*.[1] This pillar may be the real meaning of the *AN-ZAG-GAR-KI,* which looks very like an attempt to express *ziggwratu*, a tower, in an ideographic way. A very similar case is where a lady takes a girl to be wife to her son but stipulates that the wife shall treat her as mistress. If she shall say to her mother-in-law, "Thou art not my mistress," she shall be branded and sold. As long as the mother lives, they two together shall support her.[2] One may suspect that such maternal power, as is here shown over the children, arises from their having been adopted by their mother in order to provide for her in her old age. This was often done. The children may have been slaves before adoption. In the second case, the mother leaves her son all she has, or may acquire.

---

[1] $B^2$ 407. [2] $B^2$ 707.

## XI

### DIVORCE AND DESERTION

Early regulations regarding divorce

DIVORCE is regulated by the Code. The Sumerian laws seem to regard the marriage-tie as dissoluble on the part of the man by an act of simple repudiation, accompanied by a *solatium*, fixed at half a mina. The wife, however, was punished by death for repudiating her husband.[1] The Code limits the facility of divorce for the man and renders it possible for the woman to obtain.

Rights of a divorced wife

Divorce of either a wife or concubine involved her being given a maintenance. The divorced wife had the custody of her children, if any. They were not disinherited by the divorce. The divorced woman retained the marriage-portion which she had brought to the home. She had a share with her children in the divorced husband's property at his death. If he married again, the children of both marriages shared equally. She was also free to marry again, but apparently not until her children had come into their share of the late husband's property, therefore not during his life.[2]

Grounds of divorce

Divorce was permitted on the ground of childlessness. The husband gave back to his wife all her marriage-portion. Also he had to give the bride-price which he had paid to her parents during his courtship, and which they had returned to him, as a rule, on marriage.[3] If this bride-price had not been given, then he paid her a fixed sum of money;

[1] Law VI. [2] § 137. [3] § 138.

one mina, if he was a patrician, a third, if he was only a plebeian.[1] A slave does not seem to have had the liberty of divorce.

Protection of the wife's rights

The wife might take a dislike to her husband and set her face to leave him and deny him conjugal rights. This was probably equivalent to desertion. Then a judicial inquiry was required. If his ill treatment or neglect was made clear and she was blameless, a divorce was granted. She took her marriage-portion and went back to her family. But as this was of her own seeking, she received no alimony.[2] It is assumed that it was an unhappy marriage from the first and that there were no children.

If it were proved that she was a bad wife, she was treated as an adulteress and drowned.[3] On the other hand, even if she were a bad wife, the husband might repudiate her simply without paying any price for divorce. In this case there was no suspicion of her infidelity. Or the husband might degrade her to the position of a slave.[4] There is no mention in these cases of a return to her father's house.

Chronic illness on the part of a wife was not a ground for divorce. The husband had to maintain her. He might, however, take a second wife.[5] If she did not care to remain in his house in such conditions, she could leave him, take her marriage-portion and return to her family.[6]

Illustrations from the contracts

We have already seen that the Code regulates the questions arising out of divorce.[7] The examples at this period are but few. In one case a man put away his wife and she received her price of divorce. It is expressly stated that she may marry another man and her former husband will not complain.[8] This document is, however, little more than an agreement to abide by the terms of the divorce.

---

[1] §§ 139, 140. [2] § 142. [3] § 143. [4] § 141.
[5] § 149. [6] § 150. [7] §§ 136–40. [8] M. A. P., 91.

In another case a marriage-contract names the penalty a man shall pay for divorcing his wife.[1] In all these cases the word for divorce, *ezêbu*, is literally "to put away." But a man divorced his wife by the simple process of saying, "You are not my wife." He then paid her a fine, returned her marriage-portion and so on, as laid down in the Code.[2] It was far harder for a woman to secure a divorce from her husband. She could do so, however, but only as the result of a lawsuit.[3] As a rule, the marriage-contracts mention death as her punishment, if she repudiates her husband. The death by drowning is usually named. This was in accordance with Law V. of the Sumerian Code.

We may regard repudiation of husband and wife, one by the other, and desertion as leading to divorce; and therefore these may be appropriately considered next.

Involuntary desertion

Desertion of a wife by her husband might be involuntary. The Code deals with the case of a man captured by the enemy. If the wife were left at home well provided for, she was bound to be true to her absent husband. If she entered another man's house, she was condemned to death as an adulteress.[4] But if she was not provided for, she might enter another man's house without blame.[5] There she might bear children. But, if so, she yet had to go back to her original husband on his return. The children she had borne in his absence were to be counted to their real father.[6] That the law provides for such cases points to the existence of frequent wars, in which fortune was not always on the side of Babylonia.

Voluntary desertion

But the husband might desert his wife voluntarily. Then, if she was left unprovided for, the wife might enter another man's house. The errant husband, when he returned, could not reclaim his wife.[7]

---

[1] M. A. P., 90. [2] § 138. [3] § 142. [4] § 133.
[5] § 134. [6] § 135. [7] § 136.

We have a legal decision in a case[1] where a man had deserted his wife for twenty years and "left her to her fate, did not love her." During this time a daughter, whether real or adoptive we are not told, took care of her mother. To her the mother left property, among other things, a slave. The mother being dead, the truant husband returned and claimed the slave from the daughter. He was nonsuited.

Among the provocations which gave the wife cause for divorce was the "going out" of the husband, probably a euphemism for adultery on his part. Belittling his wife was another ground for her complaint. What this means is not quite clear, but we may regard it as persistent neglect.

[1] B[1] 2474.

# XII

## RIGHTS OF WIDOWS

The authority of the widow in the home

THE Code makes clear what was the position of the widow. She had a right to stay on in her husband's house until she died,[1] but was not compelled to do so.[2] If she remained, she was the head of the family. To her the young sons looked to furnish them with means to court a wife, and the daughters for a marriage-portion. She acted in these matters with the consent and assistance of her grown-up children. But she might elect to leave the home and remarry.

Rights of inheritance

As long as she remained in her husband's home she enjoyed to the full whatever she had brought there as a marriage-portion, whatever her husband had settled upon her, and also received a share from her husband's goods at his death. The widow's share was the same as a child's. But she had no power to alienate any of these possessions. The Code expressly declares that they were her children's after her.[3] The children had no power to turn her out. If they desired her to leave, the matter came before the law-courts, and her private wishes were consulted. If she wished to remain, she might do so, and the judge bound over the children to allow her to do so.[4]

Later usages

A very clear example of the permanence of the Code regulations on this subject meets us in the fifth year of Cambyses.[5] Ummu-ṭâbat, daughter of Nabû-bêl-uṣur, wife

[1] § 172. [2] § 173. [3] § 171. [4] § 172. [5] Camb. 273.

of Shamash-uballiṭ, son of Bêl-ebarra, a Shamash priest, who was dead, whose sons were Shamash-eṭir, Nidittum, and Ardi-Ḫar, swore to Bêl-uballiṭ, priest of Sippara, saying, "I will not remarry, I will live with my sons, I will bring up my sons to manhood, until they are numbered with the people." On the day that Ummu-ṭâbat remarries, according to her bond, the property [of her late husband] which is in the possession of Bêl-uballiṭ, the priest of Sippara, [she shall forfeit]. The tablet is defective here, but on the edge of the tablet we see that the care of her sons was given her. To remarry is expressed here by the words, "going into the *bît zikari*."

**Remarriage of a widow**

A widow could remarry at her discretion. She no longer had to be given in marriage. She was free to marry the man of her choice.[1] She might take with her her marriage-portion to her new home, but she had to leave behind any settlement which her former husband had given her, or any share of his goods that had come to her at his death. Her family were not called upon to find any fresh marriage-portion for her. But she was not completely mistress of even her marriage-settlement. If she had children of the former marriage, they and any children of her second marriage shared her marriage-portion equally. Only she had the enjoyment of it for life.[2] If there were no children of the second marriage, those of the first took all she left.[3]

**Disposal of her first husband's property**

We have assumed that when her husband died her children were old enough to care for themselves. If they were not, she had no power to enter upon a second marriage and desert her first family. She was not free to marry at all without consent of the law-court.[4] But there is no evidence that this could be withheld, if proper conditions were observed. The first husband's property was inventoried and consent for the second marriage being granted, she and her

[1] § 172. [2] § 173. [3] § 174. [4] § 177.

new husband were bound by deed to preserve the whole estate of the late husband for his children. With that proviso, the newly married pair entered into full use of the deceased's property and were bound to educate the children until grown up. They had no inducement to neglect them, as in any case none of the deceased's property could ever be theirs. If the children died, it would all revert to the family of the deceased. The newly married pair had no further interest in it than the enjoyment of it until the children could manage for themselves. They could not alienate any of it. The sale of even a utensil was not possible.[1]

[1] § 177.

## XIII

### OBLIGATIONS AND RIGHTS OF CHILDREN

Absoluteness of the paternal power over the family

It is customary to say that the father had absolute power over his children, but it is better to state only what is known with certainty regarding the extent of his power. The father could treat his child, or even his wife, equally with a slave, as a chattel to be pledged for his debts.[1] We may therefore conclude that he could sell his child. An actual example cannot be cited from early times, but they are very common later.

The son was not capable of entering into an independent contract with an outside person.[2] We may assume that this means simply while yet living in his father's house. The father had rights over what his son earned. A man could also hire out his child and take the wages.[3]

His power of preference

The father had the right to prefer one son above the rest. He could endow him with house, field, and garden. But this must be done in his lifetime and by written deed. This gift did not in any way affect the son's claim to inherit equally with his brethren on the father's death, when he took a full share over and above what he had by gift.[4]

His control of his daughters

The father had full power to dispose of his daughters in marriage. But he was expected to furnish them with a marriage-portion. This was not obligatory, being probably a matter of negotiation with the parents of the bridegroom. In later times the obligation evidently became irksome and

---

[1] § 117. [2] § 7. [3] M. A. P., p. 11. [4] § 165.

oppressive, and Law E was passed to relieve the strain. A father was bound to do his best to fulfil his promise to dower his daughter, but no more. A father could not hinder his daughter from becoming a votary.[1] If he approved her choice, he might give her a portion, as if for marriage,[2] but he was not compelled to do so. A father could give his daughter to be a concubine.[3]

The father's consent was also needed to his son's marriage.[4] He had to provide the youth with a bride-price, and secure a wife for him.[5]

**The age of majority**

It is not easy to determine when children ceased to be under the paternal power. Betrothed daughters remained in their father's house; so did married sons sometimes. Whether the birth of a child, making the young man himself a father, freed him as head of a family, or whether it was entering a house of his own, we cannot yet say.

**Punishment of unfilial conduct**

The Sumerian laws are very severe upon a child's repudiation of a father. That degraded him to the status of a slave. He might also be branded. Obviously he was disinherited. The repudiation is expressed in the words, "You are not my father," but it may be intended to cover all unfilial conduct. The Code is more explicit. If a son struck his father, his hands were cut off.[6]

**Disinheritance**

The Sumerian laws preserved the father's rights to disinherit the son by a simple repudiation, saying, "You are not my son." The son then had to leave house and enclosure. The Code limits this power. It insists on legal process and good reason alleged. Also it was not allowed for a first offence on the son's part.[7]

**Relations of mothers and sons**

The mother was in much the same position of authority as the father. A son who repudiated his mother was branded and expelled from house and city. He was not,

---

[1] § 178. [2] § 179. [3] § 183. [4] Page 127.
[5] § 166. [6] § 195. [7] § 168.

however, sold as a slave. The Sumerian laws also reserved to the mother the right to repudiate her son, and he must quit house and property. The Code gives no such power to mothers. Indeed, we find examples of a son disputing with a mother.[1] Mothers took up the father's place toward the children on the death of the father as regards marriage-portions, bride-price, and other family affairs. But they usually acted in concert with the elder children.

Duties to adoptive parents

The repudiation of adoptive parents was a very grievous sin, especially on the part of those who were children of parents who were forbidden to have children. Something worse than illegitimacy was their lot. The penalties of having the eye torn out, or the tongue cut out,[2] show the abhorrence felt for their ingratitude.

[1] M. A. P., p. 15. [2] §§ 192, 193.

## XIV

## THE EDUCATION AND EARLY LIFE OF CHILDREN

Number and importance of scribes

Much has been made of the knowledge of writing shown by the Babylonians and Assyrians. The ability to draw up deeds and write letters seems at first sight to have been widely diffused. In the times of the First Dynasty of Babylon almost every tablet seems to have a fresh *tupšar*, or scribe. Many show the handiwork of women scribes.[1] But most of the persons concerned in these documents were of the priestly rank. There is no evidence that the shepherds or workpeople could write. In the Assyrian times the scribe was a professional man. We find *aba* or *tupšar* used as a title. So, too, in later Babylonian times. The witnesses to a document can only be said to sign their names in so far as that they impressed their seals. This was done, at any rate, in early times. In the Assyrian period the only parties who sealed were the owners of the property transferred to a new owner. The whole of a tablet shows the same handwriting throughout. Anyone who reads carefully through the facsimile copies in *Cuneiform Texts* can readily see this. Different scribes, especially in early times, wrote differently, but this was still the case in Assyrian days. Yet no change of hand can be noted anywhere in one document, save where, as in the forecast tablets, a date or note was added by a different person, often in Assyrian script, to a text written in Babylonian. The only safe

[1] Page 82.

statement to make is that from the earliest times a very large number of persons existed, at any rate in the larger towns, who could write and draw up documents.

Sumerian words and expressions in the legal literature

The use of Sumerian terms and phrases in the body of a document written in Semitic Babylonian might be ascribed to a mere tradition. But they were no meaningless formulæ. The many variations, including the substitution of completely different though synonymous words, show that these Sumerian phrases were sufficiently understood to be intelligently used. In later times they either disappear altogether, or are used with little variation. They had become stereotyped and were conventional signs, doubtless read as Semitic, though written as Sumerian. Our own retention of Latin words is a close parallel. The First Dynasty of Babylon was bilingual at any rate in its legal documents, though the letters are all pure Semitic. The earlier documents show few signs of Semitic origin, though its influence can be traced as far back as we can go.

Schools

The discovery at Sippara of a school dating from the First Dynasty of Babylon is very fully worked out by Professor Scheil in *Une Saison de fouilles à Sippara*, pp. 30–54. Professor Hilprecht gives further details in *Explorations in Bible Lands*, pp. 522–28 and *passim*.

The methods of learning to write and the lessons in Sumerian are well described by these authors, and illustrated by numerous extant examples of practice-tablets. The subjects were very numerous and included arithmetic, mensuration, history, geography, and literature. As Dr. Pinches has shown by his edition of some of these practice-tablets,[1] these contain very valuable fragments of otherwise lost or imperfectly known texts.

Apprenticeship

Slaves were often bound as apprentices to learn a trade or handicraft. A man might adopt a child to teach him his

[1] P. S. B. A., xviii., pp. 250–56; xxiii., pp. 188–210.

trade, and his duty to him was sufficiently discharged by doing so.

Naming of children

We do not yet know in any authoritative way, when or with what ceremonies children were named. In the case of slaves we have a boy, still at the breast,[1] or a girl of three months, not named.[2] On the other hand, a girl still at the breast is named. Hence Meissner concludes, that at the end of one year, at latest, the child was given a name.[3] But the usage with respect to slaves is hardly a rule, and, as appears from the above, they were not consistently named.

Rearing of babies

A child seems often to have been put out to nurse. From the phrase-book we learn that a father might "give a child to a wet-nurse to be suckled, and give the wet-nurse food and drink, oil for anointing, and clothing for three years."[4] That this was not only done with adopted children is clear from the Code;[5] where we find a severe penalty laid on a wet-nurse, who substitutes another child for the one intrusted to her, without the parents' consent.

Number of children who could read and write

It will hardly do to interpret the phrase-book[6] as meaning that all children were made to learn writing. But that this was commonly done is evident from the number, both of men and women, who could act as scribes.[7]

---

[1] Nbd. 832, Nbk. 67. [2] Nbk. 100. [3] D. S., p. 24, note.
[4] II. R. 9, 28 cd. ff. [5] § 194. [6] II. R. 9, 66 cd. [7] Page 82.

# XV

## ADOPTION

Frequency and reasons for adoption

Adoption primarily means a process by which parents could admit to the privileges of sonship children born of other parents. There were many reasons which might impel them to such a course. If they were childless, a natural desire for an heir might operate. But under the Babylonian law a man might take a second wife, or a maid, if his wife were childless, to bear him children. A more operative cause was that children were a source of profit to their parents while they remained with them. But it seems that men married early. Hence this alone does not seem sufficient to account for the great frequency of adoption. Besides, in that case, what induced a parent to part with his child for adoption? It seems that the real cause most often was that the adopting parents had lost by marriage all their own children and were left with no child to look after them. They then adopted a child whose parents would be glad to see him provided for, to look after them until they died, leaving him the property they had left after portioning their own children.

Children who might be adopted

The Code admits all kinds of adoption, but regulates the custom. A man might adopt an illegitimate son, or the child of a votary or palace-warder, who had no right to children, or the child of living parents. In the latter case alone was the parents' consent necessary. We have examples of cases of adoption of relatives, of entirely unrelated persons, of a slave even.[1] We learn from the series *ana ittišu*[2] that a man might take a young child, put it out to nurse, provide the nurse with food, oil for anointing, and clothing, for a space of three years; and then have it taught a trade or profession, such as that of scribe.[3]

The method of procedure

Adoption was effected by a deed, drawn up and sealed by the adoptive parents, duly sworn to and witnessed. Such contracts definitely state the relationship, which was in all respects the same as that of a son born in matrimony. But it laid down the obligations of the son, while it stipulated what was the inheritance to which he might expect to succeed. It brought responsibilities to both parties and fixed them. The son was bound to do that which a son would naturally have done, explicitly, to maintain his parents while they lived. The parents were bound, not only to leave him property, but to treat him as a son. But, as a rule, all was matter of contract and carefully set down. If such a contract was not drawn up, although the adoptive parents had brought him up, the child must return to his father's house.[4] Only, for an artisan, it was sufficient to have taught the child his trade.[5]

So far as our examples go, some color might be given to the suggestion that adoption was always merely for the convenience of old people who wanted to be taken care of. But we know that children were adopted on other grounds. That they were children and not always grown-up men and women is clear from the above. This we may regard as adoption pure and simple. Other cases are a legal method of making provision for old age, or for other purposes for which an heir as legal representative was desirable. In the case of no legal heir, the property went back to the next of kin.

---

[1] B[1] 54. [2] II. R. 9, 28 cd. ff. [3] M. A. P., p. 15.
[4] § 199. [5] § 188.

Adoption pure and simple

That such a process did take place in Babylonia is made clear by the Code.[1] But few examples are known where a father takes into his family an additional child. The case, in which the son is not only adopted by parents who have a family living, but is ranked as their eldest son, deserves reproducing in full.[2]

Ubar-Shamash, son of Sin-idinnam, from Sin-idinnam, his father, and Bititum, his mother, have Beltum-abi and Taram-ulmash taken to sonship, and let him be the son of Beltum-abi and Taram-ulmash. Ubar-Shamash shall be their eldest son. The day that Beltum-abi, his father, and Taram-ulmash, his mother, say to Ubar-Shamash, their son, "You are not our son," he shall leave house and furniture. The day that Ubar-Shamash shall say to Beltum-abi, his father, or Taram-ulmash, his mother, "You are not my father or my mother," one shall brand him, put fetters upon him, and sell him.

Both parents of the adopted son were living. That the son is to be reckoned eldest implies that the adopting parents had other children. This is made clear in one case where the adoptive parents are expressly said to have five children.[3] In another case where a child is adopted a certain person is expressly said to be his brother.[4]

Consent of other members of the family involved

The existing members of the family had a real interest in the proceeding. For, as inheriting with them, the addition of another son could not but affect their prospects. We may wonder what influenced them to consent. That they did consent is clear from the often-occurring covenant by which they bound themselves not to object. One explanation may be that they had grown up and left home and were anxious for the welfare of their parents, but could not arrange to look after them themselves. Hence for their parents' sake they were willing to forego their share, or submit to a stranger taking precedence of them, or in some cases to give up all claim to the property in their parents'

---

[1] § 185 ff. [2] M. A. P., 95. [3] M. A. P., 98. [4] M. A. P., 97.

possession in return for being relieved of the responsibility of looking after them. Of course, when the adopted son was only taken in as one, even the eldest, among several, he would only have a share at the parents' death. But it even seems that the children might of their own motion adopt a brother to be son to their parents.[1]

Disinheritance of a son

The clause which implies disinheritance in case the parents repudiate the son, or he repudiates them, could only be enforced by a law-court.[2] But it was nevertheless most regularly inserted in the contract. In one case the document merely consists of it,[3] leaving us to infer that an adopted son was concerned. But this is not absolutely certain. The son might have been rebellious to his mother, who was therefore minded to cut him off, and this may be the result of her bringing her son before the judge. The judge was bound to try and conciliate the parties.[4] Hence, not infrequently the son was bound over not to repeat the offence on pain of disinheritance, while the mother retained her right to disinherit. There was no mention of his being sold for a slave, or branded, as was usual when a son was adopted and then repudiated his parents.

According to the contracts entered into by the parties, parents could repudiate adopted sons. This was contrary to the law by which the consent of the judge was needed for disinheritance. It seems to be an attempt to contract without the support of the law. The son was then to take a son's share and go away.[5]

Form of adoption

The word *aplûtu*, abstract of *aplu*, "son," and therefore literally "sonship," being also used to denote the relation of a daughter to a parent, came to denote the "share" which a son or daughter received. If a man adopted a son, he granted him an *aplûtu*, or "sonship," and this carried with it a material property. But the father, while still living,

[1] M. A. P., 94. [2] § 168. [3] M. A. P., 93. [4] § 168. [5] M. A. P., 98.

might grant the son his *aplûtu* and stipulate for maintenance during the rest of his life. Such a grant begins with *aplûtu ša* B, where B is the son. But it by no means follows that B is an adopted son. The question is only decided for us when the parentage of B is given. If he is said to be the "son of C," then we know that A giving him "sonship" must mean that A adopted him. But if B is merely indicated as the son of A, we cannot tell whether he was born to A, or only adopted by A.

**Phrases which express the idea**

So when the property given to B is in his power to dispose of later as he may choose, this privilege is expressed by the words, "he may give his sonship to whom he chooses." The choice is sometimes expressed as "that which is good to his heart," or "in his eyes," or "whom he loves." A modified choice is often mentioned, as when it is said that a votary may leave her "sonship" after her to whom she likes "among her brothers."

**Settlements which assume adoption**

We have a large number of documents which make reference to the *aplûtu* of a certain person, which we can render here by "heritage." These are especially common on the part of votaries. As we have seen, they were not supposed to have children of their own, but possessed the right to nominate their heir within limits. In return for exercising this right in favor of a certain person, they usually stipulated that such person shall maintain them as long as they live and otherwise care for them. Even outside actual deeds of heritage, we find references to property derived from votaries subject to certain duties. Such dispositions of property are closely related to a will or testament, but anticipate the death of the testator. They are really settlements for the future, which exactly answers to the title given them by the Babylonian scribes, *ridit warkati.*

The following example makes these details clear:[1]

---

[1] B[2] 565.

The heritage of Eli-eriṣa, votary of Shamash, daughter of Shamash-ilu. Belisunu, votary of Shamash, daughter of Nakarum, is the caretaker of her future life. One-third *GAN* of unreclaimed land in Karnamkarum, next the field of Issurîa, one *SAR* house in Ḫalḫalla, next the house of Nakarum, one-third *SAR* four *GIN* in Gagim, one maid Shala-beltum, price ten shekels of silver, all this for the future in its entirety, what Eli-eriṣa, votary of Shamash, daughter of Shamash-ilu, has or shall acquire, she gives to Belisunu, votary of Shamash, daughter of Nakarum. Every year Belisunu shall give to Eli-eriṣa three *GUR* of corn, ten minas of bronze, and twelve *ḲA* of oil.

Precautions against suits

The *aplûtu* thus given was in many cases an alienation of property on which some relative had claims. Even where their consent was not necessary it was desirable that they should not involve the heir in legal processes. Hence, such relatives are called up to covenant that they will raise no objection to the heir's peaceable succession.[1]

Duties of adopted child to parents: support

The obligation to support the adoptive parent is emphasized. The amount of sustenance varies much. Another list of yearly allowances reads one shekel of silver, woollen yarn, six *ḲA* of oil, four *išinni Shamaš̌h*, ten *ḲA* of fat, one side, two *GUR* of corn. Many others could be instanced, but they make no great addition to our knowledge.

Service

The obligation might be service; as when a lady adopts a maid to serve her for life and inherit a certain house.[2] In another case a lady adopts a son to bring up her daughter and give her to a husband. "If he vexes his adoptive mother, she will cut him off. He shall not have claim on any of the goods of his adoptive mother, but shall inherit her field and garden."[3] Evidently the mother intended her personal effects to be her daughter's and to form her marriage-portion. The obligation did not always last long. Thus we find that Lautum, who was adopted by a votary and was herself a votary, two years later was in a position to adopt as her daughter another votary.[4] She handed on

---

[1] $B^1$ 368. [2] $B^2$ 375. [3] $B^3$ 2484. [4] $B^2$ 609.

the same property, indicating that her adoptive mother was dead.

The adoption of a child by a lady of fortune was evidently a good settlement for the child, and usually the real parents raised no objection. We even find the father of a girl adopted by a lady, making an addition to her heritage in the form of a gift to the adopting mother on her effecting the deed of adoption. He gave them two male and two female slaves. Here also the girl covenanted to support the adoptive mother.[1]

Punishment for neglect of these duties

Occasionally the adopted child did not carry out his duties. This was good ground for disinheriting him. But disinheritance was not to be inflicted without the sanction of the judges.[2] Hence we find that when a lady had adopted a daughter who failed to give her food and drink, the judges summoned them to the great temple of Shamash in Sippara, there cut off the daughter from her heritage, took away the tablet of adoption granted her, and destroyed it.[3]

Care of aged parents

A curious case is where A, the daughter of B and C, endows D to take care of B and C. As long as D lives A covenants to allow her so much. When she dies A will herself perform the duties.[4] Here A evidently expected her parents would not live long, but also D must have been aged, or infirm, as A contemplates the chance of her parents outliving D. This is not a case of adoption, but is so similar in purpose to those above as to deserve a place here.

Inheritance rights

Occasionally, however, the adopting parent reserved the usufruct of the property for life only, fixing by deed the rightful heir.[5] This was, in effect, a will or testament, since the inheritance did not take effect until after the death of the testator.

---

[1] B[1] 2489. [2] § 168. [3] B[2] 360. [4] B[2] 2460. [5] B[2] 2179.

# XVI

## RIGHTS OF INHERITANCE

The division of an inheritance

THE division of property among the children invariably followed the death of the father. We have a very large number of contracts bearing on this custom. The contract sets forth the particulars of the division and includes a sworn declaration on the part of the recipients to make no further claim. There were certain reservations to be made in the case of minors, for whom a portion had to be set aside to provide for their making the proper gifts to the parents of their brides on marriage.

Usage as illustrated by the contracts

The Code deals at length with the laws of inheritance, which are best treated under the head of marriage. The actual examples occurring in the documents of the period serve to illustrate the practical working of these laws, but hardly add to our knowledge. They are usually occupied with the division of property among brothers. Sometimes we have some light on the reservations made in favor of other members of the family. Thus two brothers divide the property of their "father's house" and of their sister, a votary. The sister did not take her property, but the brothers were trustees for her enjoyment of it during her life, when it reverted to them in full.[1] The document merely states the amount of one brother's share and the other's agreement to be content with the division. In another case, where four brothers share the property of their

[1] M. A. P., 105.

"father's house," no details of their shares are given, but only their agreement to abide by the division made.[1] In another case the eldest brother allots to each of two younger brothers a share and takes a woman slave and her children as his portion. He is said to do this of his "own power," *ina emur ḳamanišu*, and to have given them this of his "own graciousness," *ina tûbâtišu.* The brothers swear to make no further claim on the "grant," *maršîtu*, of their father. Either the property to which they were legally entitled had already been allotted them, or possibly they had no legal claim on any. The eldest brother is a high official, a *pa-pa*, and perhaps had succeeded his father in office. The father's property would then be the endowment of his office, a grant from the king, and as such inalienable from the office to which the eldest son had succeeded. The three slaves may have thus been all the private property of the father which was available for division. But the context seems to suggest that what the brothers received was a concession from the eldest brother on which they had no claim. He may in consideration of his succeeding to his father's appointment have made this concession to his brothers as a consolation.[2] In another case a mother gives certain sums to her three sons. She had still left two sons and two daughters, and the first three agree to make no claim on all that she and these four children have or shall acquire.[3] It is noteworthy that one of the three receives ten shekels as the *terḫatu* of the wife he shall marry. He was evidently not of marriageable age, or, at any rate, still unmarried. In such a case the Code directed that on partition of the father's property, a special sum should be laid aside for this necessary present to the bride's father.[4] So we find two brothers giving a sister a share consisting of one-third *SAR* of a house, next her brother's, one maid, a bed and a

[1] M. A. P., 106. [2] M. A. P., 107. [3] M. A. P., 109. [4] § 116.

chair, with the promise that on the day that she marries and enters her husband's house she shall receive further two-thirds *GAN* of land and slaves.[1] The list of property is often given, especially where brothers give shares to their sisters. Sometimes the relationship is less close. Thus a man shares with two sons of his father's brother, *i.e.*, with two cousins, ten *SAR* of unreclaimed land, taking three and a half *SAR* as his share.[2] Sometimes the property included the mother's marriage-portion. Thus three brothers divide their property and two of them, as her sons, share their mother's marriage-portion:[3]

Division of property between three brothers

One *SAR* of built land and granary, next the house of Ubarrîa and next that of Bushum-Sin, two exits to the street, the property of Urra-nâṣir, which he divided with Sin-ikisham and Ibni-Shamash. From mouth (?) to gold the share is complete. Brother shall not dispute with brother. By Shamash, Malkat, Marduk, and Sin-mubaliṭ they swore. Nine witnesses. Thirteenth year of Sin-mubaliṭ.[4]

The property which fell to Urra-nâṣir was a house occupying one *SAR* of land. The text means not that the three men, Urra-nâṣir, Sin-ikisham, and Ibni-Shamash, divided the house among them, but that at the division this house was the share of the first named. What the two, Sin-ikisham and Ibni-Shamash, had as their share we are not here told. But the three agreed not to call in question the division of property, which probably came to them from their father or mother. Fortunately we know in this case what the others got. Thus we find:

One *SAR* of built land, (and) granary, next the house of Ibni-Shamash and next the street, its exit to the street, the property of Sin-ikisham, which he divided with Ibni-Shamash and Urra-nâṣir. From mouth (?) to gold the share is complete. Brother shall not dispute with brother. By Shamash, Malkat, and Sin-mubaliṭ they swore. Nine witnesses. Thirteenth year of Sin-mubaliṭ.[5]

---

1 B[1] 33. 2 B[1] 12. 3 B[1] 14. 4 B[1] 60. 5 B[1] 31 = M. A. P., 103.

And again:

One *SAR* of built land, (and) granary, next the house of Sin-ikisham and next the house of Ishtar-Ummasha, two exits to the street, the property of Ibni-Shamash, which he divided with Sin-ikisham and Urra-nâṣir. From mouth (?) to gold the share [is complete]. Brother shall not dispute with brother. By Shamash, Malkat, Marduk, and Sin-mubaliṭ they swore. Nine witnesses. Thirteenth year of Sin-mubaliṭ.[1]

Thus we see that each brother, if they were brothers, obtained exactly the same share, one *SAR* of land on which a house was built. Two of them, Sin-ikisham and Ibni-Shamash, were next door to each other. Ibni-Shamash had the street on the other side of him, in fact, occupied a corner house. The third brother, Urra-nâṣir, had a house in another part of the town. We therefore must understand the word "divided" in the sense "obtained on division." In the second and third case the word rendered share is literally "all." But the first text shows that "all is complete" means "the share is complete." The meaning of the expression, "from mouth (?) to gold," is still obscure. It is not certain that *bi-e* really means "mouth." But as Meissner has shown,[2] it exchanges with the ideogram for "mouth." He therefore suggests that the whole phrase means "from the first verbal discussion of the division to its consummation by payment the partition of the property is now at an end." That seems probable enough, but we may yet find a different explanation. If this be correct, it is of interest to note that while silver seems to have been the usual money, this phrase seems to assume that gold would be used in payment. A curious parallel is the fact that while in later times we always find the order gold and silver, in Sumerian texts it is silver and gold. We must not press this too far, but it really looks as if in early

[1] B[1] 46 = M. A. P., 104. [2] M. A. P., p. 145.

times silver was more valued, or at any rate, less in use than gold.

It will be noted that the second text omits Marduk from the oath, while the others name him. The third text omits *gamru*, "is complete." The nine witnesses and the date are the same for all three. In the first and last the names of the witnesses only are given, but in the second the name of the father is added to several of them.

**The great difficulty of interpreting details in testamentary documents**

In the case of testamentary documents, using the phrase in a loose way to cover gifts embodied in a deed, we usually find a list of property donated. These lists give rise to insuperable difficulties to the translator. The difficulties are not so much due to the imperfections of our knowledge of Babylonian methods of writing as to the practical impossibility of finding exact terms in one language for the terms relating to domestic furniture in another. Even in the case of languages so well known to us as French and German are, we are obliged to transfer their words unaltered into our own tongue. The most skilled translator must leave a French or German *menu* untranslated. We know for instance that the signs, *GIŠ-GU-ZA* were used to denote the Babylonian *kussû*. When a god or king sat upon a *kussû* we may be satisfied with the rendering "throne," but when we find a lady leaving her daughter six *kussê* we feel that "throne" is rather too grand. But whether we elect to call them chairs, stools, or seats, we are guilty of some false suggestion. A careful examination of the sculptured and pictured monuments may give us a clearer idea of what seats were used. The reader may consult Perrot and Chipiez, or the dictionaries of the Bible, under the articles: chairs, couches, *et cetera*, for illustrations. Unless we can find a picture with a named article upon it we are still left a wide margin of conjecture. The picture of Sennacherib receiving the tribute and submission of

Lachish gives the contemporary representation of a *kussû nimedu*, but we cannot argue that every *kussû* was of the same pattern.

We may decline to attempt a solution and merely give the original word, we may make a purely arbitrary rendering, or we may accompany the original word with an approximate indication of what is known of its nature. In neither case do we translate, for that is clearly impossible. But the reader needs a word of caution against the translations which show no signs of hesitancy. They are not indicative of greater knowledge, but of less candor. Further, to scholars a reminder is needed that even the syllabaries and bilingual texts do not give exact information. Thus alongside *GIŠ-GU-ZA* we find a number of other ideograms, all of which are in certain connections rendered *kussû*, adequately enough no doubt, but that they all denoted exactly the same article of furniture is far from likely. A closer approximation to an exact rendering may come with the knowledge of a large number of different contexts, each of which may shade off something of the rough meaning. One of the great difficulties of the translator is that the same word often occurs again and again, but always in exactly the same context. This is especially the case in the legal documents, filled as they are with stock phrases.

**Disinheritance in the Sumerian laws**

According to the Sumerian laws disinheritance appears to have been simply the result of repudiation of a child by a parent, who has said to him, "You are not my son." The penalty for a child's repudiation of parents is to be reduced to the condition of a slave. There may also be a reference to renunciation on the part of an adopted child, but there are no legal documents to clear up the point.[1]

**In the Code of Ḫammurabi**

The Code is much clearer. Here the father is minded to cut off his son. But the disinheritance must be done in

[1] See page 39.

legal form. The father must say to a judge, "I renounce my son." The judge must then inquire into the grounds of this determination. A grave fault must be alleged. What this was we are not told. But rebellious conduct, idleness, and failure to provide for parents are probable. A parent had the right to his son's work. An adoptive parent had a right by the deed of adoption to maintenance. If the fault could be established as a first offence, the judge was bound to try and reconcile the father. If it was repeated, disinheritance took place legally. It was done by a deed duly drawn up. The Sumerian laws show that a mother had the same power as the father. Whether this was only exercised when there was no father, or whether a wife could act in this way independently of her husband in disinheriting children, does not appear. But possibly she had power in this respect only over her own property.[1]

It has been suggested that disinheritance sometimes took place as a legal form and with consent of a child, in order to admit of his adoption into another family or to free the parents from responsibility for the business engagements of the son.

In the case of adopted children

An adoptive parent, who had brought up a child and afterwards had children of his own, could not entirely disinherit his adopted child. He was bound to allow him one-third of a child's share. But he could not alienate to him real estate.[2]

[1] §§ 168, 169. [2] § 191.

# XVII

## SLAVERY

The slave a chattel

In modern thought slavery concerns personal rights. But it was not thus regarded by the Babylonians, for the slave was an inferior domestic, and, like the son in his father's house, *minor capitis*. That he was actually a chattel is clear from his being sold, pledged, or deposited. He was property and as such a money equivalent. He might be made use of to discharge a debt, according to his value. Hence, while some account of slavery belongs with the discussion of the family, it is also a part of the section dealing with property, since the slave was a piece of property.

Rights of a slave

But the slave had a great amount of freedom, and was in no respect worse off than a child or even a wife. He could acquire property, marry a free woman, engage in trade, and act as principal in contract with a free man. Only, his property, at his death, fell to his master. He was bound to do service without pay, though he had the right to food and drink. He could not leave his master's service at his own will, but he might acquire enough property to buy his freedom. He was tied to one spot, not being allowed to leave the city, but might be sent anywhere at command.

Complexity of the evidence regarding slavery

His status was, however, a complex of seeming inconsistencies. Yet it was so well understood that we rarely get any hints as to the exact details. It is only by collecting a vast mass of statements as to what actually occurred that we can deduce some idea of the actual facts. Professor Oppert in his tract, *La Condition des Esclaves à Babylone, Comptes Rendues*, 1888, pp. 11 ff.; and Dr. B. Meissner, in his dissertation, *De Servitute Babylonico-Assyriaca*, have gathered together the chief facts to be gleaned from the scattered hints in the contracts. Professor Kohler and Dr. Peiser discussed the question thoroughly in their *Aus Babylonische Rechtsleben.* Many articles discussing the contracts, and most of the histories touch upon the subject. We shall come back to it later under the head of Sales of Slaves. It is very difficult to disentangle facts from the mass of scattered hints, often consisting of no more than a word or two in a long document.

Its very early existence

The institution of slavery dates back to the earliest times. We cannot in any way attempt to date its rise.

Already in the stele of Manistusu we find a slave-girl used as part of the price of land and worth thirteen shekels;[1] while nine other slaves, male and female, are reckoned for one-third of a mina apiece. This remained a fair average price for a slave in Babylonia down to the time of the Persian conquest. For the variations, see later under Sales of Slaves.[2] The Code shows that the slave was not free to contract except by power of attorney,[3] and that it was penal to seduce him from his master's service,[4] or to harbor him when fugitive.[5] It fixes a reward for his recapture,[6] makes it penal to retain a recaptured slave,[7] and deals with his re-escape.[8] It shows that he was subject to the "levy."[9] It also determines the position of a slave-woman who bears children to her master,[10] or of a slave who marries a free woman.[11] In each case the children are free. It fixes the fees to be paid by the slave's master for his cure,[12] deals

[1] D. E. P., ii., p. 25. [2] Chapter XXII. [3] § 6. [4] § 15.
[5] § 16. [6] § 17. [7] § 19. [8] § 20.
[9] § 16. [10] § 119. [11] § 175. [12] §§ 218, 223.

with injuries done to a slave,[1] damages being paid to his master;[2] enacts that if captured and sold abroad he must be freed, if re-patriated,[3] and a native of Babylonia, otherwise he returned to his master.

Sale of slaves

By far the greatest number of references to the slave condition occur in documents relating to the sale of slaves. These may be summarized here. One peculiarity always marked the sale of a slave, it was not so irrevocable as that of a house or field. For a slave might not be all he seemed. He might be diseased, or subject to fits, he might have vices of disposition, especially a tendency to run away. A female slave might be defective in what constituted her chief attraction. Hence there was usually a stipulation that if the buyer had a legitimate cause of complaint he could return his purchase and have his money back. In fact, an undisclosed defect would invalidate the sale. These defects might be physical, inherent, contingent, or legal.

Diseases regarded as just cause for a repudiation of the contract to buy a slave

There seems to have been a dreaded disease called the *bennu*. Professor Jensen[4] has shown how largely it bulks in the literature, and what dire effects are ascribed to it. But it was not the only severe disease from which men suffered then. It is associated with several others as bad. Hence in legal documents we may take it as a typical example of a serious disease, which would so detract from the value of a slave that the purchaser would not keep him. It is evident that it was something that the purchaser could not detect at sight. Perhaps it was a disease which took some time to show itself. It is mentioned in the Code and in the sales of slaves of the First Dynasty of Babylon. It also occurs in Assyrian deeds of sale, down to the end of the seventh century B.C. The Code and the contemporary contracts allow one month within which a plea could be raised that the slave had the *bennu*. The purchaser could

[1] § 99. [2] Cf. § 251. [3] § 280. [4] K. B., vi., p. 389.

then return him and have his money back. In the Assyrian deeds one hundred days is allowed.

In the Assyrian deeds *ṣibtu* is also allowed a hundred days. This is often associated with *bennu* in the mythological texts as equally dreaded. It affected the hands or the mouth. We may render it "seizure," and think of some form of "paralysis."

Legal defects

The objections which come under the head of legal defects are summed up in the Code as a *bagru*, or "complaint." In the contracts and Code this could be pleaded at any time. So in Assyrian times a *sartu*, "a vice," could be the ground for repudiation at any time. This might arise from the disposition of the slave. The sale might also be invalidated by a claim on him for service to the state; by a lien held by a creditor; by a claim to free citizenship. But we are not yet in a position to state definitely what was the exact nature of these claims. Doubtless the recovery of further codes will fix them finally.

In later Babylonian times Law B specially provides for the return of the slave at any time, if a claim be made on him.

Assyrian usages regarding slaves

In Assyrian times sales of slaves are very frequent, and we learn much more about the status of the slave. The slave was certainly a social inferior, but probably had more freedom than any other who ever bore the name. He certainly had his own property and could contract like a free man. A young slave lived in his master's house up to a certain age, when his master found a wife for him. This was usually a slave-girl. The female slaves remained in the house as domestic servants to old age, unless they were married to a slave. Married slaves lived in their own houses for the most part. Many such men seem to have taken up out-door work, gardening, agricultural labor, or the like, on their master's estates. Others engaged in business on their own account. But from all the master had a certain income. This was, within a little, the average interest on the money-value of a slave. And that interest was usually twenty-five per cent. per annum in Assyria.

Right of a slave to the enjoyment of his property and family

Theoretically a master owned his slave's property. What this ownership amounted to is hard to say. But the slave was rarely separated from it. His family at any rate was sacred. When sold, he was sold with his family. This, of course, does not exclude the sale of a young man at a time when he would naturally leave his father's home. Young women were taken into domestic service, and after a time sold. But there was none of that tearing of children from parents, which so shocked people in the modern examples. It is probable that a slave could not marry without his master's consent. He certainly could not live where he liked. But he was free to acquire fair wealth, and his property was so far his own that he could buy his own freedom with it.

The serfs

In Assyria there was a large body of serfs, *glebae adscripti*. They could be sold with the land. But they were free to work as they chose. Usually they cultivated a plot of their master's, but often had lands and stock of their own. They were not free to move, and probably paid a rent, one or two thirds of their produce. But they were mostly on the metayer system, and could claim seed, implements, stock, and other necessary supplies from their master. This class evidently possessed privileges highly esteemed, for their ranks were recruited from all classes of artisans in the towns, cooks, brewers, gardeners, washermen, and even scribes. Some of these were probably free men, others certainly had been slaves.

Advantages of slavery

The three classes, domestic slaves, married slaves, and serfs, were continually exchanging their condition. Not a few free men, whether from debt, judicial sentence, or choice, were added to these classes. For these men, if dependent, were cared for and provided with the necessaries of life. They were, if domestic, clothed, housed, and fed; if they married and lived out, they were given a house, and either were provided with land that brought them a living, or engaged in business.

Liability for forced labor

The army and corvée, or levy for forced labor, were chiefly obtained from the slaves, and above all from the serfs. A head of a family, or mother, was not liable. But young men and women had to serve a certain number of terms of service, seemingly six.[1] Hence it was of importance to the buyer of a slave to receive a guarantee that this claim had been satisfied.

Opportunity to acquire skill as artisans

We have many examples of slaves who were skilled artisans. They had been taught a handicraft. Later we shall come across cases of apprenticeship of slaves to learn a craft. But all the artisans were not slaves. Indeed, some of the craftsmen, as goldsmiths, silversmiths, carpenters, were wealthy persons.

The slave an independent asset

As a rule, though the slave is named, his father is not. But, just as in mediæval times, a serf's father is named. The serf's holding seems to have been hereditary. But we have too few examples to be sure of our ground here. The slave's father was not concerned in the sale, and that may be the sole reason why he is not named. Fathers sometimes sold their children to be slaves, then they are named. Such sales are not so unnatural as they appear. It was a sure provision for life for a child to sell him as slave to a family in good position.

The later disappearance of the serf

In the later Babylonian times, the almost total disappearance of the serf has been noted as very remarkable. But this may be entirely due to the nature of our documents. The temples owned a great deal of land and their slaves were in the condition of serfs.

---

[1] See *Assyrian Doomsday Book*, p. 24.

Slave sales

In later Babylonian times we have a very large number of examples of slave sales. So far as the formula of a deed of sale is concerned, there is nothing to distinguish from a sale of the ordinary type, thus marking the slave as a chattel.

Guarantees exacted in such deeds:

But there are several clauses, which directly illustrate the possession of slaves, their position and liabilities. One clause, frequent when slaves were either pledged or sold, was a guarantee on the part of the owner against a number of contingencies. These are not easy to understand.

Against rebellions (?)

First we have the *amêlu siḫû*. *Siḫu* means rebellion or civil war. Sennacherib was slain in such an uprising.[1] It may be that then the slave would be impressed for defence of law and order. Or it may be that *amêlu siḫû* is the rebel, or mob, who might carry off the slave. Or the contingency contemplated may be that the slave should turn rebel and refuse to do his master's bidding. The fact that a ship was also guaranteed against *amêlu siḫû*,[2] renders this less likely. A ship could not turn rebel. It is not unlikely that slaves often joined in the rebellions.

Against flight

That a slave would escape by flight was always a danger. The slave had great freedom and many opportunities of getting away. The only security was that wherever he went he was likely to be recognized as a slave and anyone might recapture him. However, the captor had a right to a reward and so the owner would have to pay to get him back, besides losing his services for a time. Hence a slave who had a fancy for running away was likely to be troublesome and costly. That might lead to his being sold. But the purchaser protected himself by a guarantee on the seller's part that the slave would not run away. Then if the slave fled and was brought back, the captor gave a receipt for the sum paid him, and the owner reclaimed it from the seller.

---

[1] K. B., ii., p. 282. [2] Cyr. 310, Nbk. 201.

The captor might retain the slave until he was paid.[1] In other cases the seller had to recover the slave for the buyer. In Assyrian times the seller guaranteed also against death. Here it has been argued that the guarantee meant only that the slave had not fled or was not dead at the time of sale. This is not likely in the case of death. Surely no man could buy a slave who was dead. He would not pay, if the slave was not delivered. But he might bargain for recompense, if the slave died within a short time after purchase, as the seller might have had reason to know that he was ill.

Against untimely death

A guarantee was also given against the *pakirânu*. This is literally "the claimant." What claim he had is not stated. When the slave was pledged, this might be a creditor to whom he had previously been pledged. But it covers all claims on the slave.[2]

Against unexpected claims

Another indemnity is the *arad šarrûtu*, or in the case of female slaves, the *amat šarrûtu*. This was the status of an *arad šarri*, or *amat šarri*, king's man or maid. The king, or state, had a right to the services of certain slaves. How long this was for, how it was discharged, and how a private person could give a guarantee against it, we do not exactly know. It may have been limited to slaves taken in war; it probably consisted in forced service; it may have been for a limited period, so that the guarantee amounted to an assurance that it was over. But it is possible that it would be compounded for, or a substitute provided. At any rate the seller held the buyer indemnified against this claim.[3]

Against over-exaction in the public service

There was also a guarantee against *mârbanûtu*, the status of a *mâr banû*, or "son of an ancestor." The difficulty which this raised was that, if a man was a scion of a noble family, he might be redeemed by it. The same result would follow from his being adopted. Hence some con-

Against redemption as men of family

[1] Z. A., iii., p. 86. [2] Cyr. 146. [3] Cyr. 146; Camb. 15.

sider *mâr banû* to mean "adopted son." But it does not always mean that. We have no good example of a slave being redeemed on this ground. But we know that they sometimes laid claim to be free men. This would of course involve a loss and at any rate a trouble to the owner. But we have not yet very full information on the point.

Against illegal enslavement

Finally there is mentioned a claim called *šušanûtu*. This occurs in Persian times only[1] and may be the status of a *šušanu*, *i.e.*, a Susian, or one of the conquering race. Such it may have been illegal to buy or hold in slavery. But in Assyrian times an official in the service of the royal house is called *šušanu*. We do not yet know what his duties were, but it may be that this official was one who could be called up for service at any time and therefore was undesirable as a slave.

The branding or tattooing of slaves

The *abuttu* which the Code[2] contemplates a mistress putting on an insolent maid and so reducing her to slavery, or which the phrase-books contemplate a master laying upon a slave, or which an adoptive parent may set on a rebellious adopted son before selling him into servitude,[3] has usually been taken to be a fetter. But in the case of a man, who being sold as a slave, had escaped and was claimed by the levy-master, we find the latter saying, *ellita abuttaka gullubat*, "thy *abuttu* is clearly branded," or tattooed. Hence it may only be a mark.

The other ways of indicating servitude

There is frequent mention in early times of a mark upon slaves. The Code[4] talks of marking a slave, but in a way that is difficult to understand. The verb usually rendered "brand" has been shown by Professor P. Jensen[5] to include incised marks. Hence the penalty which was once rendered "shear his front hair" is thought to mean "brand his forehead." The Code fixes a severe penalty for the putting of an indelible mark on a slave without his owner's consent.

---

[1] Dar. 212. [2] § 103. [3] M. A. P., 95. [4] § 226. [5] K. B., vi., p. 377.

This could hardly be enforced for merely giving the slave a bald forehead, like the Hebrew *peôt*, or like a "tonsure." The mark borne on the forehead by Cain, or by the "sealed" in the Apocalypse, is far more to the point as a parallel. The slaves also wore little clay tablets with the name of their owner inscribed upon them. There are a number of these preserved in the Louvre. On one now in the British Museum we have this inscription: "Of the woman Ḫipâ, who is in the hands of Sin-êresh. Sebat, eleventh year of Merodach-baladan, King of Babylon."[1] How these were attached to the slave is not very clear. But they must have been anything but an indelible mark. In the later Babylonian times we have[2] a slave marked by a sign on his ears and a white mark in his eye. Both may denote natural marks.[3] A more definite example is a slave "whose right hand has written upon it the name of Ina-Esagil-lilbur";[4] and another "on whose left hand was written the name of Meskitu."[5] These were the names of the owners, not of the slaves themselves. This renders it probable that the branding and the like was always an incised mark, a species of tattoo, which of course was indelible. That the same person who tattooed men should brand animals, or even shear them, is not an insuperable objection. But there is no reason to suppose that the brander ever was a sheep-shearer.

Significance of slave-names

In respect to the names of slaves we may regard them with some interest as helping to determine the sources from which slaves were recruited. Some bear good Babylonian names, and perhaps when the father's name is also Babylonian we may conclude that they had been born free, but were either sold into slavery by the head of the family, or, having once been adopted, had been repudiated and reduced to slavery again, or had been sold for debt. We have exam-

[1] K. 3787 K. B., iv., p. 166 f. [2] Camb. 291. [3] *De serv.*, p. 20.
[4] P. S. B. A. 83, p. 104. [5] P. S. B. A. 84, p. 102.

ples of all such cases. A father and mother sold their son;[1] a mother who had adopted two girls repudiated them again;[2] a brother gave a younger brother as a pledge.[3]

Foreign-born slaves

When the slave's name is not Babylonian or Assyrian, a foreign nationality is nearly certain. These names are very valuable when they can be assigned to their nationalities, as confirming the historical claims of the kings to conquest. Sometimes they are actual gentile names, as Miṣirai, "Egyptian," Tubalai, "man from Tubal." But many may have been directly purchased abroad and sold to Babylonians. A great many foreign slaves doubtless received native names. Thus an Egyptian woman was called Nanâ-ittîa.[4] Some of the names of slaves are true Babylonian, but of a rare and odd form, which has caused some to imagine them to be foreign. But this is not necessary. Servants are often renamed after the families to which they belong, and finally become known by names which were never theirs. Masters seem sometimes to have given their own names to slaves. Their names are often contracted,[5] and some even appear to have had two.[6]

Various methods of making slaves

The slaves were not only captives taken in war, but were bought abroad, and not a few were reduced to that condition from being freeborn citizens. Slavery awaited the rebellious child or the contentious wife. But it was not allowed by the Code for a man to sell his maid outright, who had borne him children. And if he sold his wife or child to pay a debt, the buyer could not keep them beyond a certain time. But in all periods parents sold their children, and there does not seem to be any clause demanding any future release.

A slave's right to hold and use property

The slave had private property which was secured to him. He paid a sort of rent for it. This was an annual

---

[1] Nbk. 70. [2] Nbk. 625. [3] Nbk. 311.
[4] Camb. 334. [5] Nbd. 697. [6] Z. A., iii., 135.

fixed sum called his *mandattu*, the same word as for the tribute of a prince to his overlord. In the case of a female slave this was twelve shekels *per annum*. Further, he paid a percentage on his profits.[1] The slave might hold another slave as pledge, lend money, and enter into business relations with another slave even of the same house. He might borrow money of another slave. Hence he was very free to do business. But when he entered into business relations with another master's slave, or a free man, he sometimes met with a difficulty. He seemingly could not enforce his own rights against a free man. At any rate, we find that in such cases his master assumed the liability and pleaded for him. In fact, the master had to acknowledge his undertakings, though he did not guarantee them. Subject to this protection from his master, the slave was free to engage in commerce. He lent to free men, entered into partnership, and owned a scribe.

A slave's evidence not good against a free man

Here is an example illustrating one of the above points.[2] S had taken a loan of L. His master, A, became aware of it and guaranteed its repayment. He then put S into L's hands as his pledge to pay it off. Now, A died, and his son, B, sells S to C, as part of his own property. But L still holds possession of S. C demands S from L. L says "Not until my money is paid off. If C will do this he may have S. But until he can prove that it has been done he cannot have S." The proof probably lay in B's hands, if he had preserved it from his father A's records. Delay is granted for C to produce the proof that S has worked off the debt. It is clear that the evidence of S was not admitted on this point.

A slave's value proportioned to his producing power

That in the case of some slaves their value to their master consisted in their *mandattu* is clear from the fact when a master sold a slave and did not at once hand him over, the

[1] A. B. R., i., pp. 1 ff.

[2] Nbn., 738.

seller had to pay a proportional amount of this fee to the buyer.[1] Of course, in transferring a slave to another owner, the seller could not separate him from his property. That was his own. A slave who had acquired a fair amount of wealth, or was earning well in trade, would produce a higher income to his master and sell for more. What was sold then, was an interest, the master's, in his slave's work. Hence prices varied very much. We are not always able to see what was the reason of the high price, but it was evident then to those who made the bargain. An average price in the later Babylonian era seems to have been twenty shekels, the interest on which at the usual twenty per cent. would be four shekels. This, then, was the annual value of a slave above his keep. If the keep amounted to about eight shekels *per annum*, that gives the value of a slave's work as twelve shekels yearly. This is what an unskilled slave was worth to his master. If, then, a man married a slave-girl, he ought to pay her master about twelve shekels a year for his loss of her services. Of course, the master retained his right over her, but it seems to have been a tacit understanding that he could not sell her away from her husband. So really what he sold was, after all, only a right to income from her husband of twelve shekels a year. The children were also his born slaves, if the father was his slave. We do not know how matters would be arranged if the man was slave to one master, the wife to another. Probably this was provided against by the master giving his slave a wife from his own maids, or buying a slave-girl as wife for him.

The history of the slave Bariki-ilu

It occasionally happens that we can trace the history of a particular slave for some time. Thus, Bariki-ilu was pledged for twenty-eight shekels to Aḫinûri, in the thirty-fifth year of Nebuchadrezzar.[2] In the next year we find

---

[1] Nbn. 573. [2] Z. A., iii., p. 87.

him in the possession of Piru, his wife Gagâ, and a cousin Ziria. What they gave for him does not appear. But they now sold him for twenty-three shekels to Nabû-zêr-ukîn. He must have fled from his new master, for four years later, the same three people pledged him.[1] But he seems to have been unsatisfactory as a pledge. For next, we find that Gagâ's daughter (Piru having probably died), being about to be married to Iddin-aplu, this slave was set down as part of her marriage-portion. She gave him over to her husband and his son. In their possession he remained awhile, but on the death of his mistress, was handed over to the great banker, Itti-Marduk-balâṭu. These events, extending from the thirty-fifth year of Nebuchadrezzar to the seventh year of Nabonidus, were all put in evidence when Bariki-ilu tried later to prove that he was a free man. He pretended to be the adopted son of Bêl-rimâni. He had to confess that he had twice run away from his master and had been many days in hiding. Then he was afraid and pretended to have been an adopted son. This, if proved, would have freed him. But he confessed that it was a pretence, and had to return to his servitude. The case was decided in the tenth year of Nabonidus.

A runaway slave not always returnable

It seems clear that when a slave ran away to his old owners, they did not always deliver him up again to the man who bought him of them. They probably had to return the purchase-money. The buyer probably would not accept him again.

Apprenticing slaves to a trade

One feature which the later Babylonian contracts show us for the first time, but which probably was always in force, is the apprenticing of slaves to a trade. Instances of this are fairly numerous. The person to whom the slave was apprenticed was usually a slave himself. The teacher was bound to teach the trade thoroughly. The owner of the

[1] Nbk. 408.

slave gave him up to the teacher for a fixed term of years, differing for different trades. He had to furnish a daily allowance of food and a regular supply of clothing. At the end of the term, the slave might remain with his teacher on payment of a fixed *mandattu* or income to the owner. Penalties were fixed for neglecting to teach him properly. The trades named are weaving, five years' term;[1] baking, a year and a quarter;[2] stone-cutting, four years;[3] fulling, six years;[4] besides others not yet recognized.

Fee paid by service

The teacher had no fee, but only the apprentice's work for his trouble. The owner was therefore bound to allow the apprentice to remain a fair time.

Relative proportion of slaves to free men

A question of considerable interest which needs to be worked out is the relative number of slaves in the population. In early times the impression one gets is that they were few. Even in the time of the First Dynasty of Babylon, the evidence at the disposal of Dr. Meissner in 1892 did not allow him to exceed four as the number in the possession of one man at a time. But since then further evidence is available. Thus we read of twelve slaves at once, seven males and five females, given by a father to his daughter, at Sippara.[5] In Assyrian times the number in an average household rarely exceeds one or two, but we have as many as thirty mentioned at one time.[6] So in later times there are generally only one or two in a household, but the number is occasionally much more.

Price of a slave

As to the value of a slave, we have in very early times an average set down as twenty shekels, with examples as low as thirteen shekels. In the time of the Second Dynasty prices varied from as low as four and a half shekels for a maid, or ten shekels for a man, up to eighty-four shekels.[7] The Code estimates the average value of a slave as twenty

---

[1] Cyr. 64. [2] Cyr. 248. [3] Cyr. 325. [4] Cyr. 313.
[5] S. 10. [6] A. D. D., No. 424. [7] M. A. P., p. 7.

shekels.[1] In Assyrian times the price of a single male slave varies from twenty to one hundred and thirty shekels, but the usual price is thirty shekels. A female slave could be had for as little as two and a half shekels, but might cost as much as ninety shekels. A common price was thirty shekels. In later Babylonian times also, prices vary widely, but the commonest price and usual pledge-value was twenty shekels.

---

[1] § 252.

# XVIII

## LAND TENURE IN BABYLONIA

Distinction between real and personal property

THE idea of real as opposed to personal property is common in Babylonian law; for we notice that in the Code, while certain persons may inherit from the goods of their parents, they may not inherit land, garden, or house.[1] He then had no share in his father's house; he was not one of the family. The distinction is important, for, as we shall see later, the word "house" had a wider signification than mere bricks and mortar.[2] It was the ancestral estate. Over it the family had rights. It went back in default of heirs to the family of the last owner. We are therefore confronted with private ownership of land, but also with a sort of entail.

Entailed property

The amount of land might be increased by purchase, but there is a strong presumption that it thus became family property and did not remain at the disposal of the buyer. For if so, in the case above the law should have stated that the parent could not donate land that was family property, but might do so with what he had bought. This does not exclude the possibility of sale. Only the family had apparently the right of pre-emption.[3]

Natural features of Babylonia in their influence on property rights

In looking back upon the primitive state of the country, its natural features must be taken into account as helping to shape the course of development. In such a low-lying country as the land between the Euphrates and the Tigris,

---

[1] § 191. [2] Page 188. [3] Page 122.

floods naturally occur every year. Every spot of land that stood above the level of the annual floods was thereby marked out for a residence. Throughout the literature of Babylonia the hill or the mountain is a refuge and a place protected by the gods. But when the floods were gone, man's great need for his land was water. Hence irrigation was synonymous with cultivation. The unclaimed land grew rank with grass and natural food for cattle, but dried up to dust in the summer. Hence the control of the flood, its diversion into desired channels, regulation, storage, and all the processes implied by canals and irrigation were forced upon the inhabitants of Babylonia by stern necessity. The only alternative was to migrate with flocks and herds to higher lands when the floods came.

Primitive land tenure

Settled society was ultimately founded upon the cultivation of a plain. Every eminence might become a hamlet occupied by the abodes of men, whose fields were water meadows. The meadows which grew their corn lay around the village and below its level; and beyond those which were needed to grow crops lay the pastures. But for security the cattle and sheep must come back, before the floods came, to the village, there to be folded and fed, as it seems, upon straw and also grain. The land of the village extended itself in time, as the population grew and needed more corn. More and more of the unreclaimed land beyond the cornfields was brought into cultivation and the flocks went farther afield for pasture. This continued until the pastures forming the outlying ring had met the pastures of another village.

Ownership of cultivated land

Such is an ideal sketch of the growth of land tenure. But in historical times this simplicity had vanished. Land was owned, not merely held. It does not appear that pasture was owned, even as late as the First Dynasty of Babylon. It seems that the flocks were confided to shepherds, who were bound to bring them back from the pastures and expected to account for all they took out and for a reasonable increase in the flock from breeding. The pasture was common land; at any rate, to the sheep-owners of the same village. No one claims to buy and sell pasture land, only cultivated land, fields, gardens, and plantations, ultimately irrigated land. But unreclaimed land, that is, such as only required cultivation to make it fields and gardens, is often sold, or let, to be reclaimed. Was this a trespass on the pasture held in common? If so, it was not resented as such. We do not know yet how a man acquired a title to such unreclaimed land. Perhaps to have brought it into cultivation sufficed originally to establish title.

Theoretical ownership of the land by the local deity

A settled hamlet soon had its temple. Some think that the god was ideally landlord of all the village land and that every title represented simply the rental of the land from the nominal owner. We do indeed find the temples as owners of vast estates and, like monastic institutions in the Middle Ages, letting lands and houses. To the temples poor men went for temporary accommodation for sowing, for wages at harvest-time, and for ransom from the enemy. These they had a right by custom to receive without paying interest. Undoubtedly the temples became the first centres of progressive civilization. The *patêsi*, as chief-priest of the god, was the regent of the community. In process of time, as villages combined and grew into towns and districts, the *patêsi*, in virtue of his town's supremacy, became the king, who, as regent of the state and representative of the gods, owned all. We know that, in later times, the king in Babylon was the adoptive son of Bel-Merodach.[1]

Private ownership absolute in historical periods

In historical times no such conditions prevail. Doubtless the tribal ownership had become theoretically transferred to the god, or to the town. That the town had a

[1] Z. A., iii., 369.

theoretical personality of its own is clear enough from the oaths sworn to confirm a sale. Men swore by the gods, the king, and also by Sippara, or Kar Sippara. But there is no indication that points to the god, or the town, or the king as having any power to intervene to prevent a sale, or to claim payment for consent. It is clear that the land was sold subject to its dues, and they were many. But the private ownership, subject to such reservation, was absolute. The one danger to a purchaser was that the family of the seller should claim a right of redemption and annul the sale. Against this the seller undertook to indemnify him.

Right to retain ancestral estates

Exact statements as to the rights possessed by the family to reclaim land sold by a member of the family are not to be found, but they are to be inferred with certainty from a few notices which we have. Thus,[1] a man claimed a certain plot of land as ancestral domain which two others had sold. There are several such cases among the legal decisions of the First Dynasty of Babylon. In most of the Assyrian deeds of sale we have a long list of representatives of the seller, who are explicitly bound not to interfere and attempt to upset the sale.[2] Their right existed or they would not be called upon to enter into a contract not to insist upon it.

Different kinds of real property

From the point of view of the ancient Babylonian, as from that of the modern lawyer, there was a great similarity about all classes of real property. The deeds of sale or conveyances, as well as the leases, treated them with much the same formula. It was the land which was the main consideration. It was as land, built upon indeed, but essentially as land, that the house was sold. The house is rarely described by what to modern views would be its most important features, the number of stories, rooms, conveniences, and the like. Instead its area was stated. This is remarkable, as we do not buy houses by the area. We

[1] M. A. P., 42. [2] A. D. D., § 600.

need not suppose that the building actually covered all the land sold. In fact, we often see that it had a garden. But it was *bîtu epšu*, a "built-on plot" of land, according to the Babylonian conveyancer. Perhaps there was in this usage a recollection of how fast the Babylonian house of sun-dried brick sank down to a mound of clay, perhaps, too, a far-off echo of the nomad's scorn for the town-dweller, in both cases a recognition that the land was the one thing permanent, the one thing that could not "run away."

Terms used in descriptions of real property

The plot of land was the *bîtu*, Hebrew *beth*, represented by the Sumerian *Ê*. When it had the additional advantage of a house upon it, it was *bîtu epšu*, a "built-on plot." Gradually the edifice, in towns at least, absorbed the whole significance, and in common parlance *bîtu* meant a "house," but in legal phraseology it always retained its inclusive meaning of the plot of land. Even as late as the Assyrian Empire it retained some shade of a still earlier meaning, that of a plot, parcel, or share, just what it meant when the first settlers divided the land among them. Thus one might use *bîtu* of a "lot" of slaves, or of a lot of land including its slaves and cattle. That *bîtu* is to be referred to a root *banû*, "to make," may still be true, though *banû* cannot have come to mean "build" when *bîtu* was formed from it. If *bîtu* was originally the "house," perhaps only a tent-house, then it could mean all that constituted the house, the man's house in a wider sense, as in tribe names, like Bît Adini or the phrase, "House of Israel." But *bîtu*, when used of a house, does not carry with it the implication of bricks and mortar, only of a fixed site occupied for dwelling. The edifice was implied by the addition *epšu*, marking the site "built upon." So a house was "landed property"; land was of various sorts, one of which is "built on land." To be accurate one must also specify the kind of building.

The field was called *eḳlu* (compare Acel-dama, "the field of blood"), denoted by the Sumerian *A-ŠA G-GA*. The term does not denote open waste land, but a cultivated plot. Indeed, it is probable that its Sumerian name implies "irrigation." In any case it was fenced, if only by a raised ridge; it was cultivated and watched over; the birds were scared away, robbers and stray animals driven off. So much at least is expressed in as many words in the undertakings of tenants to treat a field properly. The field was also *bîtu* as land, usually "*bîtu*, so much *eḳlu*."

The garden was reckoned as land, but here a fuller specification was needed. For a plot of land, a garden, *kirû* was not exact enough. It was usual to designate further of what sort it was, whether vegetable garden, orchard, or palm-grove. The scribe would even add "planted with such and such a crop." The term might include vineyards. In many cases the actual number of bushes, or fruit-trees, or vine-stocks, would be named. But it was always primarily land, and as such *bîtu*, with the qualifications enumerated.

Systems of land measures: (1) computation by area

For land measures there were two systems in use, one purely areal, the other with a reference to the average yield. In the former case the scale of measures was discovered and formulated by Dr. G. Reisner, in the *Sitzungsberichte Berliner Akademie*, 1897, p. 417 f., and is completely known. In this scale *1 GAN = 1,800 SAR, 1 SAR = 60 GIN, 1 GIN = 180 ŠE*. We do not know how these words *GAN, SAR, GIN, ŠE* were read; they may be ideograms or Sumerian words. There was also a very large measure of area, *3,600 GAN*, perhaps called a *karu*. Mr. Thureau-Dangin has further shown that the *SAR* was the square of the measure *GAR-DU*, which seems at one time to have measured *12 U*. The *U* is often taken to be a cubit, but seems at this time to have been nine hundred and ninety millimetres, which is sometimes called "a double cubit." On these suppositions the *SAR* would be a square, each side measuring about twenty-two yards, about one-tenth of an acre, or four ares on the metrical system. But it is certain that both in early times and during the First Dynasty of Babylon the *GAR* was only *12 U*, and the *U*, if a cubit, would not be much over eighteen inches. This would make the *SAR* a square of about eighteen feet on each side. The fact that a *SAR* was a fairly common size for a house seems rather against the smaller area. What is yet wanted is some cuneiform statement of the size or area of something which can be exactly identified and measured. With further exploration this is almost sure to be found.[1]

(2) Computation by an average yield

The other system applied to land the names of measures of capacity used for measuring crops. We read of so many *GUR* and *ḲA* of land, where *1 GUR = 300 ḲA*, as shown by Dr. Reisner. We may guess that a *GUR* of land was so called because it took a *GUR* of corn to sow it, or because it yielded a *GUR* of corn as an average harvest. These are mere guesses and we must remain in ignorance until further evidence connects a *GUR* of land on one side with its length and breadth, or some other relation between the *GUR* and the *GAN* can be deduced. Then we shall want to know the size of the *GUR* of corn, of which at present we have no knowledge. But already in Susa a broken pot has been found with its original contents marked upon it. When others are found, from which an approximate estimate of contents can be made, and an inscription read giving the capacity, we shall be able to make a definite statement. At present the data are insufficient and what the metrologists write is only ingenious speculation.

Descriptions and plans of plots of land

A piece of land had, so to speak, an individuality of its own. Once marked out, and that probably from time immemorial, it was rarely divided. It seems probable that

[1] Cf. also Appendix.

corn-land at any rate was divided into long, narrow strips. But the plots became gradually of all sizes and shapes, as the many plans of estates show. The lengths of the sides are usually given on such plans, and much labor has been expended with small result on reconciling the given dimensions with the area ascribed to the plot. But it is certain that these were often recorded merely for purposes of identification. The area of the field was well known, and its average crop also, without any need of resort to calculations.

Boundary-stones

These plots often bear their owner's name, and that long after he had passed away. The boundary-stones of the field were sacred. Not a few were inscribed with some sort of history of the plot. Especially was this the case when the land was granted to fresh owners, by sale, or charter. No inconsiderable portion of what we know of history is derived from inscribed boundary-stones. They are the oldest monuments and rarely deeply buried. Hence they are easy to find. They have even been brought to London, as ship's ballast, in times before they could be read. They would be invaluable, if found *in situ*, for a modern survey of the country and a reconstruction of its ancient history. As a rule they are splendidly preserved.

Inviolability of landmarks

In ancient days great importance was attached to their preservation. The kings taxed their powers of cursing in order to terrify men from removing their neighbor's landmark. The dangers to the stone contemplated were its removal to another place, its being thrown into the water, or into the fire, its being built into a wall,[1] being buried in the dust, placed where it cannot be seen, put in a house of darkness,[2] erased and overwritten with other records.[3] Akin to the crime of encroaching upon old landmarks was that of building upon or otherwise encroaching on the highway. To do this might subject the builder to the danger of be-

Encroaching on the highway

[1] Melishiḫu. [2] Merodoch-baladan I. [3] Marduk-nâdin-aḫi.

ing hanged, as a warning on a gallows erected above his own house.[1]

The king's power over land

That the land was sold subject to certain territorial obligations, we can glean from many hints. One of the most important is that, when a favorite, or well-deserving official, had acquired a large estate, the king by charter granted him an immunity from these obligations. These charters were often inscribed on large blocks of stone or water-worn pebbles of great size, and seem to have been set up as boundary-stones. Some were reproduced from tablets written on clay.[2] They are very numerous and in some periods of the history are the only monuments that have reached us. A glance through any history of Babylonia will show the reader how much depends on them. But here our only concern is with the light they throw on land tenure and its conditions. One of the points which at once becomes clear is that, although the king was representative of the god and titular head of all the tribes, he could not appropriate land just where he chose. Manistusu, King of Kish, when he was seeking to acquire a fine estate to present to his son, Mesilim, had to buy land at what seems to have been an average price. He paid for the land in corn at three and one-third *GUR* of corn per *GAN*, the *GUR* being worth one shekel of silver. This was the price. But, as was usual later in private purchases, a present to the former owner was given. The list of these presents is most interesting,—silver and copper vessels and rich vestments being the chief items. Of great importance is the reference to the leading men of each hamlet as sellers. The king's own land was a definite area, so definite as to be cited as a boundary.[3]

Recognition of private rights of possession

A celebrated passage in Sargon's cylinder[4] says, "according to the interpretation of my name, Sharru-kînu, righteous

---

[1] I. R. 7, 12 ff. [2] D. E. P., ii., 91.

[3] Scheil, *Mémoires de la Délégation en Perse*, Tome II. [4] I. R. 36, 40–42.

king, which bade me observe right and justice, repel the impious, not oppress the weak; as the great gods had bidden me, I gave money for the pieces of land, of each city; according to written contracts, in silver and bronze, to their owners, in order to do no injustice; and to those who would not take money,[1] a field for a field, where they preferred, I gave." That this was no idle boast is proved from the tablet which records how Sargon, in the year B.C. 713, having taken possession of some lands in Maganuba to form part of his new city of Dûr-Sargon, found that he was displacing an old endowment given by Adadi-nirâri to the god Ashur. It was held by a family descended from the original recipients. Sargon increased their holding and charged it with an increased monthly offering to the temple.[2] He gave "field for field," but also added largely to the endowments. He acted much the same in Babylonia, where the Suti had encroached upon the lands of the people. He drove out the invaders, restored the lands, but laid them under obligations, *kidinûtu*, making them render a monthly due to the temples, as before.

Royal grants to temples and favorites

On the other hand, we find that the kings granted large grants of land to temples and private persons. From what source these grants were made does not appear. Probably from his own personal property. The property so presented was free of imposts. But we may not assume that the king was always the poorer. The beneficiary may have bought the land and presented it to the king, to be received back free of imposts in perpetuity.

Thus, Nazimaruttash[3] presents a large estate to Merodach, and another to Kashakti-Shugab, his servant. Kurigalzu[4] granted an estate to Eṭir-Marduk for his conduct in a war against Assyria, and Bitiliashu confirmed it. A coppersmith

[1] Like Araunah the Jebusite. [2] A. D. D., No. 809.
[3] Scheil, *Mémoires de la Délégation en Perse*, Tome II. [4] Idem.

who fled from the land of Ḫanigalbat made a fine specimen of his work for Bitiliashu, and the king rewarded him with a grant of land.[1] Adadi-shum-uṣur made another grant of land to an unknown servant of his.[2] Melishiḫu made a grant of land to his son, Merodach-baladan I.,[3] and granted it exemption from all imposts. Another grant he made to a servant of his.[4] So when Shamû and Shamûa, his son, two priests of Eria in Elam, fled from their own king and took refuge with Nebuchadrezzar I., he espoused their cause, plundered Elam, brought back their god, Eria, to Babylon, and they having taken the hands of Bêl, the king granted them an estate in Babylonia and freed it from imposts.[5] Nabû-aplu-iddina granted an estate to a namesake of his, which, however, seems to have been claimed as ancestral property.[6] Melishiḫu granted lands to Ḫasardu, a servant of his.[7] Merodach-baladan I. granted lands to Marduk-zâkir-shumi.[8] Marduk-nâdin-aḫi granted Adadi-zêr-iḳisha, for his services against Assyria, lands in the district of Bît-Ada, which seem to have been ancestral domains of one Ada.[9] Some fragments of clay copies of similar grants by Adadi-nirari,[10] Tiglath-pileser III.,[11] Ashurbânipal,[12] and Ashur-eṭil-ilâni[13] are preserved in the British Museum's Collections from Nineveh. They all appear to record grants to favorite officials, who had deserved well of the king.

Restoration of ancestral estates

The king also appears as not only confirming grants made by his predecessors, but as restoring ancestral property, or temple endowments, which had come into other hands, on suit of the legal descendants of the original owners. Thus, certain land which had come into the possession of Târim-ana-ilishu and Ur-bêlit-muballiṭat-mîtûti, was claimed by

---

[1] Scheil, *Mémoires de la Délégation en Perse*, Tome II., p. 95.
[2] Idem, p. 97. [3] Idem, pp. 99 ff. [4] Idem, p. 112.
[5] C. T., ix., No. 92987. [6] C. T., ix., No. 90922. [7] K. B., iv., pp. 57 ff.
[8] K. B., iv., pp. 60 ff. [9] K. B., iv., pp. 68 ff. [10] A. D. D., Nos. 651–56.
[11] A. D. D., Nos. 658, 659. [12] A. D. D., Nos. 646–48. [13] A. D. D., Nos. 649, 650.

Marduk-kudur-uṣur in the reigns of Adadi-shum-iddina and Adadi-nâdin-aḫi, and finally granted him in perpetuity by Melishiḫu.[1] The land which Gulkishar, King of the Sea Land, gave to a goddess had remained in her possession 696 years, until, in the time of Nebuchadrezzar I., the Governor of Bît Sin-mâgir had secularized it. Bêl-nâdin-apli restored it.[2]

Granting of especial privileges

A rather different grant was made by Nebuchadrezzar I. to Ritti-Marduk for his services against Elam. This faithful vassal had been governor of a district on the borders of Elam, but the privileges of his country had been much curtailed by a neighboring King of Namar. They were now restored and apparently augmented. They were, that the King of Namar had no right of entry, could not levy taxes on horses, oxen, or sheep, nor take dues from gardens and date-plantations; could not make bridges nor open roads. The Babylonians, or men of Nippur, who came to live there were not to be impressed for the Babylonian army. Further, the towns of the district were freed from dues to the Babylonian governors.[3] Marduk-nâdin-aḫi in his first year remitted some obligations on an unknown estate.[4]

Temple endowments

Of another kind are the monuments recording the actual endowments of temples by certain kings. A very fine example is the stone enclosed in a clay coffer referring to the endowments of the temple of Shamash at Sippara. It records the restorations made by Simmash-shiḫu, É-ulmash-shâ-kin-shum, Nabû-aplu-iddina, and Nabopolassar at wide intervals. There are, however, no lands concerned.[5]

An illustration

A very archaic tablet in the E. A. Hoffman Collection, of the General Theological Seminary, New York City, published in the *Journal of the American Oriental Society*,[6] which seems to be older than the celebrated Blau monuments and which Professor G. A. Barton would date about

---

[1] K. B., iii., pp. 154 ff. [2] K. B., iv., p. 64. [3] K. B., iii., pp. 164 ff.
[4] K. B., iv., pp. 90 ff. [5] K. B., iii., pp. 174 ff. [6] Vol. xxiii., pp. 19 ff.

5500 B.C., deals directly with a presentation of land to a temple. In it the area of the land is given in *GAN* and the sides in figures only, probably denoting the lengths in *U*. Being written in very archaic, semi-picture writing, and some of the signs not yet being identified with certainty, it will not do to build much upon it. All the sides but one appear to be thirty-six thousand and fifty, that one being thirty-six thousand, while the full area is three thousand and five *GAN*. This gives the *GAR* as roughly = fifteen *U*.

The metayer system

Land was let under a variety of systems of tenure. The metayer system was one of the most common and persistent. The use of this term is justified by the similarity of actual cases to what is known to prevail in Italy, under this name. It is a co-operative system. The landlord not only allows his land to be cultivated for a consideration, but finds the means to meet expenses. He provides bullocks, tools, seed, and many other things, according to the usage of the locality.

Illustrations from the Code

In the Code of Ḫammurabi we have proof of the existence of the system. A man finds[1] his tenant tools, oxen, and harness, but hires him to reside on the field and do the work. Actual examples are rare among the contemporary contracts. But Amat-Shamash, a votary, let out,

> "Six oxen, among them two cows; an irrigator, Amêl-Adadi; two tenders of an ox-watering machine, his nephews; three watering-machines for oxen; a female servant who tended the machines; half a *GAN* of land for corn-growing; to Gimillu and Ilushu-banî. They shall make the yield of the field according to the average (?). They shall cause the corn to grow and measure it out to Amat-Shamash, daughter of Marduk-mushallim. In the time of harvest they shall measure out the corn to Amat-Shamash."

In spite of several obscurities due to uncertain readings, which render the translation doubtful in places, this must be regarded as a good example of the kind.[2]

---

[1] § 253. [2] B[2] 509.

There are fewer data from the Assyrian period, but the frequent loans, *ana pûḫi*, without any interest, at seed-time or harvest, may be due to this relation between landlord and tenant.[1] From the Assyrian period

The best example is to be found in the time of Cyrus,[2] where a certain Shulâ proposes to take the fields of Shamash, in the district of Birili, in the county of Sippara. It was sixty *GUR* of corn-land. The temple was to find him twelve oxen, eight laborers (literally irrigators), three iron ploughs, four harrows (or hoes), and five measures of seed-corn, which also included food for the laborers and fodder for the oxen. At the end of the year he was to hand over three hundred *GUR* of corn as the temple share. From the Persian period

Another good example from the time of Artaxerxes I.[3] relates to the assignment of two trained irrigation-oxen and seven *GUR* of corn for seed by a member of the Murashû firm to three brothers, who undertake to pay seventy-five *GUR* of corn *per annum* for three years. It does not appear that they hired the land as well. Here the hirer returns more than ten times his loan as yearly rent.

The usual method of hiring land was on shares. The Code contemplates that this would be for a proportion fixed by contract, either one-half or one-third of the produce going to the owner, in the case of a field or irrigated meadow and two-thirds in the case of a garden.[4] The difference was due to the fact that in the former case the owner furnished the land only, possibly with its water-supply; in the latter case he also furnished the plants. In the contemporary contracts we have but few cases where the crop is shared. In these cases the owner and tenant share equally.[5] The tenant was also to erect a *manaḫtu*, or "dwelling." It was needful that he should reside on the The system of shares

---

1 A. D. D., p. 21. 2 Cyr. 26. 3 Hilprecht, B. E. P., ix., p. 40.
4 §§ 46, 64. 5 M. A. P., 76, B2 460.

property to take care of the crop. This was stipulated for and the clause added that he should hand over the dwelling to the landlord. For such dwellings compare the "cottage in the wilderness" of Isaiah l. 8.

Duties of tenants

The tenant, of course, was bound to cultivate the land. The duties which fell to his share were "to plough, harrow, weed, irrigate, drive off birds,"[1] but these duties are but rarely stipulated. The Code protects the tenant, however,[2] from any unfair compulsion in the matter, so long as the landlord gets his fair rent.

Fixed rental

Fields were also let at a fixed rent, usually payable in kind. The contracts of the First Dynasty of Babylon give a large number of examples of this sort. The kinds of field are distinguished as *AB-SIN*, or *šerû*, and *KI-DAN*. The average rent for the former was eight *GUR* of corn per *GAN*; of the latter, eighteen *GUR* per *GAN*. The former class may include land with corn standing upon it, or simply corn-land; the latter land as yet unbroken, or fallow. The latter class seems to have been much more fertile.

This rent later became more fixed because the average yield per area was set down in the lease and the yield in corn was estimated in money according to the ordinary value of corn. Thus the rent is stated to be so much money.

Improving lease

Land was often let to reclaim, or plant. The Code lays down as law what was evidently a common practice. In the case of waste land given to be reclaimed the tenant was rent free for three whole years. In the fourth year he paid a fixed rent in corn, ten *GUR* per *GAN*.[3] Land let to be turned into a garden was rent free for four years. In the fifth year the tenant shared the produce equally with the landlord.[4]

---

[1] M. A. P., p. 12, note 3, p. 143, No. 77. [2] § 42. [3] § 44. [4] § 60.

Contracts illustrating this form of lease are quite common in the time of the First Dynasty of Babylon.

Manorial obligations

Freedom from various obligations might be granted by royal charter. In fact, it is from these charters that we know of the existence of the obligations for the most part. The land so freed was called *zakû.* Land sold is often said to be *zakû,* and we may suppose it was so because it had once been freed by charter. But this is not quite certain. The charter was granted to a person and his heirs. Doubtless, as long as they held it, it would be free, but it is not clear that they could sell it as freed forever. But we only know that some land was free. On whom then fell the obligations? So far as they were due to the king, they may have been abolished, but such obligations as repairs of the canal banks must surely have been taken up by others. If not, the granting of charters must have been a fruitful source of trouble and distress to the land.

Their basis in the obligation of fair maintenance

The obligations were of various kinds. Some were directly extensions of the duty of a tenant to exercise proper care of the estate. A very prominent duty was the care of the canals. To see that they were kept in proper order was the mark of good government. To allow them to fall into disrepair was probably the result of weak government, or the exhaustion due to defeat in war. But it very soon led to the impoverishment of the country. The Code contemplates the care of the canal banks, or dikes, as the duty of the land-owner adjoining.[1] It holds him responsible for any damage done to the neighbors' crops by his neglect to close a breach, or leaving the feed-pipe running beyond the time needed to water his field. But the canal was also liable to silt up or become choked with water-weeds, and the care of dredging it out was that of the district governor. He might carry out this duty by summoning the riparian

[1] § 53.

owners to clean out the bed of the canal,[1] or by a levy for the purpose. Soldiers, or at any rate, forced labor, might be used.[2] Later, in the time of Nebuchadrezzar I., we find men, hired for the purpose, called *ḳallê nâri*, or canal laborers.[3]

---

[1] K. L. Ḫ., p. xxxvii. [2] Ib., p. 16. [3] C. T., IX., No. 92987.

# XIX

## THE ARMY, *CORVÉE,* AND OTHER CLAIMS FOR PERSONAL SERVICE

The levy

THERE was always a militia, *Landwehr*, or territorial levy of troops. Each district had to furnish its quota. These are called *ṣâbê,* or *ummanâte.* We have no direct statements about them, but a great multitude of references. They were called out by the king, *adki ummanâtîa,* "I called out my troops," is a stock phrase. The calling out was the *dikûtu.* Not easily to be distinguished from this was the *šisîtu* of the *nâgiru.* That officer seems to have been an incarnate War Office. It is not clear whether he always acted solely for military purposes. The "levy" seems to have been equally made for public works. The men were "the king's men," whether they fought or built. The obligation to serve seems to have chiefly affected the slaves and the poorer men, the *muškênu.* In the Code of Ḫammurabi[1] it was punishable with death to harbor a defaulter from this "levy."

Forced labor

Claims might also be made for work on the fields. This was called *ḫubšu* and we know little about it more than that Sargon II. charged his immediate predecessors on the throne with having outraged the privileges of the citizens of the old capital Asshur, by putting them to work on the fields.

The obligation to provide a soldier for the state was tied

[1] § 16.

to a definite plot, or at any rate, to all estates of a certain size. The *ilku*, or obligation of the land, was transferred with it. In Assyrian times, the military unit was the bowman and his accompanying pikeman and shield-bearer. The land which was responsible for furnishing a "bow," *ḳaštu*, in this fashion, was itself called a "bow" of land.[1]

Exemption of certain cities

Some cities claimed for their citizens a right of exemption from "the levy." In Sargon's time, we find that cities like Asshur had been subjected by Shalmaneser IV. to this service, and Sargon restored their rights. He freed them from *dikûtu mâti*, *šisîtu nagiri*, and *miksu kâri*.[2] The city had not known the *ilku dupsikku*. Later, we find an officer, Tâb-ṣil-ešarra,[3] complaining that, when he was desirous of doing some repairs to the queen's palace in Asshur, of which city he was *šaknu*, Sargon's freeing of the city had rendered the *ilku* of the city unavailable to him.[4]

In the so-called "Tablet of warnings to kings against injustice,"[5] the cities of Borsippa, Nippur, and Babylon are freed from *dupsikku* and *šisîtu nâgiri*. This was drawn up in the time of Ashurbânipal, but whether it was original with him is not clear. At any rate, later, under Cambyses and Darius, these cities were again subject to the "levy."

Classes subject to the levy

This obligation to perform forced labor, or serve in the army, fell on the agricultural population primarily. Indeed, it seems that the men who discharged it might be called upon to do field labor, and it was an aggravation of the insults put upon the old capital Asshur, that its citizens were set to do field labor.[6] On all country estates, there were a number of serfs, *glebae adscripti*, sold with the estate, but not away from it. These, as the Ḫarran census shows, often had land of their own. But they were bound to till the soil for the owner. They included the *irrišu*, or

[1] A. D. D., ii., p. 172. [2] A. O. F., i., p. 404. [3] H. A. B. L., p. 89.
[4] A. D. D., ii., p. 174 f. [5] C. T., xv., 50. [6] A. O. F., i., p. 404 f.

irrigator, the husbandman in charge of date-plantations, gardens, or vineyards. From these were drawn the men who served in the army as "king's men," and on public works. They seem to have been liable to five or six terms of service, season's work probably, or campaigns, and then were free. At any rate, the heads of families seem to be free. The daughters as well as sons were subject to service, probably to repair to the great weaving houses in the towns. We read of these weaving establishments from early times. M. Thureau-Dangin has called attention to their occurrence in the Telloh tablets of the Second Dynasty of Ur.[1]

Service at the royal weaving establishments

The amounts of wool assigned to different cities to work up are the subject of many tablets.[2] In the great cities, the temples or the palaces were the home of this industry; but quantities of stuff were served out under bond to private establishments to be worked up and returned or paid for. The work on these industries constituted the *amat šarrûti*, or obligation to serve as "king's handmaid." It lay also upon slaves. It is doubtful whether the obligation included domestic service. From the second Babylonian Empire we have a host of tablets relating to these weaving accounts. They will be found fully discussed by Dr. Zehnpfund in his *Weberrechnungen*.[3]

Obligations of slaves to the state

The married slave, even in the city, usually lived in his own house. His children were born to slavery, but were usually not separated in early life from their parents. They entered their master's service, and might be sold when grown up. They might learn a trade and so earn a living, paying a fixed sum to their master. They might become agricultural laborers, and so attain a fixity of tenure as serfs. But on all these subject classes, slaves, whether

[1] Rev. Ass., III., p. 140. [2] A. D. D., 951 ff.
[3] B. A. S., i., pp. 492–536, 632–36.

domestic or living out, serfs, and artisans, there lay the obligation to do forced work for the king. After a certain number of terms of service, they were exempt.

Public obligations

The obligations to public institutions which existed in Babylonia in later times have not yet been made the subject of a thorough study. Kohler and Peiser have noted several of the more important indications, and to them we owe what has been done up to the present.

To take a share in the expense of warfare

The most noteworthy obligation was what they call the *ḳablu.* This has the same sign as so commonly used in the phrase, *ḳablu u taḫâzu*, for "war and fighting." But it is also the ideogram for *šisîtu*, the call of the *nâgiru* to war or the corvée. There is no doubt that it indicates the levy for war. The *rikis ḳabli* was the money due from certain persons to furnish a soldier for the war. Thus we have seventy shekels paid to a certain man, in the fifth year of Darius, to go to the city Shiladu.[1] Again, a certain Bêl-iddin had to find twenty-five shekels to pay a substitute to go for him to the presence of the king.[2] Another man paid the wages of a soldier for two years.[3] This was an *æs militare.* In another case we find the *rikis ḳabli* for a horseman for a certain troop, for three years. It consisted of an ass worth fifty shekels, thirty-six shekels for its keep, twelve coats, twelve breastplates (?), twelve *mušapallatum*, twelve leather *mîṭu*, twenty-four shoes, thirty *ḲA* of oil, sixty *ḲA* of bdellium sixty *ḲA* of some aromatic, all as equipment, *ṣiditum*, to go to the camp (?). This may be described as *æs equestre.*[4] So[5] the burgomaster of Babylon paid *rikis ḳabli* for three years for a certain soldier, receiving the amount from single citizens. How this arose, what dues it was a composition for, and whether it antedates Persian times, are details not yet clear.

To pay dues for the land

Besides the personal obligation to contribute "work," *dullu*, a liability for contributions in kind, *ilku*, dues from

[1] Dar. 164. [2] Dar. 156. [3] Dar. 481. [4] Dar. 253. [5] Camb. 276.

the land, existed. We are in the dark as yet as to the exact form these took. In the Code, the *ilku*, or duty from an estate held as the benefice of an office, was the fulfilment of the functions of the office.[1] The word does not seem to denote contributions. But the word literally is what "comes" of any holding, income, or what is "taken" from it. In a charter of Melišhiḫu,[2] we have a long list of powers which could be exercised by the king's officials over land. They are levies or forced contributions of wood, crops, straw, corn, wagons, harness, asses or men, rights to abstract water from canals, to drink from the water, to pasture herbage, or set on the royal flocks or herds, to pasture sheep, to construct roads or bridges. These are referred to as either a *dullu* or *ilku*. The governor is named as likely to demand right of pasture for his flocks and herds or work for roads and bridges. But we are left without information as to the proportion these levies bore to the property. All we can conclude is that the king had a right to impress such things or such labor. Few, if any, other documents are so full and explicit as to the dues exacted from the land, but all these dues are mentioned again, one or two together, in almost all the charters.

**The temple tithe**

This is one of the most important dues from land. It was paid to the temple. Some are inclined to see it in the *niširtu*, from which many charters exempt land; but others consider this merely a word for "diminution," or levy in general. There is no means of deciding yet as to the time at which the tithe first became a fixed institution.

**In Assyria**

There seems to be no trace in Assyrian times of any payment of a tithe. The tithe *rab ešrite*, which has been rendered "tithe collector," is more likely to be a commander of ten, a decurion.[3]

---

[1] § 35. [2] D. E. P., II. [3] A. D. D., § 236.

Common among Neo-Babylonians

The evidence for the existence of tithe in the later Babylonian period is very full. All seem to have paid it, from the king downward. Nabonidus paid, on his accession, to the temple at Sippara, five minas of gold. It was a very large sum, but may have been a sort of succession duty rather than an income-tax.[1] It is curious that we also find Belshazzar named as paying tithe, due from his sister, and that when the Persian army was already in possession of Sippara.[2] This shows that the Persians were friendly invaders and respected the rights of private property and of the temples. Belshazzar also paid tithe, through his major-domo, to Bêl, Nabû, Nêrgal, and Bêlit of Erech.[3]

Often paid collectively

It was paid for a group of persons by one of their company, or perhaps we might say that certain persons collected tithe from their district and paid it in. Thus we have a document recording the payment by one man of the tithe due from a number of shepherds, cultivators, and gardeners, in the city of Maḫâz-Shamshi.[4] In the time of Artaxerxes I., Hilprecht has shown that in some cases "the bow" of land also paid tithe.[5]

Usually in kind

Tithe was usually paid in kind, on all natural products, corn, oil, sesame, dates, flour or meal, oxen, sheep, asses, and the like, but also was liquidated by a money payment. The tablets relating to it are very numerous, but in nearly every case amount to no more than a receipt for its payment.

Tithe became property apparently and was negotiable. So at least appears from Nebuchadrezzar 270. We thus have property in income from land.

Octroi duties

The various dues, *miksu*, seem to have been a sort of octroi duty. They were levied at the quay, *miksu kâri*, at the ferry, *miksu nibiri*. They are only mentioned in the

---

[1] Nbn. 2. [2] Sayce. [3] Nbd. 270.
[4] Nbk. 220. [5] B. E. P., ix., p. 36.

charters, granting exemptions from them, to certain estates or their owners. Closely related to these were the *mikkasu*, which seem to be some sort of due or tax levied upon all *naturalia*, and even upon the dues which were paid into the temples. We have frequent mention of them in later times, in the temple accounts.

# XX

## THE FUNCTIONS AND ORGANIZATION OF THE TEMPLE

The great importance of the temple

THE temple exerted an overwhelming financial influence in smaller towns. Only in certain large cities was it rivalled by a few great firms. Its financial status was that of the chief, if not the only, great capitalist. Its political influence was also great. This was largely enlisted on the side of peace at home and stability in business.

Varieties and origin of temple dues

The importance of the temple was partially the result of the large dues paid to it. These consisted primarily of a *ginû*, or fixed customary daily payment, and a *sattukku*, or fixed monthly payment. How these arose is still obscure. They were paid in all sorts of natural products, paid in kind, measured by the temple surveyor on the field. Doubtless, these were due from temple lands, and grew out of the endowments given to the temple. These often consisted of land, held in perpetuity by a family, charged with a payment to the temple. The land could not be let or sold by the temple, nor by the family. Such land was usually freed from all other state dues. The endowment was thus at the expense of the state. An enormous number of the tablets which have reached us from the later Babylonian times concern the payment of these dues. They mostly consisted of corn and sesame, or other offerings, and the tablets are receipts for them. In Assyrian times the *ginû* also included flesh of animals and birds. In some few cases we have long lists of these daily dues, accompanied by precious gifts in addition. The gifts were perishable, but were accompanied by a note specifying them, and the good wishes or purpose of the donor.[1] These notes were preserved as mementos of the donor's good-will.

The temples as owners of rented land

Temples, however, also possessed lands which they could let. They also held houses which they might let.[2] In fact, the temples could hold any sort of property, but apparently could not alienate any. Some lands the temple officials administered themselves, having their own work-people. We have mention of these lands from the earliest times (*e.g.*, the very early tablet referred to above),[3] right down through the Sumerian period. We have almost endless temple accounts, many of which relate to the fields of the temple, giving their dimensions and situation, with the names of the tenants, or serfs, and the rents or crops expected of them. Then, in the First Dynasty of Babylon, we find the lands, gardens, courts, *et cetera*, of the gods named. We no longer have the temple accounts, but the private business transactions of the citizens, whose neighbors are often the gods themselves, as direct land-owners. In Assyrian times the mention of temple lands is very common. In later Babylonian times there is abundant evidence of the same custom. Dr. Peiser devotes a considerable portion of the introduction to his *Babylonische Verträge* to this subject. How the temple became possessed of these lands we do not know. We do know of large gifts of land by kings, rich land-owners and the like, but we do not know whether originally the temple started with land. When a king speaks of building a temple to a god, we may understand that he really rebuilt it, or erected a new temple on the site. Before kings, the *patêsis* did the same. But did a *patêsi* precede a temple or *vice versâ?* and did the first founder, or the town, grant the first temple lands?

---

[1] A. D. D., 998–1092. [2] Nbd., 428, 439. [3] Page 196.

Their income from private sources

The temples had further a variable revenue from private sources. There were many gifts and presents given voluntarily, often as thank-offerings. The temple accounts give extensive lists of these from the earliest times to the latest. They were of all sorts, most often food or money. But they were often accompanied by some permanent record, a tablet, vase, stone or metal vessel, inscribed with a votive inscription. These form our only materials for history in long spaces of time.

Share of the temple in the sacrifices

Sacrifices were, of course, largely consumed by the offerers and those invited to share the feast. But the temple took its share. The share was a fixed or customary right to certain parts. For one example, the temple of Shamash at Sippara had its fixed share of the sacrifice, taking "the loins, the hide, the rump, the tendons, half the abdominal viscera and half the thoracic viscera, two legs, and a pot of broth." The usage was not the same at all temples. In the temple of Ashur and Bêlit at Nineveh we have a different list.[1] For the parallels with Mosaic ritual, and the Marseilles sacrificial tablet, see Dr. J. Jeremias, *Die Cultus Tafel von Sippar*. The list was drawn up by Nabû-aplu-iddin, King of Babylon B.C. 884–860.[2]

Sometimes sold for cash

This was of course a variable source of income, depending upon the popularity of the cult and the population of the district. It was also perishable and could not be stored. It is certain that in some cases this source of income was so large that the temple sold its share for cash.[3] This must be carefully distinguished from the *ginû* and *sattukku* mentioned on page 208, which were constant and regular supplies.

The temple as a business institution

The temple was also a commercial institution of high efficiency. Their accumulations of all sorts of raw products

---

[1] A. D. D., Nos. 998–1013, etc.

[2] Haupt, *Journal of Biblical Literature*, xix., p. 60.

[3] Nbk. 213 with Nbk. 396.

were enormous. The temple let out or advanced all kinds of raw material, usually on easy terms. To the poor, as a charity, advances were made in times of scarcity or personal want, to their tenants as part of the metayer system of tenure, to slaves who lived outside its precincts, and to contractors who took the material on purely commercial terms. The return was expected in kind, to the full amount of advance, or with stipulated interest. Also in some cases, especially wool and other clothing stuffs, in made-up material. Definite fabrics, mostly garments and rugs or hangings, were expected back. Some quantity was needed for garments and vestments for temple officials, some for the gods. But a great deal was used for trade. We have references to temple treasuries and storehouses from the earliest times to the latest.

The temple as a place of deposit and traffic

The temples did a certain amount of banking business. By this we mean that they held money on deposit against the call of the depositor. Whether they charged for safe-keeping or remunerated themselves by investing the bulk of their capital, reserving a balance to meet calls, does not yet appear. But the relatively large proportion of loans, where the god is said to be owner of the money, points to investment as the source of a considerable income. Here a careful distinction must be made between the loans without interest, or with interest only charged in default of payment to time, and those where interest is charged at once. The latter are banking business, the former were probably only the landlord's bounden duty to his tenant by the custom of his tenure. The temples also bought and sold for profit.

The temple staff

The greater officials, of course, appear often at court. The king was accompanied by a staff of priestly personages. They frequently appear in the inscriptions and on the monuments. His court reproduced that of the gods above. The officials in one answered, man for man and office for office, with those above.

The priestly influence over the king

The king, by his religion, could do nothing without religious sanction. The support of the priestly party was essential. In the more unsettled times they were to a great extent king-makers. To estrange the priests was a dangerous policy always. Besides their immense wealth they had the sanctions of religion on their side. To all men certain things were right, and the priests then had what right there was on their side. A king was under obligation to come to Babylon to take the hands of Bêl-Merodach each New Year's Day. If he did not, he not only offended the priests, but also committed a wrong in the eyes of his people.

Their influence on the whole predominantly ethical

But the kings were often inclined to rely upon conjurers, soothsayers, magicians, and the like. It would be a fatal mistake to confuse these with the priests. The best kings were those who set their face against magic and supported the more rational local or national worships. Sargon II., Esarhaddon, Nebuchadrezzar II., are examples of the latter, while Ashurbânipal is a great example of the magic-ridden kings. Ḫammurabi apparently strove to put down magic. The eternal struggle between the "science"(falsely so-called) of magic and divination on the one hand and the higher claims of religious duty on the other, is the key to much that is misunderstood in the politics of the time. It would be too much to say that the priestly party were always on the side of morality, or that they were not often allied with the soothsayers, but it is certain that what ethical progress there was, was due to them. In religious texts alone have we aspiration after higher ideals. Who can fancy a wizard troubled about ethics?

Honors paid to priesthood

The priest proper, *šangû*, was a person of the highest rank. He appears very little on the whole. His chief function was to act as mediator between god and man, as over the sacrifice offered.

He had public duties outside his priestly office. He inspected canals.[1] He often acted as a judge. Additional duties

There was a college of priests attached to some temples, over which was a *šangû maḫḫu* or "high-priest." Their college

The general idea that *mašmašu*, "charmer"; *kalû*, "restrainer"; (?) *maḫḫû*, "soothsayer"; *surru*; *lagaru*; *šâ'ilu*, "inquirer"; *mušêlu*, "necromancer"; *âšipu*, "sorcerer"; all properly "magicians," are subdivisions of the general term *šangû*, is yet to be proved. Except when, in rare cases, the same man was both, the scribes carefully distinguish them. The idea seems to arise from the same modern confusion of thought which starts by calling an unknown official first a eunuch, then a priest. We do not yet fully know the functions or methods of these officials. They remain to be studied.[2] Their exact functions uncertain

The *ḳêpu*, or "warden," was over the temple servants. He let the temple lands. He inspected the temple slaves and work-people.[3] The warden

The *šatammu* was over the revenues. This name is clearly connected with the *šutummu* or storehouse. The steward

Certain officials, as surveyors or measurers, scribes, *et cetera*, may have been of priestly rank and held these offices as well. But as a rule, a man appears with an official title, without our being able to see whether he was a priest or not.

The temple kept its artificers, who had board and wages. It had its serfs, or land laborers, not actual slaves, but The workmen

---

[1] Camb. 19.

[2] Professor H. Zimmern has made a splendid beginning in his *Beiträge zur Kenntniss der Babylonischen Religion* by determining the functions of the *barû*, the *âsipu*, and the *zammaru*. He calls them all "priests." But he does not show that either was a *šangû*. It may really be so, but why confuse what the Babylonians kept distinct?

[3] Cyr. 292.

free except for their duty to the temple. They lived on the produce of their holdings, subject to a fixed, or produce-rent.

There were temple slaves, who performed the menial offices without wages, but were clothed and fed.

Within these classes doubtless came some of those who appear as slaughterers, water-carriers, doorkeepers, bakers, weavers, and the like. A temple also had its shepherds, cultivators, irrigators, gardeners, *et cetera;* but it is far from easy to determine the exact degree of dependence in each case. The temple even had its own doctor.[1]

Similarity of the temple to the monastic system

In all these cases we may compare the monastic institutions of the Middle Ages. We are not as a rule able to see whether they were "lay brothers," or had become "clerics," as well as "clerks." But there is no sign of celibacy. Even the priests were married.

Attached to the temple were votaries.[2] In not a few cases the above offices might also be held by women, even such an office as surveyor might be held by a woman. There were many female "clerks." All the temple staff were maintained by the temple, boarded, fed, and clothed, at the temple expense. But private persons might undertake to keep a definite temple official, perhaps were bound to do so, by the terms of some endowment.[3]

Hereditary rights

The right to serve in certain offices was hereditary in some families. As these multiplied, the office was held in turn by members of the family for a short time, so that it may well be that an individual priest only exercised his functions for a very limited part of the year.

Origin of clan names

Great families took their clan name from their office; for example, the Gula priests in later Babylonian times, or as the *mandidu*, "measurer," or "surveyor," attached to a temple, became a clan name.

---

[1] Cyr. 352. [2] Page 76. [3] Nbd. 773.

Proprietary rights to share in temple incomes

Hence arose property in temple incomes. That these were considerable we know from the lists of temple accounts. These form the bulk of the earliest documents. From them we learn that each day certain officials received certain allowances, mostly food and drink. From later documents we learn that men apparently not connected with the temple had become lay impropriators of the temple allowances originally intended only for temple officers.

These rights negotiable

The right to receive these was a valuable and negotiable asset. Thus we read of a right to five days per year in the temple of Nannar, sixteen days per year in the temple of Bêlit, and eight days in the shrine of Gula as being the *namḫar* of Sin-imgurâni and Sin-uzili.[1] This was confirmed to them by a legal decision in the time of Rîm-Sin. We read also of a right to act as *šatammu*, for six days per month, in the temple of Shamash.[2] In later times the *mandidûtu*, or surveyorship, to the temple of Anu, Ib, and Bêlit-êkalli, exercised in the temple, storehouse, and field, was sold, shared, and pledged.[3] Another such right was given on condition that it was not sold for money, granted to another, pledged, nor diminished in any way, and should pass to the possessor's daughter on his death.[4] The porter's post at Bâb Salimu was given as a pledge. Shares in these incomes were regularly traded in, sold, and pledged.

Other endowments of office

The position of a priest, or other official, carried with it an endowment. On this point the Code is very explicit for the cases of the *ridû ṣâbê* and the *bâ'iru*, officials charged with the collection of local quotas for the army and public works. They were recruiting sergeants, press-gang officers, and post-office officials. The office was endowed by royal grant. They were liable to be called on in the discharge of their duties to make lengthy journeys and be absent from home for a length of time, even years. In their absence,

[1] M. A. P., 41. [2] $B^2$ 2175 A. [3] P. A. S., II., 8. [4] P. A. S., II., 23.

their duties could be delegated to a son, if old enough, otherwise a substitute was put in. They could claim reinstatement within a certain time. But their endowment was inalineable from the office and could not be treated as private property.

Also the great offices at court

Quite similarly the great state officials in Assyria had endowments which were not personal, but went with the office. Thus we learn from the Ḫarran census that certain lands paid rent or crops to certain offices.

These rights maintained by inheritance

In later times the rights to income are very prominent, perhaps solely in virtue of the class of documents which has reached us. Occasionally we are able to learn exactly what they were. For example, the surveyor for the temple of Anu had a right to two *GUR* of corn, two *GUR* of dates, fifty *ḲA* of wheat, six *KA* of sesame, on every eighteen *ḲA* of land. When the corn and dates were harvested, on one *GUR*, six *ḲA* were levied.

The relation to the state

It is not clear that a temple had any direct duties to the state. Peiser thinks that they collected dues for the state. Certainly they had attached to them the king's storehouses. Certain amounts were paid in for certain state officials. In the Code of Ḫammurabi we see that a temple might be called upon to ransom a member of the town who had been taken captive.

The loaning of money

In certain circumstances the king's officials might borrow of the temples.[1] Thus Nikkal-iddina borrowed of the temple of Bêlit of Akkad a vessel of silver, weight fifteen minas, when the Elamites invaded the land.

Forced loans

Some kings laid hands on the treasures of the temple for their own use. Doubtless this was done under bond to repay. The cases in which we read of such practices are always represented as a wrong. When Shamash-shûm-ukîn sent the bribes to the King of Elam, Ummanigash, he spoiled

---

[1] A. D. D., No. 930.

the treasuries of Merodach at Babylon, of Nabû at Borsippa, and of Nêrgal at Cutha, and this was reckoned one of his evil deeds, which led to his downfall. But if he had been successful and had repaid his forced loans, doubtless it would have been excused, and his memory would have been blessed.

The temple a trading institution

Much confusion is introduced by the fact that we do not know when a temple official acts in his own private capacity and when on behalf of the temple. The deeds, which do not expressly state that the money or property belongs to the god, or the temple, may often be only concerned with private transactions, but were preserved in the temple archives on account of the official position of the parties. But there are plenty of cases, where no doubt exists, to justify us in regarding the temple as acting in all the capacities of a private individual, or a firm of traders.

# XXI

## DONATIONS AND BEQUESTS

Alienation of property

ALIENATION of property might be complete or partial. Of complete alienation we may instance donation, sale, exchange, dedication, testament. The latter was rarely complete in Babylonia. Examples of partial alienation are loan, lease, pledge, deposit.

Importance of the fact of ownership

We may note as a common mark of all these transactions the care taken to fix and define ownership. The transfer is "from" A to B. In early times the property is usually first stated to belong to A. Then he is often said in Assyrian times to be the *bêlu* of it, its full and legitimate owner. The new owner had to be satisfied that A was competent to part with it. This is often made clearer by saying, in later times, that no one else has any claim upon it. Hence arise guarantees against defeasor, redemptor, *et cetera*. This subject of guarantees is most interesting, though often obscure. The investigation of the varied rights which were likely to interfere with freedom of transfer is most important.

Peculiar forms of assignments

In certain cases we shall find a sort of hypothecation of property, as when it is assigned as security, but not given up. The possession is not free, but it is not alienated. We have also a *donatio retento usufructu*, which only gives a reversion of the property. Here also certain rights may be reserved against the ultimate possessor.

Another interesting point is that property may be credited to a man, and set off against other liabilities, so that he may never actually be in possession, but only nominally passing it on to others, and even, eventually, it may come back to the first owner, who may never part with it at all.

Restrictions on free gifts

Undoubtedly men were at liberty in daily life to make presents one to another. But the rights of the family were so strong that for the most part all the property of the parents was jealously regarded as tied to the children, or other legal heirs. When a man died, his property was divided according to a rigid law of inheritance. When a woman left her father's house to be married, the father gave her the share of his goods which fell to her, without waiting until his death to divide his substance. In this case she had nothing further at his death. But the property was not her husband's, though he and she shared its use; it was entailed to her children. If she had none, it went back to her father's house: to her brothers, if she had any, or to her father's other heirs. Unless a man legally adopted his natural sons, they did not inherit. Hence neither man nor woman was wholly free to give. But, hedged about with consents and reservations, donations took place.

The conditions of any gift

We have a great variety of types of donation, not always easy to classify, and often obscure, in some details. The common characteristics are that deeds of gift were duly executed, sealed, and witnessed; and that the consents of the parties, whose expectations were thus diminished, or restricted, had to be obtained.

Establishment of a daughter who became a votary

A daughter might be portioned off for marriage and this involved a gift, which might be treated as a donation, but rather comes under the head of marriage-portion, in the chapter on marriage. Precisely the same portioning took place when the daughter either became a votary or was dedicated to the service of a god. Such gifts may be included here. They usually contain a list of property: sharing houses, land, slaves, jewels, money, clothes, household furniture, even pots of honey or jars of wine. As a rule, in our present state of knowledge, nothing that could pretend to be an accurate translation can be given of the items of such a gift, only a general idea of the nature of the whole. Such a gift, however, evidently set the lady up in an establishment of her own, with all she could require for maintenance and comfort for the rest of her life.

Rights in a gift made by a votary

Here these donations split up into separate classes. The recipient might have only a life interest in her gift, or it might be hers outright. The latter case could not be presumed. The heirs of her parents, "her father's house," would maintain their claim at her death, unless they had specially contracted to waive it. Then the clause was inserted that she might "give her sonship to whomever she pleased," *ašar eliša tâbum aplûtsa inadin.*[1] By "sonship" is meant "heirship." Such cases do not seem common and are probably to be explained as due to the fact that as a votary she had no legitimate heir. It is important to note that there is no hint that, if she died without heirs, the temple would inherit.

Gifts made by a father to a daughter

A modified freedom is allowed by a father who gives his daughter house, land, sheep, slaves, and the like, but limits her power of gift to her brothers. But among them she may "give it to him who loves and serves her."[2] It is assumed that one of her brothers will care for her and manage her estate and be rewarded by the reversion of it. As a rule, it is only a life interest which the recipient has.

A different sort of gift is where the donor reserves to himself a use of the property as long as he lives, or stipulates for a life allowance from it. These are usually accompanied by formal adoption. The recipient is one who has not already a claim to inherit, but undertakes the care or maintenance of the donor. Such gifts are best classed under

[1] M. A. P.. 7. [2] B[1] 675.

adoption, even where the fact of adoption is not stated. When a parent makes an arrangement of this kind with a son or daughter, these were possibly adopted by a previous act. At any rate, it seems likely that such a child was either unmarried or again free to wait upon the donor. But whatever the actual state of relationships, we find a mother giving property to a daughter, reserving the use of it as long as she lives.[1] Similarly a brother undertakes to give one shekel *per annum* to his brother. Here the grounds of the undertaking are not stated, but a contract to do this is duly sealed and witnessed.[2] Further, maintenence is stipulated for, though the relationship is not stated, nor grounds given. This may not be based upon a gift, but follow the order of some judge, for other reasons.[3]

Pin-money for a wife

The husband might settle upon his wife a fixed amount of property. This was frequently done and was called the *nudunnu*. It might include a house, two maids, clothes, jewelry, and household furniture.[4] Here the sons are expressly said to have no claim, she may give it to whoever serves her and "as her heart desires." Probably she was a second wife without children, and is thus secured a life of comfort and the faithful service of her step-sons. As a rule these gifts are best considered under the head of marriage, but they were also free gifts on the donor's part. The wife in any case had her right to inherit with her step-sons, if her husband made no such settlement.

Consent of heirs to the disposal of property

The consent of the legal heirs of the donor to such alienation of their reversionary rights was needed. Thus in one case, when a man gives his daughter a house, his son appears as the first witness.[5] A father and his son give their daughter and sister a house, which she is free to give to her son, "whom she loves."[6] Had the house merely come to

---

[1] B[1] 39. [2] M. A. P., 6. [3] B[2] 324.
[4] B[2] 2504. [5] B[2] 544. [6] B[2] 729.

her as her share in the usual way, it must have been shared by her sons. If she had none, then her brother would be the next heir. That she can leave it as she will must be a matter of legal instrument. The brother must consent to the exception to the rule.

Donation in Assyria

In Assyrian times, donation is rarely represented within the group of documents which have reached us. Here is one case:[1]

> The household which Bêl-nâ'id gave to his daughter, Baltêa-abate. A house in Nineveh, before the great gate of the temple of Shamash. (Then come the servants, a *šaḳu* or head man, a washerman, a *šaknu*, and others, male and female, in all eleven souls.) Dated the fourteenth of Adar, in the Eponymy of Marduk-shar-uṣur. Nine witnesses.

This may be donation, or adoption, or even a marriage-portion.

At all times, a difficulty arises from the phraseology of the deeds of gift. When we are told that "A has given B such and such things," we do not know the ground of the gift. "To give for money," *nadânu ana kaspi*, is the usual expression for "to sell." In the older documents *šarâḳu*, "to present," often occurs, but has in most cases the derived technical sense "to dower," or "give a marriage-portion." Hence, we are not able to judge whether what appears as "gift" may not really be "a sale," or some payment meant to complete the portioning off of a daughter, on marriage or taking vows.

In the Second Babylonian Empire

There are, however, a large number of deeds of gift which have reached us from the Second Babylonian Empire. The characteristic formula may be taken to be *ina ḫûd libbišu iknukma pâni ušadgil*, "in the joy of his heart (*i.e.*, of his own free will, implying that no consideration was taken *per contra*) he has sealed and placed at the dis-

[1] A. D. D., No. 619.

posal of." As a rule, we may suspect these to be "gifts" to which the recipient had a right. Thus, mother to son,[1] brother to sister,[2] man to wife and daughter,[3] mother to daughter,[4] are not free from suspicion. But when a man gives maintenance to wife and son,[5] brother gives dower to sister,[6] father-in-law gives son-in-law arrears of his daughter's dower,[7] and wherever there is a hint that the "gift" was a *nudunnû*, or a *šeriḳtu*, we may regard the case as not properly "donation," but "dower."

The following example shows the limitations on free gift that still remained in later times.[8] Zêrûtu had married and had a son, Shâpik-zêri. Then he had an intrigue with Nasikâtum, daughter of the Sealand scribe, who bore him a son, Balâṭu. He gave Balâṭu a house, but did not adopt him. After Zêrûtu died, Shâpik-zêri demanded the house as his father's heir. The judges gave it to him and also the deed of gift. An example

The dedication of land to a temple or of a child to the service of a god may be considered as examples of free gift; but they are of a nature deserving separate consideration. We have already noticed some cases of such donations by the kings. We know from the Code that a father might dedicate a child as a votary,[9] and he might portion that child; but this did not bring a free gift to the temple, for the family had the reversion of the votary's property. Dedications

As a further example of dedication by a private owner, we may take the following:[10]

As temple of the god Lugalla (the king) and his consort Shullat, Nûr-ilishu, son of Bêl-nada, has dedicated to his god one *SAR* of improved land, for his life (salvation), has devoted it to his god. Pîsha-Shamash shall be the priest of the temple. Nûr-ilishu shall lay no claim to the priesthood. The curse of Shamash and of Sumulâ-ilu be on him who disputes the settlement. Seven witnesses. To the chief priest of a temple

1 Nbd., 65. 2 Nbd. 1098. 3 Nbd. 334. 4 Nbd. 368. 5 Nbd. 113. 6 Nbd. 258. 7 Nbd. 348. 8 Nbk. 109. 9 § 180 f. 10 B[3] 704.

This is total alienation. The donor is not making an indirect provision for himself, but waives all claims to be the chief priest of the temple.

Of children to Shamash

Here is an example of a dedication of children :[1]

> Tablet of Ishtar-ummi and Aḫatâni, daughters of Innabatum. Innabatum, daughter of Bur-Sin, has dedicated them to Shamash. As long as Innabatum lives, Ishtar-ummi and Aḫatâni shall support her, and after Innabatum, their mother [is dead], no one among her sons, their brothers, shall have any claim on them for anything whatever. They have sworn by Shamash, Malkat, Marduk, and Apil-Sin. Fifteen witnesses (of whom the first two are probably the brothers, the rest females, probably all votaries of Shamash and members of the convent.)

In another case, a mother dedicates her son to Shamash,[2] with the stipulation that the son shall support her as long as she lives.

To secure divine favor

In Assyrian times we have an example[3] of a dedication of a son to Ninip, by his mother, with consent of her brothers and their sons. A father also dedicates his son to Ninip[4] for the well-being of Ashurbânipal, King of Assyria. This is interesting as showing that the dedicator acquired merit, which he could transfer to another. Both tablets are defective. In another case, Aḫi-dalli, the lady governor of one quarter of Nineveh, purchases a large estate and presents it to some god "for the health of the king."[5] Votive tablets giving the presentation of various articles to some god are common enough at all periods.

Testaments or bequests

Testamentary devolution of property was not the rule in Assyria or Babylonia, where the law of inheritance was so firmly fixed that it would be naturally illegal. As a rule, children did not inherit under their fathers' will, but by right. However, the Code allows a father to give his mar-

---

[1] B[8] 2183. [2] B[2] 349.
[3] A. D. D., 640. [4] A. D. D., 641. [5] A. D. D., 643.

ried or vowed daughter power to leave her property as she will,[1] and it is probable that he had the same power over at least some of his property. The very frequent cases of adoption, where the adopted child becomes heir, on condition of supporting the parent as long as he lives, and the cases of gift *retento usufructu*, are a sort of testamentary disposition of property.

This developed with time into something very like testament. But we always have to bear in mind that conditions may have been understood which are not actually expressed.

Later Babylonian examples

Some examples from later Babylonian times will serve to illustrate how near these transactions came to testament. A very interesting case is where a son, probably childless, if not unmarried, and perhaps not in good health, gives his father his property. The document is very involved, but the chief points are these: A married B and they had a daughter C, who married D. The son of C and D is the testator. He leaves to his father D all the property which he inherited from A and B, which they had left to their daughter's son. It consisted of a house, fields, and slaves. He leaves it to his father "forever," only he is to retain the enjoyment of it as long as he lives. He therefore expects his father to survive him.[2]

Here is another interesting example:[3]

The division which A made with his sons B and C. The benefice of dagger-bearer (official slaughterer) in the Ishḫara temple he assigns to B. The benefice of the shrine of Papsukal in the temple of Bêlit-shami-erṣiti, situated on the bank of the canal, and the sown corn-field on the Dubanîtu canal he gave to his younger son C. All his property out in business he assigned to his mother and his two sisters. Certain dates in the possession of two of his debtors he gave to his two sisters. A fugitive slave, not yet recovered, to his mother and sisters. The house, which by a former deed he had

[1] § 178. [2] Cyr. 277. [3] A. B. R., ii., 20 f.

given to his mother and sisters, shall be theirs according to the former deed. As long as his mother lives, she shall enjoy the property formerly assigned her. The benefice of the dagger-bearership in the temple of Ishḫara, which he had formerly assigned to his mother, she has freely intrusted to his son B. As long as she lives, B and C shall live in the house with her. The income of his mother his sons shall enjoy with her. She shall give marriage-portions to his sisters, her daughters, from her own marriage-portion.

This is very like a last will and testament. The man clearly expected to die shortly. He had married and had two sons, but seems to have lost his wife. He had evidently brought his mother and sisters to live with him. He provides for his sons, his mother, and sisters. Evidently his mother is the guardian of the boys. She is expected to leave the boys all the property that was his and to dower the sisters from her own fortune.

# XXII

## SALES

Alienation of property in perpetuity was a matter for serious consideration, where all property was as much that of the family as of the individual. A change of ownership, particularly in the case of land or house, also directly concerned the neighbors. Hence the deeds of sale are imposing documents. Whether the object sold was a piece of land, a house, or a slave, the same general treatment was accorded to it. Their importance

There were the same formalities as in all deeds. First the purchaser approached the vendor and there was an interchange of ideas, often through a third party, prolonged over a considerable space of time. When etiquette had been satisfied and all the preliminary haggling was over, the parties agreed upon a scribe, who was made acquainted with the terms of the sale, already verbally agreed upon, and he set down in the imperishable clay the legal instrument which should bind the parties to their contract forever. The formal preliminaries

Undoubtedly both parties took a copy, and it seems clear that a third was deposited in the temple archives as a sort of registration of title. It seems probable that each party sealed the copy held by the other, but this surmise awaits confirmation. As a rule, the same seal seems to have been used for all copies, and the witnesses in early times also affixed their seals. A more exhaustive study must be made before this can be regarded as certain. Even where dupli- The registration of titles cates exist in our museums, it has been usual to publish only one.

The method of identifying the property transferred and the parties concerned

As a rule, the scribe followed a very definite plan. First he made clear the identity of the property. This was the specification. In the case of land, neighbors were set down, boundaries given, in some cases the size of the plot. In each sale the specification is very important. The personal identity of the parties was usually sufficiently fixed by appending to their names those of their fathers. In many cases, the office or rank held by a party is added. Occasionally the name of the grandfather, or clan-father is added. When either party was a stranger, his nationality, or city, or tribe, is given. As a rule, the same information is attached to the names of witnesses. These notes of personal identity are very valuable, for they furnish means for reconstructing long genealogies, and they throw much light on the intercourse of varied peoples. Babylonia seems always to have had a very mixed population.

Means of protecting the buyer from fraud

Having made it impossible for any mistake to arise as to the property sold or the parties concerned, the scribe proceeded to guard against errors regarding the nature of the transaction. The house or other property "was sold," "the money paid," "in full," and so on. Then he sought to make it clear that there could be no withdrawal from the bargain, nor after-claims raised. There was danger that the family might put in a claim to the property. An illustration of this is a suit brought to reclaim a house sold, which was the claimant's reversion—an actual redemption of ancestral property. From such perils the buyer was protected by heavy penalties on the seller, who in fact engaged to indemnify him.

The legal verbiage

These and many other complicated questions must have long been the subject of consideration in Babylonian legal circles. As a consequence, the scribe usually drew up the deed, in set terms, with a formula consecrated by long use, every turn of which was important.

The following is a good example of the way a scribe drew up a deed of sale:[1]

A specimen deed of sale

> Tappum, son of Iarbi-ilu, "has bought two *GAN* of field, in the Isle, next to the field of Ḫasri-kuttim, and the field of Sin-abushu, son of Ubar-Ishtar, from Salatum, daughter of Apilia, the *GI-A-GI (?)* and has paid its full price in silver. The business is completed, the contract is valid, his heart is content. In future, man with man, neither shall take exception. By the name of Shamash, Marduk, Sin-mubaliṭ and the city of Sippara, they swore."

Then follows a list of about twenty witnesses, the names of whose fathers are also given. Usually the date is added. Here, however, it is either omitted or has been lost.

The body of the document in Sumerian

In this particular case the words within quotation marks are written in Sumerian. The variations are slight as a rule, but enough to show that the scribe understood what he wrote and could make correct changes when needful. The use of such a large amount of Sumerian in these deeds, along with Semitic names and specifications, has often been compared to the retention of Latin words in the body of legal documents in European countries, almost to the present day. It will be noted that this portion constitutes the formal body of the document, and might well have been kept ready written, blanks being left to fill in the names and specifications. It is not, however, easy to find proof that this was done in early times.

Later deeds often in Semitic only

Somewhat later, in the time of the First Dynasty, a number of these Sumerian words and expressions are replaced by their Semitic equivalent. Indeed, some deeds are Semitic only. We can by comparison make a fairly complete study of Sumerian legal terms. To some extent this was already done by the scribes who drew up the series of

[1] M. A. P., p. 37.

phrase-books called *ana ittišu.* But many new forms occur in these deeds.

The specifications of the deeds the items of permanent interest

To translate all the contract-tablets would be useless, for all the deeds of sale are exactly alike, except the names of parties, witness, or neighbors, and the specification of the property. The repetitions were necessary, for each deed required an exact statement. But it is sufficient, having once noted the style of document, to call attention to the peculiarities of the specifications.

The earnest money

Very interesting are the references to earnest money, or the gift presented to close the bargain. As early as the time of Manistusu [1] we find not only a price paid, but also a present given to the seller as a good-will offering. These are of a most varied and valuable nature.[2] As already pointed out by Meissner,[3] in the purchase of a slave for four and a half shekels, a little present of fifteen *ŠE*, or one-twelfth of a shekel, was thus added. Likewise when another slave and her baby were sold we find that in addition to the price of eighty-four shekels, one shekel is thrown in as a present.[4] I do not recall the occurrence of this custom in Assyrian times, but in the later Babylonian documents it is common. There it is often referred to as the *atru*, or "over-plus." Thus we find that in the sale of a house in the time of Nebuchadrezzar III.,[5] besides the "full agreed price," *šîmu gamrûtu*, of half a mina of silver, the buyer gave one shekel of silver, *kî atri*, "as an addition," and "a dress for the lady of the house." The whole payment thus made of thirty-one shekels was called the *šibirtu.* So in the time of Darius (?) we find that, in addition to the full price of three minas, five shekels of silver, the buyer adds, *kî atri*, six shekels of silver and a dress for the lady of the house, making three minas, eleven shekels of silver as the *šibirtum*,[6]

Common in later Babylonian deeds

[1] D. E. P., ii., p. 1—f. [2] See p. 236. [3] M. A. P., p. 96.
[4] B. 320. [5] K. B., IV., p. 298 f. [6] B. V., p. 168.

or simply to a price of two minas of bright silver he adds two shekels, *ki pi atar*, making a *šibirtu* of two minas, two shekels of bright silver.[1]

The notary's fee

Equally interesting are the sums charged as fees to the scribe. This was paid to him expressly for obtaining the seller's seal or nail-mark as a conclusion of the contract.[2] Thus at the end of a deed or sale of a single male slave, executed by three owners by affixing three impressions of the same seal, and drawn up by one scribe, we read "Seven shekels of silver for their seal." The price was about one hundred and forty shekels. Thus the scribe received a fee of five per cent. on the sale price.[3] The ratio was not constant. It might be as low as two per cent. Thus in the case of a sale of a slave by two owners, who made four nail-marks in lieu of seals, we read "one mina of bronze for their nail-marks." There was but one scribe, and the price was fifty minas of bronze.[4] Hence we cannot think that this fee was paid for the scribe's seal, as some have done. The seal, or nail-mark, was not "the authenticating subscription by the notary," but by the seller.

Assyrian deeds of greater length

In Assyrian times the deed of sale was a much longer document. The same general form is observed, but the document starts with a heading giving the information that the seller had sealed the document, or, in the absence of a seal, had impressed his nail-mark. No one but the seller ever seals or impresses his nail-mark. The seller is usually described as the *bêlu*, or "legitimate" owner of the property made over. Then first after the seal, or in a space left for it, comes the specification of the property. Next it is stated that the buyer has made a bargain and taken the property for so much. But the bulk of the document is devoted to a contract that the seller, his representatives, heirs, and as-

[1] K. A. S., p. 48.
[2] A. D. D., pp. 35 ff.
[3] A. D. D., No. 173.
[4] A. D. D., No. 176.

signs, shall never rescind the sale, or bring any suit to recover possession, under specified and heavy penalties. The wording of these passages recalls most strikingly the imprecations of the kings in their charters upon those who, in after times, should dare to render their gifts inoperative. This grand style is one of the many indications that for the Assyrian period most of the deeds we have were drawn up on behalf of the king's household.

Various interests regarded as having claims which must be distinctly met

It is usually stated that the purchase is complete, the full price paid and delivery of possession made. But in some cases this was a mere conventional statement, and both payment and delivery were delayed. There was to be no return of the goods, no turning back from the bargain; the pleading of a suit of nullity of sale is expressly barred. It is of interest to notice who were regarded as competent, or likely to take action to recover the property. Sons, grandsons, brothers, brothers' sons, are all named. The enumeration clearly included females of the same nearness of kinship. Sisters are actually named. All these relatives are included in the term "his people." In some cases the *šaknu*, or governor of the district, is named, especially where slaves are sold, or the estate involved the transfer of serfs. The *šaknu* clearly had rights over lands and slaves within his district. The transfer of property might act injuriously to his rights. It was usual to stipulate that he had no such rights. How they had been annulled we do not know. Perhaps by some previous charter conferring exemption. The *ḫazânu* also appears to have had the right to intervene. The country seems to have been split up into districts which were called on to furnish fifty units, each consisting of an archer and a spearman or shield-bearer. Hence, the *rab ḫanšâ*, or "captain of fifty," was really in command of a hundred men. Whether this obligation lay on a group of a hundred families or not, it is clear that the transfer of ownership of land might lead to embarrassment of the official. Hence, the *rab ḫanšâ* was likely to intervene also. There was service on public works also concerned in the matter. Whatever official was *bêl ilki*, or had right to "the levy," might intervene. The chief of a certain district was called a *rab kiṣir*; he was also commander of a section of the army, and he had the right to intervene. Other officials as the *šâpiru*, *ḳurbu*, are named, but in all cases the nature of the claim must have been similar. The object of the buyer was to stipulate that the seller should hold him exempt from such claims. How this could be done does not appear.

The oath to observe the contract made between the parties still appears, but is not common. As before, these oaths are of interest, for the light which they throw upon local cults. The gods were invoked as being the avengers of wrong. The decision of the king was also still regarded as a source of vengeance, since he was bound to see right done.

Occasional use of the oath of confirmation

The penalties most commonly invoked were payments to the treasury of a temple. These were in the nature of forfeits. The sum set down in the deed rarely bears any exact relation to the value of the property, but is merely a large amount. Usually, a sum in both silver and gold is stated, but no relation between the relative worths of the metals can be deduced. The forfeit might take the form of presenting two or more white horses to the god. In a few cases, the penalty consisted in the devotion of a child, usually the eldest son or daughter, to a god. The verb used for "devoting" a child literally means to "burn." This seems to point to an earlier sacrifice of children by fire. But variants show that it was now used in a more general sense of dedication. The "cedar wood of Ishtar" is named as the spot where a daughter was to be dedicated. Further,

Penalties for the failure to carry out a contract

other objects might be dedicated as a forfeit. A great bow of bronze to Ninip of Kalḫu is named.

A deterrent penalty was to return the price "tenfold" to the seller. Once or twice the penalty is "twelvefold." A further penalty was to pay a talent of lead to the governor of the city or state. Very curious is the penalty of being required to eat a mina of some food, possibly a magical compound, and drink an *agannu* pot of some drink. That this drink was taken from a bowl inscribed with magical formulæ seems to be the best way of reading the signs. The penalty was, therefore, an ordeal. Then, if the contention was right, the plaintiff would be immune; if he was merely litigious, perhaps he would be sick or even die.

Rights of the purchaser

Finally, it is often laid down that, if either party (especially the seller) shall attempt to bring a suit about the property, the judge shall not hear him, or if he insists, he shall lose the action. Throughout it is clear that the buyer tries to make the seller contract to waive all rights to recover his property, but he holds to certain rights of his own. Thus, in the sale of slaves, a clause is frequently inserted which claims a hundred days within which to set up a claim to repudiate the purchase, on the ground that the slave is afflicted with certain diseases, the *ṣibtu* and *bennu*, the character of which is not exactly known. Also he bargains that a blemish may be at any time an excuse for annulling the bargain. These really amount to demanding a guarantee from the seller that the slave was free from disease or other undisclosed weakness.[1]

Late tablets include the details of bargaining

The later Babylonian tablets do not illustrate much that is of great interest. They often record the initial verbal discussion. Thus we find that when A bought of B, some phrase like the following is recorded: A said thus to B: "Give me thy property and I will give thee so much silver."

[1] For details see A. D. D., iii., pp. 288–368.

Then we read that "B listened to him and gave A his property and A gave him so much silver." It is a curious little touch of verisimilitude.

Deferred payments

Sales usually were for the full price, or the agreed price, paid down at once. This is expressly stated. But in the later Babylonian times we have some examples of deferred payment, which may also have been common during earlier periods. Thus, a man sold a slave for fifty shekels and received twenty-five shekels as advance price. The rest was to be paid later.[1] The payment was probably made soon. Thus we find a lady selling four female slaves to a certain man and taking a bond of him to pay four shekels, the balance of the price, on the second of Kislev, a week later.[2] The interval might be two days only;[3] but sometimes a much longer period of grace was allowed—as much as two months and seven days—although the purchase was taken away at once.[4]

Return of purchase on failure to pay

It is occasionally stipulated that if the purchase-money is not paid by a certain date, the object purchased shall be returned. Thus S, having sold B some slaves, took a bond of him that, if B did not pay in a week, he would return them.[5]

Retention of purchase without settlement

A long retention of the thing purchased—especially when it was profitable—without payment, was of course a loss to the seller. Hence, we find the seller of a slave taking a bond of the buyer that, if he did not pay on the date fixed, he should return the slave and his *mandattu*, or the income which a slave paid to his master.[6]

Fraud

A distinct case of fraud occurs[7] in the sale of a slave belonging to A by his brother B without A's knowledge. To make the matter worse, B had the contract drawn up in A's name. This was doubtless represented to be a case of agency, but there is no conclusive evidence.

---

[1] Page 104. [2] Nbd. 807. [3] Camb. 114. [4] Nbk. 103. [5] Camb. 165. [6] Nbk. 103. [7] L. 19.

The records of sales found at an early date

One of the earliest inscriptions, the stele of Manistusu, records the purchase of large estates to form a possession for his son Mesalim, afterwards King of Kish. The whole inscription is splendidly published in photogravure in the *Mémoires de la Délégation en Perse*, Tome II., pp. 1–52. It is divided into a number of sections each recording a separate purchase. One example will suffice as characteristic of all:[1]

> A field of seventy-three *GAN*, its price being two hundred and forty-three and seven-fifteenths *GUR* of corn, at the rate of one shekel of silver a *GUR* of corn; price in silver, four minas, three shekels, and one "little mina," the price of the field, and half a mina, six shekels and a fraction of silver, as a present to close the bargain; one garment for A, son of B, in presence of C, priest of Zamama (god of Kish); one garment for D, son of E. Total, two garments present for the field. Total, two men serfs of the field and food and money for the sons of C, priest of Zamama.

Their varied information

Here are many noteworthy pieces of information. The price of corn is fixed with relation to silver. It remained the same down to late Babylonian times. A present was given in addition to the price, as in many sales even to the latest times. The serfs go with the land. Certain food and money allowances are reserved to the priest C and his descendants. This was probably a territorial charge. Many other points of interest are furnished by the other sections. Thus, among the presents given are numerous vessels of gold, silver, and copper. The garments are of various kinds. The men who receive presents do not appear to be merely the sellers, but also elders of the city or district. This indicates a tribal or district right of control over the alienation of land. The boundaries of the estates are often given and are of great interest for topography. A number of persons are named as witnesses to the separate sales. In one

---

[1] Col. 8, l. 5.

way or another some five hundred persons and about forty places are named. Over forty titles or names of professions are given. Among them we note many familiar in later times, the *abrakku*, *nagiru*, *patêsi*, *Šakkanak*, as well as a king. We see already judges, merchants, scribes, irrigators, boatmen, carpenters, singers, shepherds, seers, branders, as well as slaves. We read of sheep, asses, goats, oxen. And all this from one inscription. It is a fine example of the kind of information this class of documents may afford. Not least in importance is the fact that many Semitic, as well as Sumerian, names and words occur.

**Method of legally describing real estate**

In the case of landed property the deeds of sale usually specify its position. In the case of fields and gardens four neighbors are often specified. Their plots of land then completely enclosed the plot concerned. What rights of access to such a plot existed does not appear, but where the boundaries were low mounds or ridges, it may be assumed that the tops of these were common to all for access and carriage. In towns, more usually three neighbors are named, the fourth side is often said to be on the street. Sometimes four neighbors are given for a house, but then an exit, *mûṣû*, is specified, which doubtless means a right of way through, or past, another house to the street. When more than four neighbors are named, it is probably the case that on one side the plot was conterminous, at least partly, with two of them. Very commonly only two neighbors are given, one each side. We may then presume that there were streets or lanes both front and back. If we could press the term *bîtu* to mean "house," we might conclude from many cases that the old Babylonian cities contained streets of houses, which were one conterminous block of buildings. But they seem in very many cases to have had some open ground, and often gardens were attached.

These boundaries are of great interest both from the

Importance of these boundary inscriptions

point of view of population and geography. Were we able to consult all the documents which were once stored in the archives of one great temple, we might map out a city and assign each plot to its owner; and then extend our map and the names of owners to the fields and plantations which lay around the city. For outside the city walls the *ugaru* or town-land extended to a considerable distance from the city walls. We may even soon be able to determine what was the approximate extent of this margin about the city, a belt of land often called a *ḳablu* or "girdle."

Many of the details puzzling

Usually the plots are said to be in a city whose name is given. Thus we conclude the close proximity of Laḫî, Ishkun-Ishtar, Malgia, Ḫalḫalla, to Sippara. Indeed, they were probably conterminous with it. Often the plot is stated to be in some quarter, or ward of the city. For the most part the names of these wards, as for example Gagim, Karim, are difficult to understand. Why or how they obtained these names we cannot tell. It is noteworthy that one ward was called Amurru, "the Amorite land." Much has been made of this by Professors Hommel and Sayce, but we are still far from clear ideas on the point. With respect to other indications of locality, it must be noted that they are usually at the end of the first line at the right-hand top corner of the tablet, and have suffered defacement more often than any other detail, so that they are often illegible.

Plots often, but not invariably rectangular

From many considerations it appears that most of these plots were rectangular, but it is curious to note that many plans of houses and fields exist which show that this was not always the case. Perhaps it was the irregularity of the outline which made plans necessary and they may be an indirect witness to the rarity of such a feature.

Plans of houses

As a rule the private houses seem to have been small and to have had a few small rooms. The palaces, or mansions of the great, had much more extensive conveniences. One reads of several specially defined rooms, but their names do not as a rule tell us much of their use. Wash-houses, shops, stables, granaries, and vacant plots, as well as gardens and orchards, are often attached. Apparently one had to leave the house to enter these. The houses were built of brick and their roofs were supported by strong beams. In many plans, while the doorways for internal communication are carefully marked, there seems to be no access from the street. Perhaps this is a peculiarity of the architect's ideas of a plan, the door to the street being understood. At any rate, doors, bolts, posts, and a lintel are frequently named. These were often put in by the tenant and, like the beams, taken away by him. A door might be pledged alone. But it is possible that some houses had no door proper, being entered by steps leading to the roof. This may be the explanation of the oft-mentioned *mûṣû* or right of way out, either between, through, or over, other house property. When a house had other houses touching it on each of four sides, something of the kind was necessary.

Probably the house did not usually have an upper story; but, perhaps, as a remarkable exception, an "upper house" is occasionally mentioned. There is reason to think that some were in the form of a quadrangle, around an inner court; as there are wells, or fountains, mentioned as being "within the house." In some parts of the city, at any rate, the block of buildings was continuous. But there were many streets, and canals also, in the cities. The streets, *suḳê*, were as a rule only narrow lanes or passages. As shown by the excavations at Nippur, houses stood for a long time. When first used, the floors were above the street level, but after the footpaths had been some time in use, they rose to the level of, and finally above, the floor, so that there were steps leading down into the house.[1]

It seems evident that great efforts were made to provide drains for the foundations; and perhaps other sanitary appliances were found in the better class of houses. But we must await more extensive exploration, not necessarily in the more important mounds, before we are able to give a clear account of an ancient Babylonian house.

Description of houses in the contracts of sale

In the sale of a house it was often stated that the house was in good condition.[2] In this respect many particulars might be recited, or the whole summed up in one concise phrase. In the early Babylonian documents no good example is yet published in which all the points are mentioned. We must refer to an example of Assyrian times,[3] where all the chief points occur together. Early Babylonian tablets mention nearly all of these items, but only one or two at a time. Thus we have a note that the beams and doors are sound. Wood was scarce, and a tenant usually stipulated to take away the beams and doors, if he put them in. The fact that a man might pledge a door[4] suggests that the modern theory of interchangeable parts was anticipated in Babylonia, so that a door would as a rule fit any house.

---

[1] One such plan is published by King (L. Ḫ., ii., p. 242) and discussed by him later (L. Ḫ., iii., p. 255 f.). There are many others in our museums, several of which have been published (*Receuil de Travaux*, xvii., pp. 33 ff.; *Saison de fouilles a Sippar*, pp. 125, 126, 128). The plans of the buildings excavated at Khorsabad form our most perfect specimen of an Assyrian city and palace. Besides the original sketches and plans in Botta's *Nineve*, excellent studies of them will be found in Perrot and Chipiez, *Assyrian and Babylonian Art*. There are also many plans of the early cities and palaces in De Sarzec's *Découvertes en Chaldée;* also, *Receuil de Travaux* and *Revue d'Assyriologie passim*.

[2] Good examples of deeds of sale of this class of real property will be found in Dr. Meissner's A. P., pp. 31–35. The principal terms used in such conveyances are well discussed and for the most part correctly explained in his commentary (pp. 119–23). In all these cases we have the phrase, *bîtu epšu*. Dr. Meissner also regards as "houses" the plots of land called *Ê KI-GAL* and *Ê KISLAH;* they are, however, mentioned later with some other plots of land where *Ê* denotes a "plot," not necessarily a "house."

[3] Page 244.

[4] K. 1297.

What the beams were for is far from clear. To carry screens or curtains of skins over a central court seems most likely. Actual roof-beams were probably included in the "roof" itself, which is mentioned separately from the beams. The threshold, or perhaps, rather, the lintel of the doorway, may be meant; and, with the door-posts, be included under beams. The bolt or crossbar of the door is often associated with these beams.

The streets mentioned as boundaries

Streets are more frequently named as boundaries of a house than in any other connection. The "great street," or "wide street," occurs continually. Whether this was the main street of Sippara, or only one principal thoroughfare, is not always clear. Streets are often named after a god; thus the street of Lugal-amgaba, of Ishtar, of Bunene, of Bêlit-nuḫshi occur. They were named after people; Immerum the king, or Kât-Ninsaḫ, whose house adjoined the street named after him. The gate of Sin and his garden are named. Canals, especially the *Nâr tupsarrûti*, the *Nâr Bilîa*, are named. Roads, as that to Ishkun-Ishtar, are sometimes given.

A deed of the First Babylonian Dynasty

The following is a good example of a deed of sale at the time of the First Dynasty of Babylon,[1] translated literally and illustrating the usual order of words:

One and two-thirds *SAR* of land built on,
next to the house of Nabi-ilishu,
and next to the house of Ilushu-ellatzu;
upper end, the house of Ḫaiabni-ilu,
its exit to that of Immarum,
*šar irbitim*
which is his own also;
from Nabi-ilishu,
Lamazi, the votary of Shamash,
daughter of Kasha-Upi,
by her written order

[1] $B^2$ 476.

has bought,
its full price
in cash has paid.
In future, party with party,
they shall not dispute.
By the name of Shamash, of Marduk,
and of Apil-Sin they have sworn.

Then follow the names of five witnesses, but there is no date given.

Its interesting historical information

The house was in Sippara, since it is known that Nabi-ilishu resided there.[1] The "exit," that is to say, the front door, opened on the road to the house of Immarum. The scribe means to say that Ḫaiabni-ilu, who was a neighbor, owned the house of Immarum. It appears that Immarum was *šar irbitim*, "king of the four quarters," a title often borne by Babylonian kings. There is a great probability then that Immarum was no other than the Immerum, once King of Sippara, in the reign of Sumu-lâ-ilu. It is not necessary to suppose him still alive. This deed was executed in the reign of Apil-Sin, whose father, Ṣâbum, had reigned fourteen years after the death of Sumu-lâ-ilu. Further, one of the witnesses, Sin-ublam, is said to be a son of Immerum.

Thus we may conclude that Immarum, or Immerum—the difference in spelling is slight for these times—King of Sippar, bore the title of "king of the four quarters," and as such was still remembered in Sippara. The exact meaning of the term has been disputed, but Sippara was a fourfold city: Sippar the great, Sippar Amnânu of the goddess Anunitum, Sippar Edinna, and Sippar Iḫrurum are named in the tablets of this dynasty. Perhaps the four quarters of Sippara are meant.

Lamazi, the buyer, daughter of Kasha-Upi, votary of

---

[1] B[2] 476.

Shamash, bought another house in the nineteenth year of Sinmubaliṭ,[1] borrowed a quantity of lead in the first year of Ḫammurabi,[2] and bought a female slave in a year of Ḫammurabi's reign, the date of which is not yet fixed.[3] The name Lamazi is common and was borne by several votaries of Shamash whom we know to be daughters of other men than Kasha-Upi. But she may well be the same as the lady who figures without such marks of identity in several other documents. For example, she is named as being a neighbor of Ilushu-ellatzu.[4]

The phrase *ina šapiriša*, "by her order," occurs often. It implies that Lamazi acted through an agent, when she borrowed the lead, she acted through a *mâr šipri*, a messenger and agent. She bought her other house in the same way. This does not imply any disability on the part of women to enter into business, for they were as free and competent to act as men. Nor does it arise from her being a votary of Shamash, for these ladies are concerned in by far the larger part of the transactions recorded at Sippara. It is merely the fact that on these occasions, as was frequently done, Lamazi employed a business agent, who is not named. Her father, Kasha-Upi, is referred to again as buying a house from the sons of Nabi-ilushu,[5] where we learn that the latter was a son of Shamash-ina-mâtim and brother of Kasha-Upi. Lamazi was therefore a niece of Nabi-ilushu.

Mention of the business agent

It will be noted that the price paid for the house is not given. This is often the case. But more commonly the price is named. As Dr. Meissner has already pointed out, prices varied greatly. Houses in a small provincial town like Tell Sifr naturally did not bring the same price as those in Sippara. But variation was probably even more due to situation and size. The lowest price per *SAR* was

Mention of the price of a house

---

[1] B² 332. [2] B² 1058. [3] B² 331.
[4] B² 2192. [5] B² 2190.

four shekels, the highest thirty shekels. This gives a wide margin.

An Assyrian deed for sale of a house

While there are many examples of the sale of houses in Assyrian times, they do not as a rule exhibit any important peculiarities. The best example comes from Erech[1] and may be taken as a representative specimen:

> The house of Ina-êshi-eṭir, son of Nabû-eṭir, a well-built house, furnished with door-frames, a roofed house, the door and crossbar of which are firm, in the quarter of Bît Kuzub-shamê-erṣiti, which is in Erech; upper side next Sulâ, Nabû-nâṣir and Bêl-aḫê-erba, sons of Eṭeru; lower side next Ereshu, son of Shama; upper end next Ṣillâ, son of Nabû-aḫiddin; lower end next Ereshu, son of Nabû-bêlâni; on each side the house of Ina-êshi-eṭir, son of Nabû-eṭir, more or less, so much as there is, for one mina fifteen shekels of silver, as price, he has intrusted to Ereshu. It is given, received, paid for, freed. An exception to the sale cannot be taken, there is no going back, neither shall implead the other. Hereafter, in future, in days to come, neither brothers, sons, family, relations on either side of the house of Ina-êshi-eṭir shall arise and lay claim or cause claim to be laid on this house, shall alter or complain saying [the usual pleas are understood here but omitted]. If so, he shall pay twelvefold. At the sealing of this tablet were present [then follow the names of five witnesses]. Dated in the twentieth year of Ashurbânipal. Ina-êshi-eṭir has impressed his nail-mark in lieu of a seal.

Various parts of the house

This example contains a full description of a house. The specification is rarely so full. But doors are always named, as many as six, in one case. Most of the Assyrian deeds of sale mention various adjuncts of the house. Thus the *tarbaṣu* or "court" is named. This was perhaps an attached walled enclosure.

It is the name given in the Code to the fold where sheep and oxen are kept.[2] Vines might grow in it,[3] and butter was kept there. A *bît kutalli*, or out-house, is named. Often *bît rimki*, or "wash-house," is also mentioned. This

[1] K. B., iv. p. 170 f. [2] § 266. [3] H. W. B.

was a chamber within the house, and may be rather meant for lustration, than for ordinary washing. One house had three of these rooms.[1] Sometimes there was a *bûru*, a "well," or cistern, within the house.[2] A "shop," or *bît ḳâtâti*, was often attached.[3] Stables, *bît abusate*, are named.[4] What is meant by *bît irši* is difficult to determine, perhaps some chamber fitted with beds and couches.[5] The *bît akulli* had a well in it, but what it was is not clear.[6] The *bîtu elîtu*[7] may be an "upper story." If so, most houses were one-storied only.

Another interior apartment is called a *kimaḫḫu*. This has usually been taken to be a "tomb." We know that the old Babylonian kings were buried in the palace of Sargon. But this was when the palace was no longer the abode of the living. Ashurbânipal's charter to his faithful general and tutor-in-arms, Nabû-shar-uṣur,[8] seems to contemplate that general's being buried in the palace, though this is not certain. However, the explorations of Nippur demonstrate the existence of vaults for burial, built over with brickwork. It may be that such vaults did exist within the house, and were sold with it. The burial-vault

A "portico," *bît mutirrêti*, is named once.[9] Beside the "great house," *bîtu dannu*, or *bitannu*, a "second house," *bît šanû*, is mentioned. The exit from the house, *mûṣû*, a way to the street, was often named, being very important where the house was bounded on four sides by others.

Most of the houses, of which we have deeds of sale, were situated in Nineveh itself. Occasionally, the house is shut in by more than three others, most often only by three. Then the fourth side is said or implied to be on the street. Block houses in Nineveh

---

[1] A. D. D., 320.
[2] A. D. D., Nos. 325–40.
[3] A. D. D., Nos. 341, 342.
[4] A. D. D., Nos. 326–34.
[5] A. D. D., Nos. 326–32.
[6] A. D. D., Nos. 340–49.
[7] A. D. D., Nos. 329–40.
[8] A. D. D., No. 646.
[9] A. D. D., No. 340.

Hence, we may be sure that in parts of Nineveh, there were continuous blocks of houses, on each side of a street. Sometimes, however, we have a garden, or orchard, as one boundary.

Size not mentioned

Contrary to the practice in Babylonia, the size of the house is rarely given. We have the size of the *bîtu akulli* given, in one case,[1] as forty-three cubits long and twenty cubits broad. What seem to be the dimensions of an ordinary house were twenty-two by fourteen cubits.[2]

The usual cost

Houses in Assyria sold for from half a mina up to twelve minas; but as long as we are so ignorant of the form, nature, and dimensions of the house and its adjuncts, the information is of very little interest.

Side buildings

A number of other buildings or parcels of land were sold with houses or separately. Thus, we read of a *papaḫu*, or chamber, which was beneath an adjoining beer-shop.[3] The beer-shop is often mentioned, and was a state-regulated institution.

Unimproved land

A term which was long somewhat of a puzzle, the *kigallu*, usually written *Ê-KI-GÀL*, or *Ê-KI-DAN*, is shown definitely by the Code[4] to be a plot of uncultivated land. This might be rented for cultivation and was not necessarily poor land, for it was expected to yield ten *GUR* per *GAN*. But it might also lie in a city bounded on four sides by houses,[5] or, as often, by three houses and the street. It was then, of course, a building site. Its price was usually about two shekels per *SAR*, but might be as high as eight shekels per *SAR*.[6]

Granaries

Another common object of sale was a building called *Ê KISLAḪ*, shown by the Code[7] to be really a "granary," or barn, read *maškanu*. These are usually in the city, and the prices paid for them varied from one-third of a shekel[8]

---

[1] A. D. D., No. 349. [2] A. D. D., No. 345. [3] M. A. P., 25. [4] § 44.
[5] B[2] 377. [6] B[2] 446. [7] § 113. [8] S. 67.

to fifteen shekels[1] per *SAR*. They might be surrounded by houses on all four sides, or by a canal, road, and street.[2]

The term *bîtu* means not only "house," but "field"

These examples serve to show that *bîtu* as often denoted a "plot" of land as a "house."[3] In Assyrian times we find the same usage. A fairly common object of sale is what I take to be a "fuller's field," or a "bleaching ground," *bîtu ḳakḳiri pûṣê*. It was usually in the city, of small size, given in cubits each way, or a trifle over a homer in area. It was near a stream. It sold for a very high price. Once we find half of it used as a garden. It seemed to have been fenced in. Unfortunately, no one example is perfectly preserved; and the deeds are of no special interest beyond the peculiar nature of the plot.[4]

Sales of gardens

The gardens in the time of the First Dynasty of Babylon are generally said to be planted with dates, and sold for "full" price. Once two shekels are given for a garden of fifteen *SAR*.

These sales less frequent in Assyrian times

There are not many examples of these sales in Assyrian times, but they give some welcome information. There is nothing peculiar about the sale formula. The only interest is in the specifications. The garden is usually said to be planted with the *iṣu tillit*, almost certainly "the vine." Hence, we may regard them as "vineyards." The number of plants in them is often given, being as high as two thousand four hundred.[5] Of other plants grown in a Babylonian garden we can recognize with more or less certainty in The Garden Tablet,[6] garlic, onion, leek, kinds of lettuce,

---

[1] B² 2192. [2] B² 2518.

[3] A plot of land or house called *Ê burbalum* is sold (B¹ 280, B² 838, B² 2462), but there is no information given as to its special nature; so also a *bît kidim* (B² 2444a), but there is no means of deciding what it was. A term applied to land which may be read *ḳirubû* is perhaps to be taken as "arable land" (*M. A. P., p. 122*). But the occurrences are not sufficient to fix the meaning clearly. It was bounded by a house and the street.

[4] A. D. D., Nos. 350–58.

[5] A. D. D., No. 362.

[6] Z. A., vi., pp. 291 ff.

dill, cardamom, saffron, coriander, hyssop, mangold, turnip, radish, cabbage, lucerne, assafœtida, colocynth.

Other gardens are said to be *kirû urḳîtu*, "vegetable gardens." In later times the date-plantations are continually in evidence. Beyond the specification, "planted with dates," and certain obscure references to the condition of the crop at the time of sale, there is nothing to be noted.

Sales of fields: in First Dynasty of Babylon

The sales of fields are very numerous. They were usually situated outside the city walls, in the *ugaru*, or town-land. They were not, however, reckoned outside the "town." For the town extended beyond its walls, like a parish in England; and was bounded, as a rule, by adjoining towns. In the case of Sippara, many of these *ugarê* are named; but as a rule, the names do not explain themselves. Thus, Azarim, Ḫiganim, and Shikat Malkat may be named after persons or temples. Other names, like Shutpalu, Nagû, Iblê, Tapirtum, may well be significant. Certainly, Ebirtim appears to mean "across" the Euphrates. Once the field is said to be in Sippara,[1] once in Ḫalḫalla,[2] but we cannot press these statements to mean "within the walls" of those cities. Usually, the boundaries of a field are four other fields, with now and then a road, or canal. The price per *SAR* varied from one-thirtieth of a shekel[3] to more than a mina. Very frequently, indeed, the price is simply said to be "full."

In Assyrian times

The fields in Assyrian times are often mentioned. Nearly always when a field, *eḳlu*, is sold, it is somewhere else referred to as *bîtu*, or plot, usually of so many homers in size. There is nothing distinctive about the sale formula. The specifications give most interesting and valuable data as to the topography of the land around Nineveh.[4] The accessories of a field may be named. Sometimes it was corn-land, *šê zêr*, part was *tabrû*, "open land," part *adru*, enclosed by

[1] B[1] 43. [2] B[2] 330. [3] B[1] 194. [4] A. D. D., Nos. 359–413.

a wall or fence. Pits or wells, canals or ditches, courts or folds, occur frequently as adjuncts of a field.

Great estates

Larger estates are built up of the simple elements which we have noted. Sometimes the estate was so large as to be styled a "city," *alu šê*. These "cities" are generally called after the name of some one, probably a former owner. But the number of people sold in them does not justify the use of any larger designation than "hamlet." A large estate, with a few people on it, obviously its bailiffs and the serfs of its landlord, constituted the *alu*. Hence, this term, like *bîtu*, must have a wider signification than that usually given it. Such hamlets were, doubtless, the germs of future cities, but the term evidently denotes simply a settled abode of a group of people.

Plans of estates

From very early times the Babylonians drew plans of estates, which are in many ways very instructive. The seated statue of Gudea, found by De Sarzec at Telloh, has a plan of his city upon a tablet on his lap, accompanied by a scale of dimensions or a standard of length.[1]

Professor Oppert, Dr. Eisenlohr, M. Thureau-Dangin, and others have discussed at length the plan of a field,[2] which has the sides of several plots given in linear measure and the areas in square measure. From this was obtained a great variety of results regarding the relations between the measures.[3]

---

[1] This plan is published in *Découvertes en Chaldée*, plate 15 ff.

[2] Published best in *Rev. Ass.*, iv., p. 13 f.

[3] Much earlier plans will be found, pp. 21 ff. They are ascribed to the age of Sargon I. and Naram-Sin. A plan, or rather map, of Babylon was also published by Dr. Peiser. [*Z. A.*, iv., 361 ff.] This is rather geographical than cadastral, and, perhaps, mythical, since it refers to the king Shamash-napishtim-usur, who may be the Shamash-napishtim of the flood story.

A number of other plans are given, or referred to, by Father Scheil in *Rec. des Trav.*, xvii., 1 and 2, pp. 33 ff. A good many more appear in *Une Saison de fouilles a Sippar*. There are many others in the great museums and in private hands. For conclusions regarding linear and square measures, cf. Appendix III.

# XXIII

## LOANS AND DEPOSITS

Records of loans of an early period

In the first epoch there are many examples of loans. The characteristic word *ŠU-BA-TI,* or *ŠU-BA-AN-TI,* which means "he has borrowed," has been used as a title and they are often called *ŠUBATI* tablets. They are the receipts given for the loans by the borrowers. Here is an example:

"Sixty *GUR* of corn, royal quality, from L have been received by B." Date. Seal of borrower.

In place of corn we may have money, dates, wool, or almost anything. Sometimes a date for repayment is given. In the examples there are usually no references to the interest to be paid for the loan. They may be regarded as advances made to temple tenants, or serfs, to be repaid at harvest from crops.

Their value for chronology

The greatest value of these tablets lies in their dates. The dates are usually events. Many of these have already been collected and registered, especially by Dr. H. Radau.[1] But there is even more to be done, when further examples are published. Many tablets contain two dates referring to loans contracted at different times. By this means the sequence can gradually be determined. The seals are also of great interest and often of value, as may be seen from Dr. Radau's work.

Advances of all sorts were freely made both with and

[1] E. B. H., pp. 254 ff., etc.

without interest. For convenience we may separate money from corn loans and advances of all kinds of commodities; but we must not forget that corn, at any rate, was legal tender; and silver loans might be repaid in corn. This, however, was early recognized as an inconvenience and it is quite common to find a direct stipulation that what was lent shall be repaid in kind. It soon became usual to state that if the loan was repaid otherwise, it must be according to a fixed ratio between silver and corn.

Second Epoch. Repayments in kind or its stated equivalent

A very large number of loans take the form of *Abstract schuldscheine*, loans without statement of any cause for the debt. They are merely promises to pay, that is, acknowledgments of indebtedness. Thus we read: "Five shekels of silver which A has given to B. On such a date B shall pay five shekels of silver to A." A penalty may be added for not paying on the fixed date. Usually this takes the form of interest. The rate is one shekel *per mina* each month, or twelve shekels *per mina yearly*, that is, twenty per cent. There is no clear case of money lent as an investment to bear interest. That was done in quite another way. The lender entered into relationship with an agent, to whom he furnished capital and who traded with the money and repaid it with interest.

Promissory notes

Most of the loans were evidently contracted to meet temporary embarrassment. Usually it was in connection with the need of cash to pay the expenses at harvest-time. The loan was then repaid at harvest. It might be repaid in corn.[1] The time was usually short—fifteen days is named.[2] The lender had his reward in obtaining his money's worth in corn, when its price was cheapest. But he was evidently not expected to charge interest. A similar kind of loan is half a mina of silver to pay the price of a piece of land. Here the money was lent until the land was bought,

Temporary loans at harvest-time

[1] B² 2524.

[2] M. A. P., 15.

and was to be repaid with interest of three *GUR* of corn.[1] So half a mina for certain land to be paid, when the land was cultivated.[2]

Loans for the payment of taxes

Another reason for borrowing was the need of money to pay taxes, *ana ilkim suddanim.*[3] In one of these cases the stipulation is added that the borrower shall bring the receipt of the tax-collector and then may take back his bonds.[4] Here the "sealed tablet" is in one case the receipt for the tax, in the other the receipt which the borrower gave for his loan. But there is no mention of his repayment. Perhaps the lender owed the tax, half a mina, and as it was a considerable sum, sent it by a third party, but made him give a receipt for it. But such a receipt would differ in no respect from the sort of bond mentioned above, and would render the messenger liable to repay the money; so he was to have his receipt back, on handing over the tax-collector's receipt showing that he had paid the tax.

The temple as places of temporary loans

In several cases the god is represented as lending the money. It is obvious that such advances were made from the temple treasury.[5] It is usual from such instances to expatiate on the temple, or the priests, as the great money-lenders. This is a view easily misunderstood. It is quite true that the temples were great landowners, and had steady incomes, and possessed treasuries; but there is no evidence that they lent on usury. It seems rather that these loans without interest (except as a fine for undue retention of the loan) were a kindly accommodation. We know that under certain circumstances a man might appeal to the temple treasury to ransom him from the enemy. He might also borrow in case of necessity without interest. Money-lending proper existed, but was kept in narrow bounds by the temple itself.

---

[1] B² 2519. [2] M. A. P., 19. [3] B¹ 218.
[4] *Kanik mušaddinim utbalunimma kanikšu illikû*, B² 754. [5] *M. A. P.*, 8, 9.

Current coin

In view of the many questions that arise as to the nature of the money at this period, it should be noted that the silver is often said to be *kanku;* literally "sealed." Whether this means that the silver bars, or ingots, were sealed while the metal was soft enough to receive a mark which would authenticate its weight and purity, or whether it means that the money was enclosed in sealed sacks, is hard to say. Against the latter may be urged that such a small sum as one and two-thirds shekels would not be sealed up.[1] But it may be that *kanku* means "sealed for," that is, acknowledged by the receipt.

Loans of corn

Even more common than money loans are the corn loans. Here the loans were generally for a short time just before harvest, when the repayment was expected. The period is usually short, five days,[2] or a month.[3] Interest is sometimes demanded, at the rate of *one hundred ḲA per GUR*, or one-third, that is, *thirty-three and a third per cent.* This was probably the rate *per mensem, four hundred per cent. per annum.* But in one case the interest is *one hundred ḲA per GUR per annum,*[4] once it is expressly said to be nothing,[5] usually it is not referred to at all. Sometimes a loan was partly in money, partly in corn.[6]

Other loans of produce

Other things were lent, as sesame, skins, bricks, and the like, but these loans exhibit no peculiarity. They are merely letting the borrower have goods on credit, to be paid for, or returned, after a time.

We may take, as an example of this kind of transaction, a rather more complicated case:[7]

Record of a loan

Two and seven-thirtieths of a *GUR* of corn, Shamash standard measure, which Ilu-kasha, son of Sharru-Shamash, gave to Belshunu, Ilushu-abushu, and Ikash-Ninsaḫ. Ilu-kasha brought the corn and returned one *GUR* and one-tenth and took for himself two hundred

[1] $B^1$ 218. [2] $B^3$ 771. [3] $B^1$ 642. [4] $B^1$ 655.
[5] *M. A. P.*, 24. [6] $B^2$ 1182, S. 76. [7] $B^2$ 869.

and twenty *ḲA*. Later he paid one-tenth of a *GUR* to Ilushu-bânî, Ikash-Ninsaḫ, and Shumma-Shamash, and they remitted in all three *GUR*, the former and later debt.

In the second case only one of the former debtors is left. The loan was partly repaid, a fresh loan contracted, and then partly repaid. It is not clear whether the arrears were remitted or extracted by distraint. Nor is it clear whether Ilukasha was debtor or creditor. As a rule such points are clear. It is only the conciseness of the formula which here causes the obscurity.

Loans or allowances in series

Another fairly common type of document contains a number of sections, each containing the record of one sum. But it is not clear that these were loans. They may be allowances for food or salary. Thus in B[1] 247 we have so much corn for the women weavers, so much more for the votaries, so much for other officials, from the first of one month to the thirtieth, so much for the Sutî who was watching the field, so much for a boatman, and so on. These are perhaps a temple steward's accounts. Their interest lies only in the incidental notices. We also note that here a month had thirty days. It is interesting to find that the celebrated Sutî nomads who later gave so much trouble, were already in the country and were employed to watch the fields. Was this watching done on the principle of "setting a thief to catch a thief"? Perhaps it was necessary to employ a Sutî as custodian, of course at a salary, if one was to preserve the crop from the depredations of his fellow-tribesmen.

Some of these tablets expressly state the amount of corn loaned, giving the date for repayment.[1] Hence we see what a narrow margin divides the proper bond from the mere receipt, or even the memorandum of the loan.

---

[1] B[2] 687.

A number of tablets deal with advances of wool or woollen yarn made by temple officials to weavers and dyers to work up. As a rule they contain a number of words connected doubtless with the weaver's craft which are not yet made out. The following is a fairly simple example:[1] Formal advances of working materials

One talent of wool belonging to the palace, price ten shekels of silver, property of Utul-Ishtar the *abi ṣâbê*, which Ishme-Sin, son of Sin-bêl-aplim, Marduk-mushallim, son of Sin-idinnam, Ilushu-ibni and Bêlshunu, sons of Sin-eribam have borrowed. The day that the tax-collector of the palace demands it they shall pay the money of the palace.

Elsewhere the time of loan may be stated, two months for example.[2] The price is always reckoned at six minas of wool for a shekel. It seems that the borrowers were not obliged to repay until a certain date, or until a demand was made for certain taxes. They then must pay in silver.

In the Assyrian examples of money-loans the same general features constantly recur. The most common are loans *ana pûḫi*, which may be taken to mean "for consideration," as the word *pûḫu* means an "exchange." But there is never any statement of what the consideration was. Some have thought, that as the bond was invariably given to the creditor to be broken up on the repayment of the loan, the exchange referred to was a restoration of the bond in return for the money. But the consideration, which is a legal presumption, may have lain in the fact that the borrowers were tenants on the metayer system and had a right to borrow of their landlord, free of interest, at seed-time and harvest. On such loans interest is only demanded when the debtor fails to repay at the fixed date. Assyrian loans *ana pûḫi*

The rate of interest charged as a penalty for non-payment or late payment was *twenty-five per cent. per mensem, three hundred per cent. per annum.* This interest was intended Usual rate of interest

[1] B² 684. [2] B² 701.

to secure prompt payment, but was not unfair in view of the increase of value obtained by investing it in corn and then sowing that. Other rates were one-third and one-eighth, but there is no fixed rate of interest for the loan of money, except when it was *ana pûḫi*.

For the use of corn

The interest on corn was *thirty ḲA per homer*. Some think the homer had sixty *ḲA*, which would make the interest fifty per cent. But no case has yet been found which gives the number of *ḲA* in a homer.

The coinage

The money lent is often said to belong to a god. Ashur, Ishtar of Arbela, or Ishtar of Nineveh, are the most common. Sometimes it is said to be in "Ishtar heads," which has been taken to mean ingots stamped with a head of Ishtar. The frequent reference to the mina of Carchemish alongside the king's mina is eloquent as to the commercial eminence of the old Hittite capital.

An example is the following:[1]

> Sixteen shekels of silver, from A to B, *ana pûḫi*, he has taken. On the first day of Tammuz he shall pay the money. If not, it shall increase by a quarter. Dated the eleventh of Nisan, in the Eponymy of Bêl-ludâri. Three witnesses.

Loans on property often mere advances of material

Loans or advances were also made of various kinds of property. Thus we have an advance of ten minas of silver, Carchemish standard, seventy-five sheep, one cow, made by Ashurbânipal's chief steward to four men, *ana pûḫi*. The sheep and cow they are to return in Adar. If they do not return the sheep, they must breed them. The interest on the money is to be one-third. Dated the twenty-fifth of Tebet, B.C. 664. Thirteen witnesses. Such a loan seems to be on the metayer system.[2]

Property on approval

Here again we have an exceptional case:[3]

L lends two dromedaries, "which they called double-

---

[1] A. D. D., No. 1. [2] A. D. D., No. 115. [3] A. D. D., No. 117.

humped," to three men, who shall return them on the first of the month, or pay six minas of silver. If they do not pay the money, interest shall accrue at the rate of five shekels per mina. Dated the fourteenth of Tishri, B.C. 674.

These animals were rare and evidently highly valued. What could the three borrowers want with a pair of such animals? Were they for exhibition in a menagerie? Perhaps they were for breeding. We may have here a case of goods taken on approval, for a fortnight or so, perhaps for sale to another party.

The same lender lent to the same three men, two hundred sheep, one hundred and fifty goats, two hundred and thirty yearling lambs, in all five hundred and eighty small cattle. They were to return the animals by a fixed date, or pay. Dated the seventh of Iyyar, B.C. 673. The same lender had lent seventy-two sheep to two other men, in Sivan, B.C. 680. They had to return the sheep in Ab, or pay for them at the market-rate in Nineveh. Bêl-êresh acted as agent for the borrowers.[1]

Other goods, such as wine, or oil, were advanced. Here we probably have to do with the transactions of the royal chief steward and the king's agents. For example:[2] A loan of wine

L intrusts five homers of wine, according to the royal measure, to D. On the first of Nisan he shall return the wine, otherwise he shall pay for the wine according to the market-rate in Nineveh. Dated fifth of Adar, B.C. 674. Five witnesses.

Again:[3]

L advances six homers of pure oil, price ten *KA* of bronze per homer, to D, the major-domo at Carchemish. He shall repay the oil in Sebat; if not, it shall be doubled. Dated twenty-first of Ab, B.C. 681. Six witnesses. Of oil

---

[1] A. D. D., Nos. 118, 119. [2] A. D. D., No. 124. [3] A. D. D., No. 127.

We may deduce the interesting fact that Esarhaddon was at Carchemish in Ab, B.C. 681. The advance was made for the use of the royal household there.

Of corn

Advances of corn were made exactly as in the earlier times. Thus:[1]

L advances thirty homers of corn to D, the messenger from the city of Maganiṣi, by the hands of E, a colonel in the army. He shall pay the corn in Marchesvan, in the city of Maganiṣi, or pay the full value of it in Nineveh. Dated the seventeenth of Sebat, B.C. 665. Eight witnesses.

The peculiar shape of the tablets recording loans of corn

One peculiarity of the corn loans is that they are chiefly recorded upon what have been called heart-shaped tablets. These were lumps of clay through which a string passed and came out at the upper shoulders. The string was probably tied around the neck of a sack containing the corn. They thus served both as labels, seals, and as bonds. Many of them have Aramaic dockets, which have been collected and edited by Dr. J. H. Stevenson, in his *Assyrian and Babylonian Contracts, with Aramaic reference-notes.*

These loans made by the king

Thus the above example bears the words in Aramaic, "barley, assignment, which is from Nabû-dûri." These Aramaic legends, in the case of such labels, may have served as addresses. But the general purpose is obscure. All the corn advances seem to have been made by officials of the royal household to inferior officers, in charge of farms or otherwise dependent for supplies.

Often made just before harvest

They show by their dates that the corn was usually advanced just before harvest, when corn was dearest. Some of them name the reapers; others give the number of them. We conclude that these advances were made as food for the harvesters, or as wages for their labor. Occasionally, however, the loan was made at seed-time. Most of the loans are *ana pûḫi*,[2] which supports the view that the meaning of this

Sometimes at seed-time

[1] A. D. D., No. 128. [2] P. 256.

phrase is really "for management expenses" and presupposes the metayer system.

Closely connected with money or other loans are receipts for payment. These are somewhat rare. The more usual practice was to break the tablet, or promise to pay, which was returned to the debtor. But we have two good examples, thus:[1] Receipts for payment of a loan of money

The four minas of silver, interest, belonging to C, which were due from D, D has paid and given to C. One with the other, neither shall litigate. Dated seventh of Sivan, B.C. 683. Three witnesses.

Here we are not aware of the circumstances which lead to the loan. But, in one case, we have records both of the loan and its repayment, thus:[2]

Baḫiânu advanced two homers of corn, for food, to Nabû-nûr-nammir; and one homer each to Latubashâni-ilu and Ṣabutânu, *ana pûḫi*. Dated the twenty-ninth of Elul, B.C. 686. Of a loan of corn

And we find also:[3]

Ṣabutânu and Latubashâni-ilu repay each one homer. Nabû-nûr-nammir does not repay. Dated Iyyar, B.C. 685.

Whether or not the defaulter paid later is not known; but we probably owe our knowledge of the repayment to the fact that all three did not pay together. We note that each paid exactly what he borrowed. No interest was charged.

In one case we have a receipt for a fine, or damages, imposed by a law-court. Thus:[4] Of a fine

Forty minas of bronze, without rebate, which the *sukallu* imposed as a fine. Paid to the *šakintu*. Dated the tenth of Adar, B.C. 693. Four witnesses.

There is no statement who owed, or paid, the fine. But the lady governor who received the money gave this receipt for it.

---

[1] A. D. D., No. 155.
[2] A. D. D., No. 134.
[3] A. D. D., No. 135.
[4] A. D. D., No. 162.

Explicitness of the Code regarding legal responsibility

The Code makes very clear the legal aspect of this transaction. A minor or a slave could only deposit under power of attorney.[1] A deposit was not recoverable unless made by a deed, or delivered in presence of witnesses and duly acknowledged by a receipt.[2] The receiver was liable for all loss occurring to the goods in his possession on deposit, even when the loss was such as involved the loss of his own goods as well.[3] For corn, the Code fixed a yearly fee for warehousing of one-sixtieth the amount deposited.[4]

The bond destroyed on payment

As we learn from the few actual cases which occur, the receipt given for the goods was returned to the recipient on the return of the goods and the tablet broken as cancelling the responsibility. One form which it might take is illustrated by the following:[5]

> Ten shekels of silver, which according to a sealed receipt was deposited for the share of Ṣili-Shamash, he has taken from Ṣili-Ishtar and Amêl-ili, his brothers. His heart is contented; he will not dispute. Oath by Ḫammurabi, the king. Seven witnesses. Fourth year of Ḫammurabi.

Here apparently three brothers share, but one being absent the two hold their brother's share for him, giving a sealed receipt for it. This the judge delivered to him and he claimed and received his share.

Examples of deposit rare

Actual examples of deposit are rare; probably because our collections refer to temple transactions, rather than to private family deeds. We have a deposit of lead,[6] from which we learn that silver was worth twice as much as lead. It was to be sent from Ashnunna, on demand. Here is another:[7]

> "Concerning the silver which Zikrum and Ṣabitum gave to Ṣili-Ishtar on deposit. They have received it; their hearts are content. They gave up their bond and it was broken."

Receipts

[1] § 7. [2] § 123. [3] § 125. [4] § 121.
[5] M. A. P., p. 27. [6] B² 1058. [7] M. A. P., p. 28.

Instead of a receipt by the recipient there is often found a list concluding with the word *apkida*, "I have intrusted." Then comes the date and the names of witnesses. It is not clear, however, that these things were meant to be returned. They may only be memoranda of allowances given out. They chiefly occur in Scheil's *Saison de fouilles à Sippar*.[1]

No examples in later literature

In Assyrian documents no examples of this kind of transaction are found. Nor are any very clear examples producible from later Babylonian times. But it must not be overlocked that some cases, where a receipt is given for a sum or quantity of goods, without mention of interest to be paid, may very well be acknowledgments of a deposit; they have usually been taken to be loans.

[1] S. 62, 69, 73, etc.

# XXIV

## PLEDGES AND GUARANTEES

Pledges given as security in early times

VERY little is known about pledges in early times, though Meissner had argued for their existence from certain passages of the series *ana ittišu*, such as "on account of the interest of his money he shall cause house, field, garden, man-servant, or maid-servant, to stand on deposit"; followed later by, "if he bring back the money he can re-enter his house; if he bring back the money, he can plant his garden again; if he bring back the money, he can stand in his field; if he bring back the money, he can take away his maid; if he bring back the money, one shall return his slave."[1] Consequently the creditor held the pledge in his possession until the loan was returned, when he had to give it back. The pledges here mentioned are antichretic, that is, such that they produce an income or return to the holder, which is a set-off against the interest of his money.

Similarity of this custom to distraint

The Code recognizes the taking of property in satisfaction of a debt.[2] But this is rather a process of distraint upon the goods of the debtor, in case of non-payment, than a case of pledge. Since it was usually expected that the property so taken would be returned on payment of the debt, we can hardly distinguish it from pledge. Indeed, where a debtor gave up his wife, child, or slave to work off a debt, we have a case of antichretic pledge for the debt and interest.

---

[1] M. A. P., p. 9, and notes 1 and 2.

[2] §§ 114, 115.

The practice in later periods

In times subsequent to the First Babylonian Dynasty, the pledge is common. As a rule, it is antichretic, such that income or profit derived from the pledge is a fair equivalent for the interest of the loan. The lender acquires the right of enjoying the pledge. As a rule this is assigned him absolutely, so that no account is needed to be kept of interest on one side and profit on the other. If the profit exceeds the interest due, the excess may be returned, or it may be credited towards the discharge of the debt. If the interest exceeds the profit on the pledge, then the amount by which the loan exceeds the capitalized profit must pay interest.

Very frequent in Assyria

In Assyrian times loans on security are fairly common. Here also we have antichretic loans, where the profit on the pledge was a set-off against the interest of the money. The pledge is expressly stated to be "in lieu of interest." But it seems that the property was often expected also to extinguish the debt. Or it was merely pledged, as a security, which the creditor would keep in case he could not get his money back. We may illustrate these by examples:[1]

A loan secured by land and seven slaves

The lady Addati, the *šakintu*, lends two minas of silver, Carchemish standard, exact sum, to D, the deputy of the chief of the city. In lieu of the two minas of silver, a plot of twelve homers of land in the outskirts of Nineveh, Kurdi-Adadi, his wife and three sons, Kandilânu and his wife, in all seven people, and twelve homers of land, are pledged. On the day that one returns the money, the other shall release the land and people. Dated the first of Marchesvan, B.C. 694. Ten witnesses.

The point about the phrase, "exact sum," seems to be that the advance was made without any rebate. Here the security is worth little more than the loan. Its profits would, however, be a good security for the interest of the loan. No time is given for repayment, but the creditor

---

[1] A. D. D., No. 58.

undertakes to accept repayment and release the pledge at any time.

Again:[1]

A loan secured by a vineyard and slaves

The lady Indibî lends sixteen minas of silver, royal standard, to D. In the month of Tishri, he shall pay the money in full; if not, interest shall be two shekels per mina monthly. A vineyard in the village of Bêl-aḫê, next to that of Ḫabašu, next to that of Si'-banik, next to that of the chief scribe; also these slaves, Dâri-Bêl, his wife, three sons, and two daughters, along with his household, four fat cows (?); Ḫudi-sharrûtu and his daughter; all are pledged as security. If they die or run away, the loss shall be D's. The day that D shall refund the money, with the interest, his slaves and vineyard shall be released. Dated the ninth of Ab, B.C. 688. Six witnesses.

Or again:[2]

A loan secured by a field

Five homers of land belong to D, in the city Kâr-Au. The lender L gives D two-thirds of a mina of silver. This two-thirds of a mina of silver L shall acquire from the field and when D thus has given L his money back, he shall release the field. Dated the sixteenth of Iyyar, B.C. 680.

In the following case a maid is assigned outright for a loan. It is doubtful whether this is a sale, or a pledge:[3]

By the service of a maid

In lieu of money, Bêlit-ittîa, the maid of the *šakintu*, is assigned to the lady Sinki-Ishtar. As long as she lives, she shall serve her. Dated the fourteenth of Iyyar, B.C. 652.

By the borrower's service

A very similar case occurs in the loan of corn and a cow by the *bêl paḫâti* of the Crown Prince, to a certain Nargî of the city of Bamatu. Nargî was to serve the lender for the corn and cow. When his service had become equivalent to the value of the advance, he could go free.[4]

Antichretic pledge was very common in later Babylonian times. The most typical examples are houses. The lender

---

[1] A. D. D., No. 66.
[2] A. D. D., Nos. 73, 74.
[3] A. D. D., No. 76.
[4] A. D. D., No. 152.

has a house in pledge. To him it is rent-free until the loan is repaid. Hence the common phrase "rent is nought, interest is nought." There was then no reckoning made one against the other.[1] The creditor might not, however, care to take the pledge in perpetuity against interest of a loan, never repaid. Usually a date was fixed for repayment, at which time the debtor was bound to take back his pledge. Thus a house might be pledged definitely for three years.[2]

In later Babylonian times by the free use of a house

A reckoning might also be made, to check off profit against interest. Thus D pledges a field to L, but on condition that, if in any year the crop is less than will meet the interest due, he shall pay the difference; but if, on the other hand, it be worth more, he shall take the balance.[3]

Relations between profits and interest

The value of the pledge might, however, be such that it would outweigh both loan and interest. At any rate, it should be as valuable as the loan. Hence it could not be used as a further pledge to another. There is often a guarantee that the pledge given has not been already pledged, that no other creditor has a lien upon it.

Second mortgages barred

In these cases the creditor enters into possession of the pledge and enjoyment of it. He has some responsibilities towards it. He cannot destroy it, or waste it. As a rule, he assumed full liability for all cases for wear and tear. He also fed and clothed a slave pledged to him. Now and then we find the debtor responsible for clothing the slave pledged by him.[4] It is not essential, however, to the idea of pledge that it should come into the possession of the creditor, only it is hypothecated to him. This practice was very common in later Babylonian times.[5]

The creditor's responsibility

Such pledges give an eventual possession. Something like a reversion occurs in the pledge of a share not yet di-

Pledges often anticipated and readily transferable

[1] Nbd. 655. [2] Ev. Mer. 24. [3] B. V., p. 282 f.
[4] Nbk. 408. [5] Dar. 294.

vided.[1] Thus a sum was borrowed on the understanding that if not returned by the proper time, a slave shall be handed over as an antichretic pledge.[2] The man who gives a pledge may not be in actual possession of it, but pledges it on the understanding that he will hand it over as soon as it becomes his. Thus B bought a slave and her two young children for sixty-five shekels, but before they were handed over, he pledged them for fifty-five shekels. Nine months later he sold them for sixty shekels.[3]

Mortgages

A common case is where the debtor pledges all he has to the creditor, a pledge usually greatly in excess of the value of the loan and its interest for a reasonable term, but remains in possession himself. Hence the creditor has only a right over the pledge, a lien upon it, but no usufruct. For this hc had the bond. This also gives only an eventual possession.

The creditor in free use, within his needs, of pledged property

We often meet with after-pledge. The creditor, being in possession of the pledge, might traffic in its profits. If he held a house as pledge, he was not bound to live in it, but could sublet it. Hence he might pledge the rent of it. Or he could repay himself his loan by repledging the house to another. He could also pledge the loan which was due to him. This makes a rather complicated case.

Possible complications

Thus L makes an advance $a$ to D and receives a pledge $p$. He may then pledge both $a$ and $p$. If these are given to two separate persons, $a$ to A and $p$ to P, then P has a cause for uneasiness. If D comes in and pays up $a$, he has a right to the pledge $p$ which is in P's possession. But the money he advanced is not thereby paid to him. Further, A has a right to the money $a$ just paid in by D, which is all that is in evidence. Hence L will have succeeded in getting two sums, and unless he can succeed in realizing his investments of them, is called on to pay both A and P with

[1] Dar. 144, 235. [2] Nbn. 655. [3] Nbn. 765, 772, 832.

one amount. Either A or P may suffer. But if L pledges both *a* and *p* to one man C, then C is quite independent of the relations of L to D. Now D simply has to pay C and gets his pledge back. C is sure of his money.

Method of securing the holder of a second mortgage

Such a transfer of the responsibility of D from L to C was effected by handing over to C, with the pledge, also D's bond to L. C now holds this bond, which, with his pledge, D wishes to get back. The following is a complicated case illustrating these points:[1] D had a house and pledged it to L, who lived in it. Two others were guarantees that D would repay the loan. The pledge was antichretic, "rent nothing, interest nothing." Now L wanted money; so he pledged the house to C. But he did not wish to vacate. So he hired it of C, at such a rate that he would repay C's loan in about five years. It is clear that this house was not good security for C, since D might turn out L at any time by repaying him. L would then owe money to C for which C had no security at all. But L in addition pledged all his own property, his slave, and all his goods in town and country. Further, he not only pledged the house, but handed over D's bond to him. C thus held the house in after-pledge, and the advance with its security in pledge. He was therefore amply secured, since D must pay him.

Now L died and was succeeded by his son M. L had already paid nearly a third of his debt. M thus owed less interest on the loan still due and was accepted by C as tenant at a lower rent. By this means M really made a small profit to himself. In three years M had paid off the whole sum borrowed by his father, and due from him as heir and executor, so he gave back his father's bond to C, also D's bond to L. Now D paid back his loan to M. His bond to L was destroyed. The claim of C on D was annulled, the guarantees of D were free. A final deed of settlement was

[1] Nbk. 132, 142, 172.

drawn up, in which C acknowledged that he had no claims on D or M, nor on D's sureties. He had to say this, because he was not only creditor to M, but as long as he held transferred to him the pledge of D, and the credit of L, he was a creditor with claims on D also. Further, M declares that he has no credit on D.[1]

The occasion for guarantees

A guarantee arises from certain persons undertaking to fulfil a responsibility which is legally incumbent on another, in case he fails to do so himself; or to secure that he shall fulfil it himself. Thus, guarantees are very frequent at all times, especially in the later Babylonian period, and are of many different kinds.

Guarantees for debt

A guarantee for debt was an additional security to the creditor. Of course, the original debtor is the security that the guarantor shall not lose. A good example showing all sides is the following bond for three minas due from D to L. G and W come in and guarantee that D will pay; if not, they will. To protect themselves, they take as a pledge of D some of his people. But D paid and received back his people, so that the bond was returned to D.[2] Why D did not give his people as pledge to L direct is not clear. G and W were probably persons of greater credit and perhaps related to D. The guarantor was sometimes called on to pay. Thus G guarantees for D, is called on to pay and D repays him.[3] The guarantor was legally protected against the defaulting debtor.[4]

For appearance

A guarantee for appearance may have been only to come and pay, as when G guarantees the creditor, a temple, that D will come on a fixed date, and pay his debt; or if not, G will himself pay.[5] It may be a guarantee that a man will not go away; by which may be meant escape payment, or fail to appear for judgment. This is called a guarantee

---

[1] Such is an actual case traced through its phases by Kohler and Peiser.—A. B. R.
[2] Dar. 319. [3] Dar. 310. [4] A. B. R., ii., p. 73. [5] A. B. R., p. 6.

"for the foot of" the person thus indorsed. The "foot" is said to be in the "hand" of him who demands the guarantee. It often refers to debt. G guarantees for the foot of D, out of the hand of L. If he goes away, G will pay thirty-five *GUR* of dates. Here G is the mother of D.[1] So, probably on account of debt, G guarantees for the foot of D, his son-in-law, from the hand of L;[2] again, G guarantees for D to L that D will come on a certain day. G takes the responsibility for all D owes to L, and will pay if D does not come.[3] Or, G guarantees for D and E that they will not leave for another place. If they do, he will pay six minas.[4]

For a witness's appearance

But the appearance may be needed for a different purpose. G guarantees to bring a witness to Opis, and give witness against L that one who was guarantee for the foot of someone to L shall return at the right time. If the guarantee shall prove that L was paid, he is free; if not, he is bound to pay.[5]

D owed L a debt. L ceded this debt to M, but had to guarantee that D will come and pay.[6]

Joint responsibility

Solidarity is in some cases a form of guarantee. Thus two men D and E owe a debt to L. Each is taken as guarantee for the other that they will pay.[7] This is one of the commonest forms of guarantee. The debt could then be recovered in its entirety from either.

Against theft

An example of a guarantee against theft is also found.[8]

Of full value of property sold

A warrant against defects in a slave is very common. The seller warrants that if the slave prove to have certain undisclosed defects, vices, or liabilities, which would detract from his value to the buyer, the seller will indemnify the buyer. This indemnification seems to be effected by a return of the purchase-money and accepting the slave back.

---

1 Cyr. 147. 2 Nbk. 342. 3 Nbk. 86. 4 Nbk. 83.
5 Nbk. 366. 6 Cyr. 119. 7 Nbd. 133. 8 Dar. 93.

But, in some cases, the seller returned part of the purchase-money according to a fixed scale of allowances. In the sale of an estate, the seller guarantees that he will indemnify the buyer in case of any defect of title to sell, or any lien upon the estate.

Against suits at law

Very common at all times was a personal guarantee not to dispute the compact entered into. In fact, this may always be said to be assumed. The oaths by which parties swore to observe the terms of the compact are a form of this guarantee. The penalties, so prominent in Assyrian times, are voluntary undertakings to forfeit stated sums, if found attempting to go behind the contract.

Of the value of securities

As the pledge did not always leave the debtor's possession, the creditor only had a lien upon it. Hence the giver of the pledge had to guarantee that no creditor had a previous lien upon it. This is also extremely common. A slave pledged for debt might run away. His labor as the offset against the interest was thus annulled. The borrower then becomes liable for the interest lost to the creditor.[1]

[1] Dar. 431, 434, Nerig. 39.

## XXV

### WAGES OF HIRED LABORERS

Free labor in demand

DESPITE the existence of slaves, who were for the most part domestic servants, there was considerable demand for free labor in ancient Babylonia. This is clear from the large number of contracts relating to hire which have come down to us. The variability of the terms agreed upon is witness for the existence of competition. As a rule, the man was hired for the harvest and was free directly after. But there are many examples in which the term of service was different—one month, half a year, or a whole year.

Slaves or dependants secured from owners

One might hire labor from the master of a slave, or from the parents of a young man, not yet independent, and then the wages were small, a shekel or two. These wages were paid to the master or parents, not to the laborer himself.

Reapers for the harvest had half a shekel,[1] or two shekels,[2] each. The first may be the daily wages, the latter the price for a specific job. It is probable that the *GUR* of corn for ten days also represents the wages for the whole period.[3]

Wages subject to adjustment

Average wages have been estimated by Meissner[4] to be six shekels per year, according to the Code, and some actual examples of contracts. But it was evidently a matter of agreement, for we have rates as low as four shekels and as high as eight. Usually the employer paid down a sum, for example, a shekel, as earnest-money; the rest was paid by

---

[1] $B^1$ 327. [2] $B^2$ 2425. [3] M. A. P., 57. [4] A. P., 10.

a monthly or daily rate, or in a lump sum at the end of the term of service. Occasionally the wages might be paid down at the start, but this was rare and the amount less.

Often paid in produce

Very frequently, of course, the wages were paid in corn instead of money. Many difficulties lie in the way of finding an equivalent of the shekel in corn. Harvest labor was probably far dearer than any other, because of its importance, the skill and exertion demanded, and the fact that so many were seeking for it at once. Further, after harvest, when the wages were paid, corn was at its lowest price. Meissner's actual examples show that two hundred and fifty *ḲA* might be accepted as yearly wages. We have such a variety of rates that it is difficult to draw any clear conclusion, but two young slaves at harvest could earn three hundred *ḲA*, and for a whole year the wages might be over six hundred *ḲA*, or even as much as three *GUR*, or nine hundred *ḲA*.[1] The Code names ten *ḲA* as daily wages. The average value of a *GUR* of corn was a shekel, hence this gives a yearly rate of twelve shekels. In this case we may suppose that the laborer supported himself.

The labor duly guaranteed

The laborer had to be bound to perform his task. A penalty was attached to his failure to appear at the proper time, and guarantees were sometimes taken for his appearance. In other cases it is stipulated that the penalty for non-appearance shall be fixed by the king's decision.[2]

Duration of service fixed

It was usual to name expressly the time of his commencing and leaving off his work. These clauses are incidentally of importance as fixing the names and sequence of the months at this period. Thus, from the example below we see that the month Tirinu preceded Elul.

Living usually included

Of course, the employer took all responsibility for the slave whom he hired. He fed and clothed him during his term of service. If he suffered any injury, the employer

[1] S. 61. [2] B[2] 2455.

had to compensate the master. Occasionally the slave clothed himself,[1] and then his wages were higher.

As an example we may take the following:[2]

Nâmir-nûrshu from Rutum, Rîsh-Shamash, son of Marduk-nâṣir, for wages, for one year, has hired. His wages for one year, twenty-four *ḲA* of oil, he shall pay, and he shall clothe him. In Elul he shall enter, in Tirinu he shall leave. Two witnesses. Dated in the reign of Ḫammurabi.

Assyrian contracts name both wages and time-limit of work

In the Assyrian times we have certain examples of advances of corn, or money, at harvest-time for the payment of reapers, which have already been noticed under loans.[3] An advance of money and food to workmen may perhaps be put here. But it is also a contract ṭo do work. It reads thus:

Shamash-bâni-aplu, Latubashâni, Ukîn-abîa, Aḫu . . . in all four workmen. Two talents of bronze, three homers one *ŠE* of cooked corn. On the tenth of the month they shall do the work. All the repairs and the beams they shall make fast. They shall fix the balks, and set up the roof. If the bricks are not sufficient . . . the month they do not give, they shall work and finish. Then follow seven witnesses. Dated on the sixth of some month, B.C. 734.

Unfortunately, parts of the tablet are injured and so the sense is not at all clear; but the workmen seem to have had four days in which to do the work. The price offered was considerable.

In later Babylonian times we do not obtain much further information. Here is a good example:[4]

From the twentieth of Nisan to the tenth of Ab, Zamama-iddin, son of Shamash-uballiṭ, son of the smith, shall be at the disposal of Nabû-usallim, son of Limnîa, and he shall pay him as his wages ten shekels of silver. He shall pay half the wages in Nisan and the rest in Tammuz. Whoever breaks the contract shall pay five shekels of silver.

---

[1] B² 938. [2] B² 1137. [3] Page 251. [4] Nbn. 210.

The hire is nearly thirty shekels a year, as in the next example:[1]

Bultâ, son of Ḫabaṣiru, son of the oxherd, has put himself in the hands of Marduk-nâṣir-apli, son of Itti-Marduk-balâṭu, son of Egibi, for wages of half a mina of silver for one year. From the first of Sebat shall Bultâ be at the disposal of Marduk-nâṣir-apli. Bultâ has received one-third of a mina of silver from Marduk-nâṣir-apli.

---

[1] Dar. 215.

# XXVI

## LEASE OF PROPERTY

In case of lease, the specifications of the house are usually the same as in a sale. But this is often not so full, since the identity of the house is less in evidence. A very interesting text referring to the sale or lease of a house next to the palace, in the district of Tirḳa, a house belonging to gods Shamash, Dagan, and Idur-mêr is published by M. Thureau-Dangin in *Revue d'Assyriologie.*[1] It belonged to the King of Ḫana, whose seal it bears. His name was Isarlim, son of Idin-Kakka. The receiver was Kaki-Dagan's son. The oath was by Shamash, Dagan, Idur-mêr and Isarlim the king. The names are very interesting—Igid-lim, an official of the god Amurrû; Idin-abu, king's son; Ili-esuḫ, a judge; Idin-Nani, son of Idin-Marduk; Sin-ukûr, son of Amur-sha-Dagan; Iazi-Dagan; Ṭuri-Dagan; Ṣilli-Shamash. These prove that the land of Ḫana, already known by a votive offering of one of its kings, Tukulti-mêr, was largely Semitic. The names are either of the Babylonian or Aramaic type. It is, of course, not easy to date, as the style of writing in Ḫana may have been different from that in Babylonia at the same epoch.

Form of house-rental

Meissner estimates the average rent of a house to be one shekel per annum. But there are noteworthy variations which, with our available data, cannot be explained. Perhaps the best way is to take account of the size of the

The rental variable

[1] IV., p. 85 f.

house, usually given in the Babylonian fashion by the area of its ground-plan. Rents were often paid in corn, but are so variable that a value for corn in money cannot safely be deduced.

The usual conditions of tenancy

A small part of the rent was usually paid as earnest-money to close the bargain. In the case of short leases the rest was paid on quitting the house, in longer leases half-yearly. Usually the term of tenancy was carefully stated. It was most commonly one year. The cost of repairs fell on the tenant, according to the Code,[1] but he was forbidden to make any alterations until he had paid over the earnest-money. The Code perhaps only means to forbid his closing the door and fastening it, until the deposit was made. The landlord, in fact, preserved the right of free entry until then.

Fields rented for a limited term

The usual term of lease for fields was three years. It is not possible as yet to explain why three years was stipulated, but it was probably due to something more than an accident of custom. Possibly a rotation of crops or an alternation of crop and fallow may have been in vogue.

Usual conditions of tenancy

According to the Code the tenant was bound to keep the land in good condition. His duties included the ploughing or trenching, sowing the seed, snaring or driving off the birds and stray beasts, weeding, watering, and harvesting. Gardens he had to fence. The watering-machines were of great importance and had to be kept in order. They were worked by oxen—often as many as eight oxen were required to work them. A certain amount of stock was frequently leased with the land. It is not clear that oxen were used for the plough; they may have been kept for the watering-machines.

Land often taken on shares

The landlord was in a very real sense a partner with his tenant, though he may be described as a "silent partner."

[1] § Y.

In the case of the great temple landowners it seems to have been the custom to supply a very large amount of the tenant's necessities. Seed-corn was frequently furnished, also corn for food for farmer and men, until the crop was gathered. The stock and farm implements were also provided by the landlord. This metayer system of leasing land probably accounts for loans without interest. It is not clear that such a system was already in vogue in early times.

Stipulations regarding improvements

In hiring a field it might be stipulated that the lessee should place a dwelling upon it,[1] *manaḫtu ana eḳlim išakkanu.* Here the field was at a distance from the city, "beyond the upper stream." If the crop was to be properly looked after, protected from birds, stray beasts, and robbers the farmer must live there some part of the year. There was no dwelling. The lessee was therefore called on to erect a dwelling. Probably a simple edifice sufficed. At the end of the tenancy the tenant was called on to resign this building.

Varying rentals

There were two sorts of land. That called *AB-SIN* or *šeru'*, seems always to have paid six to eight *GUR* of corn per *GAN*. The other sort, *KI-DAN*, probably read *kigallu*, and certainly meaning land, not cultivated but to be brought into cultivation, was exceedingly variable in quality. It is set down for a rent of from three up to eighteen *GUR* per *GAN*, but some land is rented at seventy-two *GUR* per *GAN*.[2]

Allowances for maintenance sometimes a part of the agreement

On account of the hire, some deposit was usually made, which seems to bear no direct relation to amount of rent. But while this was in many cases money—one to three shekels—a number of cases exhibit a list of quantities of food and drink. What these were it is difficult to say, as the terms are written ideographically. But joints of meat, pieces of flesh, drinks, bread and oil, seem to be intended. The

[1] B² 361. [2] B² 797.

custom is obscure. Possibly these are set down as weekly or monthly rations secured on the whole rent and to be set off against it later. That the quantities are in some sense distributive is certain, "so much each," but whether "each person," "each day," "each month," or "each year" is not stated. One plausible suggestion is that the landlord, like the votary in the Code whose brothers do not content her, let the farm to a man who covenanted to support or maintain him. The contention is strengthened by the fact that the cases known to us are all female landlords, and may actually be examples of what the Code contemplates. Having only a life interest in the property and being without capital, they could not afford to wait until harvest to receive the rent, but needed a frequent allowance for maintenance.

Life leases rare

One such tablet known, but difficult to localize

The lease of an estate for a term exceeding a few years was always rare. One is found on a tablet which is one of the most interesting of all those supposed to be of the First Dynasty of Babylon. The script and the language recall Assyrian types most vividly and it is full of non-Babylonian names, which suggest Hittite, or even Armenian, origin. Unfortunately, it is not dated. It might well have been found at Kalaḫ, or Asshur, and belong to somewhat early Assyrian times, perhaps before Assyrian independence of Babylonia. Not one person named in it occurs in the other tablets of the Bu. 91–5–9 Collection—a thing which cannot be said of another of them. If this was really found with them, we can only suppose that centralization was carried to such a pitch that important legal documents, even when executed as far away as Assyria, or Mesopotamia proper, had to be sent in duplicate to the capital of Babylonia. Or was it possible that the principal party came to the capital with this document in his possession, deposited it in the temple archives there, and died, leaving no one to reclaim it.

Dr. T. G. Pinches gave a transcription and translation of the text in the *Journal of the Royal Asiatic Society*, 1897, pp. 589 ff., with many interesting and valuable comments:

Six homers of corn [land] belonging to Ishtar-KI-TIL-LA, son of Teḫip-TIL-LA, Kibîa, son of Palîa, Urḫîa, son of Ithip-sharru, and Irishenni, son of Iddin-PU-SI, have taken for three homers of land, to harvest and transport. As long as Ishtar-KI-TIL-LA lives, Kibîa, Urḫîa, and Irishenni shall transport the crop of three homers of land and shall deliver the same in caldrons. If Kibîa, Urḫîa, and Irishenni do not harvest and transport and deliver the same in caldrons, and the corn perish, they shall pay in full one mina of silver and one mina of gold to Ishtar-KI-TIL-LA. Each is surety for the other. Before Aḫli-Têshup, son of Taishenni; before Ukuia, son of Geshḫai; before Shellu, son of Wantia; before Kushshu, son of Ḫulukku; before Durar-Têshup, son of Gil-Têshup; before Aḫli-Babu, the *ḫazânu*, son of Nubananu; before Zinu, son of Kiannibu, the scribe.

The names of the witnesses seem to be North Semitic

The names of the witnesses are here given in full because of their exceptional interest. Until we are sure of his nationality it is scarcely safe to suppose the principal's name was really pronounced Ishtar-kitilla—the latter part of the name may well be an ideogram. The name of his father ending also in *TIL-LA* suggests that that group of signs is separable. If so, the signs read Ishtar-KI may perhaps be ideographic also. It is evident that Teḫip is from the same root as Ithip, and the form looks Semitic.

Kibîa, Palîa, Urḫîa are Semitic, but Irishenni and Taishenni remind one of the Erisinni, of the son of U'alli, King of the Mannai in Ashurbânipal's time. Still, neither can be said to be non-Semitic with certainty, when we recall the many names ending in *enni* or *inni* formed from verbs and compare the names formed from *erêšu, erêsu*. Names containing the name of the god Teshup were known long ago, as Ḫu-Teshup, Kali-Teshup, Kili-Teshup, where the other element of the name does not seem to be Semitic. Egyptian records give us other compounds of the name of this god, who was the sky-god among the pre-Semitic peoples of Mesopotamia.

Here we have Aḫli-Teshup, Gil-Teshup, and Durar-Teshup. With the former, Professor Hommel compares Aḫlib-shar. With the next compare the Mitanni name Gilîa, also Gilûa. Aḫli-Babu is a closer parallel.

Of the other names, Shellu, Kushshu, Ḫuluḳḳu, and Zinu seem to be Semitic; at any rate they occur frequently, or in cognate forms, well known among the Assyrians and Babylonians. The others are all very unfamiliar. We are as yet so imperfectly acquainted with the onomastics of the nations surrounding the Semites that it is hazardous to attempt to locate these people. Supposing them to be all of one race, they may belong to a colony settled near Sippara, but the whole style of the language is so unlike the Sippara documents that we can hardly suppose that to be the case.

# XXVII

## THE LAWS OF TRADE

The fitting-out of traders by capitalists a very early practice

THE oldest form of business in Asiatic life is *commenda:* the commendatist gives a fixed sum of money to the agent with which he does his business. The former takes a fixed share of the profit, say half, in addition to the original sum invested. The agent usually secures guarantees for the capital. This method of carrying on business is customary in the early times. The Code regulates the relations between principal and agent. The former is called *tamkaru*, usually rendered "merchant," and the latter is *šamallû*, often rendered "apprentice." The merchant is, however, a trader in many ways, and in the Code he is usually named, where we expect lender or creditor. Hence there is little doubt that his name is derived from *magâru*, or *makâru*, with a meaning "to traffic" (?). He seems to have been a monied man, who was ready to make to cultivators advances on their crops—a practice always liable to great abuses, which the Code aims to check.

The agent repaid the value of the outfit with interest

The merchant principal also furnished goods, among which are mentioned corn, sesame, oil, wool, wine, and manufactured articles. The agent did the trading, and regularly rendered his accounts to his principal. He travelled from place to place to find a market for his goods, or to make purchases, which could be profitably sold at home. The principal paid no salary, but received again his capital, or the value of his goods, and an interest or share of the profit.

It is clear that the merchant also moved from place to place, and there is evidence that many of them were foreigners. The travelling agents with their goods formed the caravan.

Legal memoranda essential as security

This kind of trading was regulated by the Code.[1] Unfortunately, the opening sections of the part dealing with the relations of principal and agent are lost; but from what is left we see that it insisted on exact accounts being taken, on both sides, of the amounts of money or value of goods thus invested. If the merchant intrusted money to his agent, he was to take a receipt for it. If the agent received goods, he was to enter their money value and obtain his principal's acknowledgment of the amount of his debt. If he suffered loss of goods from his caravan by bandits, or in an enemy's land, he could swear to his loss, and be exempt from repayment to his principal. But if he did not prosper in his business, or sold at a loss, he had to make good the capital, at least, to his principal. The Code leaves nothing to chance. If the agent is foolish enough not to obtain a sealed memorandum of the amounts received, or a receipt for what he pays to his principal, it is enacted that money not sealed for cannot be put in the accounts. Much was clearly left to the good faith of the agent. The principal was tolerably secure of receiving back his money and had hope of profit. Against that he had to set possible loss by robbery of the caravan. But he was not bound again to employ the same agent. An agent detected defrauding his principal had to pay threefold. But it speaks well for the Code as protector of the weak that it made the capitalist who defrauded the agent repay sixfold.

This business done mainly by caravans

From the contemporary documents we learn that the name for the business was *girru*. That this was also the name for an "expedition," warlike as well as peaceable, points to its connection with the caravan trade. The sign

[1] §§ 100–107.

for *girru*, also used for *ḫarrânu*, a "journey," came in later times to be used for all kinds of business transactions. That the relations noted in the Code actually were carried out in practice, many tablets show. Thus we read:

> One shekel of silver, price of one hundred and eighty *ŠE*, and three shekels of silver which Zuzana lent Aplâ son of Edishu, for five *years*, to enter on his *girru*. He shall pay one hundred and eighty ŠE and three shekels of silver to take back his sealed receipt.[1]

Here the capital intrusted was a quantity of corn worth a shekel, and three shekels in money. This was in order to enter on a business journey. The agent Aplâ had to return the capital in full, as the Code enacts, to take back his bond. There is no agreement as to profits, which might be wanting; that was left to be understood. As a rule, the time was shorter, generally "one year." The agent appears to have often borne the name of *muttalliku*, "one who wanders about," "a hawker." The same may be denoted by *AḪ-ME-ZU-AB*, a group of signs whose reading is not yet clear, but may be a variant of the ideogram for *šamallû*.

Business was also done, as the Code shows, as speculation in futures. Thus[2] we read: Speculation not unknown

> Sibbat-asê-iddina hired as "business" the produce of a field from three men. The produce of the business was to be three and seven-fifteenths *GUR* of corn, according to the standard measure of Shamash paid in Kar-Sippar, and one shekel was to be profit.

This was what he had to pay, and evidently, if the crop yielded more, that was his profit; if less, he had to stand the loss. Similarly, other crops were let on the terms that at harvest, or at the end of the "business," a specified amount should be paid.

We learn from many hints, that caravan trade was always active. The name of Ḫarran in Mesopotamia is supposed Caravan trade

1 B[1] 549. 2 B[1] 110.

to be derived from the numerous caravan routes that crossed there. The Tell el Amarna tablets tell us of the complaints made by the kings of Babylonia of the robbery of caravans in districts nominally under the control of Egypt.

These dealings frequent in later times

In the more private documents of the later Babylonian times, there is again plentiful evidence that this form of trade was common. The money was loaned out "to buy and sell." It was given *ana ḫarrânu*, "for hawking trade." Then whatever profit was made upon the money, the agent "will give" to the principal. The agent binds himself to undertake no other agency. He gives a guarantee for the money. The principal had no further responsibility for the business, and would not meet any further call. It is obvious that in a sense the principal and agent were partners, and many transactions in later times are difficult to distinguish from cases of partnership in the ordinary sense.

Importance of the canals for commerce

It has long been recognized that the canals controlled the prosperity of the country, but it is only lately that their importance as waterways has been fully realized. In the early period we read of flour sent by ship to Nippur for certain officials.[1]

Navigation laws for shipping of great number and variety

The Code has much to say about ships. Temples owned them, as well as private persons. It was a crime, punishable with death, to steal a ship.[2] We read of fees for building or navigating various ships.[3] The responsibilities and damages in collisions and wrecks are apportioned.[4] A shipowner might hire a captain to navigate a ship for him, or might hire the captain and ship together. The usual freight included corn, wool, oil, and dates, but many other things were also carried. The wages of a captain was six *GUR* of corn yearly. There are frequent references to ships in the contemporary letters.[5] They were named ac-

[1] E. A. H., 27. [2] § 8. [3] § 234. [4] §§ 235, 236. [5] K. L. Ḫ., *passim*.

cording to their carrying capacity, which was five or more *GUR*. A ship of seventy-five *GUR* is named. They carried wood, for King Ḫammurabi ordered seven thousand two hundred pieces of *abba* wood to be brought to Babylon, three hundred pieces in a ship. A number of boat captains or perhaps shipping agents were ordered to proceed from Larsa to Babylon and arrive with their ships in Adar. He gave orders for the furnishing of the crews. We further have a correspondence concerning the invasion of certain fishing rights by boats from another district. In the contemporary contracts we meet with several long lists of ships divided into little groups, of five, six, or seven, each with its captain named, each group under a head captain, all set down as at anchor at the port of Shamash, or the like.[1] There is a case of the hire of a boat of six *GUR* freight by two persons for two months.[2]

In Assyrian tablets

In Assyria, canals served chiefly for water-supply. Except when the Assyrian kings went outside their own lands to Babylonia or Mesopotamia, we hardly read of ships. Sennacherib's ships were built abroad and served abroad. There is no hint of their ever coming up to the walls of Nineveh. The contracts only once mention a ship[3] in which booty was brought from somewhere.

Boat hire a regular stipulation in Babylonia

In the later Babylonian times there are many references to the hire of boats and their crews. They appear to be a regular conveyance of goods:[4]

> One shekel and a quarter of silver for the hire of a ship which brought three oxen and twenty-four sheep from the king's son [Belshazzar], for Shamash and the gods of Sippara. Further, fifty *ḲA* of dates for the rations of the two boatmen.

Thus the receiver paid carriage and expenses. The daily hire of a boat is now one shekel, and the wages of the crew

---

[1] S. 160. [2] S. 244. [3] A. D. D., No. 468. [4] Nbd. 401.

amount to half as much.[1] A boat might be bought for twenty shekels or half a mina.[2] The wages of the boatmen included corn, dates, salt, and onions. The freight was exceedingly varied as before. One boat appears to have carried fresh meat.[3]

The maintenance of roads

There are less obvious references to roads in the literature; but that they were in excellent condition has been conjectured from the many evidences of postal service and ready carriage even in early times. Convoys travelled from Agade to Lagash as early as the time of Sargon I.[4] Innumerable labels are found on lumps of clay with the name and address of the consignee. These were attached to consignments of money and goods.

A regular tariff for land-transportation

The Code contemplates consignments being sent from a great distance, even from abroad.[5] It regulates the charges for a wagon, with oxen and driver,[6] or a wagon alone.[7] There are several cases in the contracts of the hire of wagons, for varied prices per year, one-third of a shekel[8] to twelve shekels;[9] but it is not certain that these were for conveyance from place to place. They may have been for agricultural purposes only. The usual means of conveyance seems to have been by asses.

Roads in Assyria of prime importance

In Assyrian times we find it part of the duty of a founder of a city to open up the roads leading to it.[10] The land was intersected with roads in all directions, so that a field often had two roads as its boundaries. The whole plain outside Nineveh was cut up by roads, which here take the place of the canals of Babylonia. In this period we find horses and camels in use as beasts of burden as well as the asses.

---

[1] Nbd. 1019. [2] Nbd. 180. [3] Cyr. 343. [4] K. L. Ḫ., p. xxi.
[5] § 112. [6] § 271. [7] § 272. [8] B[1] 564.
[9] S. 572. [10] K. B., vi., p. 106.

# XXVIII

## PARTNERSHIP AND POWER OF ATTORNEY

Partnership in business common from early times

ASSOCIATION, or partnership, makes its appearance very early and in a highly developed state. Some forms are very simple, as when two or more men buy or hire a piece of land together. There may, or may not, be any family relationship between the partners. In some cases we learn nothing about the terms of partnership. But where we are able to discern them, they follow the natural course that profits were divided, *pro rata*, according to the capital contributed. More obscure is the question how far the personal exertions of each partner were pledged to the benefit of the firm. There is a suggestion that some partners were content with furnishing capital, and obtaining a fair return upon it, while the others were actively engaged in the business of the firm. Prolonged study and comparison are, however, needed before all these points can be definitely decided.

Origin of the word for partner

The name for a "partner" is *tappû*, and the sign *TAP* serves as ideogram. This sign consists of the two horizontal strokes used to denote "two," and may have been used to denote "union," or partnership, and so from its name *tap* have given rise to the name for "partner." In the new Babylonian times the ideogram is the sign usually read *ḫarrânu*, also formed of the two horizontal strokes crossed by two connecting strokes or bonds. There is little doubt that in early times this was read *girru*, when denoting "business," undertaken in association. Later the dualism of the partnership was marked by the addition of the dual sign to *ḫarrânu*. That both *ḫarrânu* and *girru* are used as words for "way," "journey," "expedition," may well point to the prominence of the idea of trade journeys with caravans. But partnerships were made with less ambitious aims and confined to holding and sharing in common varied sources of income.

The usual conditions

To make a partnership, *tapputam epêšu*,[1] it seems that each partner contributed a certain amount of capital, *ummânu*.[2] Yearly accounts were rendered and the profit then shared. This took place by a formal dissolution of partnership, when each partner took his share. This in no way prevented a renewal of partnership. For the satisfaction of the partners sworn declarations as to the property held in common and the profit made were deposed before judicial authorities. These often take the form of a suit by one partner against the other, but it seems that they might be only formal suits to clear up the points at issue and secure a legal settlement.

Always legally defined

A considerable number of tablets are drawn up to embody a settlement on dissolution of partnership. Some do not make any reference to a law officer as arbitrator; but all contain a careful setting-forth of each partner's share and an oath to make no further claim. It is practically certain that these were drawn up with the cognizance of the local law-court.

The Code silent

The Code has nothing to say as to partnership, unless its regulations on the point were embodied in the lost five columns.

A good example of partnership documents is the following:[3]

Erib-Sin and Nûr-Shamash entered into partnership and came into the temple of Shamash and made their plan. Silver, merchandise,

---

[1] M. A. P., 78. [2] M. A. P., p. 13. [3] $B^2$ 358.

man-servant, and maid-servant, abroad or at home, altogether they shared. Their purpose they realized. Money for money, man-servant and maid-servant, merchandise abroad or at home, from mouth to interest, brother with brother will not dispute. By Shamash and Malkat, by Marduk and Ḫammurabi, they swore. Then follow seventeen witnesses. The document is not dated.

The word for plan, *ṭêmu*, means the basis of partnership, that is, its terms. Here it was "share and share alike." The phrase *babtum*, "merchandise," includes all the material in which they traded, excluding the living agents. The phrase *ša ḫarrânim*, literally "on the road," may well have denoted the merchandise not in warehouse, but in circulation. Whether *ḫarrânu* actually referred to a caravan may be doubtful. We often read of goods *ša suḳi*, "on the street," in the same sense, "out on the market." If the partners dealt in corn, and had a quantity lent out on interest, that was *ša suḳi*. Whether a distinction between *ša ḫarrânim* and *ša suḳi* was kept up is not clear. But if they invested their capital in merchandise which they sent to a distant market for sale, the former phrase would be more appropriate, while if they bought wool to manufacture into cloth or garments and to sell in the bazaars of their own town, *ša suḳi* would be more suitable. The gate of the city was a market, and money or goods *ša bâbi*, "at the gate," was as we should say "on the market." In contrast to these phrases, *ina libbi alim*, "in the midst of the town," answers to our "in stock." While the term *mitḫariš* literally means "altogether," "without reservation," it implies exact equality of share. The *amâtu* was the "word," literally, but, applied to business, means the agreement as to their mutual transactions. The completion of that was reached when they took the profits and divided them. It might include the mutual reckoning of profit and loss. The phrase "from mouth to interest" is very idiomatic. The

Explanation of the terminology

"mouth," or verbal relationships, included all they said, the terms they agreed upon. The word "interest" here replaces the more usual "gold;" both mean the "profit," or the balance due to each. Usually we have the words "is complete," the idea being that no verbal stipulation has been overlooked, no money or profit left out of reckoning.

Evidence of long-established commercial customs

As will be remarked, such pregnant forms of expression evidently presuppose a long course of commercial activity. They can only have arisen as abbreviations of much longer sentences. Clear enough to the users of them, they do not admit of literal rendering, if they are to be intelligible to us. But they are eloquent witnesses of an advanced state of commerce.

In Assyrian literature

Traces of partnership are difficult to find in the Assyrian tablets which have reached us. We must not confuse with partnership the holding in common of property or lands, which may be due to heritage. Two or more brothers may sell their common property, for greater ease of division, but they are not exactly partners.

In later Babylonian times such evidence common

In the later Babylonian times, as is natural to expect with the larger number of private documents, there is much evidence regarding the many forms of association for business. We have such simple forms as the following:[1]

One mina which A and B have put together for common business. All that it makes is common property.

Or thus:

Two minas each, A and B, have as *ḫarrânu*. All that it makes, in town and country, is in common. Rent of the house to be paid from capital.[2]

The many varied details

They had a house, as shop and warehouse, the rent of which was a charge upon the business. Slaves might be partners with free men, even with their masters. A part-

---

[1] Nbn. 199. [2] Nbk. 88.

ner might merely furnish the capital or both might do so, and commit it to the hands of a slave or a free man with which to do business. The slave took his living out of such capital, and the free man received either provisions or a fixed payment. Thus we read:[1]

Five minas and six hundred and thirty pots of aromatics belong to A and B as partners. This stock is given to C, a slave, and D, another slave, with which to do business. Whatever it makes is A and B's in common. C and D take food and clothing from the profits where they go.

It is not unlikely that each slave was to look after his own master's interests. For we read:[2]

Six minas belong to A and B and are given to C the slave of B as capital. A and B share what it makes. A will give another slave D to help C.

Even women entered into business as agents. We read:[3]

Two-thirds of a mina belonging to A and B are given to a free woman with which to trade.

A formal dissolution of partnership

As in earlier times, the dissolution of partnership usually involved a reference to the law-courts. Thus we have[4] a reckoning before judges of two brothers and a third who were in a partnership from the eighth year of Nabopolassar to the eighteenth of Nebuchadrezzar. "The business is dissolved" (*girru paṭrat*). All the former contracts were broken and shares are assigned to each. The first two brothers were in possession of fifty shekels which were to be divided.

Reckonings

Provisional reckonings were constantly made at frequent intervals, but did not involve dissolution of partnership, nor need to be referred to a law-court.[5]

---

[1] Nbn. 572. [2] Nbn. 653. [3] Nbn. 652.
[4] Nbk. 116. [5] A. B. P., ii., 59.

Some cases are interesting for additional items of information. Thus we note:[1]

A manufacturing partnership

Two partners put in each fifty *GUR* of dates. Whatever it makes is to be in common. They take a house in Borsippa for one year at rent of half a mina. The rent is to be paid out of profits. B holds the house and apparently carries on the business. At the end of the year he returns it and all the utensils to A.

It seems likely that he carried on some kind of manufacture. A held the south house, next door. B also paid the tithes. A similar case where some manufacture from dates is supposed, is thus stated:[2]

A lends one hundred *GUR* of dates, fifty *GUR* of corn, sixty large pots, to B and C two of his slaves, on a partnership. They are to take in common whatever it makes, in town and country. The venture is to last three years. But, in this case, they are to pay interest two minas *per annum.* At the end of the three years, the two slaves returned all.

They were given a house for which they paid no rent.

Power of attorney recognized and frequently used

Closely allied with agency is the power of attorney. In the Code[3] a son in his father's house could not contract, buy or sell, or give on deposit, except by power of attorney empowering him to act for his father. The same was true of the slave. The contemporary documents contain many references to business done by agents on the order of their principals.[4] The Assyrians also make frequent mention of persons acting as *bêl ḳâtâti*, having the power of another's hands, being in fact allowed to act as their attorney or agent. The king was represented in the law-courts by his agent.[5] Sometimes the agent was called *bêl paḫâti* of the king's son.[6] It even seems to be the case that *ḳâtâtu* acquired the sense of agency, or business, and *bît ḳâtâti* came to

[1] Dar. 280. [2] Dar. 395, 396. [3] § 7.
[4] Page 243. [5] A. D. D., No. 94. [6] A. D. D., No. 152.

mean a "shop," or bazaar. In many cases "agency" was expressed by *ša ḳâtâ*, "by the hands of." Aliens had to act through such an agent.[1] When three men borrow a quantity of straw, one alone sealed the receipt and bond to repay, and was said to be *bêl ḳâtâti ša tibni*, "agent for the straw."[2] A female slave was sued for property said to be due from her master, in his absence. A free man, perhaps the judge, was *bêl ḳâtâti* for the woman that her master would take up the case on his return, and undertook to satisfy the suitor, if she could not do so.[3]

Protection of the rights of the principal

In later Babylonian times the phrase survived. The commissary acted "with the hand" of his principal. We may take this to be the hand-sign, or seal, representing written authority. It involved a reckoning with his master, and naturally gave rise to a number of delicate questions. If a man bought a house for another, having been commissioned so to do, his principal must of course pay the price. But was he bound to accept his agent's selection? Could he not demur regarding the price? One of these points at least was dealt with by the later Code. Law A deals with the man who has concluded a purchase for another, without having a power of attorney from him in a sealed deed. If he has had the deed made out in his own name, he is the possessor. Of course, he can sell again to his principal, but he could not do so at a profit. Nor is the principal under any obligation to accept the purchase at the price the agent gave for it. Actual examples are far from rare: A buys a field, crop, date-palms and all, for C and D. This purchase was made on condition that all copies of the transaction be destroyed. The condition was not observed, as we still possess one of them. Later A received from C, one of his principals, about half the price he had paid. But it does not appear that D ever paid his share, and this is

[1] A. D. D., No. 307. [2] A. D. D., No. 151. [3] A. D. D., No. 166.

why the condition was not carried out. Presumably A and C remained owners of the field.[1]

Representative action

There is no limit to the varieties of agency or representative action. At all periods we meet with a brother, usually the eldest, acting for his other brothers. A brother acting with the hand of his brother also occurs in the time of Evil Merodach.[2]

Power of attorney over funds

The power of attorney was also given to receive money and give a receipt, under seal.[3] Again: A bought some slaves of B and paid in full. B gave receipt for the money, but did not undertake to deliver the slaves at A's house. A can send a messenger or agent to take the slaves, and B agrees to deliver them to such. Whatever is born or dies from among the slaves is credited to A.[4]

---

[1] Nbn. 132, 133; A. B. P., p. 11.
[2] Ev. Mer., 13.
[3] Dar. 386.
[4] A. B. P., ii., 34.

# XXIX

## ACCOUNTS AND BUSINESS DOCUMENTS

Account-books

THERE are lists which are not formal contracts, but may have been used as legal evidence. The stewards of the great temples, of the palaces, and even of wealthy men in business, kept most careful accounts. These lists have some features peculiar to themselves and are not without considerable interest.

Those of the first epoch mainly temple accounts

The tablets which have reached our museums from Telloh, Nippur, and elsewhere, belonging to the ages before the First Dynasty of Babylon, are for the most part temple accounts. They often concern the offerings made by various persons, often officials of high standing, and some may well have been the notes sent with the offerings. But many were drawn up as records of the receipts for a certain day, month, or year. Interesting as they are for the class of offerings, for the names of offerers, or of priests, and for the cult of particular gods, or the localities near Telloh and Nippur, and often containing valuable hints for the history and chronology of those times, they do not give us the same insight into the daily life of the people that the longer legal documents do, in later periods.

Receipts for loans

An important class consists of receipts for loans. Those drawn up at full length and witnessed, have already been considered. But the majority may only contain a list of articles delivered, with the name of the receiver, the lender being the holder as a temple official, while the receiver is a subordinate. These may have been as effective as the fuller bonds, but they furnish little information, except regarding the current prices of articles.

Accounts of repairs or expenses

Some tablets are concerned with hire. The amounts paid by the temple for repairs, fresh robes for gods and officials, even maintenance of the workmen, are all set down with their totals for a week, or a month.

Records of measurements

An important class consists of the records of the measurements, length, breadth, and area of fields, together with the amounts of corn which they were expected to produce. Were these available for a widely extended area, we might be able to map out the district round the temple from whose archives they come.

The conditions of service with flock and herds

The temples and large landowners had great flocks and herds. Consequently, there is much evidence concerning the pastoral occupations of the people of Babylonia. The Code regulates the relations of the shepherds and herdsmen to the flock-masters.[1] Thus an owner might hire a shepherd, *nâkidu*, for his sheep or cattle, at the wages of eight *GUR* of corn *per annum*. The shepherd or herdsman took out the flock or herd to the pasture and was responsible to the owner for them. They were intrusted to him, and if sheep or ox were lost through his fault, he had to restore ox for ox and sheep for sheep. If he was hired and had received satisfactory wages, he had no power to diminish, or abstract from, the flock or herd for his keep or private use. He entered into a contract with the owner, and that stipulated for the restoration of the entire flock or herd, together with a proper increase due to the breeding of the flock or herd. He had to make any deficiency good, by statute.[2] This applied also to the stipulated profit in wool or other produce. It seems clear that his own profit was any excess above the stipulated return. Otherwise it is difficult to see

---

[1] §§ 261–67. [2] § 264.

what source he had from which to make good the loss to his master. He was forbidden to alter the agreement into which he had entered in any particular, or to sell any of the flock, under penalty of a tenfold restitution. He was, however, protected from liability for loss by wild beasts or accident. But, if the loss was due to his fault, by neglecting to keep the fold secure, he had to make up the loss.

**Herdsmen's accounts**

It is obvious that he gave a receipt for what was intrusted to him and made his account on return from the pastures. These accounts are plentiful among the temple accounts in the earliest periods, but being written for the most part in Sumerian, have still many obscurities for us. As a rule, each deals with the liabilities of one man, whose "account," *nikasu*, it is said to be. At the beginning are recounted the details of his trust, so many oxen, cows, sheep or goats, of varied ages and qualities. Here it is very difficult to translate. Anyone who knows the variety of names which are given to an animal by agriculturists according to its age, sex, and use, need not be surprised to find that the Babylonians had many names for what we can only render by "sheep." As a rule, we know when the ram, ewe, or lamb is intended. But this by no means exhausts the variety. Anyone who glances through an Arabic lexicon must notice how many different names the Arabs have for the camel in its different aspects. But in our case we often have no clew to what was meant by the signs beyond some variety of sheep, ox, or goat. At any rate, the first section enumerates the cattle or sheep delivered to the herdsman. Then follows a section devoted to those "withdrawn," taken back by the owner, or exacted as some due from the flock. Others are noted as taken for sacrifice, used for the wages or support of the herdsman, or else dead or otherwise missing. These the herdsman was allowed to subtract and then had to return the balance. There are similar lists of asses or goats. The tablets hardly lend themselves to connected translation because of the absence of verbs. The following is an example:

Forty-three ewes, forty-three rams, seven ewe-lambs, seven he-lambs, three she-goats, one sucking kid, to start with. Expended in ewes and rams, none; six ewes, seventeen rams, snatched away; no lambs lost: no ewes, one ram, no lambs. Total: one hundred and four to start with. Total expended: none. Total: twenty-three snatched away. Total: one lost. Namḫâni, shepherd. Overseer: Duggazidda. At Girsu. The year after the king devastated Kimash.

The meaning of the words is somewhat conjectural. "Expended" may mean used for the shepherd's own maintenance. "Snatched away" means probably deducted for revenue purposes, about one in five. The scribe did not write "none." He merely left a blank.[1]

Lists of second epoch unavailable

The similar lists for the second epoch are not yet available for study. Only one[2] appears to have been published,[3] but there are many still unpublished. It is not easy to translate them, because, though many Semitic names occur, there is still a tendency to use the old Sumerian, or ideographic writings. Such a list as:

Eight oxen, twenty-three work-oxen (for watering-machines), eleven milch cows, sixteen steers, sixteen heifers. In all seventy-four oxen (or cattle) belonging to Marduk-uballiṭ in the hands of Bêlshunu, fifth day,

may serve as an example, but does not convey much information to us. These lists are chiefly valuable for the means of comparison they afford. A three-year-old ox was worth half a mina of silver.[4]

The Assyrian lists indicate new varieties of animals

For Assyrian times we have a few interesting examples, just enough to show that the same customs survived. There

[1] E. A. H., 14. For fuller details the reader should consult Radau's *Early Babylonian History*.

[2] B[2] 447. [3] In C. T., vi., p. 24. [4] B[2] 448.

are no less than thirty-five kinds of sheep and goats, and fifteen kinds of cattle named in the lists; also eleven kinds of birds. Here is a specimen list of asses which gives some prices:[1]

> One male working ass for one and a half minas seven shekels, one she-ass for thirty-seven shekels, a second she-ass for one mina, a third she-ass for one royal mina, a fourth she-ass for thirty-two shekels, in all five and a half minas two shekels.

There is nothing to show for whom or why the list was drawn up, but if the total is correct, we learn that a royal mina was worth one mina forty-six shekels of the ordinary standard. The lists of horses are now very numerous, some dozen varieties being distinguished. Many of these lists give the numbers of horses of different kinds which entered a certain city on a certain day.[2] The horses are often distinguished as coming from certain countries, being called Kusai, or Mesai, horses. The camels are frequently mentioned, and we learn that one was worth a mina and a third.[3] Dromedaries are also named[4] and seem to have been worth three minas apiece.

Memoranda regarding wool

Wool accounts play an important part in documents of the early times. They may be regarded as of two kinds. The first are shearers' accounts returned by the shepherd of a flock; the second are concerned with the amounts of wool given out to weavers.

The four kinds of wool

Shearers' accounts enumerate four sorts or qualities of wool. The best was called royal wool, that which was of the highest quality. The others were second, third, and fourth quality. Poor wool and black wool are also named. Sometimes we are told from what part of the sheep's

[1] A. D. D., No. 732.

[2] They are published by Professor R. F. Harper in his *Assyrian and Babylonian Letters, passim.*

[3] H. A. B. L., p. 690.

[4] A. D. D., No. 117.

body it was taken. Other terms applied are less easy to recognize. This wool was received by weight.

Black wool very highly valued

The weavers' accounts give a list of quantities of wool, with the same distinctions as to quality, and the price at which it was assessed. This was doubtless the sum to be paid by the weaver, if the wool was not returned made up. The values attached show very clearly the difference in quality. Thus, while two looms of royal wool were worth thirty minas, seven looms of second quality went for the same value, eleven looms of third quality for a talent, and thirty-two looms of fourth quality for one talent, one loom of another sort for one talent, and the same amount of black wool for the same value.[1] It is evident that the black wool was highly valued. The loom, literally, "beam," of wool, was some measure, perhaps what would occupy one weaver. The price was probably fixed in silver. The price of the same quality varied from time to time.

Sheep-shearing

In the letters of Ḫammurabi and his successors there are frequent references to the shearing, and orders for the inspection of flocks and herds.[2] The Code does not refer to sheep-shearing, though it mentions wool. The shearing was concluded by the New Year feast in Nisan. In the contemporary contracts there are several wool accounts. As a rule, one talent, or sixty minas' weight, of wool was served out to several men who were to pay for it, to the palace, at the rate of one shekel of silver *per mina*.

The weaving accounts

In Assyrian times we have great wool and weaving accounts. Some deal with the huge amounts of wool received as tribute from the great cities of the empire and then served out to bodies of weavers in various palaces with specifications of the species of cloth or sorts of garments which were to be returned. In the later Babylonian times we have a large number of wool accounts recording

[1] E. A. H., 50. [2] K. L. Ḫ., pp. xlvi. ff.

the amounts given out from the temple to various persons to weave or make up into garments.[1]

Memoranda regarding skins of animals

Skins are also named in the accounts. They are distinguished as the skins of certain kinds of animals. Various amounts are credited to different persons, but whether as giving or receiving, and in what capacity, is not clear. Sheep and goat skins are most common, but ox and cow hides are named.

Leather

The Code does not refer to these, nor the letters of Ḫammurabi and his successors, but we have lists of skins and carcasses of animals.[2] The purpose of the lists is not clear. In Assyrian times there are frequent references to hides. There was a distinct grade of official called a *ṣârip taḫšê*, "dyer of skins." Large quantities were bought in the markets of Kalaḫ and Ḫarrân. The price was about two shekels of silver for a skin.[3] The articles made of leather are very numerous; shoes, harness, pouches, even garments, are named. It was used for buckets, baskets, bottles, shields, and many other things not clearly recognized.

Amounts allowed for the food of animals

Fairly frequent also are accounts of the quantities of corn expended for the keep of flocks and herds. The amounts allowed *per diem* are the chief items of interest. Sheep were allowed from one to one and a half *ḲA* a day, lambs half a *ḲA*, oxen six to eight *ḲA*.[4] In the Code we find allowances for the keep of animals. There are very frequent lists in Assyrian times of amounts of corn given to various animals. These also occur at later times. The amounts allowed per day are various and by no means

[1] These have been discussed by Dr. R. Zehnpfund, B. A. S., i., pp. 492–536. He has striven to identify the garments as far as possible; but when we recall that over eighty such garments are named in these lists, most of which are merely names, with no indication of their uses, it is clear that a translation is generally out of the question. We know something of their material and often of their color, but nothing further. It is curious that in many cases these names are the same for Assyrian and later Babylonian times.

[2] B² 406, 611. [3] A. D. D., No. 872. [4] E. A. H., 152.

uniform. A very good example gives as the allowance of corn for a full-grown sheep two *ḲA per diem*, for a young sheep, one *ḲA*, for a lamb one-half *ḲA*.[1]

Acknowledgment of advances

Acknowledgments of advances, or loans, occur in the first epoch. As a rule, we are not told what was the ground of the loan. The fact that these loans were to be repaid is not stated, and we may take the tablets to be merely receipts for things given out to officials who had a right to them. The substances were corn of different kinds, wine, beer, sesame-wine, butter, flour and other food-stuffs, wool, and other supplies. We sometimes learn prices from these tablets. Thus a *GUR* of corn cost one shekel.[2]

Stewards' accounts

Long lists of accounts are very common at all epochs. They relate what sums or amounts were paid out to various officials for certain goods or for wages, keep, and the like. In fact, they are stewards' accounts. Unfortunately, the way in which most collections have been formed, and even more the way in which they have since been preserved, renders it impossible for us to make the use of them which has often been made of mediæval accounts. Otherwise we could obtain from them many interesting items. They are, however, most valuable for prices and names.

The earliest mention of iron

Thus, in such lists we find mention of articles which would otherwise remain unsuspected. The first reference to iron is in the Ḫammurabi period,[3] whence we learn that a shekel of silver would buy eight times its weight of iron. Sometimes we get an important contribution to chronology. It is well known that there is no certainty as to the order of the Eponyms after B.C. 648, but we know their names for at least forty years later. Any contribution to the order of these names would be welcomed with avidity. Thus, one scribe writes: "Income from the Eponymy of Sagab to the Eponymy of Nabû-shar-aḫêshu, for six years, which was paid

---

[1] Cyr. 250; Nbd. 841. [2] E. A. H., 100. [3] B² 405.

in as maintenance, eleven talents . . . besides twenty-seven plates of silver." We cannot say whose income it was, but the previous section dealt with the income of the crown prince, and this may be only a *résumé* of the last. But we now know that from Sagab to Nabû-shar-aḫêshu was six years in all.

Thus, from the most varied and often most unpromising sources are derived those important details which make it possible to attain an exact and realistic conception of Babylonian and Assyrian history and life.

# BABYLONIAN AND ASSYRIAN LETTERS

# I

## LETTERS AND LETTER-WRITING AMONG THE BABYLONIANS AND ASSYRIANS

External form of the letters

The ancient Babylonians early discovered the convenience of written communication between friends at a distance. The origin of letter-writing is not yet clear; for, when we first meet with letters, they are fully developed. A piece of clay, usually shaped like a miniature pillow, was inscribed and then enclosed in an envelope made of a thin sheet of clay. On the envelope was written the address. As a rule, the letter was baked hard before being put into its envelope. Powdered clay was inserted to prevent sticking. The envelope, after being inscribed, was also baked hard. Of course, the letter could not be read without breaking the envelope, which was therefore a great protection to the interior letter. The envelope was naturally thrown away after being broken. Hence, extremely few envelopes have been preserved.

Their envelope

Their dates

The practice of dating letters does not seem to have been common. We have dated letters at all epochs, but they are few. In some cases the date may have been on the envelope. It is more common for the writer to give the day of the month, sometimes also the month. But the date of a letter was probably not then of any great importance.

Another method of insuring privacy

Some letters seem to have been covered with coarse cloth, on which was impressed a lump of clay, to act as a seal and bind down the edges. The lumps were then sealed with a signet-ring, or cylinder-seal. The clay envelopes were also sealed, before baking, with the sender's seal. So usual was this habit, that the word for seal, *unḳu*, is often used to denote a sealed letter. Thus when an official acknowledges the receipt of the king's "seal," it means a sealed order or rescript.

Style of the opening address

The early Babylonian letters usually open with the formula, "To A say: Thus saith B." The formula probably goes back to the times when the message was verbally delivered. These would be the words used to a messenger who had to remember the message. The verb "saith" is not expressed exactly. The word used is *umma*, which is often rendered "saying"; it introduces a direct quotation. We might render, "In the name of B." But the written letter replaced the spoken message. Some think the letter was read by a professional reader. Such readers are common still, where education is not widely diffused. It is very clear that the letter was generally written by a scribe. Thus, all Ḫammurabi's letters show the same hand, while those of Abêshu or Ammi-ditana are quite different. In the case of private letters we have less proof. But it is possible that the king sometimes wrote with his own hand. Some terms of expression render that very likely. It is, however, quite impossible to be certain on such points.

Variations of the formula

The same opening formula also appears in the Tell el Amarna letters. It is not known in Assyrian letters, but survived in Babylonia to a late period. In Assyria the formula is nearly the same; with the omission of the *ḳibi*, or "say," it reads "To A thus B." In addresses to superiors, B usually adds "thy servant." Polite letters generally add good wishes for the recipient. These are exceedingly varied. The word *šulmu* plays a great part in them. Literally it denotes "peace." "Peace be to thee" is very common. But it soon came to mean the "greeting of peace."

Thus "I have sent *ana šulmika*" means "I have sent to wish thee peace," "to greet thee." But it also takes the more general meaning of well-being. Thus *šulmu iâši* means "I am well," "it is peace with me"; not only absence from war, but health and all prosperity was included. Hence Joram's inquiry of Jehu, "Is it peace, Jehu?" means "Is everything all right?" "Be thou at peace" may be rendered loosely, "I hope you are well," in the fullest sense that "all is well with you." No consistent rendering can be given for such phrases as these.

**References to a former correspondence**

Very often letters quote the previous message of the present recipient, *ša tašpuranni*, "what thou didst send me." But the quotation is often omitted and then this becomes an awkward rendering. We have to fill up some general sentence such as, "as to what you sent about." A very difficult sort of construction arises when the writer sets down a list of questions, which he has been asked, and the answer to each. As there are no capitals, periods, or question-marks, there is often some difficulty in separating a question from its answer. This may be done differently by different translators, with startlingly different results.

**Elliptical phrases**

Very many sentences are elliptical. Thus, it was common to add at the end of the letter something like, "I leave it to you to decide." This might be put, "As the king, my lord, sees fit, let him do." But a scribe would often merely say, "As the king sees fit." Such elliptical sentences are often very difficult to complete. They were obviously clear to the recipient. To us they leave a wide margin for conjecture.

**Inscribed seals on packages**

Very early indeed in the history of Babylonia a sort of postal system had been developed. At any rate, in the time of Sargon I., B.C. 3800, an active exchange of commodities existed between Agade and Shirpurla. Packages or vessels of produce or goods were forwarded and with them small blocks of clay, impressed with seals and inscribed with the address of the recipient. These were probably used to prevent the fastenings of the packages from being untied, and on their backs may be seen the impressions of the strings which fastened the packages.[1] As it happens, no letters have yet been published from the era preceding the First Dynasty of Babylon; but we can hardly doubt that such exist.

Letters of the First Dynasty of Babylon

In the time of the First Dynasty of Babylon letters appear frequently in the collections of tablets brought to our museums. The volumes of *Cuneiform Texts from Babylonian Tablets, etc., in the British Museum, published by order of the Trustees,*[2] contain a large number of letters from copies made by Mr. T. G. Pinches. These have been made the subject of a study by Dr. Mary Williams Montgomery.[3] Mr. L. W. King, in his work, *The Letters and Inscriptions of Ḫammurabi,* published fifty-five letters of Ḫammurabi to his subordinate officer, Sin-idinnam, six letters of Samsuiluna, thirteen of Abêshu', two of Ammiditana, five of Ammizaduga, and two private letters. These were all transcribed, translated, annotated, and, with a number of other contemporary inscriptions, issued with admirable introductions, glossary, and index.[4] Nowhere can a more vivid picture be obtained of the great empire and the manifold duties of a Babylonian king. A number of the texts published in the first volume were translated and commented upon by Dr. G. Nagel under the title, *Die Briefe Ḫammurabi's an Sin-idinnam.*[5] Professor Delitzsch added some valuable notes. Dr. B. Meissner had already published the text of four letters as *Altbabylonische Briefe.*[6] Professor V. Scheil

---

[1] Heuzey, *Revue d'Assyriologie*, iv., pp. 1 ff.

[2] Vol. II., 1897; Vol. IV., 1898; Vol. VI., 1898; Vol. VIII., 1899.

[3] *Briefe aus der Zeit des Babylonischen Königs Ḫammurabi*, Leipzig, 1901.

[4] Three volumes, 1898–1900, Luzac, London.

[5] *B. A. S.*, iv., p. 434–500.

[6] *B. A. S.*, ii., pp. 557–64, 573–79.

gave the text of two letters of this period, found by him at Sippara, in the *Recueil de Travaux*[1] and noticed others, and some more in his *Une Saison de fouilles a Sippar.*[2] These are preserved at Constantinople, but the text has not yet been published. They are chiefly private letters and of a business nature. There are a great many other letters in American and European museums, the publication of which should not be longer delayed.

For the long period before the Tell el Amarna times, *circa* B.C. 1500, nothing of any extent seems to have been published, though letters are also known to exist of this period. A late copy of one such letter, addressed by Adadi-Shumnâṣir, King of Babylon, to Ashur-narara and Nabû-dâni, kings of Assyria, about B.C. 1250, is partly preserved in the British Museum.[3] Of the subsequent period

The Tell el Amarna tablets, some three hundred in number, were discovered in 1887–88, at the ruins of the palace of Amenophis IV., in Egypt. They will form the subject of a separate volume of this series. They consist of the letters or despatches sent to kings of Egypt by the kings of Babylon, Assyria, Mitanni, and the subject-rulers of many Syrian and Palestinian cities and states. From these can be obtained a very clear view of the state of Syria and Palestine just before the exodus of the Israelites from Egypt. Naturally, these letters have formed the subject of a very large literature. The most complete edition of the texts is by Winckler, *Der Thontafelfund von el Amarna.*[4] With these should be compared Dr. J. A. Knudtzon's *Ergebnisse einer Collation der El Amarna Tafeln* and *Weitere Studien zu den El Amarna Tafeln.*[5] A full transcription with trans- The Tell el Amarna letters

---

[1] XVI., p. 189.

[2] Pages 105, 106, 107, 116, 123, 124, 125, 133, 134, 135, 136, 137.

[3] Published III. R. 4. No. 5.

[4] Heft I. of *Mittheilungen aus den Orientalischen Sammlungen der Königliche Museen zu Berlin,* Speman, Berlin.

[5] *B. A. S.*, iv., pp. 101–54, 279–337, and 410–17.

lation and glossary to these texts has been given by Winckler, as *Die Thontafeln von Tell el Amarna*.[1] An excellent English translation by J. P. Metcalf is to be had. There are a few of these tablets, which found their way into private hands, or to other museums than London, Berlin, and Gizeh, whence Winckler's copies were obtained. It is a duty to science that these should now be published. In the *Bulletin de l'Institut Français d'Archéologie orientale*, t. II., published at Cairo, Professor Scheil gives the text of two more of these important letters. The explorer, Dr. F. Bliss, found another in the ruins of Lachish. It is included in Winckler's work above. Professor Sellin has lately found several tablets, which by their script and personal references are shown to belong to this period. They were found at Ta'annek, and are published by Dr. Hronzy in the *Anzeige der philos. hist. Klasse der Wiener Akademie*.[2] The interest of these additions lies in the fact that they were found in Palestine itself.

Cappadocian letters

The numerous Cappadocian tablets are now generally recognized by their language and script to belong to this period. They also show considerable affinity with the documents of the First Dynasty of Babylon, and the Tell el Amarna letters preserve many characteristic expressions.

Assyrian letters

The subsequent periods in Babylonia are represented by few letters. It is not until we come down to the end of the eighth century and the Sargonide times that we meet with many letters. The archives of Nineveh contained immense numbers. A great many of these are now in the Kouyunjik Collections of the British Museum. There they early attracted attention. Being written by the imperial officials to the kings of Assyria, they contain most valuable material

---

[1] Vol. V. of Schrader's *Keilinschriftliche Bibliothek*, Reuther and Reichard, Berlin, 1896.

[2] June 17, 1903.

for history. George Smith in 1871 gave extracts from several of them in his *History of Ashurbanipal.* A number were published in Rawlinson's *Cuneiform Inscriptions of Western Asia.* Mr. S. A. Smith, in the *Proceedings of the Society of Biblical Archæology*, 1887–89,[1] and in the second and third volumes of his *Keilschrifttexte Asurbanipals* gave some seventy more. Professor Delitzsch also published a number in his *Zur assyrisch-babylonischen Briefliteratur*,[2] and in his translations and comments laid the real foundation for their interpretation. In 1892 Professor R. F. Harper began the colossal task of publishing the text of all the letters from Nineveh, in his *Assyrian and Babylonian Letters belonging to the K Collections of the British Museum*, of which eight volumes are already published.[3]

Published texts

A considerable number of scholars have busied themselves with the translation and elucidation of these texts. Professor C. Johnston in his work, *The Epistolary Literature of the Assyrians and Babylonians*;[4] C. van Gelderen, *Ausgewählte babylonisch-assyrische Briefe*;[5] A. J. Delattre, *Quelques Lettres Assyriennes*;[6] G. R. Berry, *The Letters of the Rm. 2 Collection*, in *American Journal of Semitic Literature*, xi., pp. 174–202; F. Martin, *Lettres assyriennes et babyloniennes*—besides the many articles by other scholars on particular words or subjects—have contributed to the understanding of these difficult texts. Professor R. F. Harper has published a few preliminary studies on these texts.[7] Dr. H. Winckler not only gave several important texts in his *Texte verschiedenen Inhalts*,[8] but transla-

Translations

[1] IX., pp. 240–56; X., pp. 60–72, 155–77, 305–15.

[2] *B. A. S.*, i., pp. 185–248, 613–31; ii., 19–62.

[3] *University of Chicago Press*; Luzac, London.

[4] Baltimore, 1898. [5] *B. A. S.*, iv., pp. 501–45.

[6] *P. S. B. A.*, 1901, pp. 331–59.

[7] *A. J. S. L.*, x., pp. 196–201; xiii., pp. 209–12, xiv., pp. 1–16, 171–82; xv., pp. 129–44.

[8] Pfeiffer, Leipzig.

tions and comments on them in his *Altorientalische Forschungen*.[1]

Late Babylonian letters

The letter-texts of the latter Babylonian period at present published are extremely few. Some may be found in Strassmaier's great collection of *Babylonische Texte*, among the contracts. A list of those for the reigns of Nabonidus and Nebuchadrezzar is given in Dr. K. L. Tallqvist's *Die Sprache der Contracte Nabû-nâ'ids*, p. xviii.

Historical value of the letters

One of the uses to which the letters may be put is to illustrate the history of the time. From the letters of Ḫammurabi we can gather a great deal of information as to the civil policy of the reign. From the Tell el Amarna tablets we may reconstruct almost a complete survey of the condition of politics in Palestine. From the Assyrian letters we can rewrite the history of affairs in Armenia at the end of Sargon's reign, or the wars with Elam in Ashurbânipal's time.

General value

The letters are also a rich mine of information on all sorts of topics, and those very often on which almost all other literatures are silent. We gain here a closer and more intimate acquaintance with humanity than at any other period of ancient history. We must not expect finality in our translations for a long while to come. Fresh documents will continually be found or published that will help us to revise our views. But that is the perennial interest of the letters. We may read and reread them, always finding something fresh to combine with every new piece of information.

Methods of classification

Several different methods of classifying the letters suggest themselves. One plan would be to group those letters which illustrate some phase of civil life. Thus we may collect the references to medical cases, or the illustrations of religious life, or the contributions to astronomy and astrology. But none of these methods will be exhaustive or gen-

[1] II., pp. 52, 58, 184 f., 302 f.

erally applicable. A letter rarely deals with only one subject. The only scientific classification seems to be that adopted by Professor Harper in his edition of the Nineveh letters, or Mr. King in his letters of Ḫammurabi. This is to place together all the letters written by one scribe. Here we have two difficulties. There may be more than one scribe of the same name. Thus it is practically certain that in Professor Harper's groups of letters apparently assigned to one man, more than one person is often really involved. Again, a very large number of letters no longer preserve the name of their scribe. Only a prolonged study can reduce these difficulties; it is not likely that we shall ever quite eliminate error.

Royal letters

There is one large group that has a claim to separate consideration. Many letters are written by, or to, a king. They are on various subjects. A subdivision might be made of reports sent by officials concerning public affairs. But even these often contain side-references; and at the last we have really to consider each letter as a separate document.

## II

### THE LETTERS OF ḪAMMURABI

Great historical value of this collection

The letters of Ḫammurabi are by far the most important collection of letters hitherto published for the period of the First Dynasty of Babylon. They had a certain adventitious value at one time, because one of them was thought to contain the name of Chedorlaomer, and this association with Ḫammurabi, as Amraphel, was exploited in the interests of a defence of the historical value of Genesis xiv. Mr. L. W. King's edition of the letters, however, showed that such a use was unwarranted. But it served a much more useful end, giving us a very full picture of the times of the founder of the First Babylonian Empire. The excellent account given by Mr. King of the contents of these letters is fairly exhaustive. The importance of such sources for history cannot be overestimated. They are contemporary. They are not written to impress posterity, but with absolute fidelity to fact. We may disbelieve some of the excuses made for misconduct, but in the references to current events or general customs we have a sure witness, if only we can understand them. This is often difficult because a letter presupposes relations between the correspondents which we must conjecture.

The letters to Sin-iddinam

Since Mr. King's introduction to his first volume gives a full account of the few letters previously published, this need not be reproduced here. Of Ḫammurabi's letters fifty-three are addressed to one and the same man, Sin-iddinam.

It is doubtful whether he was the King of Larsa who bore this name, or the official who in the next reign seems to be Governor of Sippara. There are many persons who bore this name known at this period. However, several mentions of the temple of Shamash at Larsa occur in these letters and there is a certain presumption that Sin-iddinam of Larsa was the person intended.

Ḫammurabi as an administrator

Ḫammurabi's ability as an administrator, which these letters reveal, and his care even for small details of his rule, may well be the reason why his empire proved so stable. He established a tradition which was long followed by his successors. He organized his land, appointed governors, and held them responsible to himself. He had a direct interest in their doings and sent minute written instructions, demanding reports, summoning defaulters to his presence, or directing their punishment where they were. The dates for his reign, as for others of the dynasty, show, not only raids and conquests, but chiefly public works of utility. The construction or repair of canals, public buildings, temples, the ordering of justice, are works that repaid his care.

His care for the revenues of the temples

Ḫammurabi was a man of many business enterprises. The collection of the temple revenues was an object of his attention. There is no evidence that these were available for his use, but he had a personal interest in all that was right and just. To him the herdsmen and shepherds of the temple flocks and herds had to report. He often appears as restoring, rebuilding, or adorning shrines, and he was careful of his religious duties. Thus he postponed a case because of a festival at Ur, which he seems to have found demanded the presence of one of the parties.

The ordering of the calendar

He had to settle important questions concerning the calendar; whether or not reports of astronomical observations were then received is not clear, but at any rate the king decided when the intercalary months should be inserted. Thus he told Sin-iddinam there was to be a second Elul.

His supervision of justice

The administration of justice was also no small part of his work. Not only did he promulgate a code, but he also superintended its execution. There was a right of appeal to his judgment. He actively supervised his judges in the provinces. Thus a case of bribery was reported from Dûr-gurgurri and he instructed Sin-iddinam to investigate the case and send the guilty parties to Babylon for punishment. He upheld a merchant's claim against a city governor, for the recovery of a loan. He protected the landowners against money-lenders. He examined claims to land and sent instructions to Sin-iddinam to carry out his decision. Thefts of corn, loans withheld, rents, were adjudicated by him. He summoned not only the parties, but the witnesses, to Babylon. Prisoners were sent under escort, and arrests ordered.

His private property

The king's own herds and flocks were a personal care to him. They were stationed in various parts of the country. He received reports about them, or sent inspectors to report upon them. On one occasion he summoned forty-seven shepherds to come and report to him in Babylon. He ordered additional shearers to assist those already at work. He regulated supplies of wood, dates, seed, and corn. These were often sent by ship, and there is evidence of a large number of ships being employed, of varied capacities.

His building enterprises

Public buildings demanded large gangs of workmen. They were drawn from the slave and serf population. A great many letters are concerned with the supply and movements of these laborers. Whether forced labor was inflicted as a punishment may be doubted. But the *corvée* was in full operation. The hire of laborers is referred to, and it is probable that the forced laborers were fed and clothed at the expense of the state. Thus we see that Ḫammurabi was a busy man and worked hard to build up his empire. His successors, though we have fewer of their letters, seem to have been fully as active.

**The return of the goddesses of Emutbal to their homes**

It is not easy to select specimens for this period. Each letter has an interest of its own, and it is tempting to include most of them. But we may take the two letters referring to the goddesses of Emutbal, because one of them by a series of misreadings and misunderstandings was made to contain the famous reference to Chedorlaomer. The first[1] may be rendered.

To Sin-iddinam say, thus saith Ḫammurabi: Now I am sending Zikir-ilishu, the *AB-AB-UL*, and Ḫammurabi-banî, the *DU-GAB*, to bring the goddesses of Emutbal. Do thou forthwith embark the goddesses in a procession-boat (state barge) and let them come to Babylon. Let the hierodules come with them. For the sustenance of the goddesses embark food, drink, sheep, ship's furniture, and travelling expenses for the hierodules, until they reach Babylon. Appoint men to draw the ropes, and *biḫru* men, that the goddesses may come safely to Babylon. Let them not delay but come quickly to Babylon.

**The date of their capture**

These goddesses were very likely captured during an expedition to Emutbal which was a border province of Elam. It is natural to associate this with the thirty-first year of Ḫammurabi, for which the full date is:

"The year of Ḫammurabi, the king, in which by the help of Anu and Bêl he established his good fortune, and his hand cast to the earth the land of Iamutbal and Rim-Sin, the king."[2]

The transport of the goddesses was made possible by the system of canals. Intercommunication was in an excellent state, for Ḫammurabi ordered a man to be sent to Babylon from Larsa, and allowed him two days, travelling day and night. The hierodules are the female attendants of the god-

[1] K. L. Ḫ., No. 34. [2] K. L. Ḫ., iii., p. 237.

desses. The officers whom Ḫammurabi sent bear titles not yet clearly recognized. The name Ḫammurabi-banî points to a deification of the king. Whether the goddesses reached Babylon and there brought misfortune on the country and so were sent back again, or whether their restoration to their shrines in Emutbal was part of the king's policy for a pacification of the conquered country, does not appear. But we read in another letter:[1]

"To Sin-iddinam say, thus saith Ḫammurabi: The goddesses of Emutbal, which are in thy command, the troops of Inuḫsamar shall bring safely to thee. When they shall reach thee, combine the troops with those in thy hands and restore the goddesses to their shrines."

The construction of the passage seems to imply that the goddesses had protected Inuḫ-samar. The latter was in command of troops that were within Sin-iddinam's jurisdiction; for when Sin-mâgir complained to Ḫammurabi that Inuḫsamar had impressed some of his servants for military service contrary to a bond given him by the king, Ḫammurabi referred the matter to Sin-iddinam, ordering the servant to be given up.[2] It was this name Inuḫ-samar that Scheil misread as Kudur-nûḫ-gamar.

The care of the canals

A number of letters concern the canals of the country. Thus we read:[3]

"To Sin-iddinam say, thus saith Ḫammurabi: Summon the people who hold fields on the side of the Damanu canal, that they may scour the Damanu canal. Within this present month let them finish scouring the Damanu canal."

Here we are introduced to the duty which lay upon riparians to keep the canals running alongside their land in order. This was part of the *ilku*, or customary obligation. It lay with the governor to enforce it. In another letter[4] the

[1] K. L. Ḫ., No. 45.
[2] K. L. Ḫ., No. 26.
[3] K. L. Ḫ., No. 71.
[4] K. L. Ḫ., No. 5.

king complains that a canal which had been partly cleared had not been cleared as far as Erech, and so the boats could not enter that city. Here Sin-iddinam was ordered to do the work with the men at his disposal and complete it in three days. After that he was to go on with the work he had already been ordered to do. In another fragmentary letter the king orders the clearing away of the water-plants which had obstructed the course of the Euphrates between Ur and Larsa. One is reminded of the *sudd* on the Nile.[1]

A case of bribery

The case of bribery is referred to in a way that leaves it rather doubtful whether a theft may not be meant. The meaning of the word rendered "bribe" by King is unknown, and his identification of *tâtu* with *da'tu* is not certain. But at any rate the wrong was brought under the cognizance of Ḫammurabi, and he writes:[2]

To Sin-iddinam say, thus saith Ḫammurabi: Shumma-ilu-lâ-ilu saith thus, so saith he, "In Dûr-gurgurri bribery has taken place. The people who took the bribe and the witnesses who know the affair are here." Thus he saith. Now I will send this same Shumma-ilu-lâ-ilu, a *DU-GAB* and a . . . to thee. When this letter is seen inquire into the matter. If there is bribery, take the money, or what was given as a bribe, seal it up and send to my presence. The people that received the bribe, and the witnesses who know the case, whom Shumma-ilu-lâ-ilu will disclose, send to me.

A case of oppression redressed

A case of oppression by a governor is complained of, and redressed by the king. He writes:[3]

To Sin-iddinam say, thus saith Ḫammurabi: Lalu, the *kadurru*, hath informed me thus, saith he, "Ani-ellati, the governor *rabiânu*, has laid claim to [alienated] the field which I have held since . . . and [taken] the corn of the field." Thus he hath informed me. The tablet can be seen in the palace. Lalu holds two *GAN* of land. Why has Ani-ellati, the governor, laid claim to Lalu's field? Inquire into the matter. If Ani-ellati has lent on mortgage to Lalu, the *kadurru*, grant him his debt and lay the blame on Ani-ellati, who lent on pledge.

[1] K. L. Ḫ., No. 4. [2] K. L. Ḫ., No. 11. [3] K. L. Ḫ., No. 6.

It is clear that Lalu was one of those privileged officials who held lands by royal charter, and who could not be dispossessed of their land. The Code directs[1] that a governor shall not lend on mortgage to a reeve or runner or tributary, under pain of death. Although a *kadurru* is not there named, this letter makes it probable he was similarly protected. It is interesting to notice where the record was to be found. The palace, or "great house," was the residence of the governor. The tablet probably recorded the appointment of Lalu to his benefice; it therefore was his title-deed.

The depository for deeds

An interesting question may be raised here. Did Ḫammurabi mean in his own palace? It may be so, for he writes in another letter:[2]

To Sin-iddinam say, thus saith Ḫammurabi: One *GAN* of water-meadow, a field in the district of Dûr-gurgurri is an old possession of Ea-lubanî. In a tablet it is inscribed as his. Give the field to Ea-lubanî.

Now how could Ḫammurabi know this unless the tablet had been shown to him? Perhaps the claimant brought his tablet with him when he came to lay his plea before the king. That is quite possible, but it may well be that the king insisted that all title-deeds be deposited in the capital.

Restitutions ordered

An order for the restoration of stolen corn appears in another letter:[3]

To Sin-iddinam say, thus saith Ḫammurabi: Ṭummumu of Nippur hath informed me thus, saith he, "I deposited seventy *GUR* of corn in a granary in Unabu and Amêl-ili has opened the granary and taken the corn." Thus he hath informed me. Now I will send Ṭummumu himself to thee. Send and let them bring Amêlili to thee. See what they have to say. The corn belonging to Ṭummumu which Amêl-ili took let him return to Ṭummumu.

---

[1] § 34. [2] K. L. Ḫ., No. 76. [3] K. L. Ḫ., No. 12.

Another letter reads thus:[1]

To Sin-iddinam say, thus saith Ḫammurabi: Ilushu-iḳîsh, the merchant, over five, has informed me thus, saith he, "Thirty *GUR* of corn I gave to Sin-mâgir, the *Šakkanak*, and I took his receipt. I have asked for it for three years and he has not given back the corn." Thus hath he informed me. I have seen his receipt. Cause Sin-mâgir to give up the corn and its interest and give it to Ilu-shu-iḳîsh.

The title "over five" seems to be meant literally. He was a superior merchant. Like many another hint, this speaks for the strict organization of each class of the community. The *Šakkanak* was usually the superior official, "governor," of a city, or of a ward of a city. We are not told what was Sin-mâgir's district. But it was under Sin-iddinam's rule. In other letters we read of a Sin-mâgir being sent to Babylon.[2] Perhaps he refused to give up the corn.

Another letter illustrates the incidence of taxes and the relations of landlord and tenant:[3]

About taxes

To Sin-iddinam say, thus saith Ḫammurabi: As to what I sent to thee about the corn that is the tax on the field of Ibni-Martu, which is in the hands of Etil-bi-Marduk, to be given to Ibni-Martu; thou didst say, "Etil-bi-Marduk hath said thus, saith he, 'I have cultivated another field together with the field of Ibni-Martu, and the corn is all garnered in one place, let them declare on oath before God how much corn was from the field of Ibni-Martu and let them take the tax.' Thus he said. But Ibni-Martu did not agree. Saith he, 'Without Ibni-Martu one can do nothing.' Thus he said, and went away." As to what thou didst send, "the corn, as much as was in his field, should be declared before God and the tax given him." As thou didst send, let them declare before God how much corn was in the field of Ibni-Martu, and pay Ibni-Martu the corn that is the tax on his field.

The case is not quite clear, but Ibni-Martu owed a tax on his field. He had either mortgaged or let his field to

[1] K. L. Ḫ., No. 24. [2] K. L. Ḫ., Nos. 13, 41. [3] K. L. Ḫ., No. 28.

another. This tenant had not given him the corn to pay the tax and excused himself on the ground that the produce of the field was now mixed up with that of another field. Hence he could not say how much the tax should be; clearly it was proportionate to the yield. The method of solving the difficulty was that a sworn estimate had to be taken from competent witnesses and the tax levied on that basis. This course was recommended by Sin-iddinam in a previous report on the situation. The amount was to be given to the landlord, who then had to pay the tax. He clearly had no rent in corn from the land; but he could not sell or mortgage his crop except subject to the tax. The mortgagee was liable for the tax and the owner was bound to pay. The mortgagee must furnish him the means to do so; he had no right to claim the part of the crop due as tax, whatever bargain he had made with the owner of the land.

Commerce under strict control by the State

While agriculture was in the hands of free men who only paid on produce, there are indications that commerce was very strictly controlled by the State. The merchant was the only money-lender as a rule. He also seems to have acted as contractor, or farmer of taxes. The merchant, or factor, was under the king's protection and also directly responsible to him. Hence some have regarded him as a royal official. But this is hardly correct. He was to Ḫammurabi what the Jew of the Middle Ages was to the king then, or the Stock Exchange or Bourse is now. Probably we should not be far wrong in applying to him the term "publican," in the New Testament sense. He owed a certain amount to the treasury, which he recouped from the taxes due from the district for which he contracted. If he did not secure enough, he had to make up the deficit. The following letter[1] deals with what was probably common,

The collection of taxes

---

[1] K. L. Ḫ., No. 33.

namely, an evident reluctance on the part of such officials to settle accounts:

To Sin-iddinam say, thus Ḫammurabi: Concerning the chief collector, Shêp-Sin, I wrote to thee, saying, "send him with one thousand eight hundred *GUR* of sesame and nineteen minas of silver, due from him, as well as Sin-mushtal, the chief collector, with eighteen hundred *GUR* of sesame and seven minas of silver, due from him, send them to Babylon, and send with them the market rates (?) . . ." But thou didst say that these chief collectors had said, "Just now is harvest-time, after harvest we will go." Thus they said, and thou didst tell me. Now the harvest is over. On receipt of this tablet, when I have sent to thee, send Shêp-Sin, the chief collector, with one thousand eight hundred *GUR* of sesame and nineteen minas of silver, his due, and Sin-mushtal, the chief collector, with one thousand eight hundred *GUR* of sesame and seven minas of silver, his due, to Babylon; and with them thy trustworthy guard, and with all their property let them come and appear before me.

The title which I have rendered "chief collector" may be read "scribe of the merchants." The sign *PA,* read *aklu,* does in some of its connections mean "scribe," as *tamkaru* does mean "merchant." But the sign often denotes merely an overseer. Hence we may take it that this was the derived meaning. The reason may well be that over a group of shepherds or merchants, one was always set who could keep accounts. Hence the term *aklu,* properly a "scribe," came to be an "overseer." Such a high official as the *PA Martu* would be the Superintendent of Martu. The person referred to in this letter, Shêp-Sin, occurs also in two other letters of Ḫammurabi.[1] In one, Sin-iddinam is told to send him to Babylon with money; in the other, he complains of not being able to collect money due to a temple, and having to make up the deficit himself.

The officials who were under obligation to furnish men for public work and the army, doubtless often found a difficulty

**Illegal impressment for public service**

[1] K. L. Ḫ., Nos. 16, 30.

in making up their quota, and impressed men who were not strictly liable for duty. Such men as those called *KA-DUR, KAPAR, MU, PATESI,* are named on the letters as exempt from the service. But even this is not conclusive. They are not exempted because they are of these ranks, but because they have been wrongly assigned to the service. Their masters may have been exempt from the liability to furnish a man; or already engaged in royal service. Slaves and poor men were subject, as we know from the Code. Here is one of the letters on the question:[1]

To Sin-iddinam say, thus saith Ḫammurabi: Naram-Sin, the shepherd, hath said thus, saith he, "The herdsmen in my hands have been put in the *corvée.*" Thus he said. The herdsmen which are the property of Apil-Shamash and Naram-Sin shall not be put in the *corvée.* Now summon Etil-bi-Marduk and the officials and order them to return the herdsmen of Apil-Shamash and Naram-Sin, whom they have taken.

Here the *KABAR,* or herdsmen, are the employees of the shepherd, his "sheep-boys." Their absence would be a danger to the flocks. The delinquent Etil-bi-Marduk was often in fault. Several other complaints against him appear in the letters, in his capacity of money-lender.[2] On two occasions he was sent for by the king, evidently with a view to punishment. Further, a *patêsi* in his service appealed to be transferred to another master.[3]

---

[1] K. L. Ḫ., No. 3. [2] K. L. Ḫ., Nos. 18, 30, 73. [3] K. L. Ḫ., No. 38.

## III

## THE LETTERS OF SAMSU-ILUNA AND HIS IMMEDIATE SUCCESSORS

Few in number

THE discovered letters of Samsu-iluna are as yet comparatively few. They are not all addressed to one man. We may take one or two specimens.

About change of air for a goddess

Like his father Ḫammurabi, Samsu-iluna cared for the health of the goddesses, providing them with an occasional change of scene. This time it is the goddess Anunitum, who makes a journey:[1]

To Haiab . . . say, thus saith Samsu-iluna: Concerning Anunitum's going to Sippar-edina, I have sent an officer. Forthwith let Anunitum go to Sippar-edina.

The name of the official to whom the letter is sent is broken and it could be completed in several different ways. Sippar-edina was one quarter of Sippara.

Temple dues

The following letter is concerned with the supply of corn for the Shamash temple at Larsa. It is addressed to three officials:[2]

To Sin-ilu, Bîtu-rabi, and Nîḳ-Sin say, thus saith Samsu-iluna: The corn for the treasure-house of the temple of Shamash of Larsa, the property of Igmil-Sin which ye deliver, verily ye shall deliver. Forthwith, from the corn that is in your hands, give corn for the supply of food for the treasure-house of the temple of Shamash; what is now standing due make up.

The "treasure-house" may be only a "store-house" in general. Instead of "make up," we may render "buy."

---

[1] K. L. Ḫ., No. 81. [2] K. L. Ḫ., No. 49.

Fishing rights

Samsu-iluna looked into the details of his government quite as closely as his father. We see him regulating fishing rights:[1]

To Sin-iddinam, Kâr-Sippar, and the judges of Sippara, say, thus saith Samsu-iluna: They tell me that the ships of the fishermen go down to the districts of Rabî and Shamkâni and catch fish. I am sending an official of the palace-gate; when he shall reach thee [summon] the ships of the fishermen (who have been catching fish) in the districts of Rabî and Shamkâni, and let it not occur again that the ships of the fishermen go down to the districts of Rabî and Shamkâni.

Clearly each district owned its own fishing rights, as it was responsible for the repairs of the banks and scouring the beds of the water-ways in it. It is far from unlikely that Kâr-Sippar denotes some ruling body in Sippara, for in the contracts we find that cases were brought before the Kâr-Sippar. As they are associated with the judges of Sippara, they may be the town elders. Sin-iddinam here is hardly the official of Larsa to whom Ḫammurabi usually wrote, though he might have been promoted to Sippara in the meantime.

Business details

Two other letters were addressed to him by Samsu-iluna,[2] one about corn due from certain persons, the other about a contingent of men sent to strengthen the walls of Sippar-Amnanu. In another letter, the king summons to Babylon, Sin-iddinam, Ibni-Marduk, the Kâr-Sippar, and the judges of Sippara, but the letter[3] is too defaced for us to determine the reason. It was to be "at seed-time."

Letters of Abêshu'

The letters of Abêshu' are somewhat more numerous. Mr. King published thirteen. They are all more or less defective, and add nothing to our knowledge beyond the fact that the same policy of centralization went on.

Of Ammi-ditana

The letters of Ammi-ditana, two in number, are more

[1] K. L. Ḫ., No. 80. [2] K. L. Ḫ., Nos. 79, 104. [3] K. L. Ḫ., No 105.

interesting. One deals with the supply of corn for men at work on the citadel of Shagga, a town probably near Sippara. The king orders the authorities of Sippara to make up and send on the supply, and adds that the soothsayers were to be consulted as to favorable auspices for sending the corn.[1] The other deals, as do three letters of Abêshu', with tribute due in wool from Sippar-iaḫruru. The report from the superintendent of this source of revenue in each case is that the tribute is over-due and the king sends a peremptory order for it to be sent forthwith to Babylon.

Ammi-zadûga's letters, five in number, all happen to be concerned with the annual sheep-shearing at Babylon. They differ slightly, in the person addressed, and the date assigned for the shearing. Thus one[2] reads: Of Ammi-zadûga

To Ibni-Sin, son of Marduk-nâṣir, say, thus saith Ammi-zadûga: A sheep-shearing will take place in the House of the New Year's Festival. On receipt of this note, take the sheep . . . and the sheep which are sealed, which thou shall set in motion, and come to Babylon. Delay not, reach Babylon on the first of Adar.

The one letter written by Sin-iddinam[3] is addressed to the *rabiânu* of Katalla, ordering him to send the plaintiff in a suit to him. Very interesting is a letter from Tabbi-Wadi and Mâr-Shamash to Aḫâti, the wife of Sin-iddinam,[4] asking her to intercede for them with Sin-iddinam. He had himself referred them to her, perhaps because their offence immediately concerned her. They say that they are ill acquainted with the ways of the court. From several unusual forms of expression it may be concluded that they were strangers who had settled in Babylonia. They do not state either their offence or the grounds on which they would be excused, but ask for an interview, that they may remove Aḫâti's resentment against them. Of Sin-iddinam

---

[1] K. L. Ḫ., No. 56. [2] K. L. Ḫ., No. 50.
[3] K. L. Ḫ., No. 47. [4] K. L. Ḫ., No. 48.

Periphrasis for "king"

Some letters are addressed to "the man whom may Marduk make to flourish."[1] Some have taken this as a proper name. But that seems very unlikely. Others regard it as a sort of polite address to a superior. Winckler[2] suggested that it was an address to the king. The Code has made it clear that the *amêlu* was the "gentleman," or "noble," who lived in a "palace," or "great house." Hence, these letters may be addressed to any great official. But many turns of expression support the view that the king is really meant; he was thus the "First Gentleman" of Babylonia. It was not till Ḫammurabi that the title "king" was generally given. Perhaps the old nobles were slow to admit a king over them.

Freeing of runaway slaves

As an example we may take:[3]

To "the man whom may Marduk make to flourish" say, thus saith Ashtamar-Adadi: May Shamash and Marduk ever make thee flourish. The gardeners, inhabitants of Sippara, have spoken concerning their servants who fled and have been recaptured. Therefore I have sent a note thus to thee, I sent those men to thee. Accept their petition (?) and may they be acceptable to thee before Shamash. Grant their entreaty and set them free. If they come not to Babylon, do this in my name.

It is probable that recaptured runaway slaves, who would not name their owners, were forfeit to the State. The king is the only one who would have power to release such slaves. It is clear that the recipient of the letter was at Babylon.

---

[1] *Ana Amêlim-ŝha-Marduk-ubalaṭuŝhu.*

[2] A. O. F., ii., 312.

[3] V. A., Th. 793; B. A. S., ii., p. 563.

# IV

## PRIVATE LETTERS OF THE FIRST DYNASTY OF BABYLON

Many details uncertain

In these cases, as a rule, we know neither the sender nor receiver, beyond their names, and what we can gather from the letter itself. Hence a great deal must always remain uncertain. Here is a letter which comes from a prisoner, who says he is nearly starved and does not know why he was imprisoned:[1]

A prisoner's plea to his master for deliverance

To my lord say, thus saith Bêlshunu, thy servant: From the time that I was shut up in the house of the *abarakku*, thou, my lord, hast kept me alive. What is the reason that my lord has neglected me for five months? The house where I am imprisoned is a starvation-house. Now have I made the jailer carry a letter to my lord. When thou, my lord, shalt make an end of my misery, send, and the imprisonment, since it has been ended by thee, I will cause to conduce to thy blessing (I will even thank thee for). I am ill . . . ten *ḲA* of *SU-DA*, thirty-one *ḲA ZAG-ḪI-LI* . . . two *ḲA SAR-SAR EL-SAR* send me that I die not; and clothing send me that I may cover my nakedness. A *ḫubidu* has come upon me on account of thee, my lord. Either half a shekel of silver, or two minas of wool, send to me, for my service, let him bring it. Let not the jailer be sent away empty-handed. If he comes empty-handed, the dogs may eat me. As thou, my lord, and the people of Sippara and Babylon, all of them know, I am imprisoned, not for robbery, nor was I caught at burglary. Thou, my lord, didst send me with oil across the river, but the Sutû fell upon me and I was imprisoned. Speak a friendly word to the servants of the king's *abarakku*. Send, that I die not in the house

[1] B. 290 ff.

of misery. Send a *ḲA* of oil and five *ḲA* of salt. That which thou didst lately send no one gave me. Whatsoever thou sendest, send it fastened up (?).

There are many obscurities about this letter. Some are caused by the difficulty of reading the defaced characters. Some by the fact that the signs, printed here in capitals, are ideograms whose meaning is not yet clear. The prisoner, if his plea is true, was sent on an errand for his master, apparently to trade for him. He was either robbed by the nomad Sutû, or compelled to give up his oil to them. Why this led to imprisonment is not clear, unless it was regarded as furnishing supplies to the enemy. But though his master did not get him out of prison, it seems that he had sent him supplies from time to time. The word rendered "jailer" is perhaps a name, Mâr-abulli, "son of the gate." But it may be a title used as a name, "Mr. Jailer." The prisoner thinks that it is in the power of his master to put an end to his imprisonment and promises to be grateful. But he does not seem sure whether his master can do this. He asks, however, for further supplies, if he is to live. Let us hope he was released or at least fed. We may perhaps conclude that imprisonment was the punishment due for robbery and burglary.

A father reminded of a broken promise

Here is a letter reminding a father of a broken promise:[1]

To my father say, thus saith Elmeshu: Shamash and Marduk fill with well-being the days of my father perpetually. My father, be thou well, flourish; the God that preserves my father direct my father's source of grace. I have sent to greet my father. May my father's peace endure before Shamash and Marduk. From the time that Sin Amurrû named my father's name, and I answered for my fault, thou, my father, didst say, "When I shall go to Dûr-Ammi-zadûga, which is on the River Sharḳu, I will forward a sheep and five minas of silver, in a little while, to thee." This thou saidest, my father, and my expectation was from my father. But thou hast not sent;

---

[1] B[2] 212.

and now, my father, thou hast returned to the presence of Taribu, the Queen. I have sent a note to my father's presence. My father, thou shalt not ask the purport of my note, until Lashêr has brought me my father's note. My father has not sent one to bring even a single shekel, in accordance with thy promise. Like Marduk and Sin Amurrû, who hearken to my father, my ears are attentive. Let my father send and let not my heart be vexed. Before Shamash and Marduk, may I pray for my father.

The letter suggests that the father was king, by the phrase so common in the historical inscriptions, "named his name," usually equivalent to "nominated" to rule. The word rendered "fault" is *sardu*, which may be for *sartu*. There is nothing to show whether Elmeshu is a man or woman. There was an Elmeshu (the name means "Diamond") who was daughter of Ammi-ditana.[1] But the mention of Dûr-Ammi-zadûga seems to demand a date at least as late as that in which this wall or city was built. But Ammi-zadûga succeeded Ammi-ditana. Unless the latter built Dûr-Ammi-zadûga and called it after his son, we can hardly identify this Elmeshu with the daughter of Ammi-ditana. The mention of Sin Amurrû is not quite clear. We may suppose two gods, Sin and Amurrû, or take the latter name as an epithet, "Sin of the Amorites." To have "the ears attentive," is to be in a state of expectation. In the last sentence, Elmeshu seems to hint that, if she does not have a favorable answer, she will not be able to pray for her father. This may be regarded as an un-Christian attitude, but people then thought more of the efficacy of prayer; and it was a threat, if so meant, likely to have great weight with the father. But it may mean that Elmeshu being vowed to a religious life, yet needed material means to maintain her alive, and she merely hopes, by her father's continued sustenance of her, to be long spared to pray for him.

[1] B[1] 193.

Request from a tenant for the grant of a good cow

Another letter is apparently from a tenant, or serf, to his landlord:[1]

To my lord say, thus saith Ibgatum thy servant: As, my lord, thou hast heard, the enemy has carried off my oxen. Never before have I sent to thee, my lord. Now I have caused a letter to be brought to thee, my lord. Do thou, my lord, send me one young cow. I will weigh out and send five shekels of silver to thee, my lord. My lord, what thou sayest, under the command of Marduk, thy protector, what pleases thee, no one can hinder thee, my lord. My lord, do thou make her worth the five shekels of silver that I have weighed out and sent to thee. Do thou, my lord, treat seriously this request, do not trifle with my wish. Let my lord not wonder at this request, which I send my lord. I am thy servant. I will do thy will, my lord. As to the young cow, which thou, my lord, dost send, let her be on credit, and either to Baṣu, or wherever is convenient to my lord, do thou send. With Ili-iḳîsham, my brother, let the young cow come. And I, in order that my lord should quickly consent and send the young cow, will forthwith weigh out and send fifteen shekels of silver to thee, my lord.

Evidently, the wise man sent only five shekels on deposit with his brother, holding back the rest of the price, till he had seen what sort of a cow he was to get for his money. It was from this letter that Winckler[2] deduced a meaning for *ṣamâdu* something like "weigh out," "pay," whence a better meaning for *ṣimittu* than "yoke" was readily obtained. As Dr. Peiser pointed out, the word is also used in the Cappadocian tablets in a way that leaves small doubt of its meaning. It may have come to mean simply "pay," but must have ordinarily meant "measure," or "weigh," according as it was applied to grain, or money.

Authorization to compel a creditor to pay his debts

Here is a very interesting example showing how the merchants of those days transacted business at a distance:[3]

To Erib-Sin say, thus saith Ibni-Nabû, I am here (?): As to the case of Ardi-ilishu, son of Ibni-Dibbara, I gave him two-thirds of a

---

[1] B[2] 2185. [2] A. O. F., ii., p. 90. [3] B[2] 315.

mina of silver, and it was acknowledged in writing, in the presence of my witnesses. He went to Assyria. He did not give the money to Shamaiatu. I and Shamaiatu met in Daganna and disputed over the affair. Said I, "I sent thee money by Ardi-ilishu." He said, "If Ardi-ilishu has paid the money, let him [*here come some uncertain signs*]." And concerning what thou didst send about Shamash-bêl-ilâni's fourteen shekels, I did not give him the money. There is two-thirds of a mina due from Ardi-ilishu; take Ardi-ilishu and cause him to weigh out the money, and its interest, more or less, and from that take the fourteen shekels and send the surplus.

The two, Erib-Sin and Ibni-Nabû, are either partners, or agents. The former had asked the latter to pay over fourteen shekels to a certain Shamash-bêl-ilâni, either because the latter had money of his, or had promised to honor his order. But this particular order was not honored. Ibni-Nabû had intrusted a sum of forty shekels to one Ardi-ilishu, with which to pay Shamaiatu. But Ardi-ilishu had gone off to Assyria without discharging the obligation. So Shamaiatu had demanded payment and perhaps the doubtful signs express the fact that Ibni-Nabû had to pay a second time. Fortunately, he could prove that Ardi-ilishu had had the money, having taken a receipt. He seems to think that Erib-Sin can find Ardi-ilishu. Was the former resident in Assyria? If so, this must be a copy of the letter sent him. But perhaps Erib-Sin was to arrest the defaulter on his return to Sippara. At any rate, this was a warrant for so doing. That, perhaps, is why the letter was kept. If Erib-Sin could get forty shekels and the interest, he had a fair margin from which to pay the fourteen shekels, due to him from Ibni-Nabû. But he had to take risks. If Shamash-bêl-ilâni had given Erib-Sin consideration for his order on Ibni-Nabû for fourteen shekels, he was badly served.

A warning connected with the filing of a suit

Here is a letter, warning a man of a suit brought against him in his absence:

To my lord, say, thus saith Sin-taiar: May Shamash and Marduk give thee health. As to the case of the field about which thou didst send, belonging to the sons of Sin-rêmêni, which is in Bitûtu, which my lord sold me for five minas of silver; Sin-aḫam-iddinam, Marduk-taiar, and Nabû-malik, have gone about to the king, and have turned over this title to Nûr-parim. Hasten, come, save thy title from Nûr-parim.

The word of most difficulty is *nistu*, rendered "title." It may mean something different, but the "title" seems the most likely thing to be disputed.

A request for fish and other food

A letter to a father from an absent son[1] is interesting for its personal character:

To my father say, thus saith Zimri-eraḫ, may Shamash and Marduk give thee health forever. Be thou well. I have sent for thy health. Tell me how thou art. I am located at Dûr-Sin on the canal Kashtim-sikirim. There is no meat fit to eat. Now I have made them bring two-thirds of a shekel of silver to thee. For this money send some nice fish and something to eat.

A love-letter

The following is what may be fairly described as a love-letter, though the real relation between the correspondents is not certain:[2]

To Bibêa say, thus saith Gimil-Marduk: May Shamash and Marduk for my sake preserve thy health forever. I have sent for thy health. Tell me how thou art. I went to Babylon and did not see thee. I was greatly disappointed. Send me the reason of thy leaving, and let me be cheered. In Marchesvan do thou come. For my sake keep well always.

It is certain that Bibêa was a lady, perhaps the writer's wife.

Assyrian copies of old Babylonian letters

The interest which these ancient letters inspire in us was felt in the seventh century B.C., for there are two Assyrian

[1] S. 273. [2] S. 274.

copies of early Babylonian letters, preserved in the remains of Ashurbânipal's library. One was a letter from the Babylonian King Adadi-shum-uṣur to Ashur-nirari and Nabûdaian, kings of Assyria, about B.C. 1250.[1] It is too fragmentary to translate. Another[2] is a letter from a King of Assyria to his father, who is King of Babylon. The names are lost, and its contents cannot now be made out. It was a copy made for Ashurbânipal, and has his "library mark."[3]

[1] III. R. 4, No. 5. [2] K. 2, 41. [3] K. L. Ḫ., i., p. xxiii., note 2.

## V

## SENNACHERIB'S LETTERS TO HIS FATHER, SARGON

The proof that the letters are Sennacherib's

AMONG the Ninevite collections we can single out several periods where the history is supplemented by the letters. Thus Sennacherib's letters to his father, Sargon, chiefly deal with events in Armenia, which must have transpired during Sargon's last few years, when his annals and other historical inscriptions are silent. This view of them was first worked out by the present writer,[1] and later with increased material by R. C. Thompson.[2] Briefly put, the argument from them is this: a person called Sennacherib, who might be any officer from the times of Sargon onward, writes to the king, whom he does not address as his father, on the reports which have reached him from a number of officials, concerning events in Armenia. We have, however, two letters which refer to the same events, naming the same officials and certainly from the same Sennacherib. In one of them he is twice referred to as the king's son. The officials named are all found in documents of the reign of Sargon, or the early part of Sennacherib's reign. The King of Armenia is named Argista in one of these reports to the king, which belongs to the same group. The King of Assyria himself is said to be at Babylon at the time. One report quoted comes from Tabal, and is brought by the major-domo of the Princess Aḫat-abisha, probably the daughter of Sargon, who was married by him to the King of

[1] P. S. B. A., 1895, p. 220 f. [2] A. J. S. L., xvi., pp. 160-67.

Tabal. We have independent copies of these reports, quoted by Sennacherib, which enlarge our knowledge of the events. Hence, there can be no doubt that we have here Sennacherib's letters to his father, Sargon, while that king was absent in Babylonia. We are, therefore, able to reconstruct a chapter of Assyrian history, on which the historical monuments have nothing to say. The first letter reads thus:[1]

A letter concerning events in Armenia

To the king, my lord, thy servant Sennacherib. Peace be to the king, my lord. There is peace in Assyria, peace in the temples, peace in all the fortresses of the king. May the heart of the king, my lord, be abundantly cheered. The land of the Ukkai has sent to me, saying, when the King of Armenia came to the land of Gamir, his forces were utterly defeated; he, his commanders, and their forces were driven off; [*then comes a broken space from which the few traces left refer to "two commanders," someone who "came," someone or something "was captured," someone "came to me," something "of his country," something "he appointed."*] This was the news from the land of the Ukkai. Ashur-riṣûa has sent, saying, "News from Armenia. What I sent before, that is so. A great slaughter took place among them. Now his land is quiet. His nobles are dead. He has come into his own land. Ḳaḳḳadânu, his tartan, is taken, and the King of Armenia is in the land of Uazaun." This is the news from Ashur-riṣûa. Nabû-li', the commander of Ḫalṣu, has sent to me, saying, "Concerning the garrisons of the fortresses which are on the border, I sent to them for news of the King of Armenia. They report that when he came to the land of Gamir, his forces were all slain, three of his nobles together with their forces were killed, he himself fled and entered into his own land; but that as yet his camp is not attacked." This is the news from Nabû-li'. The King of Muṣaṣir, his brother, and his son, have gone to greet the King of Armenia. A messenger from Ḫupushkia has gone to greet him. The garrisons of the fortresses which are on the boundary all send news like this. The letter of Nabû-li', the major-domo of Aḫat-abisha, brought from Tabal; to the king, my lord, I have sent it on.

The second letter[2] began in exactly the same way, so far as one can judge from the traces of the first seven lines. As

[1] K. 181; H. 197. [2] H. 198.

Another letter regarding the movements of the Armenian king

before, Sennacherib quotes reports, which he has received, in the sender's own words. From what is left of the first report we learn that the King of Armenia had ordered the forces at his command to capture the commanders of the King of Assyria and bring them alive to him. The city of Kumai is named as the place where these commanders were. As yet the sender "is cut off" and has not withdrawn from his post. But, as he has heard, so he has sent to the king's son:

"Now let him quickly send forces. This is the news from Ariê: On the fourteenth of Elul, a letter came to me from Ashur-riṣûa, saying that the King of Armenia, when the Zikirtai brought things to him, at least obtained nothing, they returned empty-handed; that he went to the city Uesi with his forces and entered it, that his forces are in the city Uesi, that he and his forces are few, that they are with him with their possessions."

This seems to be the end of Ashur-riṣûa's news. A few traces refer to news from the Mannai concerning some "letter," "as yet" something has "not" happened.

"As I have heard I have sent, that the commander in the district, in the midst of the city Uesi, he and his forces are assembled; that with his troops he has set out and driven him out of Uesi, that he has not seen the roads (to some place), that he has made good the bridges, that as he has heard, whatever takes place, whether he comes with his forces, or whether he goes off free, I will quickly send to the king's son."

These fragments of the report are difficult to disentangle, as the person referred to seems sometimes to be the King of Armenia, sometimes another person. But all may be news sent from the Mannai to Ashur-riṣûa.

This is the news from Ashur-riṣûa: The land of Arzabia sends word, saying, The land of the Ukkai has broken away from me (?), that now they are killing me; you care for yourselves. I have sent my body-guards to the Ukkai. The messengers of Arzabia said, . . .

Then follow a few traces from which we gather that a messenger came to the writer and brought a present; that the "Mannai said" something, someone "returned" and "I appointed him" something, that a messenger from the land of Sadudai came to Kalaḫ, that "I received and sealed" something, and "I appointed" something. Again we have a reference to the month of Elul, a letter, and the word "brought."

These letters explained by a comparison with those of Ashur-riṣûa

This letter is very obscure from the many lacunæ. We naturally turn to the letters of Ashur-riṣûa. This man may well be the same as the witness, *shaḳû*, and scribe of the queen, at Kalaḫ in B.C. 709. We have nine letters of his referring to Armenian affairs. In one of them[1] he announces that "at the commencement of Nisan the King of Armenia set out from Ṭurushpîa and went to Eliṣada, that Ḳaḳḳadânu, his tartan, went into the city Uesi, that all the forces of Armenia have gathered to Eliṣada." The rest of the letter is obscure. At the end of another[2] he says: "I have heard, saying, "the king has come into the midst of Uesi, as yet he has not left." In the same letter he reports that "three thousand foot-soldiers, with their officers, belonging to Sêtini, his military commander, have set out to Muṣaṣir, crossed the river by night, that Sêtini has camels with him, and that Sunâ, who is in command among the Ukkai, has started with his troops for Muṣaṣir." It is clear from these that the movements here refer to the beginning of the year after that in which, in Elul, the King of Armenia was in Uesi, and before the defeat of Armenia by the Gimirri.

A mere glance at the contents of his other letters will show their connection with these events. In one,[3] he sends Naragê, a colonel, with twenty men who had plotted against the king and were caught. He mentions the capture of a second tartan, Urṣini, in Ṭurushpîa and the mission of Urṣini's

[1] H. 492. [2] H. 380. [3] H. 144.

brother, Apli-uknu, to see him there. The King of Armenia had entered Ṭurushpîa with a number of restless men. In another,[1] he reports the return to Assyria of a messenger from the Ukkai, who had gone up into Armenia; and mentions Muṣaṣir. In a third,[2] he reports that "Gurânia, Nagiu, the fortresses of Armenia and Gimirri, are giving tribute to Armenia." But that "when the Armenians went to Gimirri, they were badly defeated." The rest is so injured as to give little sense. In another,[3] he names Ariê and Ariṣâ, Dûr-Shamash, Barzanishtun, the city of Ishtar-dûri, and Shulmu-bêl-lashme; but the text is so defective that one cannot discern what he had to say about them. In another,[4] he acknowledges the king's order to send scouts into the neighborhood of Ṭurushpîa. In another,[5] he writes that "the Mannai in the cities of Armenia on the coast of the sea rebelled, that Apli-uknu, the commander of Muṣaṣir, and Ṭunnaun, the commander of Kar-Sippar, went to the borders of the Mannai, to garrison Armenia and made a slaughter there, that all the commanders are present." But these are not the only references to him. Ṭâb-shâr-Ashur[6] writes to the king that he has received a letter from Ashur-riṣûa: "Thus it is written in it, saying, a messenger of the Ukkai went to Armenia, he has sent a letter to the palace, and these are the contents of the letter, on the morning of the sixth, this letter came to me; he sent, saying, the Ukkai have heard concerning Ariê that he went against him (the king of Armenia) and his city." Then the letter becomes very defective, but we hear again of Kumai and Eliṣ (clearly the Eliṣada above). Ṭâb-shâr-Ashur again mentions Ashur-riṣûa,[7] saying that a letter of his was brought, which referred to the King of Armenia entering some city. But too little is preserved to make out the message. In a report[8] about

[1] H. 145. [2] H. 146. [3] H. 147. [4] H. 148.
[5] H. 381. [6] H. 101. [7] H. 488. [8] H. 490.

beams of wood, collected by Ashur-riṣûa, he is associated with Ariê, and Uriṣâ, evidently the Ariṣâ above, and the city Kumai. Finally, on a letter by Gabbu-ana-Ashur he is mentioned in a most significant way. The writer says: "Concerning the news which the king gave me about the garrisons of Armenia, from the time that I entered the city Kurban, my messengers went to Nabû-li', to Ashur-bêl-danân, to Ashur-riṣûa; they came to me." After a break he goes on, "Like this I have heard; the Armenian (king) has not gone out of Ṭurushpîa." After some more uncertain traces, he adds: "On the twenty-third of Tammuz I entered into Kurban, on the twentieth of Ab I sent a letter to the king, my lord." It is evident that Nabû-li', Ashur-bêl-danân, and Ashur-riṣûa were the commanders most concerned in these events. Nabû-li', we have already seen, sent reports to Sennacherib; no letters of Ashur-bêl-danân, yet published, seem to refer to these events. But clearly the king was concerned to hear from other quarters than Kalaḫ, where Sennacherib evidently was. Ashur-riṣûa is also named elsewhere on fragments not yet published.

We may now pursue the clew given by the fact that Uesi was the city which seems to have been the bone of contention. Thus Urzana, whose name recalls that of the King of Muṣaṣir, who may have been reinstated as a vassal by Sargon, writes[1] to the *nâgiru* of the palace:

"What thou didst send me, saying, Has the King of Armenia with his troops moved away? He has gone. Where is he dwelling? The commander of Uesi, the commander of the district of the Ukkai, came, they sacrificed in the temple, they say that the king has gone, he is dwelling in Uesi; the commanders returned and went away. In Muṣaṣir they sacrificed. What thou didst send, saying, Without the king's order let no one put his hand to the work, when the king of Assyria shall come, I will serve him, what I have [always] done I will keep doing, and this according to his hand (?)."

[1] H. 409.

Evidently Urzana lived in Muṣaṣir and was anxious to be thought a faithful vassal. An unknown writer[1] tells the king that

"five commanders of Armenia entered the city of Uesi, Sêteni [*of whom we heard above*] commander of . . . teni, Ḳaḳḳadânu of the writer's district, or of Ukkai, Sakuatâ of Ḳaniun, Siblia of Alzi, Ṭutu of Armiraliu, these are their names. With three underlings, they entered Uesi. Now their forces are weak and weakening (?), the forces are (?), the king has set out from Ṭurushpîa, he has come into Kaniun. What the king, my lord, sent me, saying, 'Send scouts,' I have sent a second time. The spies (?) came, these are the words they say, and the spies as yet have not started."

The whole tone of the letter and the fact that Ashur-riṣûa above acknowledges having received an order to send scouts make us think he is the unknown writer. But, of course, the king may have sent the order to other commanders as well. In an unpublished text we read that the commander of Uesi was slain.

The references to Ṭurushpîa are also significant. We know that this city was once the stronghold of Sardaurri, King of Armenia, and was doubtless still attached to its old rulers. We have a letter written by Upaḫḫir-Bêl, doubtless the Eponym of B.C. 706, and governor of Amedi. He writes in the same style as Sennacherib and Ashur-riṣûa:[2]

Concerning news of Armenia I sent scouts, they have returned; thus they say: "The commander of that district, and the deputy-commander with him, in Ḫarda, the district of the *sukallu*, keep ward from city to city as far as Ṭurushpîa; weakness is written down, the messenger of Argista has come,"

and so on. The rest does not concern us here. But another letter,[3] evidently from the same writer, gives news from Armenia and a message from Argista, which the writer says

---

[1] H. 444. [2] H. 424. [3] H. 548.

he has answered, as the king directed. It also states that the commander keeps ward in Ḫarda. Ṭurushpîa is also mentioned on fragments not yet published.

Other fragments occur which clearly belong to this group. Thus[1] a letter from an unknown writer names Ashur-riṣûa in connection with Kumai, Babutai, Ukkai, and Uliai, and narrates something about ten commanders. The loss of nine commanders in Armenia, at one time, is the subject of a very fragmentary letter,[2] but it is not clear that it refers to this period.

To the same period seems to belong another letter of Sennacherib, probably to his father Sargon.[3] It begins with precisely the same formulæ of greeting in the first seven lines. Then it goes on:

The chieftains of the land of Kumuḫai (Commagene) have come and brought tribute. Seven mule mares apiece they brought and tribute with the mules. The chieftains are in the house appointed for the Kumuḫai. They are fed at their own expense, they would journey on to Babylon [where Sargon evidently is]. They have brought *šaklâ* (?), they have received them here. As we have told the king, my lord, let him send quickly. They brought cloth and fruit each of them. The factors say that we have received seven talents from them, that the Kumuḫai are not contented, saying, "Our produce is reduced, let them bring the king's weavers and let them take charge." Let the king, my lord, send word to whom they shall assign them.

A letter about the chieftains of the Kumuḫai

Another letter-fragment only preserves the opening address.[4] Another very defective letter[5] with the same introduction refers to Dûr-Sargon,

"in the district of Kurban are excessively great floods, they go on."

We know from another source that this was the case, in B.C. 708, when the floods came into the lower part of the

[1] H. 619. [2] H. 646. [3] H. 196. [4] H. 199. [5] H. 731.

city, and the tribute could not be levied in the district.[1] Yet another fragment, opening in precisely the same manner, refers to a certain Nabû-eṭir-napshâte and the city of Kalḫu.[2] Here also we have too little left to make out any connected sense.

[1] A. D. D., 1141. [2] H. 730.

## VI

## LETTERS FROM THE LAST YEAR OF SHAMASH-SHUM-UKÎN

Another period on which the letters throw considerable light is the close of the reign of Shamash-shum-ukîn in Babylon. This was coeval with the suppression of a great combined rebellion against the rule of Assyria. From the historical texts of Ashurbânipal's reign we know the names of many of the actors in that great struggle. They are frequently referred to in the letters. Already G. Smith, in his *History of Assurbanipal*, 1871, had used the information given by some of the letters. This was utilized by C. P. Tiele in his *Babylonisch-assyrische Geschichte*. The period well known

But much more may be made out when the letters are fully available. Thus Nabû-bêl-shumâte, grandson of Merodach Baladan II., had been made King of the Sealands on the death of his uncle, Nâ'id-Marduk. When the revolt broke out, Ashurbânipal sent Assyrian troops to help Nabû-bêl-shumâte to repel Shamash-shum-ukîn. During the long process of suppressing the revolt, it is clear that Nabû-bêl-shumâte conceived the idea of reasserting the independence of the Sealands. He endeavored to gain the alliance of the Assyrian garrison, some he imprisoned, others may have joined him. On the fall of Babylon, in B.C. 648, he saw that Ashurbânipal's vengeance must overtake him, so he fled to Elam. He took with him a certain number of Assyrians, evidently to hold as hostages. Ashur- The case of Nabû-bêl-shumâte bânipal had a long score to settle with Elam. He began by demanding of Indabigash the surrender of Nabû-bêl-shu-mâte and the Assyrians with him. But before the ambassador could deliver the message, Indabigash had been succeeded by Ummanaldash. Nabû-bêl-shumâte was evidently a difficult person to lay hands upon. At any rate, Ummanaldash's land was invaded and devastated. But when the Assyrian troops were gone, he again returned to his capital, Madaktu, and Nabû-bêl-shumâte joined him there. Again Ashurbânipal sent to demand his surrender. Rather than further embarrass his host, and quite hopeless of protection or pardon, Nabû-bêl-shumâte ordered his armor-bearer to slay him. Ummanaldash attempted to conciliate Ashurbânipal by sending the body of the dead man and the head of the armor-bearer to him. Such is the story as Ashurbânipal tells it in his great cylinder inscription.

Letters about him

The letters make no less than fifty distinct references to him. The officers write many bad things of Nabû-bêl-shu-mâte, and it is plain that he had been a very vicious enemy. We have a number of letters from a writer of his name, who may well be the King of the Sealands before he broke with Assyria. Thus we read:[1]

A letter reporting the dethronement of the King of Elam

To the king, my lord, thy servant Nabû-bêl-shumâte. Verily peace be to the king, my lord; may Ashur, Nabû, and Marduk be gracious to the king, my lord. Cheer of heart, health of body, and length of days may they grant the king, my lord. As I hear, the King of Elam is deposed and many cities have rebelled against him, saying, "We will not come into thy hands." According to what I hear I have sent to the king, my lord. I have inhabited the Sealands from the time of Nâ'id-Marduk. The brigands and fugitives who came to the Gurunammu, five hundred of them, did Sin-balâṭsu-iḳbi, when he caught them, lay in fetters and hand over to Natânu, the King of the Uṭṭai, their ruler, whom the king had given them.

[1] H. 839.

Then come a number of defective lines, from which not much can be made out. But there can be little doubt that this letter was written in the days when policy still kept him faithful to Assyria. There was another Nabû-bêl-shumâte, whose letters[1] begin quite differently, and refer to horses and troops. There is even a third, a *ḳêpu* of Birati, named by Tâb-ṣil-esharra,[2] who was concerned in repelling a raid on Sippara, and is named in a contract of B.C. 686.[3] It is just possible that the second and third are the same man. But while we must exercise care in assigning the references of the letters, we have a guide in the historical connection.

Bêl-ibnî's letters

Bêl-ibnî was a very important officer who held the position of a *manzâz pâni*, having the right of access to the royal presence and a place near the king on all state occasions. He is probably to be distinguished from the Bêl-ibnî set on the throne of Babylon by Sennacherib in B.C. 702. He is a frequent writer to the king during this period. Ashurbânipal placed him over the Sealand after the flight of Nabû-bêl-shumâte. The king's proclamation to the Sealanders[4] reads thus:

Letter appointing him governor of the Sealands

> Order of the king to the Sealanders, elders and juniors, my servants: My peace be with you. May your hearts be cheered. See now how my full gaze is upon you. And before the sin of Nabû-bêl-shumâte, I appointed over you the courtesan of Menânu. Now I have sent Bêl-ibnî, my *dubašu*, to go before you. Whatever order is good in my opinion which is [written] in my letters [obey].

Then after some defaced lines, he threatens that if they do not obey,

> "I will send my troops."

This order is dated the fifth of Iyyar, B.C. 650. By that date Nabû-bêl-shumâte had fled. It is not easy to say whether Ashurbânipal had appointed a lady, once the *ḫar-*

[1] H. 832, 833, 835, 836, 837. [2] H. 88. [3] A. D. D., 9. [4] H. 289.

*imtu*, or courtesan, of Menânu, as ruler of the Sealand before Nabû-bêl-shumâte, or whether he means to call Nabû-bêl-shumâte by this opprobrious epithet. Who is meant by Menânu is hard to see, unless it be the Elamite King, Umman-minana, the contemporary of Sennacherib, who had protected the family of Merodach-Baladan II.

Letter of Ummanaldash offering to give up Nabû-bêl-shumâte

We have a fragmentary letter[1] from the King of Elam, Ummanaldash, to Ashurbânipal, which says:

Letter of Ummanaldash, King of Elam, to Ashurbânipal, King of Assyria, peace be to my brother. From the beginning, the Martenai [*Elamite name for the Sealanders, from Marratu, "the Salt Marshes"*] have been sinners against thee. Nabû-bêl-shumâte came from there. The crossing of the land . . . over against Elam I broke down, [to keep him out]. Thou hast sent letters [*or forces?*] saying, "Send Nabû-bêl-shumâte." I will seize Nabû-bêl-shumâte and will send him to thee. The Martenai whom from the beginning Nabû-bêl-shumâte brought us . . . they are people who came by water from . . . it entered into their minds and they came, they broke into Laḫiru and there they are. I will send to their border my servants against them and by their hands I will send those who have sinned against us. If they are in my land, I will send them by their hands; and, if they have crossed the river, do thou [take them].

The rest of the letter is hard to make out. It was dated on the twenty-sixth of Tammuz, in the Eponymy of Nabû-shar-aḫêshu, probably B.C. 645.

Letter of Bêl-ibnî accusing Nabû-bêl-shumâte of imprisoning his brother

Bêl-ibnî had a great hatred for Nabû-bêl-shumâte. For the latter had years before laid hands upon Bêl-ibnî's eldest brother, Bêlshunu, and put him in prison. This we learn from a letter to the king,[2] which, although the name of the writer is lost, is clearly from Bêl-ibnî. The first few lines yield no connected sense, but name Umman-shimash and the nobles with him:

When they assembled they spoke evil words against their king. From those days they kept on plundering his land. Before the

[1] G. Smith, ii., pp. 51 ff. [2] H. 460.

forces of the lord of kings, my lord, want, like a pestilence, entered the land. When the forces of the lord of kings, my lord, have arrived at Dûr-ili, they shall not take a holiday; that smitten of Bêl, accursed of the gods, Nabû-bêl-shumâte, and the sinners with him, they shall capture and give them to the lord of kings, my lord. And the Assyrians, as many as are with them, they shall release and send to the lord of kings, my lord. Bêlshunu, my eldest brother, a servant of the lord of kings, my lord, now four years ago, did that smitten of Bêl, that accursed of the gods, Nabû-bêl-shumâte, when he revolted, bind hand and foot with bronze and imprison him.

The rest is obscure, but names Ṣalmu-shar-iḳbi as sending news to the palace.

Bêlshunu's identity

The Bêlshunu here named is probably the Eponym of B.C. 648, who was then governor of Ḫindana, who also dates a letter from the king to Umman-shimash, which names Bêl-ibnî. There are over fifty references in the letters to Bêl-ibnî, most of which directly connect him with these events. His duties in command of the Sealand brought him into relations with the many Elamites, who in the frequent revolutions in that land, fled for refuge to the Assyrians. Here is one of the best of his letters to the king:[1]

His letter about the fugitive Shumâ

To the lord of kings, my lord, thy servant Bêl-ibnî. May Ashur, Shamash, and Marduk decree length of days, cheer of heart, and health of body to the lord of kings, my lord. Shumâ, son of Shum-iddina, son of Gaḫal, sister's son to Tammaritu, fled from Elam and came to the Daḫḫai. From the Daḫḫai, when I had taken him, I made him cross over. He is ill. As soon as he has completely recovered his health, I will send him to the king, my lord. A messenger is here from Natan and the Pukudu, who are in Til-Ḫumba, to say that they came before Nabû-bêl-shumâte at the city Targibâti. They took an oath, by God, one with another, saying, "According to agreement we will send thee all the news we hear." And according to contract they furnished fifty oxen for money at his hands, and said to him, "Let our sheep come and among the Ubânât in the pasture let them graze among them. Thou mayest have confidence in us."

[1] H. 282.

Now let a messenger of the king, my lord, come and make Natan learn in his mind, that "if thou dost send anything for sale to Elam, or one sheep be allotted to pasture in Elam, I will not suffer thee to live." I have sent trustworthy reports to the king, my lord.

The incident here referred to, the reception of the fugitive Shumâ, who probably on account of his illness was unable to join his uncle Tammaritu, is very similar to that related of Tammaritu himself. This King of Elam succeeded his cousin Ummanigash, whom he dethroned, but after a short reign was himself dethroned by the usurper Indabigash. He and his brothers and family and eighty-five princes of Elam, his supporters, fled by sea from Elam to the marshes at the mouths of the Tigris and Euphrates. There he fell sick. But Ashurbânipal sent him a friendly message, and he came before the Assyrian governor, and kissed the ground in token of submission. We learn that Marduk-shar-uṣur was the officer who received him, and a very mutilated letter seems to refer to it. He was probably the Rabshakeh to whom Bêl-ibnî wrote[1] complaining of certain slanders about him. So even the faithful servant was not entirely free from court intrigues. In another letter Bêl-ibnî refers to his having received and sent on to the king, Tammaritu, his brothers, family, and nobles.[2]

Many letters of this period

Like Ummanigash and Indabigash, Tammaritu corresponded with Ashurbânipal. We have letters from him to the King of Assyria and from Ashurbânipal to him. Unfortunately these letters are very imperfect, or not yet published. He is mentioned continually in the letters. There were several of the name: (1) son of Urtaku, third brother of Teumman, (2) son of Teumman, slain with his father, (3) son of Ummanigash, King of Elam, succeeded his cousin Ummanigash, whom he dethroned, (4) son of Attamitu. To which of these a reference is made is often hard to decide.

---

[1] H. 283. [2] H. 284.

## VII

## LETTERS REGARDING AFFAIRS IN SOUTHERN BABYLONIA

Their character that of forecasts or omens

ANOTHER group refers to the events at Ur, in the far south of Babylonia. Sin-tabni-uṣur, son of Ningal-iddina, was governor there during the time of Shamash-shum-ukîn's great rebellion. This we learn from some of the forecast tablets, published in George Smith's *Assurbanipal*.[1] The greater part of these tablets is unintelligible, containing a record of the omens observed, probably on inspection of the entrails of the slaughtered sacrifices. What these symptoms were cannot yet be determined. Much has been done by Boissier in his *Textes Assyriens relatifs au Présage*, and many articles contributed to various journals. The omens are generally such as also occur in the tablets published by Dr. Knudtzon in his *Gebete an den Sonnengott*, and ably discussed by him there. The tablet evidently was meant to submit these omens to some oracle that a prediction might be given on their authority. The king also usually stated his cause of anxiety and asked for guidance and direction.

Their great value

These forecast tablets, many of which are dated, are of the greatest service for the chronology of the period. They have been partly discussed by the present writer.[2] Thus the two, which refer to Sin-tabni-uṣur, announce that he is governor of Ur, and seem to inquire whether he can be relied upon to prove faithful. We may conclude that his appointment took place in Ab, B.C. 648.

[1] Pages 184, 185. [2] In P. S. B. A., etc.

A letter of the governor of Erech

From a letter,[1] which G. Smith[2] ascribes to Kudur, governor of Erech, we learn that he had heard from Sin-tabni-uṣur, who reports that a messenger had arrived from Shamash-shum-ukîn, inciting the people to rebel against Ashurbânipal. As a result,

"the Gurunammu have rebelled against me. Re-enforce me at once."

The good Kudur sent five or six hundred archers and joined Aplîa, the governor of Arrapḫa, and Nûrêa, governor of Ṣameda, and went to Ur. He was able to seize the leaders of the revolt, among them Nabû-zêr-iddin. But someone had captured Sin-tabni-uṣur. Bêl-ibnî is named, and later Nabû-ushêzib, the archer, but the text is too mutilated to make out a clear account. But it seems likely that Sin-tabni-uṣur was rescued, and being re-enforced, held out well for his master. Ashurbânipal writes to assure him of his continued confidence.[3]

The king's reply

Message of the king to Sin-tabni-uṣur: It is well with me. May thy heart be cheered. Concerning Sin-shar-uṣur, what thou didst send. How could he say evil words of thee and I hear anything of them? Shamash perverted his heart and Ummanigash slandered thee before me and would give thee to death. Ashur, my god, withholds me. I would not willingly slay my servant, and the support of my father's house. In that case, thou wouldst perish with thy lord's house. I would not see that. He and Ummanigash have compassed thy death, but because I know thy faithfulness I have increased my favor and bestowed honor upon thee. Is it not so? For these two years thou hast not caused hostility or want to thy lord's house. What could they say against a servant who has loved his lord's house and I believe it? And with respect to the service which thou and the Assyrians, thy brothers, have done, what thou sendest, all that thou hast done and the guard thou hast kept, . . . which is pleasing before me [I will reward] and return thee favors to thy children's children.

---

[1] H. 754. [2] Page 201. [3] H. 290.

The persons mentioned

It is clear that Sin-shar-uṣur and Ummanigash had been intriguing against Sin-tabni-uṣur. There are several persons of the name Sin-shar-uṣur about this time. No less than three Eponyms bear the name after B.C. 648. The *aba mâti*, or governor of Hindana, or the *arḳû* might be meant here. But there was a brother of Sin-tabni-uṣur, of this name, who perhaps coveted his post. Among the many unpublished texts which refer to him one may, perhaps, be found to explain the hostility. Nor is it clear which Ummanigash is meant. There was one of the three sons of Urtaku, who took refuge at the court of Ashurbânipal, when their father was murdered and dethroned by his brother, Teumman. When the Assyrian king espoused his cause, he was enabled by Assyrian troops to defeat and slay the usurper Teumman and take the throne of Elam. But he was faithless and allied himself with Shamash-shum-ukîn. He was dethroned by his cousin, Tammaritu, shortly before the fall of Shamash-shum-ukîn. That he, while at the Assyrian Court, should have slandered the governor of Ur, is quite in accordance with his character, but what was his purpose, or what he alleged, we do not know. There was another Ummanigash, brother of Urtaku; another, son of Umbadara; another, a son of Amedirra. The latter raised a rebellion against Ummanaldash, as we learn from a report by Bêl-ibnî.[1] After his usual salutations, Bêl-ibnî reports,

Bê-libni's letter about Ummanigash

When I left the Sealand, I sent five hundred soldiers, servants of my lord, the king, to the city Ṣabdânu, saying, "Hold a fort in Ṣabdânu and make raids into Elam, slay and make prisoners." When they went against Irgidu, a city two leagues this side of Susa, they slew Ammaladin, the sheik of Iashi'ilu, his two brothers, three brothers of his father, two of his brother's sons, Dalâ-ilu, son of Abi-iadi', and two hundred well-born citizens of that city. They had a long journey before them. They took one hundred and fifty prisoners. The sheiks of Laḫiru and the people of Nugû', when they saw that my

[1] H. 280.

raiders had extended on their farther side, were full of fear, sent word and took the oath to Mushêzib-Marduk, my sister's son, a servant of the king, my lord, whom I had appointed over the fort, saying, "We will be servants of the King of Assyria." When they had gathered their bowmen, as many as they had, they went with Mushêzib-Marduk, and marched into Elam.

Here follows a bad break in the narrative, but Iḳisha-aplu is named, and Bêl-ibnî promised to send on to the king whatever they captured and brought to him. The letter then resumes:

News from Elam: they say that Ummanigash, son of Amedirra, has rebelled against Ummanaldash. From the river Ḫudḫud as far as the city Ḫa'adânu they have sided with him. Ummanaldash has gathered his forces, and they are now encamped on the river opposite one another. Iḳisha-aplu, whom I have sent to the palace, has penetrated their designs. Let one question him in the palace.

Kudur's letters about the king's favorite

Kudur, governor of Erech, who sent news of the outbreak of rebellion in the south, gives us further information about Mushêzib-Marduk, who was a favorite with the king. After a long salutation occupying nearly the whole of the obverse, with a short reference to a certain Upaḳu, the reverse side goes on:[1]

Mushêzib-Marduk, Bêl-ibnî's sister's son, who has come two or three times into the presence of the king, my lord, on a message from Bêl-ibnî, Bêl-ibnî has appointed him concerning it (the case in hand). The gate-keepers have told him that those soldiers are not lovers of the house of my lord. It is not good for them to cross over to our midst. They will give news of the land of the king, my lord, to Elam, and if there be a famine in Elam, they will furnish them provisions. To the king, my lord, I have sent; let the king, my lord, do what he sees fit.

The king's reply

The king himself writes to Bêl-ibnî[2] in a most friendly way about Mushêzib-Marduk:

Message of the king to Bêl-ibnî: I am well. May thy heart be cheered. Mushêzib-Marduk, about whom thou didst send, in the

---

[1] H. 277. [2] H. 399.

fulness of time he shall enter my presence, I will appoint the paths for his feet (*i.e.*, make a way for his advancement). The holiday in Nineveh is not finished.

Mushêzib-Marduk is also mentioned by Nabû-zêr-ukîn, in a letter to the king,[1] in close connection with Shum-iddin, the governor of Dûr-ilu. It is not clear what the writer had to say of him, but farther on in the letter Bêl-ibnî is named. The same Nabû-zêr-ukîn is mentioned in a tablet of epigraphs,[2] where he is associated with Shamash-shum-ukîn, Tammaritu and Indabigash. He is there said to be son of Nabû-mushêṣi. In another letter he writes with Adadi-shum-uṣur, Nabû-shum-iddin, Ardi-Ea, and Ishtar-shum-êresh to the king,[3] but hardly anything remains except a mention of Nineveh. The same group of writers is elsewhere associated with Nabû-mushêṣi. Of another letter[4] from him to the king only the introduction is found.

Kudur's letters about the rebellion

Kudur, governor of Erech, was a frequent correspondent with the king. A score of letters from him to the king, or from the king to him, are preserved. They are nearly all concerned, more or less, with the events during the great rebellion. There were several others of the name, one an Elamite prince, son of Ummanaldash. The name itself may be Elamite and may point to a strong admixture of Elamite blood in Erech. The element Kudur occurs in such names as Kudur-Mabug, Kudur-Naḫunte, and Kudur-lagamar, the prototype of Chedorlaomer. There was another Kudur, son of Dakkuri, who was brought captive to Assyria with Shum-iddin. We may take as one example:[5]

To the king of countries, my lord, thy servant Kudur. May Bêl and Nabû decree peace, health, and length of days for the king, my lord, forever. Since I was in the enemy's country the Puḳudu have made an end of the Bît-Amuḳâni, servants of my lord, the king, by their attacks. The cities which were to be held for the king, my lord,

[1] H. 412. [2] K. 4453. [3] H. 332. [4] H. 513. [5] H. 275.

they captured. Let the servants of the king, my lord, march. They have occupied the cities, killed the men and ravished the women. Also they have attacked Ṣâbâ, the body-guard. The day they reached Bît-Amuḳâni, it is said, the attackers attacked the body-guard. I sent soldiers, saying, "Go, slay 'Ala' with the pike, save the garrison and take them captive." When on the king's canal they attacked Nabû-shar-uṣur, the colonel, he took them captive. Let the king, my lord, inquire of them, as he can. The king, my lord, knows how Bît-Amuḳâni is destroyed. The Puḳudu keep their land. The soldiers with us have not set out, and they are the attackers, and we abhor the alienation of territory. Let the king, my lord, give orders and the soldiers shall set out against the cities, where they dwell.

It seems that the men of Pekod (see Jer. i. 21, Ez. xxiii. 23) had made an attack upon Bît-Amuḳâni and nearly destroyed the country. Kudur moved into the country, but sent for explicit orders as to what he should do. He changes his subject rather abruptly at times and it is not quite clear always of whom he is speaking. The most obscure sentence is where he says that "we abhor the alienation of territory," literally "the sin of the land." It seems that a land sinned when it was occupied by an enemy.

Ashurbânipal was deeply attached to his faithful servant, as the following letter shows:[1]

**His affectionate letter of thanks for the king's favors**

To the king of countries, my lord, thy servant Kudur. Erech and E-anna (the temple there) be gracious to the king of countries, my lord. Daily I pray to Ishtar of Erech and Nanâ for the health of the king, my lord's life. Iḳîsha-aplu, the doctor, whom the king, my lord, sent to heal me, has restored me to life. The great gods of heaven and earth make themselves gracious to the king, my lord, and establish the throne of the king, my lord, in the midst of heaven forever. I was one who was dead and the king, my lord, has restored me to life. The benefits of the king, my lord, toward me are manifold. I will come to see the king, my lord. I say to myself, I will go and I will see the face of the king, my lord; then I will return and live. The chief baker made me return to Erech from the jour-

---

[1] H. 274.

ney, saying, "A special messenger has brought a sealed despatch to thee from the palace, thou must return with me to Erech." He sent me this order and made me return to Erech. The king, my lord, must know this.

The king had sent a doctor who had restored Kudur, when he had despaired of himself. Then he started to come and thank the king in person, but when on the road the chief baker (if that was his right title) recalled him, because a sealed despatch had reached Erech addressed to him from the king. He sends at once this letter, not having reached Erech again; at any rate, he does not refer to the contents of the despatch.

# VIII

## LETTERS ABOUT ELAM AND SOUTHERN BABYLONIA

The downfall of Elamite power

IN Elam, during the reign of Ashurbânipal, there was a protracted series of revolutions, interspersed with invasions of, or by, Assyria. The result was the utter decay of Elamite power, and after Ashurbânipal's final reduction of the country and sack of Susa, the land was an easy prey to the Aryan invaders. From the story, as told by Ashurbânipal, the Elamites richly deserved their fate, and lest we should suspect him of undue partiality, the matter-of-fact letters of his officers give us substantial grounds for crediting his view. It seems that Urtaku, who came to the throne of Elam in B.C. 675, was always on good terms with Assyria. We have a letter from Esarhaddon to him[1] in very friendly terms. It begins:

A friendly letter from Esarhaddon to Urtaku

Letter of Esarhaddon, King of Assyria, to Urtaku, King of Elam: I am well. Peace to thy gods and goddesses. There is peace in my land and with my nobles, peace be to Urtaku, King of Elam, my brother. There is peace with my sons and my daughters, peace be to thy nobles and thy land. Now what Ashur, Sin, Shamash, Bêl, Nabû, Ishtar of Nineveh, Ishtar of Arbela, the gods . . . have said, I have (fully?) accomplished.

This friendship at first maintained by Ashurbânipal

The rest is obscure by reason of lacunæ. The reverse seems to be inscribed with numerals, perhaps relating to items of presents sent. Ashurbânipal kept up the friendship, and, when a famine broke out in Elam, allowed some

---

[1] G. Sm., p. 24.

Elamites to take refuge in his land, and afterwards restored them to their country. He also sent grain into Elam itself. But, perhaps as consequence of having spied out the land, the Elamites contrived to make Urtaku attack Assyria. He was incited to this act by Bêl-iḳisha, prince of the Gambûlai, who inhabited the marshes about the mouth of the Uknû, or Blue River, perhaps the modern Karoon, bordering on Elam. Bêl-iḳisha rebelled against Assyria, and with his troops joined Elam. Nabû-shum-êresh, the *TIK-EN-NA*, apparently sheik of the district of Dupliash, another Assyrian subject, seems to have done the same. Marduk-shum-ibnî, the general of Urtaku, who led the invasion, was evidently not an Elamite, but perhaps a Chaldean, or renegade Babylonian. At any rate, the Elamites invaded Akkad and covered the land like grasshoppers. They laid siege to Babylon. On the approach of the Assyrian army, the invaders fled. Urtaku died. Bêl-iḳisha was killed by a wild boar. Nabû-shum-êresh was smitten with dropsy and died. "In one year the gods cut them off." The throne of Elam fell to Teumman, a brother of Urtaku, who maintained a hostile attitude. Dunânu, son and successor of Bêl-iḳisha, joined Teumman. Ashurbânipal accordingly invaded Elam, defeated and slew Teumman, ravaged the land of Gambulû and captured Dunânu, who was taken to Nineveh and made to march in the triumphal procession, with the head of Teumman slung about his neck, and was finally tortured to death.

The Elamites invade Babylonia

The punishment

All the time that Shamash-shum-ukîn was king in Babylon, Ashurbânipal seems to have retained the rule over Southern Babylonia. At any rate, the governors of the cities there wrote to him as their king and lord. The above-mentioned revolt in Gambulû was a direct concern of the governor of Erech, who seems to have suffered severely. As late as the twentieth year of Ashurbânipal,

Nabû-ushabshi's letters as governor of Southern Babylonia

Nabû-ushabshi was governor there. We have many letters from him to the king. One[1] refers to the above events:

To the king of countries, my lord, thy servant Nabû-ushabshi. Erech and E-anna (the temple of Ishtar at Erech), be gracious to the king of countries, my lord. Daily I pray to Ishtar of Erech and Nanâ for the well-being of the life of the king, my lord. The king, my lord, sent, saying, "Take troops and send against Gambulû. The gods of the king, my lord, assuredly know how, from the time that Bêl-iḳisha revolted from the hands of the king, my lord, and went to Elam, he plundered my father's house and went about to kill my brother."

Then comes a break, in which the fragments indicate that Nabû-ushabshi prayed daily for revenge. Then we read:

now as the king, my lord, has sent, I will go and fulfil all his bidding. If on any ground, over there, the inhabitants of Gambulû will not obey, if it be pleasing to the king, my lord, let a messenger come and let us assemble all Akkad and we will go with him, we will win back the land and give it to the king, my lord. I have sent. Let the king, my lord, do what he will. Preserve this letter.

The last request is very unusual, but we are glad it was obeyed. Another of his letters refers to the intrigues of Pir'-Bêl, son of Bêl-eṭir. This Bêl-eṭir may be the son of Nabû-shum-êresh, who, with his brother, Nabû-nâ'id, was carried captive to Nineveh, along with Dunânu, and there made to desecrate the bones of their father. But it seems possible that we have here to do with another Bêl-eṭir, as these events seem earlier in the history. After the same introduction as before, the letter[2] reads:

Pir'-Bêl, the son of Bêl-eṭir, sometime after he and his father went, some ten years ago, to Elam, came again from Elam to Akkad, he and his father. When they came, whatever was evil against Assyria, they kept on doing in Erech. Afterwards when they went back to Elam, Bêl-eṭir, his father, died in Elam; and he in March-

[1] H. 269. [2] H. 266.

esvan brought letters to me, and to Aplîa, the governor, we sent the letters on by Daru-Sharru, the body-guard.

After some broken lines:

"Now a certain servant of . . . came with him to Erech."

we read:

if he say to the king, my lord: "I have come from the land of Elam," let not the king, my lord, believe him. From the time when in the month of Marchesvan, he brought the letters and we sent them to the king, my lord, until now, he has not returned to Elam. If the king, my lord, desire to verify these words, Idûa, a servant of Kudur, who brought him to Erech, the contents are known to him [*there are some very obscure phrases in the next two lines*], and those letters, what lies are written, let him tell the king, my lord, and as to those letters, which, in the month of Marchesvan we sent to the king, my lord, by the hands of Daru-sharru, if the king, my lord, does not understand, let the king, my lord, ask Daru-sharru, the body-guard. To the king, my lord, I have sent, let the king, my lord, be aware.

Letters about presents sent to the sanctuary of Erech

One event, very characteristic of the times, is the subject of three letters. The sanctuary of Ishtar, at Erech, was celebrated far and wide, and on one occasion the King of Elam sent gifts to it. These Nabû-ushabshi seems to have been unable to possess himself of, or to send to the king. Thus, we read:[1]

To the king of countries, my lord, thy servant, Nabû-ushabshi [*after the same introduction as before*]; the sheep of the temple and of the city Puḳudu are detained in the city Ru'ua, two shepherds of them, one belonging to the temple, and the second from Puḳudu, three white horses with harness and trappings of silver, and fittings of bronze. On the trappings were written . . . which the King of Elam had sent to Ishtar of Erech. The horses, which they brought, I will now preserve. Before the king, my lord, I was afraid and in the temple I will not place them, until the shepherds bring

[1] H. 268.

the three horses. To the king, my lord, I have sent, and the bronze inscribed fittings, when I see them, I will send on to the king, my lord. What the king my lord will, let him do.

The king replied:[1]

To Nabû-ushabshi, concerning the horses about which thou didst send, as yet thou hast not sent them to me. I have sent Ashur-gimil-tirru, the *abarakku*, and troops with him. Whatever is good to do, that do; whether the River Ḫarru be dammed, or whether those people come, and as to the contents of the letter which thou didst send. Bêl-eṭir, Arbaia, the colonels, two hundred horses in their hands, I have sent to thee; let them stand on your side, let them do the work.

Evidently in consequence of this, we have another letter,[2] where both writer and recipient are unknown. It is much injured, and while there are a few sentences intelligible, it is not easy to say to what they refer. But on the reverse after the first six or seven lines, the words of the last letter are repeated verbatim. It is perhaps another letter from the king to Nabû-ushabshi. The governors of Laḫiru and Arbaḫa are said to be with the receiver of the letter.

---

[1] H. 273. [2] H. 543.

# IX

## MISCELLANEOUS ASSYRIAN LETTERS

Letters about omens and predictions

A VERY interesting group may be made up of letters concerned with omens and predictions. The Assyrian kings were firm believers in omens. They did not venture upon any great undertaking without consulting the augurs. We have numerous letters telling the king what days were propitious for certain projects which he had formed. For the most part, the whole point is obscure to us. We know neither the purpose he had, the omens relied on, nor the real grounds of the decision. Very often translation is impossible. In some cases the publication of the innumerable omen texts may give some light on the subject, but usually it is quite impossible to see how these were made to apply to the actual case. It is very like the case of Nebuchadrezzar's dream. We are without any data to work from.

About a fox's falling into a well

Here is an example of some interest, and more easily understood than many:[1]

To the king, my lord, thy servant Nabûa. May Nabû and Marduk be gracious to the king, my lord. On the seventh of Kislev a fox entered into the city, and fell into a well, in the grove of Ashur. They got him out, and killed him.

Whether this was a good or evil omen, or even an omen at all, we do not know. Nabûa is a very common name. There are fourteen or fifteen astrological reports which bear

[1] H. 142.

his name. In these he appears as an inhabitant of the city Asshur. The name occurs some forty times in the contracts, but it is clear that there were several of the name. Perhaps the scribe who appears from B.C. 668 down to post-canon times may be our writer, but, as he lived at Nineveh, that is doubtful.

Regarding auspicious days for a journey

Another case which is fairly intelligible is a letter of Balasi and Nabû-aḫê-erba,[1] on a question of auspicious days for a journey. It reads:

> To the king, our lord, thy servants, Balasi and Nabû-aḫê-erba. Peace be to the king, our lord. May Nabû and Marduk be gracious to the king, our lord. As to Ashur-mukîn-palêa, about whom the king, our lord, has sent to us, may Ashur, Bêl, Sin, Shamash, and Adad be gracious to him. May the king, our lord, see his well-being. Things are auspicious for a journey. The second is auspicious. The fourth extremely auspicious.

We have fairly frequent references to Ashur-mukîn-palêa in a way that shows that he was delicate. From a letter of Ardi-Nabû's we learn that the order of seniority in the family of Esarhaddon was Ashurbânipal, Shamash-shum-ukîn, Sherûa-eṭirat (a princess), Ashur-mukin-palêa, Sharru-shame-erṣiti-balâṭsu-(iḳbi). He is often named in the letters, usually as king's son. But despite his delicate health he survived to be made high-priest of Sin at Ḫarrân, by his royal brother, and even as late as B.C. 648 his name occurs in the contracts.[2]

Balasi's letters about astrology

Balasi is a frequent writer of astrological reports, some five and twenty being preserved, besides some fifteen letters. In the latter he is associated with Nabû-aḫê-erba no less than seven times, once with Ishtar-shum-êresh also. In these cases we probably have the same person. But the name occurs often in the contracts, and there belongs to at least three different men. Nabû-aḫê-erba was the writer of

---

[1] H. 77. [2] A. D. D., 1053.

some five and thirty astrological reports, besides some seven or eight letters, usually with Balasi. The name belongs to several persons named in the contracts.

Ardi-Êa's letters of congratulation

Ardi-Êa was also a frequent writer to the king. Besides three or four astrological reports, he wrote nine letters to the king. He is generally associated with Adadi-shum-uṣur, Ishtar-shum-êresh, Akkullânu, or Marduk-shâkin-shum. But one letter,[1] written to Sargon II., and mentioning Merodach-Baladan II., clearly belongs to another Ardi-Êa. Most of his letters are defective. The most intelligible[2] reads thus:

To the king, my lord, thy servant Ardi-Êa. Peace be to the king, my lord. May Nabû, Marduk, Sin, Ningal, and Nusku be gracious to the king, my lord. Sin, Ningal (and other gods) shall grant health, long days, to the king, my lord. Day and night I pray for the life of the king, my lord.

Adadi-shum-uṣur's letters

The great group of writers with whom he is associated is responsible for a large number of letters. Adadi-shum-uṣur wrote some thirty-five letters and five or six astrological reports. He is especially prolix in his introduction. Here is a specimen:[3]

To the king, my lord, thy servant Adadi-shum-uṣur. Peace be to the king, my lord. May Nabû and Marduk be excessively gracious to the king, my lord. The king of gods shall decree the name of the king, my lord, to the kingdom of Assyria. Shamash and Adad, in their changeless regard to the king, my lord, have confirmed him in the kingdom of all lands. A gracious reign, settled days, years of righteousness, plenteous rains, copious floods, high prices. The gods are reverenced, the fear of God increased, the temples are flourishing. The great gods of heaven and earth are exalted in the reign of the king, my lord. Old men dance, young men sing, the women and girls are given in marriage, the bridegrooms marry wives, marriages are consummated, sons and daughters are begotten, children are born. To those that have sinned and look for death, the king, my lord, has given new life. Those that for many years

---

[1] H. 30. [2] H. 28. [3] H. 2.

were captive, thou hast freed. They that many days were sick have recovered. The hungry are satisfied. The lean grow fat. The plantations are covered with fruits. Only I and Ardi-Gula among them have our soul depressed, our heart disturbed. Lately has the king, my lord, shown love for Nineveh, to his people, to his chiefs, saying, "Bring your sons, let them stand before me." Ardi-Gula, my son is he, let him stand with them, before the king, my lord. We with all the people will rejoice indeed, and dance for joy. My eyes are set upon the king, my lord. They that stand in the palace, all of them, love me not. There is not a friend of mine among them, to whom I might give a present, and they would receive it, and take up my cause. Let the king, my lord, take pity on his servant. Among all those people, I hope none of my slanderers may see the purpose of their hearts against me.

A plea for his son to be appointed to the court

Judging from the frequent mention of Ardi-Gula in other letters and that he wrote to the king about his sons, Ashurbânipal and Shamash-shum-ukîn, we may be sure the old courtier got his request, and that he was writing to Esarhaddon. The letters of Adadi-shum-uṣur concern domestic affairs, the sickness of one, an auspicious day, the health of another, rarely does he mention any news of public interest. The persons about whom he writes are the members of the royal family, Esarhaddon's children and the above-named circle of officials. The king sent him to see certain sick folk,[1] he writes about an eclipse, or a ring, or something of the sort. He usually gives a very long introduction; often the real message occupies only a few lines.

Miscellaneous letters

Marduk-shâkin-shum is another of the same group, with twenty-five letters. They are of the same domestic nature as the last. Ishtar-shum-êresh is the writer of a score of letters and about thirty astrological reports. He was evidently a younger member of the group, son of Nabû-zêr-lîshir, and chief scribe to Ashurbânipal. In the reign

[1] H. 1.

of Esarhaddon he ranked as a *mašmašu.* Akkullânu, who was an *êrib bîti*, of Ashur, writes sixteen letters and some dozen astrological reports.

Nabûa's letters about the calendar

We have seen that in the second epoch the king had to fix the time when intercalary months should be inserted. In this period the calendar was very carefully regulated by astronomical observations. As a new month began on the day on which the new moon was seen, it is clear that a month would often exceed twenty-nine days, but that a new moon might sometimes be seen on the twenty-ninth. Nabûa, the astronomer of the city Asshur, sends a number of such letters as:[1]

On the twenty-ninth, we kept watch, we did not see the moon. Nabû and Marduk be gracious to the king, my lord. From Nabûa of Asshur.

So Nabû-shum-iddin writes:[2]

To the Gardener, my lord, thy servant Nabû-shum-iddin, the *rabûte* of Nineveh. Nabû and Marduk be gracious to the Gardener, my lord. On the fourteenth we kept watch on the moon. The moon suffered an eclipse.

The gardener, or rather irrigator, may be a royal title. At present these observations are useless to us in our attempts to fix chronology, as we do not know the month and year of many of them.

The queen-dowager's importance

The queen-mother was always an important personage in the state and she had very great influence indeed at court. But probably few ladies ever obtained a higher degree of power than did Naki'a, or Zakutu as she was also called, the wife of Sennacherib and mother of Esarhaddon. She had a sister Abirami.[3] The queen-mother resided in Laḫiru, but there seem to have been more than one city of the name. Her necklace, or some part of it, is in private possession

[1] H. 825. [2] H. 816. [3] A. D. D., 70.

and has been described by Professor Scheil.[1] She survived her son, and, with her grandsons, Ashurbânipal, Shamash-shum-ukîn, and the nobles of Assyria, issued a proclamation to the empire, declaring Ashurbânipal the true heir to the throne.

Letter of Nâ'id-Marduk to her

It is, of course, uncertain whether the person addressed as mother of the king is always Zakûtu, since we cannot always date the letters. But the letter of Nâ'id-Marduk,[2] which names Ummanigash as King of Elam, was certainly addressed to her. Nâ'id-Marduk was a son of Merodach Baladan, who, in the reign of Esarhaddon, when his brother Nabû-zêr-kînish-lîshir was killed by Ummanaldash II., threw himself on the mercy of Esarhaddon and was by him made ruler of his ancestral domain of Bît Jakin, as a vassal king. He speaks for himself:

To the mother of the king, my lord, thy servant Nâ'id-Marduk. Peace be to the mother of the king, my lord. May Ashur, Shamash, and Marduk give health to the king, my lord. May they decree the cheer of heart of the mother of the king, my lord. From Elam they came to me, saying, "They have seized the bridge." When they came, I sent to the mother of the king, my lord. Now let the bridge be restored and the bolts of the bridge strengthened. They say, "They have burnt it." I have not sent them, we do not know. They came, it was gone. To the mother of the king, my lord, I will send. Do thou, my lord, send troops. The son of Ningal-iddina has gone to the King of (Elam ?) and taken the side of Ḫubanigash. [*Several lines follow with only fragments of sentences.*] "Since these are trustworthy reports, whatever the Chaldees in future send to the gods of the king, my lord. If a messenger of the King of Elam does not bring messages to me, he shall enter and I will see him, and whatever is his message, he shall explain until I understand." They came on the second of Ab, his messenger came to me to the border; he did not pass over to hinterland, and I sent my messenger to the palace. My lord, may he decide, and what is right for the house of my lord, fulfil.

---

[1] Rec. Trav., xx., p. 200.

[2] W. Sm., p. 7.

It is evident that the writer regards the queen-mother as so thoroughly identical with the king that he does not scruple to address her as "my lord." Despite several lacunæ the general sense is clear. After the break the passage in quotation-marks seems to be quoted from a report made to the writer. The sons of Ningal-iddina were Sin-tabni-uṣur, Sin-balâṭsu-iḳbi, and Sin-shar-uṣur, all of whom were in important commands in Southern Babylonia. It seems probable that the events referred to in this letter are those which led up to the Elamite invasion of Babylonia, when they came raiding as far as Sippara. Esarhaddon was away at the time in the west. There is no record of how they were driven back.

King's letter to her

Here is a letter from the king to his mother:[1]

Message of the king to the king's mother: I am well. Peace be to the king's mother. Concerning Amushe's servant, what thou didst send me, as the king's mother has told me, I will at once order. What thou hast said is extremely good. Wherefore should Ḫamunai go?

The meaning is obscured for us by our complete lack of information as to the persons concerned. We may conjecture that Ḫamunai was the servant of Amushe, but we do not know. However, we see that the queen-mother gave good advice.

Aplâ's cordial letter to her

Zakûtu must often have been a prey to great anxiety, left in command as she was in Assyria, with her warrior son nearly always away and such awkward neighbors as the Elamites. But she was on the whole faithfully served. It seems that the proud nobles of Assyria became restless during Esarhaddon's long absences, for we learn from the Babylonian Chronicle that, in B.C. 670, Esarhaddon put a number of them to death. Here is a letter, however, from an attached subject:[2]

---

[1] H. 324. [2] H. 303.

To the mother of the king, my lady, thy servant Aplîa. May Bêl and Nabû be gracious to the mother of the king, my lady. Every day I pray Nabû and Nanâ for life and health and length of days, for the king of lands, my lord, and for the mother of the king, my lady. May the mother of the king, my lady, be bright. A messenger of good news from Bêl and Nabû has come from the king of lands, my lord.

There is a suggestion in the mention of Nanâ that Aplîa wrote from Erech. He may be the Aplîa afterwards associated with Bêl-ibnî and Kudur in the south. If so, we may suppose that the messenger came from Esarhaddon, from Egypt, by way of Southern Babylonia. One would suppose that a messenger from Canaan, or the west, would reach Nineveh, before Chaldea. But, of course, the queen-mother may have been at Laḫiru. Only it is doubtful whether she lived there, while Esarhaddon was away.

It is more likely still that the Aplîa is the same as the *râb ali* of Laḫiru, who in B.C. 678 was over the house of the queen-mother there.[1]

Asharîdu's letter of loyalty

Another letter [2] conveys assurance of fidelity:

To the mother of the king, my lord, thy servant Asharîdu. May Nabû and Marduk be gracious to the mother of the king, my lord. Daily I pray to Nêrgal and Lâz for the life and health of the king, and the king's mother, my lords. There is peace in the city and temples of the king and now I keep the watch for the king, my lord.

That Asharîdu is the same as the writer of some thirty astrological reports who was the son of Dankâ, a *ḳatnu*, and servant of the king, may be doubted. He is more likely to be the author of several letters who seems to have been connected with Borsippa. Another letter [3] is from Nêrgal-sharâni in response to another about some sacrifices, sent by the queen-mother. He prays for a thousand years of rule for Esarhaddon, so there can be no mistake about the

---

[1] A. D. D., No. 301. [2] H. 254. [3] H. 368.

period. He recounts the preparations made—an ox, two sheep, and two hundred geese. But he says that Ninḳai, the handmaid of the queen-mother, for some reason, will not perform the sacrifice. The queen-mother is asked to send authority for someone to open the treasury and perform the work. The letter is defective and obscure by reason of unknown words. Nêrgal-sharâni may be the same Ashur-shum-uṣur who so often writes to the king about this time. Again Nabû-shum-lîshir writes to the queen-mother[1] about a woman, Kallati, who was intrusted to the writer in the house of Shama', and about some sheep.

Medical letters

Another group includes the letters which refer to medical treatment. Here especially Dr. C. Johnston, himself a medical man, has made a most valuable start in his Assyrian *Epistolary Correspondence*, and we can hardly do better than to follow his guidance. As a rule, what these ancient peoples said and thought of disease is very obscure to us. Many terms were then, as now, used in the medical vocabulary which were well known in ordinary language, but which were given a distinctly different technical meaning. Great attention was paid to surgery and medicine, as is shown by the clauses in the Code.[2] There are also a great number of tablets dealing with medicine, some of which have been published. Long ago Professor Sayce discussed one such text under the title, "An Ancient Babylonian Work on Medicine,"[3] and from the British Museum Catalogue fully four hundred and fifty such texts are known. Dr. C. F. H. Küchler in his *Beiträge zur Kenntniss der Assyrischen Medicin* has made great progress toward settling the reading and meaning of certain words and phrases. Dr. Baron Felix von Oefele, who has devoted much study to ancient medicine in general, has made noteworthy contributions to the study, by his articles in learned journals. Still, the

Medical records numerous

[1] H. 263. [2] §§ 215–21. [3] Z. K. F. II.

great obstacle is that so much of the materia medica, which was a very full one, is unknown; and the diseases appear under names which do not assist us in determining the meaning. The medical treatises considered affections of all parts of the body, and made much of symptoms. They prescribe roots and oils and a great variety of powdered drugs. Some of the treatment is evidently based on extended trial and observation. But also much reliance was placed on charms, and diseases were associated with demons. To drive away the demon, as well as cure the pain, was the doctor's duty. There was full recognition of the mental factor in sickness.

*Exorcism as well as healing the duty of a physician*

*A letter reporting the progress of a disease*

With considerable hesitation the following two letters from the physician Ardi-Nanâ to the king Esarhaddon are given, in which Dr. C. Johnston's rendering is closely followed. In the first, Ardi-Nanâ reports on the state of a patient, perhaps one of the young princes, who was suffering from a disease of the eyes, or perhaps facial erysipelas. He was progressing so well that the physician piously opines that some god has taken the case under his care. The gods who were special patrons of the healing art were Ninip and Gula, whose blessing the physician accordingly invokes. We read:[1]

To the king, my lord, thy servant Ardi-Nanâ. May it be peace in the highest degree to the king, my lord; may Ninip and Gula give cheer of heart and health of body to the king, my lord. It is extremely well with that poor man whose eyes are diseased. I had applied a dressing to him, it covered his face. Yesterday, at evening, I undid the bandage which held it, I removed the dressing which was upon him. There was pus upon the dressing as much as the tip of the little finger. Thy gods, if any of them has put his hand to the matter, he has indeed given his order. It is extremely well. Let the heart of the king, my lord, be cheered. In seven or eight days he will be well.

---

[1] H. 392.

There is also another letter[1] from Ardi-Nanâ to the king, but part of it is too defective to render. It begins in exactly the same way as before, save that greeting is also sent to the king's son.

For the cure which we wrought on . . . we were given five-sixths of a shekel. The day he came, he recovered, he recovered his strength, he stayed until. . . . Concerning the patient who had blood run from his nose, the messenger has told me, saying, "Yesterday, at evening, much blood ran." Those dressings are not with knowledge. They have been placed upon the breathing passages of the nose and oppress the breathing and come off, because of the bleeding. Let them be placed within the nostrils, they will preserve the breath and the blood will be held back. If it is right in the sight of the king, in the morning I will come and prescribe for him. Now let me hear his well-being.

The messenger here was a *rab MU-GI,* in which title it has been proposed to see the original of the Rabmag of Jeremiah xxxix. 3. He was a high official charged with the care of horses and chariots, and here sent to hear news of the patient. There is no evidence that he had any medical knowledge himself. In another letter,[2] Ardi-Nanâ writes concerning Ashur-mukîn-palêa, a younger son of Esarhaddon and brother of Ashurbânipal. He bids the king not to fear. The young prince seems to have been in the doctor's care. Further he writes about the health of a tooth (of the prince's ?) about which the king had sent to inquire. He had greatly improved its condition (literally, uplifted its head). In another letter,[3] also partly defective, he directs the king to anoint himself as a protection against draughts (?), to drink pure water, and to wash his hands frequently in a bowl. Presently the rash (?) will disappear. In another still more defective letter[4] he mentions the plant *martakal,* to which magical efficacy was ascribed. Another

---

[1] H. 108. [2] H. 109.
[3] H. 110. [4] H. 111.

long letter,[1] after the same complimentary opening as the others, goes on:

Continually has the king, my lord, said to me, thus, "The nature of my disease is this, thou hast not seen to it, its recovery thou hast not effected." Formerly I said before the king, my lord, "The ulcer is incurable (?), I cannot prescribe for it." Now, however, I have sealed a letter and sent it. In the presence of the king, let them read it, I will prescribe for the king, my lord. If it be agreeable to the king, my lord, let a magician do his work on him. Let the king apply a lotion (?). Shortly the sore will be loosed. This lotion of oils (?) let the king apply two or three times. The king will know if the king says . . .

The rest is obscure, simply because we do not know what the disease, or remedy, was.

Shamash-mîtu-uballiṭ, probably the youngest son of Esarhaddon, writes to the king, but whether to his father or his brother Ashurbânipal does not seem clear, about the health of a lady, in whose well-being the king seemed to take interest.[2]

To the king, my lord, thy servant Shamash-mîtu-uballiṭ. Verily peace be to the king, my lord, may Nabû and Marduk be excessively gracious to the king, my lord. Verily the king's handmaid, Baugâmelat is excessively ill, she can eat nothing. Forsooth let the king, my lord, send an order and let a doctor come and see her.

Letters regarding the appointment of officials

There is also an interesting letter concerning the appointment of a successor to a dead official,[3] sent by a writer whose name is lost:

To the king, my lord, thy servant, . . . verily peace to the king, my lord. May Ashur and Beltu be gracious to the king, my lord. Concerning the overseer of the house of the seers, who is dead, as I said in the presence of the king, my lord, to wit, his son, his brother's son, are alive. Now his son, his brother's son, and Simânai, the son of Nabû-uballiṭ, and the son of the father's brother, of Ashurnâ'id, the deputy priest, with them, shall come into the presence of the

[1] H. 391. [2] H. 341. [3] H. 577.

king, my lord. Whoever shall find favor in the sight of the king, my lord, let the king, my lord, appoint.

It is clear that succession was not purely hereditary. Even when the son was alive, he might be passed over in favor of a cousin, or for a still more distant relation. There are many other interesting cases where the king inquires for the proper persons to be placed in the offices vacated through death or deposition. For example, when Esarhaddon began to set in order the temple services, he heard the following report:[1]

To the king, my lord, thy servant Akkullânu. Peace be to the king, my lord. Nabû and Marduk be gracious to the king, my lord. In the long desuetude of the customary rights of Ashur, regarding which the king, my lord, sent word to his servant, saying, "Who among the magnates have not complied, have not given, be it much or little (their default)," yesterday I could not write to the king, my lord. Now these are the magnates who have not given their dues: the governors of Barḫalza, Raṣappa, Kalzi, Isana, Bêlê, Kullania, Arpadda; these have failed to pay their dues. Raṣappa, Barḫalza, Dikuḳina, the chief of the vineyards, Daian-Adadi, Isana, Ḫalziatbar, Birtu, Arzuḫina, Arbailu, Guzana, Sharish, Diḫnunna, Rimusu, all these have not given the barley and wheat due from them. And as to the overseer of the bakehouse, the overseer of the larder and the chief purveyors, concerning whom the king, my lord, inquired, they are removed from their posts, and this is alleged as the reason: The overseer of the bakehouse is a child, Sennacherib removed him; Ashur-zêr-iddin, the priest of Nineveh, slandered him. I was frightened at the troubles. He had not committed any great crime. . . . The overseer of the larder had broken (?) a dish of Ashur's, for this deed thy father removed him from charge of Ashur's dish, and appointed a turban-maker's son; he is without education. And concerning the chief purveyors, Sennacherib made a reduction of their allowances, and the son of the turban-maker receives the rest. Now for six years he has been dead and his son indeed stands in his office. Justice has been in abeyance since Sargon. Sennacherib was the re-

[1] H. 43.

mover. This is according to their reasons. The king, my lord, as he will, let him do.

The text is difficult, partly because some signs are defaced, partly because some words could be read more ways than one, and others are obscure. It seems quite clear that the cult of Ashur had greatly suffered. We know from the Ḫarrân census that certain lands were charged with dues to the temples, others with salaries to officials. The list of defaulters is of geographical value. The deposition of rightful temple officers and the intrusion of unworthy substitutes, on slight grounds, is charged to Sennacherib. He was evidently estranged from the cult of Ashur. Doubtless a comparison of other letters will clear up some of the obscurities, but sufficient is clear to indicate the importance of such documents.

Women's letters

It is of interest to note that we have a few letters sent by women. We may select the following:[1]

To the scribe of the palace, my lord, thy handmaid Sarai. Bêl, Bêltu (of Nineveh?), Bêltu of Babylon, Nabû, Tashmetum, Ishtar of Nineveh, Ishtar of Arbela, be gracious to my lord. Long days, health of mind, health of body, may they give to my lord. The servants of my lord, whom the governor of Bît Naialani took, seven souls in all, he gave to Marduk-erba. Now the people are here, they have come to me and say thus: "Say to the scribe of the palace, Do not cause them to enter into the house of Marduk-erba." The *šâḳu* has sealed for them, now he is with them.

Evidently the lady Sarai had great influence with the scribe of the palace; perhaps she was his wife. The reason why the governor took certain servants of his and gave them to Marduk-erba is not clear. Perhaps they were sold for some government claim. It seems that the lady wished to keep them back, but that the purchaser had called and was about to take them away, unless the scribe in some way intervened.

[1] H. 220.

Private letters

A few quite private letters found their way into the archives of Nineveh, unless indeed this is a mere freak of the discoverers. Thus:[1]

Note from Marduk to Kurigalzu, his brother: Bêl and Nabû seek the peace of my brother. Wherefore have I not seen thy messenger? Until he enter Borsippa, when I see thy messenger, my heart shall drink the wine of joy. Let my brother send so many pots.

Here is another from Borsippa:[2]

Note from Bêl-upaḳ to Kunâ, his father: Peace be to my father. Daily I pray to Nabû and Nanâ for my father's health of life and I have fulfilled the duty to Ezida (the temple of Nabû at Borsippa) for thy sake. When I inquired of Mâr-bîti (a divine name) for thy sake, a fixed time of peace was taken up to the fourth day. Thy workman is informed concerning everything whatever is safe according to his (the god's) word.

Reports and lists

As before remarked, many letters are notices of the movements of horses. These are really obscure in that we do not know what the real purpose of the reports was. They are very similar to many reports which lack the form of address that marks a letter. Many of the terms applied to the horses are also obscure and there is no way to translate them. In other cases we have reports to the king or his officials on various every-day subjects. A list of slaves assigned to one or more men, a list of guests, men of high rank, sent to stay with certain officials, lists of furniture and effects, including books, sent to Ḫarrân with one of the princes, all serve to throw light upon the daily life at the court of Nineveh. Incidentally we have many hints for history as well as life and manners. But such lists and reports do not lend themselves to translation.

Inquiries of the oracles

A group of texts, very similar to the letters, only with an especial character of their own, are the inquiries addressed by Esarhaddon and Ashurbânipal to the oracle of

[1] H. 345. [2] H. 219.

the sun-god. Their great interest lies in the fact that they usually state the events which cause the king's anxiety and so make important contributions to history. But the larger part of them consist of a detailed statement of what omens have been observed by the augurs on examining the entrails of the sacrifices. On these it is probable that the sun-god was to base his opinion. He would know and declare what they portended.

Metrology

Occasionally a letter serves to make a contribution to some subject which is of interest apart from the events of the day. Thus, information is furnished regarding metrology in a letter primarily concerned with materials for the repair of a temple or palace.[1] There we read of "six articles of *mismakanna* wood, six *KA* apiece, one cubit long and one cubit thick." The thickness is clearly a cubit each way, and we learn that a cubit cube contained six *ḲA*. There are many letters and fragments which concern beams of wood and stones sent from great distances for buildings and repairs. When these are all published and considered together, no doubt they will clear up the difficulties which at present render translation impossible.

Diary of a journey

A fragmentary report—it may have been a letter—gives a diary of a journey. If we could complete it, or find a few more like it, we should have a knowledge of geography such as we have not for any other part of the world for early times.[2] We may summarize it as follows: On the sixth, the writer went from Bagarri to Sarî, from Sarî to Arzuḫina, from Arzuḫina to Tel-Arzuḫina. He stated the distances from city to city, but these are now lost. This was the first journey. The second journey was from Tel-Arzuḫina to Dûr-sisite. The third journey was from Dûr-sisite to Maturaba, from Maturaba to Dûr-Taliti. The fourth journey was from Dûr-Taliti to Babiti, from Babiti to Lagabgalagi. The fifth

---

[1] H. 566. [2] A. D. D., No. 1096.

journey was from Lagabgalagi to the river Radânu, thence to Asri. The sixth journey was from Asri to Arrakdi. The seventh journey was from Ḫualsundi to Napigi, thence to Dûr-Ashur. Here we get the whole distance from Arrakdi to Dûr-Ashur as *two kaspu, twenty-four uš, twenty-four u.* The identification of these places would be of enormous value for a determination of the Assyrian measures of length. The distances are correct to the cubit. The eighth journey was from Dûr-Ashur to Tarzini, thence to Banbala. The ninth journey was from Banbala to Ishdi-dagurrai, thence to Gupni-Bêl-Ḫarrân, *one kaspu, five uš, fifty-four u.* The tenth journey was from Gupni-Bêl-Ḫarrân to Dûr-Adadi-rîmâni, thence to Dûr-Tukulti-apil-esharra, on the seventeenth. Several of these places are already known. Others may be identified with some certainty. The whole would have a great value if preserved complete.

# X

## LETTERS OF THE SECOND BABYLONIAN EMPIRE

Business letters

Some Babylonian letters of the Second Empire are to be found in the great collections published by Strassmaier. For the most part they are of a business nature, asking for some payment to be made or some object sent on.

Thus,[1] one reads:

Order for seed

Note from Nabû-shum-lîshir to Bêl-uballiṭ and Ki . . . my brothers. Bêl and Nabû decree the well-being of my brothers. Two *GUR* of dates to Bêl-nâṣir, two *GUR* to Shamash-pir'-uṣur, from the store for seed let my brothers give. Adar the ninth, year eleven, Nabonidus, King of Babylon.

Or,[2]

Another for supplies

Note from Shamash-erba to Ḫâr-ibnî, my brother: When I send Shamash-uballiṭ to thy presence, do thou send ninety *ḲA* of meal by his hand. Verily thou knowest. Besides the twelve *ḲA* of meal before is this. Adar the thirteenth.

A somewhat longer but imperfect letter[3] reads:

Explanation of the filling of an order

Note of Nadinu to the priest of Sippara, my brother: Verily, peace be with thee. To my brother, may Bêl and Nabû decree the well-being of my brother. When to my brother I [send], to the presence of my lord. . . . Thou, my lord, knowest why seeds for the *kêpu* of Raḫza I sent, and money for the seeds I gave him. He received it. Let me hear news and the welfare of my brother.

---

[1] Nbd. 574. [2] Nbd. 1134. [3] Nbk. 460.

Of some interest for the nature of public works is:[1]

Note from Shâpik-zêr to Ḫâr-ibnî, my brother: The gods decree thy well-being. Give ninety-six *ḲA* of meal to the men who are digging the canal. Kislîmnu, the twentieth, fifth year, Cyrus, King of Babylon, king of lands.

Or this:[2]

Note from the priests to Ḫâr-ibnî, our brother: The gods decree thy welfare. Give thirty-six *ḲA* of meal to Ardi-Ḫâr, for the king's men who dig the canal. Kislîmnu the twenty-fifth, year five, Cyrus, King of Babylon, king of lands. Requisition for supplies for canal digging

The following is another of the best-preserved letters of this period:[3]

Note from Nêrgal-aḫ-iddin to Iddin-Marduk, my father: Bêl and Nabû decree the health and well-being of my father. Concerning the money my father sent; the money is little, which has been given for dates. Two minas of silver is needed. Let my father send it. Concerning that (?), as it is good to thee. I have none. See, Nabû-mattûa I have sent to my father. The governor has gone to Babylon. As long as he is not here (?) at his side, he demands. Let me hear news of my father. Whether it be corn or whether it be anything that is with me, I will give to my father. Thy word is indisputable with me. Request for some money

For the most part the others are fragmentary and of no special interest. It is noteworthy that they all begin with much the same form of greeting. Fragmentary notes

Dr. T. G. Pinches published the text of three letters of this period in *Recueil des Travaux*.[4] Two are very fragmentary; the third reads thus:

Note from Suḳâ to Bêl-zêr-ibnî, my father: May Bêl and Nabû decree health and wealth to my father. Now I am going without the ass. Give the ass to Shamash-eṭir; let him send it. Give him the clothes (?).

---

[1] Cyr. 207. [2] Cyr. 209.
[3] Cyr. 376. [4] XIX., p. 104 f.

Here is an interesting letter:[1]

Note from Daian-bêl-uṣur to Shirḳu, my lord: Every day I pray to Bêl and Nabû for the health of my lord's life. Concerning the lambs, which my lord sent, Bêl and Nabû know that there is a lamb from before thee. I have set the crop and fixed the stable. I have seen thy servant with the sheep; send thy servant with the lambs, and direct that one lamb from among them be offered as a gift to Nabû. I have not turned so much as one sheep into money. On the twentieth I worked [or sacrificed] for Shamash. I saw fifty-six. From his hands I sent twenty head to my lord. The garlic which the governor received from my lord, the owners of the field, when they came, took possession of; the governor of fields sold it for money. I am deprived of the yoke of the harrow (?). As to what my lord said to me, saying, "Wherefore hast thou not sent a messenger and measured out the crop?" Forthwith (?) I will send to thee, let a messenger of thy appointing (?) take it and keep it.

Several words in this text are not found elsewhere, but very strangely we know much about the persons. Shirḳu, whose other name was Marduk-nâṣir-aplu, son of Iddinâ, was of the important commercial house of Egibi, and lived in the reign of Darius. He was a great ship-owner, and had the tolls of a certain bridge. He travelled to Elam in the fifth year of Darius. A great many of his business transactions are detailed by Dr. Pinches.[2] Daian-bêl-uṣur and his wife Nanâ-bêl-uṣri were slaves of Shirḳu, who pledged them with their six children, at one time. In the sixteenth year of Darius their master gave them as part of her dowry, to Amat-Bau, daughter of Kalbâ. They lived in the town of Suppatum.

The reader has now before him a few specimens of this extremely valuable but very obscure class of literature. As time and study avail to clear up the obscurities, much more will be learned of the life and customs of these ancient peoples. Enough may have been given to stimulate research,

[1] Peek-Pinches, No. 22.

[2] Peek-Pinches, pp. 85 ff.

and interest a wider circle of readers. It is the writer's hope that many may be led, even by these scattered and disjointed specimens, to undertake such studies as may render more perfect his slight contribution and rescue from oblivion the heroes of a bygone civilization.

# APPENDIX

# APPENDIX

## I

### THE PROLOGUE AND EPILOGUE TO THE CODE OF ḪAMMURABI

The prologue and epilogue of the Code are very difficult to translate. Often the phrases are simply stock expressions which occur in most of the royal inscriptions. The meanings of many of these have degenerated to mere titles of courtesy and their original significance is obscure. But early translators found no difficulty in guessing the most complimentary things to say, and more recent scholars in their efforts to be exact become grotesque. When an ancient king called himself a "rabid buffalo" it doubtless gave him satisfaction, but it would be very rude for us to do so. On the other hand, it is very tiresome to an English reader to read a sentence of three hundred lines in length before coming to a principal verb. Such a sentence, a string of epithets and participles, is here broken up into short clauses and the participles turned into finite verbs. This is done, not because the translator is entirely ignorant of grammar, but in pity for the reader. This further necessitates turning the third person singular, in which the king speaks of himself, like a modern acceptance of an invitation to dinner, into the more simple direct narration in the first person. Anyone who wishes to compare this translation with the original will please recall that this is done for ease in understanding, not because the original was misunderstood.

A more serious difficulty is, that, as it was customary to apply the same honorific titles to both a god and the king, it is often uncertain to which the original meant to apply them. This may have been left intentionally vague. Some translators have taken on themselves to settle to which they will refer the epithet, to the god or to the king. Such translations are only interesting as a record of private opinions. They settle nothing, do not even give a presumption in favor of anything. It is more honest to leave the translation as vague as the original, when this can be done. This part of the stele is full of rare words, or what is just as bad, words which invariably occur in the same context. If a king calls himself by some strange honorific title, it is no assistance to understanding the meaning of it that a score of successors should do the same. Of many words, all we can conjecture is that the king was honored by them. There is nothing to indicate what they really meant. In some cases "mighty" is as likely to be correct as "wise." There is no reason why we should prefer either rendering. Both can hardly be right, neither may really be. Some king may once have prided himself on being an expert potter, as a modern monarch might on being a photographer. If he called himself on a monument a "superb potter," all his successors would keep the title, though they never made a pot in their lives. We have only to peruse the titles of modern monarchs to be sure of the fact. It is, therefore, to be hoped that no one will build any far-reaching theories upon logical deductions from the translations given here or elsewhere of such honorific titles.

## PROLOGUE TO THE CODE OF ḪAMMURABI

When the most high God (Anu), king of the spirits of heaven (Anunnaki), (and) Bêl, lord of heaven and earth, who settles the fates of all, allotted to Marduk, the first-born of Ea, the lord God of right, a rule over men and extolled him among the spirits of earth (Igigi), then they nominated for Babylon a name above all, they made it renowned in all quarters, and in the midst of it they founded an everlasting sovereignty, whose seat is established like heaven and earth; then did God (Anu) and Bêl call me by name, Ḫammurabi, the high prince, god-fearing, to exemplify justice in the land, to banish the proud and oppressor, that the great should not despoil the weak, to rise like the sun over the black-headed race (mankind) and illumine the land, to give health to all flesh. Ḫammurabi the (good) shepherd, the choice of Bêl, am I, the completer of plenty and abundance, the fulfiller of every purpose. For Nippur, and Dûrili (epithet of Nippur or part of it?), I highly adorned Ê-KUR (the temple of Bêl there). In powerful sovereignty I restored Eridu and cleansed Ê-ZU-AB (temple of Ea there). By onslaughts on every side (the four quarters) I magnified the name of Babylon and rejoiced the heart of Marduk my lord. Every day I stood in Ê-SAG-GIL (the temple of Marduk at Babylon). Descendant of kings whom

Sin had begotten, I enriched the city of Ur, and humbly adoring, was a source of abundance to Ê-NER-NU-GAL (the temple of Sin at Ur). A king of knowledge, instructed by Shamash the judge, I strongly established Sippara, reclothed the rear of the shrine of Aya (the consort of Shamash), and planned out Ê-BAB-BAR (temple of Shamash at Sippara) like a dwelling in heaven. In arms I avenged Larsa (held by the Elamite, Rim-Sin), and restored Ê-BAB-BAR (temple of Shamash at Larsa) for Shamash my helper. As overlord I gave fresh life to Erech, furnishing abundance of water to its people, and completed the spire of Ê-AN-NA (temple of Nanâ at Erech). I completed the glory of Anu and Ninni. As a protector of my land, I reassembled the scattered people of Nisin (recently reconquered from the Elamites) and replenished the treasury of Ê-GAL-MAḪ (temple of Nisin). As the royal potentate of the city and own brother of its god Zamama, I enlarged the palace at Kish and surrounded with splendor Ê-ME-TE-UR-SAG (the temple at Kish). I made secure the great shrine of Ninni. I ordered the temple of Ḫarsagkalama Ê-KI-SAL-nakiri, by whose assistance I attained my desire. I restored Kutha and increased everything at Ê-SID-LAM (the temple there). Like a charging bull, I bore down my enemies. Beloved of TU-TU (a name of Marduk) in my love for Borsippa, of high purpose untiring, I cared for Ê-ZI-DA (temple of Nabû there). As a god, king of the city, knowing and farseeing, I looked to the plantations of Dilbat and constructed its granaries for IB (the god of Dilbat) the powerful, the lord of the insignia, the sceptre and crown, with which he invested me. As the beloved of MA-MA (consort of IB), I set fast the bas-reliefs at Kish and renewed the holy meals for Erishtu (goddess of Kish). With foresight and power I ordered the pasturages and watering-places for Sirpurla and Girsu and arranged the extensive offerings in Ê-50 (the temple of "the fifty" at Sirpurla). I scattered my enemies. As the favorite of Telitim (a god), I fulfilled the oracles of Ḫallab and rejoiced the heart of GIS-DAR (its goddess). Grand prince, whose prayers Adad knows well, I soothed the heart of Adad, the warrior in Bît Karkara. I fastened the ornaments in Ê-UD-GAL-GAL (temple there). As a king who gave life to Adab, I repaired Ê-MAḪ (temple at Adab). As hero and king of the city, unrivalled combatant, I gave life to Mashkan-Shabri and poured forth abundance on SIT-LAM (temple of Nêrgal there). The wise, the restorer, who had conquered the whole of the rebellious, I rescued the people of Malkâ in trouble. I strengthened their abodes with every comfort. For Ea and DAM-GAL-NUN-NA I increased their rule and in perpetuity appointed the lustrous offerings. As a leader and king of the city, I made the settlements on the Euphrates to be populous. As client of Dagan, who begat me, I avenged the people of Mera and Tutul. As high prince, I made the face of Ninni to shine, making the lustrous meals of NIN-A-ZU secure. I reunited my people in famine by assuring their allowances within Babylon in peace and security. As the shepherd of my people, a servant whose deeds were acceptable to GIS-DAR in E-UL-MASH (temple of Anunit) in the midst of Agade, noted for its wide squares, I settled the rules and set straight the Tigris. I brought back to Asshur the gracious colossus and settled the altar (?). As king of Nineveh I made the waters of Ninni to shine in Ê-DUP-DUP. High of purpose and wise in achievement for the great gods, descendant of Sumu-lâil, eldest son of Sin-muballiṭ, long descended scion of royalty, great king, a very Shamash (or sun) of Babylon, I caused light to arise upon Sumer and Akkad. A king who commanded obedience in all the four quarters, beloved of Ninni am I. When Marduk brought me to direct all people and commissioned me to give judgment, I laid down justice and right in the provinces, I made all flesh to prosper. Then—(*the words of the Code are the completion of the sentence. The king implies that its regulations were the outcome of this legislative decision*).

## THE EPILOGUE

The judgments of righteousness which Ḫammurabi, the powerful king, settled, and caused the land to receive a sure polity and a gracious rule.

I am Ḫammurabi, the superb king. Marduk gave me to shepherd the black-headed race, whom Bêl had assigned me. I did not forget, I did not neglect, I found for them safe pastures, I opened the way through sharp rocks, and gave them guidance. With the powerful weapon that Zamama and Ishtar granted me, by the foresight with which Ea endowed me, with the power that Marduk gave me, I cut off the enemy above and below, I lorded it over the conquered. The flesh of the land I made to rejoice. I extended the dwellings of the people in security. I left them no cause to fear. The great gods chose me and I am the shepherd that gives peace, whose club is straight; of evil and good in my city I was the director. I carried all the people of Sumer and Akkad in my bosom. By my protection, I guided in peace its brothers. By my wisdom, I provided for them. That the great should not oppress the weak, to counsel the widow and orphan, in Babylon, the city of Anu and Bêl, I raised up its head (the stele's) in Ê-SAG-GIL (temple of Marduk there), the temple whose foundation is firm as the heaven and earth. To judge the judgment of the land, to decide the decisions of the land, to succor the injured, I wrote on my stele the precious words and placed them before my likeness, that of a righteous king. The king that is gentle, king of the city, exalted am I. My words are precious, my power has no rival. By the order of Shamash, the judge supreme, of heaven and earth, that judgment may shine in the land; by the permission of Marduk, my lord, I set up a bas-relief, to preserve my likeness in Ê-SAG-GIL that I love, to commemorate my name forever in gratitude. The oppressed who has a suit to prosecute may come before my image, that of a righteous king, and read my inscription and understand my precious words and may my stele elucidate his case. Let him see the law he seeks and may he draw in his breath and say: "This Ḫammurabi was a ruler who was to his people like the father that begot them. He obeyed the order of Marduk his lord, he followed the commands of Marduk above and below. He delighted the heart of Marduk his lord, and granted happy life to his people forever. He guided the land." Let him recite the document. Before Marduk, my lord, and Ṣarpanitum, my lady, with full heart let him draw near. The colossus and the gods that live in Ê-SAG-GIL, or the courts of Ê-SAG-GIL, let him bless every day before Marduk, my lord, and Ṣarpanitum, my lady.

In the future, in days to come, at any time, let the king who is in the land, guard the words of righteousness which I have written on my stele. Let him not alter the judgment of the land which I judged nor the decisions I decided. Let him not destroy my bas-relief. If that man has wisdom and is capable of directing his land, let him attend to the words which I have written upon my stele, let him apprehend the path, the rule, the law of the land which I judged, and the decision I decided for the land, and so let him guide forward the black-headed race; let him judge their judgment and decide their decision, let him cut off from his land the proud and violent, let him rejoice the flesh of his people. Ḫammurabi, the king of righteousness, to whom Shamash has granted rights, am I. My words are precious, my deeds have no rival. Above and below I am the whirlwind that scours the deep and the height. If that man has hearkened to my words which I have written on my stele and has not frustrated justice, has not altered my words, has not injured my bas-reliefs, may Shamash make lasting his sceptre; like me, as a king of righteousness, let him guide his people in justice.

But if that man does not hearken to my words which I wrote on my stele, forgets my curses, fears not the malediction of God, sets aside the judgment which I judged, alters my words and destroys my bas-reliefs, effaces my inscribed name and writes in his own name; or, for fear of these curses has charged another to do so; that man, be he king, lord, patêsi, or noble, whose name is ever so renowned, may the great god (Anu), the father of gods, who named my reign, turn him back, shatter his sceptre in pieces, curse his fortunes; may Bêl the lord who fixes the fates, whose command is not set aside, who extended my sovereignty, cause for him an endless revolt, an impulse to fly from his home, and set for his fortune a reign of sighs, short days, years of want, darkness that has no ray of light and a death in the sight of all men. May he decree with his heavy curse the ruin of his city, the scattering of his people, the removal of his sovereignty, the disappearance of his name and his race from the land. May Beltu, the great mother, whose command is weighty in Ê-KUR, the lady who made my plans prosperous, make his words in the matter of justice and law to be hateful before Bêl. May she bring about the downfall of his country, the loss of his people, the efflux of his life like water, by the order of the Bêl, the king. May Ea, the grand prince, whose destiny takes premier rank, the messenger of the gods, who knows all, who has prolonged my life, distort his understanding and intellect, curse him with forgetfulness, dam up his rivers at their source. In his land may Ashnan (the deity of wheat), the life of the people, not grow. May Shamash, great judge of heaven and earth, who governs the creatures of life, the lord of help, cut off his sovereignty; judge not his judgment; carry away his path; annihilate the march of his armies; cast an evil look upon him to uproot his rule, and fix for him the loss of his land. May the evil sentence of Shamash quickly overwhelm him; deprive him of life among the living above; and below in the earth, deprive his ghost of water. May Sin, the lord of the sky, the god who creates, whose ray is splendid among the gods, deprive him of crown and throne of kinship; surround him with a great shirt of pain, a heavy penalty, that will not leave his body, and make him finish his days, month by month, through the years of his reign, in tears and sighs. May he multiply for him the burden of royalty. May he grant him as his lot a life that can only be likened to death. May Adad, lord of abundance, great bull of the sky, and the earth, my helper, withdraw the rain from the heavens, the floods from the springs; destroy his land with hunger and want; thunder in wrath over his city, and turn his land to deluge mounds. May Zamama, great warrior, first born of Ê-KUR, who goes at my right hand on the battlefield, shatter his weapon and turn for him day into night. May he place his enemy over him. May Ishtar, the lady of conflict and battle, who prospered my arms, my gracious protector, who loved my reign, in her heart of rage, her boundless fury, curse his sovereignty; turn all his mercies to curses, shatter his weapon in conflict and battle, appoint him trouble and sedition, strike down his heroes, and make the earth drink of their blood, scatter the plain with heaps of the carcasses of his troops, grant them no burial; deliver himself into the hands of his enemy, cause him to be carried in chains to the enemy's land. May Nêrgal, the powerful one of the gods, who meets with no rival, who caused me to obtain my triumphs, burn up his people with a fever like a great fire among the reeds. With his powerful weapon may he drink him up, with his fevers crush him like a statue of clay. May Erishtu, the exalted lady of all lands, the creator-mother, carry off his son and leave him no name. May he not beget a seed of posterity among his people. May Nin-karrak, the daughter of Anu, the completer of my mercies in Ê-KUR, award him a severe malady, a grievous illness, a painful wound, which cannot be healed, of which the physician knows not the origin, which cannot be soothed by the bandage; and rack him with palsy, until she has mastered his life; may she weaken his strength. May the great gods of heaven and earth, the Anunnaki, in their assembly, who look after the halls and the courts of this Ê-bar-ra (temple of Shamash at Sippara, where the stele was clearly set up), curse with a bitter curse his dynasty, his land, his soldiers, his people, and his subjects. May the judgments of Bêl, which in his mouth are irrevocable, curse him and quickly overcome him.

# II

## CHRONOLOGY

The following tables make no pretence to finality. In Babylonian history no date before B.C. 747 can be considered absolutely fixed. In Assyrian history the Eponym Canon certainly goes back to about B.C. 893. Then scattered notices in later writers enable us to approximate to earlier dates and the varied synchronisms between Assyrian and Babylonian kings render the dates probable, as far back as the First Dynasty of Babylon. There is only one fixed date before that, the period of Sargon I., which depends on a statement of Nabonidus.

The sequence of monarchs is, however, very probably correct. As knowledge increases, more names will be added to fill up the gaps, and dated documents will give the lengths of the reigns. A discussion of the grounds for the dates cannot be given here. The reader may refer to Dr. P. Rost, in the *Mittheilungen der Vorderasiatischen Gesellschaft*, 1897, No. 2, and *Orientalistische Litteratur-Zeitung*, 1900, pp. 143, 175, 212. Radau's *Early Babylonian History* may be consulted for the earliest dates.

In the early periods, a vertical line between two names denotes that the second was son of the former. This is often all we know, but it is useful to mark the fact, as we cannot then insert other rulers between them. Names printed in capitals are either Sumerian or their true pronunciation is unknown. When these capitals are in Roman type, we know that they were kings or Patesis; when they are printed in italic, we only know that they were the parents of those whose names follow. We do not then know whether they reigned or not.

For Assyrian chronology, see *Annals of the Kings of Assyria*, by Budge and King, 1902.

## ASSYRIA

### EARLY PATESIS, DATES CONJECTURAL, ORDER UNCERTAIN

Ushpia,

Ilushuma,
|
Irishum, circa B.C. 2100
|
Ikunum,

Ishme-Dagan, circa B.C. 1930
|
Shamshi-Adad I., circa B.C. 1910

Igur-kapkapu,
|
Shamshi-Adad II.,

Bêl-upaḫḫir (?),
|
Shamshi-Adad III.

### EARLY KINGS, DATES CONJECTURAL

| | CIRCA B.C. |
|---|---|
| Bêl-ibni, . . . . . . | |
| Sulili (?), . . . . . . | |
| Bêl-kapkapu, . . . | 1700 |
| Ashur-bêl-nishêshu, . . | 1500 |
| Puzur-Ashur, . . . . . | 1470 |
| Ashur-nâdin-aḫê, . . | 1430 |
| Ashur-uballiṭ, son, . . | 1420 |
| Bêl-nirari, son, . . . | 1400 |
| Pudi-ilu, son, . . . | 1397 |
| Adad-nirari I., son, . . | 1395 |
| Shulmanu-asharid (Shalmaneser) I., son, . . | 1380 |
| Tukulti-Ninip I., son, . | 1340 |
| Ashur-nâṣir-pal I., . . | 1330 |
| Ashur-narara, . . . . | 1300 |
| Nabû-daian, . . . . . | 1295 |
| Bêl-kudur-uṣur, . . . | 1290 |
| Ninip-apil-esharra, . . | 1285 |
| Ashur-dan, son, . . . | 1260 |
| Mutakkil-Nusku, son, . | 1250 |
| Ashur-rêsh-ishi, son, . . | 1220 |
| Tukulti-apil-esharra (Tiglath-pileser) I., son, . | 1200 |
| Ashur-bêl-kala, son, . | 1090 |
| Shamshi-Adad IV., brother, | 1080 |
| Ashur-nâṣir-pal II., . . | 1050 |
| Erba-Adad (?), . . . | |
| Ashur-nâdin-aḫê, . . | |
| Ashur-erbi, . . . . . | |
| Tukulti-apil-esharra (Tiglath-pileser) II., . . | 950 |
| Ashur-dan II., son, . . | 930 |
| Adad-nirari II., son, . . | 911 |

#### DATES CERTAIN FROM EPONYM CANON

| | B.C. |
|---|---|
| Tukulti-Ninip II., son, | 890 |
| Ashur-nâṣir-pal III., son, | 884 |
| Shulmanu-asharid (Shalmaneser) II., | 859 |
| Shamshi-Adad V., | 824 |
| Adad-nirari III., | 811 |
| Shulmanu-asharid (Shalmaneser) III., | 782 |
| Ashur-dan III., | 772 |
| Ashur-nirari II., | 754 |
| Tukulti-apil-esharra (Tiglath-pileser, Pul) III., | 745 |
| Shulmanu-asharid (Shalmaneser) IV., | 726 |
| Sharru-ukin (Sargon) II., | 721 |
| Sin-aḫê-erba (Sennacherib) son, | 704 |
| Ashur-aḫ-iddin (Esarhaddon), son, | 680 |
| Ashur-bâni-pal (Asnapper) son, | 668 |
| Ashur-etil-ilâni, son, | 625 |
| Sin-shum-lîshir, | (?) |
| Sin-shar-ishkun, | (?) |
| Fall of Nineveh, | 607 |

## III

## WEIGHTS AND MEASURES

### I. WEIGHTS

1 shekel = 180 *šê*.
1 mina = 60 shekels.
1 talent = 60 minas.

The weight of the mina may be reckoned in round numbers as 500 grams.

### II. MEASURES OF CAPACITY

*Early Scale*

1 GIN = 180 *šê* (?).
1 ḲA = 60 GIN.
1 GUR = 300 ḲA.

*Later Scale*

1 GUR = 180 ḲA.

### III. MEASURES OF LENGTH

1 ell (U) = 60 *ubanu*.
1 *ḳânu* = 6 ells.
1 GAR = 2 *ḳânu*.
1 KASBU = 1,800 GAR.

On other measures see *A. D. D.*, ii., pp. 197–218. The ell is about half a metre.

### IV. MEASURES OF SURFACE

1 GIN = 180 *šé*.
1 SAR = 60 GIN.
1 GAN = 1,800 SAR.

The area of the SAR was one GAR square, or 6 metres square. Areas were also measured by the amount of corn required to sow them, or their average yield, that is by the GUR and ḲA.

### V. MEASURES OF TIME

1 day = 12 double hours.
1 month = 30 days, average.
1 year = 12 months, average.

Further details may be obtained from Zimmern's *Das Princip unserer Zeit-und Raumteilung*, in the *Berichten d. philolog. histor. Classe d. Königl. Sächs. Gesellschaft der Wissenschaften zu Leipzig*. November 14, 1901.

## IV

## BIBLIOGRAPHY OF THE LATER PERIODS

### The New Babylonian Empire

**Nabopolassar.**—Strassmaier published nineteen texts in *Z. A.*, iv., pp. 141–45, of which three are transcribed and translated in *K. B.*, iv., pp. 177–81. Dr. Pinches gave another, *C. T.*, iv., p. 14, and another in Peek-Pinches, p. 3. Dr. Moldenke gave nine other texts in his *Cuneiform Texts from the Metropolitan Museum of Art, New York*.

**Nebuchadrezzar II.**—Strassmaier published 460 texts in *Hefts V.-VI.*, of the *Babylonische Texte*, of which thirty-one are transcribed and translated in *K. B.*, iv., pp. 180–201, and forty are discussed in Kohler-Peiser's *Aus Babylonischen Rechtsleben.* Two texts are published by Pinches, *C. T.*, iv., p. 38, two more in Peiser's *Babylonische Verträge*, six texts from the Liverpool Museum were published by Strassmaier in the *Actes du VI. Congrès Internationale des Orientalistes, 1883.* Some of the above texts belong, however, to the reign of Nebuchadrezzar III.

**Evil-Merodach.**—Evetts published twenty-four texts in *Babylonische Texte, Heft VI., B*, of which *K. B.*, iv., pp. 200–3, gives transcriptions and translations of two. Kohler-Peiser discuss eight in *Aus Babylonischen Rechtsleben* and add one more. Strassmaier published two from the Liverpool Museum in the *Actes du VI. Congrès Internationale des Orientalistes, 1883.*

**Neriglissar.**—Evetts published seventy-two texts in *Babylonische Texte, Heft VI., B*, pp. 25–82. Of these four are transcribed and translated in *K. B.*, iv., pp. 202–7 and Kohler-Peiser discussed fourteen in *Aus Babylonischen Rechtsleben.* In *Babylonische Verträge*, Peiser published another; and Strassmaier published three from the Liverpool Museum in the *Actes du VI. Congrès Internationale des Orientalistes, 1883.*

**Laborosoarchod.**—Evetts published six texts, *Babylonische Texte, Heft VI., B*, pp. 85–90. Of these, one is transcribed and translated in *K. B.*, iv., pp. 206–7. Strassmaier published four in the *Actes du VIII. Congrès Internationale des Orientalistes, 1889.*

**Nabonidus.**—Strassmaier published 1134 texts in *Babylonische Texte, Heft I.–IV.* Of these, *K. B.*, iv., pp. 206–59, gives transcriptions and translations of fifty-six, and three fresh texts from copies by Peiser, Pinches, and Revillout. Kohler-Peiser discuss sixty-five of them in *Aus Babylonischen Rechtsleben* and add one more. Pinches published two, *C. T.*, iv., pp. 30–41, and four in Peek-Pinches. Dr. Peiser gave another in *Keilschriftliche Acten-Stücke*, No. 3, two from the British Museum. Strassmaier published six from the Liverpool Museum in the *Actes du VI. Congrès Internationale des Orientalistes, 1883.* Dr. Moldenke gave forty-two texts in his *Cuneiform Texts in the Metropolitan Museum of Art, New York.*

## Persian Period

**Cyrus.**—Strassma.er published 384 texts in *Babylonische Texte, Heft VII.*, of which *K. B.*, iv., pp. 253–85 gives transcriptions and translations of twenty-four, and Kohler-Peiser discussed thirty-four in *Aus Babylonischen Rechtsleben,* adding four new texts. In *Keilschriftliche Acten-Stücke*, Peiser gave two more; in *Babylonische Verträge,* fourteen more. Strassmaier gave two from the Liverpool Museum, in the *Actes du VI. Congrès Internationale des Orientalistes, 1883.* Pinches published another in Peek-Pinches, Dr. Budge another in *Z. A.*, vii., p. 219.

**Cambyses.**—Strassmaier gave 441 texts in *Babylonische Texte, Heft VIII.–IX.*, but in these no distinction is made between the reigns of Cambyses and Cyrus, Cambyses alone, Cyrus alone. *K. B.*, iv., pp. 260–63 gives transcription and translation of four, followed by twenty-five of Cambyses alone and fourteen of Cyrus alone. Kohler-Peiser discussed twenty-one in *Aus Babylonische Rechtsleben.* Peiser gave seventeen more in *Babylonische Verträge* from the Berlin Museum and one from the British Museum. Strassmaier gave three from the Liverpool Museum, and one in possession of Golenischeff in the *Actes du VI. Congrès Internationale des Orientalistes.* Pinches published one in *C. T.*, iv., one in Peek-Pinches. Dr. G. A. Barton published two in the *American Journal of Semitic Languages, January, 1900.*

**Barzia.**—Strassmaier published nine texts, *Z. A.*, iv., pp. 147 ff., of which four are transcribed and translated, *K. B.*, iv., pp. 294–98. Peiser gave three more in *Babylonische Verträge.* Strassmaier published one from the Liverpool Museum in the *Actes du VI. Congrès Internationale des Orientalistes, 1883.*

**Nebuchadrezzar III.**—In *K. B.*, iv., pp. 298–303, three are transcribed and translated from those published above and ascribed to Nebuchadrezzar II.

**Darius.**—Strassmaier has published 579 texts in *Babylonische Texte, Heft X.–XII.*, of which *K. B.*, iv., pp. 302–11 gives transcription and translation of nine. Kohler-Peiser discuss ninety-six in *Aus Babylonischen Rechtsleben* and add seven more. Pinches published six in *C. T.*, ii., p. 2; iv., pp. 21, 32, 41, 43, 44; and twelve in Peek-Pinches. Peiser gave fifteen in *Keilschriftliche Acten-Stücke,* and fifty-five in *Babylonische Verträge* from the Berlin Museum, twenty-four from the British Museum. Dr. G. A. Barton gave twenty-seven in *American Journal of Semitic Languages, January, 1900.* Strassmaier gave six from the Liverpool Museum in the *Actes du VI. Congrès Internationale des Orientalistes, 1883.* Dr. Budge published three in *Z. A.*, iii., pp. 216 ff.

**Shamash-erba.**—Strassmaier published one text of this period in *Z. A.*, iii., p. 157 f.

**Xerxes.**—Evetts published four texts, *Babylonische Texte, Heft VI., B*, pp. 91–94; of these *K. B.*, iv., pp. 310–11 gives transcription and translation of one. Pinches published one, *C. T.*, iv., p. 34, Dr. G. A. Barton gave one in *American Journal of Semitic Languages, January, 1900.* Strassmaier published seven in the *Actes du VIII. Congrès Internationale des Orientalistes, 1889.*

**Artaxerxes.**—Professor Hilprecht and Dr. Clay have published 119 texts with transcriptions and translations of twelve, in the ninth volume of the series of Cuneiform Texts of the collections of the University of Philadelphia. Kotalla has given transcriptions and translations of others in *B. A. S.*, iv. Dr. Peiser gave a transcription and translation of one from his own copy, *K. B.*, iv., pp. 312–13. Kohler-Peiser give two more in *Aus Babylonischen Rechtsleben.* Dr. G. A. Barton gave four in *American Journal of Semitic Languages, January, 1900.* Strassmaier published nine in the *Actes du VIII. Congrès Internationale des Orientalistes, 1889*, and one in *Z. A.*, iii., p. 158.

### Macedonian Period

**Alexander IV.**—Strassmaier, *Z. A.*, iii., p. 150, transcribed and translated one, also *K. B.*, iv., pp. 312–13. Pinches gave one, *C. T.*, iv., p. 39.

**Seleucus II.**—Oppert, *Doc. Jur.*, pp. 301 ff., gave two, one given again, *K. B.*, iv., pp. 312–17. Pinches gave another, *C. T.*, iv., p. 29. Strassmaier published one in *Actes du VIII. Congrès Internationale des Orientalistes, 1889*; and one, *Z. A.*, iii., p. 152f.

**Demetrius.**—Strassmaier published two, *Z. A.*, iii., pp. 148–50.

**Antiochus III.**—Strassmaier published one, *Z. A.*, iii., p. 150 f., transcribed and translated also, *K. B.*, iv., pp. 316–17.

### Arsacide Period

Strassmaier published sixteen texts, *Z. A.*, iii., pp. 143 ff., one is given in transcription and translation, *K. B.*, iv., pp. 318–19.

# INDEX

# INDEX

Superior Roman numerals refer to sections of the early Babylonian laws, superior arabic numerals to the laws of the Code of Ḫammurabi, and superior capitals to the later Assyrian or Babylonian laws.

## Reprints of the Legal Classics Published by The Lawbook Exchange, Ltd.

### ☙Admiralty & Maritime Law ☙

**Flanders, Henry. [1824-1911].** *A Treatise on Maritime Law.* Boston: Little, Brown and Company, 1852. xvi, 444 pp. Reprinted 1999 by The Lawbook Exchange, Ltd. ISBN 1-886363-72-2. Cloth. $75.

**Marsden. R.[eginald]. G.[odfrey], ed.** *Documents Relating to Law and Custom of the Sea.* [n.p.]: The Navy Record Society, 1915-6. Two volumes. xxxiii, 561; xl, 457, [5] pp. Reprinted 1999 by The Lawbook Exchange, Ltd. LCCN 99-24138. ISBN 1-886363-96-X. Cloth. $175.

**[Twiss, Sir Travers].** *The Black Book of the Admiralty, with an Appendix.* Monumenta Juridica. Edited by Sir Travers Twiss. Four volumes. 4, xciii, 491, [2]; 4, lxxxvii, 500, 31; 4, lxxxvi, 673, [1], 31; 4, clii, 559, 32 pp. LCCN 97-38809 ISBN 1-886363-39-0. 1871. Reprinted 1998 by The Lawbook Exchange, Ltd. Cloth. $495.

### ☙ Law & Literature ☙

**Barton, Dunbar Plunket.** *Shakespeare and the Law.* With a foreword by James M. Beck. Boston: Houghton Mifflin Company, 1929. xl, 167 pp. Reprint available October 1999 by The Lawbook Exchange, Ltd. LCCN 99-26602. ISBN 1-58477-000-7. Cloth. $60.

**Darrow, Clarence.** *A Persian Pearl. And Other Essays.* East Aurora, NY: The Roycroft Shop, 1899. 175 pp. Reprinted 1997 by The Lawbook Exchange, Ltd. ISBN 1-886363-27-7. Cloth. $50.

**Darrow, Clarence S.** *An Eye for an Eye.* New York: Fox Duffield & Company, 1905. 213 pp. Reprinted 1996 by The Lawbook Exchange, Ltd. ISBN 1-886363-07-2. Cloth. $40.

**Davis, C.K.** *The Law in Shakespeare.* Washington, D.C.: Washington Law Book Co., [1883]. 303 pp. Reprinted 1999 by The Lawbook Exchange, Ltd. ISBN 1-886363-75-7. Cloth. $60.

**Gest, John Marshall.** *The Lawyer in Literature.* London: Sweet & Maxwell, Limited, 1913. xii, 249 pp. Reprint available November 1999 by The Lawbook Exchange, Ltd. LCCN99-18365. ISBN 1-886363-90-0. Cloth. $60.

**Holdsworth, William S.** *Charles Dickens as a Legal Historian.* New Haven: Yale University Press, 1929. 157 pp. Reprinted 1995 by The Lawbook Exchange, Ltd. ISBN 1-886363-06-4. Cloth. $40.

## ଓ Legal Biography ଓ

**Foss, Edward.** *A Biographical Dictionary of the Judges of England From the Conquest to the Present Time 1066-1870.* London: John Murray, 1870. xv, 792 pp. Reprint available December 1999 by The Lawbook Exchange, Ltd. LCCN 99-12577. ISBN 10886363-86-2. Cloth. $100.

**Richards, John T.** *Abraham Lincoln The Lawyer-Statesman.* Boston: Houghton Mifflin, 1916. Frontis. Illustrated. xii, 260 pp. Reprint available October 1999 by The Lawbook Exchange, Ltd. LCCN 99-20587. ISBN 1-886363-94-3. Cloth. $60.

## ଓ Legal Codes ଓ

**[Field Codes]. [New York 1850-1865]. New York Field Codes. 1850-1865.**
**Vol. I.** *The Code of Civil Procedure of the State of New-York, Reported Complete by the Commissioners on Practice and Pleadings. 1850.*
**Vol. II.** *The Code of Criminal Procedure of the State of New York, Reported Complete by the Commissioners on Practice and Pleadings. 1850.*
**Vol. III.** *The Civil Code of the State of New York, Reported Complete by the Commissioners of the Code. 1865.*
**Vol. IV.** *The Penal Code of the State of New York, Reported Complete by the Commissioners of the Code. 1865.*
**Vol. V.** *The Political Code of the State of New York. 1860.*
With a new introduction by Michael Weber. Reprinted 1998 by The Lawbook Exchange, Ltd. Five volume series. [8], xcvi, 791; liii, [1], 486; cxii, 776; lxiv, 406, clxvii; xlvii, 607 pp. ISBN 1-886363-40-4 (set). Cloth. $495.

**Livingston, Edward.** *A System of Penal Law, for the State of Louisiana: Consisting of A Code of Crimes and Punishments, A Code of Procedure, A Code of Evidence, A Code of Reform and Prison Discipline, A Book of Definitions. Prepared Under the Authority of a Law of the Said State. To Which are Prefixed a Preliminary Report on the Plan of a Penal Code, and Introductory Reports to the Several Codes Embraced in the System of Penal Law.* Philadelphia: James Kay, Jun. & Brother, 1833.v, 745 pp. Reprint available November 1999 by The Lawbook Exchange, Ltd. LCCN 99-11403. ISBN 1-886363-83-8. Cloth. $95.

## Legal Dictionaries

**Anderson, William C.** *A Dictionary of Law, Consisting of Judicial Definitions and Explanations of Words, Phrases, and Maxims, and an Exposition of the Principles of Law: Comprising a Dictionary and Compendium of American and English Jurisprudence.* Chicago: T.H. Flood and Company, 1889. viii, 1140pp. Reprinted 1996 by The Lawbook Exchange, Ltd. ISBN 1-886363-23-4. Cloth. $125.

**Black, Henry Campbell.** *A Law Dictionary. Containing Definitions of the Terms and Phrases of American and English Jurisprudence, Ancient and Modern. And Including the Principal Terms of International, Constitutional, Ecclesiastical and Commercial Law, and Medical Jurisprudence, with a Collection of Legal Maxims, Numerous Select Titles from the Roman, Modern Civil, Scotch, French, Spanish, and Mexican Law, and Other Foreign Systems, and a Table of Abbreviations.* St. Paul, Minn.: West Publishing, 1910. 1314 pp. Reprinted 1995 by The Lawbook Exchange, Ltd. ISBN 1-886363-10-2. Cloth. $125.

**Black, Henry Campbell.** *A Dictionary of Law. Containing Definitions of the Terms and Phrases of American and English Jurisprudence, Ancient and Modern. Including the Principal Terms of International, Constitutional, and Commercial Law; with a Collection of Legal Maxims and Numerous Select Titles from the Civil Law and Other Foreign Systems.* St. Paul, Minn.: West Publishing, 1891. x, 1253 pp. Reprinted 1991 by The Lawbook Exchange, Ltd. ISBN 0-9630106-0-3. $125.

**Bouvier, John.** *A Law Dictionary Adapted to the Constitution and Laws of the United States of America, and of the Several States of the American Union; with References to the Civil and Other Systems of Foreign Law.* Philadelphia: T. & J.W. Johnson, 1839. Two volumes. 559; 28 pp. Reprinted 1993 by The Lawbook Exchange, Ltd. ISBN 0-9630106-7-0. Cloth. $130.

**Burrill, Alexander M.** *A New Law Dictionary and Glossary: Containing Full Definitions of the Principal Terms of the Common and Civil Law, Together with Translations and Explanations of the Various Technical Phrases in Different Languages, Occurring in the Ancient and Modern Reports, and Standard Treatises; Embracing Also All the Principal Common and Civil Law Maxims. Compiled on the Basis of Spelman's Glossary, and Adapted to the Jurisprudence of the United States; with Copious Illustrations, Critical and Historical.* New York: John S. Voorhies, 1850. Two volumes. xviii, 1099 pp. Reprinted 1998 by The Lawbook Exchange, Ltd. LC 97-38481. ISBN 1-886363-32-3. Cloth. $175.

**Holthouse, Henry James.** *A New Law Dictionary, Containing Explanations of Such Technical Terms and Phrases As Defined in the Works of Legal Authors, in the Practice of the Courts, and in the Parliamentary Proceedings of the Houses of Lords and*

*Commons, To Which Is Added An Outline of An Action at Law and of A Suit in Equity. Edited, from the Second and Enlarged London Edition, With Numerous Additions, by Henry Penington.* Philadelphia: Lea and Blanchard, 1847. viii, [17]-495 pp. Reprinted 1999 by The Lawbook Exchange, Ltd. ISBN 1-886363-67-6. Cloth. $75.

**Jacob, Giles. [1686-1744].** *The Law-Dictionary: Explaining the Rise, Progress, and Present State of the English Law; Defining and Interpreting the Terms or Words of Art; and Comprising Copious Information on the Subjects of Law, Trade, and Government. Corrected and Greatly Enlarged by T[homas] E[dlyne] Tomlins.* New York: Printed for, and Published by I. Riley, 1811. Originally six volumes, viii, 531; [2], 543; [2],618; [2], 472; [2], 553; [2], 471pp. Reprint available December 1999 by The Lawbook Exchange, Ltd. ISBN 1-886363-68-4. Cloth. $495.

**Rapalje, Stewart and Lawrence, Robert L.** *A Dictionary of American and English Law with Definitions of the Technical terms of the Canon and Civil Laws. Also, Containing a Full Collection of Latin Maxims, and Citations of Upwards of Forty Thousand Reported Cases, in which Words and Phrases Have Been Judicially Defined or Construed.* Jersey City: Frederick C. Linn & Co., 1888. Two volumes. xxxviii, 1380 pp. Reprinted 1997 by The Lawbook Exchange, Ltd. LC 97-38484. ISBN 1-886363-33-1. Cloth. $195.

**Stimson, Frederic Jesup.** *Glossary of Technical Terms, Phrases, and Maxims of the Common Law.* Boston: Little, Brown, and Company, 1881. iv, 305pp. Reprinted 1999 by The Lawbook Exchange, Ltd. ISBN 1-886363-70-6. Cloth. $60.

**Tayler, Thomas.** *The Law Glossary: Being a Selection of the Greek, Latin, Saxon, French, Norman and Italian Sentences, Phrases, and Maxims, Found in the Leading English and American reports, and Elementary Works.* New York: Lewis & Blood, 1856. 580 pp. Reprinted 1995 by The Lawbook Exchange, Ltd. ISBN 1-886363-12-9. Cloth. $65.

## ∞ Legal History ∞

**Bar, Carl Ludwig von.** *A History of Continental Criminal Law.* Boston: Little, Brown, and Company, 1916. lvi, 561 pp. Reprint available September 1999 by The Lawbook Exchange, Ltd. LCCN 99-32341. ISBN 1-58477-013-9. Cloth. $90.

**[Brandeis, Louis D.]. [1856-1941].** *Brandeis on Zionism. A Collection of Addresses and Statements by Louis D. Brandeis with a Foreword by Mr. Justice Felix Frankfurter.* Washington, D.C.: Zionist Organization of America, [1942]. viii,

156 pp. Reprinted 1999 by The Lawbook Exchange, Ltd. ISBN 1-886363-60-9. Cloth. $65.

**Corwin, Edward.** *The Doctrine of Judicial Review: Its Legal and Historical Basis and Other Essays*. Princeton: Princeton University Press, 1914. ix, 178 pp. Reprint available December 1999 by The Lawbook Exchange, Ltd. LCCN 99-32362. ISBN 1-58477-011-2. Cloth. $60.

**Darrow, Clarence and William J. Bryan.** The *World's Most Famous Court Trial. Tennessee Evolution Case. A Complete Stenographic Report of the Famous Court Test of the Anti-Evolution Act, at Dayton July 10 to 21, 1925, Including Speeches and Arguments of Attorneys.* Cincinnati: National Book Company, [1925]. [4], 339 pp. Reprinted 1997 by The Lawbook Exchange, Ltd. LC 97-38485. ISBN 1-886363-31-5. Cloth. $65.

**Dawson, John P.** *A History of Lay Judges*. Cambridge, Mass.: Harvard University Press, 1960. viii, [2], 310 pp. Reprinted 1999 by The Lawbook Exchange, Ltd. ISBN 1-886363-69-2. Cloth. $75.

**Evans, E.P.** *The Criminal Prosecution and Capital Punishment of Animals.* New York: E.P. Dutton, 1906. x, 384pp. Reprinted 1998 by The Lawbook Exchange, Ltd. LC 98-12801. ISBN 1-886363-52-8. Cloth. $65.

**Forsyth, William.** *History of Trial by Jury* [*Second edition*]. Jersey City: Frederick D. Linn, [1875]. x, 388 pp. Reprinted 1994 by The Lawbook Exchange, Ltd. ISBN 0-9630106-8-9. Cloth. $65.

**Forsyth, William.** *The History of Lawyers. Ancient and Modern.* Boston: Estes & Lauriat, 1875. Illustrated. xvii, 404 pp. Reprinted 1996 by the Lawbook Exchange, Ltd. ISBN 1-886363-14-5. Cloth. $60.

**Fortescue, Sir John. [?1394-1476?].** *The Governance of England: Otherwise Called The Difference between an Absolute and a Limited Monarchy. A Revised Text edited with Introduction, Notes, and Appendices by Charles Plummer.* London: Oxford University Press, 1885. xxiii, 387pp. Reprinted 1999 by The Lawbook Exchange, Ltd. ISBN 1-886363-79-X. Cloth. $65.

**Futrell, William H.** *The History of American Customs Jurisprudence.* New York: Published privately, 1941. 314pp. Reprinted 1998 by The Lawbook Exchange, Ltd. LC 98-11342. ISBN 1-886363-51-X. Cloth. $60.

**Greenidge, A.H.J.** *The Legal Procedure of Cicero's Time*. Oxford: The Clarendon Press, 1901. xiii, 599 pp. Reprint available December 1999 by The Lawbook Exchange, Ltd. LCCN 99-26771. ISBN 1-886363-99-4. Cloth. $85.

**Harris, Virgil M.** *Ancient, Curious, and Famous Wills.* Boston: Little, Brown, and Company, 1911. xiv, 472 pp. Reprinted 1999 by The Lawbook Exchange, Ltd. LCCN 99-20588. ISBN 1-886363-93-5. Cloth. $75.

**Henderson, Gerard Carl.** *The Position of Foreign Corporations in American Constitutional Law. A Contribution to the History and Theory of Juristic Persons in Anglo-American Law.* Cambridge: Harvard University Press, 1918. xix, 199 pp. Reprint available November 1999 by The Lawbook Exchange, Ltd. LCCN 99-18233. ISBN 1-886363-89-7. Cloth. $50.

**Holdsworth, William S.** *Essays in Law and History.* Edited by A.L. Goodhart and H.G. Hanbury. Oxford: At the Clarendon Press, 1946. xv, 302 pp. Reprinted 1995 by The Lawbook Exchange, Ltd. ISBN 1-886363-13-7. Cloth. $50.

**Holdsworth, W.S.** *The Historians of Anglo-American Law.* New York: Columbia University Press, 1928. 175 pp. Reprinted 1994 by The Lawbook Exchange, Ltd. ISBN 0-9630106-9-7. Cloth. $50.

**Langdell, C.C. [1826-1906].** *A Selection of Cases on the Law of Contracts. with References and Citations. Prepared for Use as a Text-book in Harvard Law School.* Boston: Little, Brown & Co., 1871. xvi, 1022 pp. Reprint available September 1999 by The Lawbook Exchange, Ltd. LCCN 99-28293. ISBN 1-58477-001-5. Cloth. $120.

**[MacDonell, Sir John and Edward Manson].** *Great Jurists of the World.* Edited by Sir John MacDonell and Edward Manson. With an Introduction by Van Vechten Veeder. Boston: Little, Brown, and Company, 1914. Illustrated. xxxii, 607 pp. Reprinted 1997 by The Lawbook Exchange, Ltd. ISBN 1-886363-28-5. Cloth. $95.

**Maitland, Frederick W., et.al.** *A General Survey of Events, Sources, Persons & Movements in Continental Legal History. By Various European Authors.* With an introduction by Albert Kocourek. Boston: Little, Brown, 1912. liii, 754pp. Reprinted 1998 by The Lawbook Exchange, Ltd. LC 98-11159. ISBN 1-886363-47-1. Cloth. $110.

**Maitland, Frederic William.** *Roman Canon Law in the Church of England: Six Essays.* London: Methuen & Co., 1898. vii, 184 pp. Reprinted 1998 by The Lawbook Exchange, Ltd. LC 98-22357. ISBN 1-886363-57-9. Cloth. $65.

**Maitland, Frederick W., et.al.** *Select Essays in Anglo-American Legal History. By Maitland, Pollock, Holmes, Beale, Holdsworth and Others.* Boston: Little, Brown, and Company, 1907. Three volumes. 847; 823; 862 pp. Reprinted 1992 by The Lawbook Exchange, Ltd. LCCN 91-77977. ISBN 0-9630106-0-1. Cloth. $195.

**Maitland, Frederick W., Montague, Francis C.,** *A Sketch of English Legal History.* Edited with Notes and Appendices by James F. Colby. New York: G.P. Putnam's Sons, 1915. x, 234pp. LCCN 98-11337. ISBN 1-886363-50-1. Reprinted 1998 by The Lawbook Exchange, Ltd. Cloth. $50.

**[Nichols, J.].** *A Collection of all the Wills, Now Known to Be Extant, of the Kings and Queens of England, Princes and Princesses of Wales, and every Branch of the Blood Royal, from the Reign of William the Conqueror, to that of Henry the Seventh Exclusive: With Explanatory Notes and a Glossary.* London: J. Nichols, 1780. x, 434 pp. Reprinted 1999 by The Lawbook Exchange, Ltd. LCCN 99-17114. ISBN 1-886363-87-0. Cloth. $75.

**Pollock, Frederick and Frederic William Maitland.** *The History of English Law before the Time of Edward I.* Cambridge: Cambridge University Press, 1898. Two volumes. xxxviii, 688; xiv, 691 pp. Reprinted 1996 by The Lawbook Exchange, Ltd. ISBN 1-886363-22-6. Cloth. $165.

**Merriam, C.E., Jr.** *History of the Theory of Sovereignty Since Rousseau.* New York: Columbia University Press, [1900]. x, [11]-233 pp. Reprinted 1999 by The Lawbook Exchange, Ltd. LCCN 98-32385. ISBN 1-886363-76-5. Cloth. $65.

**Reeve, Tapping. [1744-1823].** *The Law of Baron and Femme, of Parent and Child, Guardian and Ward, Master and Servant, and of the Powers of the Courts of Chancery; with an Essay on the Terms Heir, Heirs, Heirs of the Body. Third Edition, With Notes and References to English and American Cases by Amasa J. Parker and Charles E. Baldwin, Counselors-At-Law.* Albany: William Gould, 1862. xlvi, 677pp. LCCN 98-36057. ISBN 1-886363-58-7. Reprinted 1998 by The Lawbook Exchange, Ltd. Cloth. $75.

**Schwartz, Bernard, editor.** *The Code Napoleon and the Common-Law World. The Sesquicentennial Lectures Delivered at The Law Center of New York University December 13-15, 1954.* New York: New York University Press, 1956. x, 438pp. LCCN 98-34100. ISBN 1-886363-59-5. Reprinted 1998 by The Lawbook Exchange, Ltd. Cloth. $65.

**Schwarz, Philip J.** *Twice Condemned: Slaves and the Criminal Laws of Virginia, 1705-1865.* [Baton Rouge: Louisiana State University Press]. [1988]. xvi, 354pp. Reprinted 1998 by The Lawbook Exchange, Ltd. LCCN 98-4424 ISBN 1-886363-54-4. Cloth. $75.

**Tucker, Henry St. George.** *Commentaries on the Laws of Virginia. Comprising the Substance of a Course of Lectures Delivered to the Winchester Law School. With an Introduction by David Cobin and Paul Finkelman.* Richmond: Shepherd and Colin, 1846. Two volumes. 34, 468; 24, 512 pp. Reprinted 1998 by The

Lawbook Exchange, Ltd. LCCN 97-10313. ISBN 1-886363-26-9. Cloth. $175.

**Vinogradoff, Sir Paul.** *Outlines of Historical Jurisprudence.* London: Oxford University Press, 1920. Two volumes. 428; x, 315 pp. Reprinted 1999 by The Lawbook Exchange, Ltd. LCCN 98-42298. ISBN 1-886363-64-1. Cloth. $150.

**Walker, James.** *The Theory of the Common Law.* Boston: Little, Brown and Co., 1852. xxiv, 130pp. Reprinted 1998 by The Lawbook Exchange, Ltd. LCCN 98-9522. ISBN 1-886363-45-5. Cloth. $65.

**Warren, Charles.** *History of the Harvard Law School and of Early Legal Conditions in America.* New York: Lewis Publishing Company, 1908. Three volumes. xiv, 543; iv, 560; 397 pp. Illustrated. Reprint available September 1999 by The Lawbook Exchange, Ltd. LCCN 99-29193. ISBN 1-58477-006-6. Cloth. $275.

**Wiener, Leo.** *Commentary to the Germanic Laws and Mediaeval Documents.* Cambridge: Harvard University Press, 1915. lxi, 224 pp. Reprint available October 1999 by The Lawbook Exchange, Ltd. LCCN 99-23969. ISBN 1-58477-005-8. Cloth. $60.

## ☙ Legal Reference and Bibliography ☙

**Benedict, Russell.** *Acts and Laws of the Thirteen Original Colonies and States: Constituting the extraordinary collection of Hon. Russell Benedict.* New York: American Art Association, 1922. [272]pp. Reprinted 1998 The Lawbook Exchange, Ltd. LCCN 98-20196 ISBN 1-886363-56-0. Cloth. $85.

**Eller, Catherine Spicer.** *The William Blackstone Collection in the Yale Law Library. A Bibliographical Catalogue.* New Haven: Yale University Press, 1938. Reprinted 1993 by the Lawbook Exchange, Ltd. xvii, 113 pp. Cloth. LCCN 99-38826. ISBN 0-9630106-5-4. $40.

**Finkelman, Paul.** *Slavery in the Courtroom. An Annotated Bibliography of American Cases.* Washington:Library of Congress, 1985. Illustrated. xxvii, 312pp. Reprinted 1998 by The Lawbook Exchange, Ltd. LCCN 98-11284. ISBN 1-886363-48-X. Cloth. $85.

**Friend, William L.** *Anglo-American Legal Bibliographies. An Annotated Guide.* Washington, D.C.: United States Government Printing Office, 1944. xii, 166 pp. Reprinted 1996 by The Lawbook Exchange, Ltd. ISBN 1-886363-21-8. Cloth. $65.

**Hicks, Frederick.** *Men and Books Famous in the Law. With an introduction by Harlan F. Stone.* Rochester, New York: Lawyers Co-operative Publishing, 1921. 259 pp. Reprinted 1992 by The Lawbook Exchange, Ltd. LCCN 92-070809. ISBN 0-9630106-2-X. Cloth.$50.

**Jackson, E. Hilton.** *Latin for Lawyers. Containing I: A Course in Latin, with Legal Maxims and Phrases As a Basis of Instruction. II. A Collection of Over One Thousand Latin Maxims, with English Translations, Explanatory Notes, and Cross-References. III. A Vocabulary of Latin Words.* London: Sweet & Maxwell, 1915. viii, 300 pp. Reprinted 1992 by The Lawbook Exchange, Ltd. LCCN 92-074408. ISBN 0-9630106-4-6. Cloth. $50.

**McNamara, M. Frances.** *Ragbag of Legal Quotations.* Albany: Matthew Bender & Company, 1960. xi, 334 pp. Reprinted 1992 by The Lawbook Exchange, Ltd. LC 92-074141. ISBN 0-9630106-3-8. Cloth. $50.

**Maxwell, W. Harold and C.R. Brown.** *A Complete List of British and Colonial Law Reports and Legal Periodicals. Arranged in Alphabetical and in Chronological Order with Bibliographical Notes.* **[With]:** *Check List of Canadian and Newfoundland Statutes.*[Third Edition]. Toronto: The Carswell Company, Limited, 1937. viii, 141, 49 pp. Reprinted 1995 by The Lawbook Exchange, Ltd. ISBN 1-886363-11-0. Cloth. $70.

**[Worrall, John and Edward Brooke].** *Bibliotheca Legum Angliae. Or, a Catalogue of the Common and Statute Law Books of This Realm, and Some Others Relating Thereto: Giving an Account of Their Several Editions, Ancient Printers, Dates, and Prices, and Wherein They Differ. [With a Supplement to 1800]. Part I Compiled by John Worrall, Part II and Supplement Compiled by Edward Brooke. Parts I, II and Supplement bound in one volume.* London: Printed for Edward Brooke, 1788-1800. 316; 264; 48 pp. 1788-1800. Reprinted 1997 by The Lawbook Exchange, Ltd. ISBN 1-886363-29-3. Cloth. $110.

## ☙ Legal Sources ☙

**Bouvier, John. [1787-1851].** *Institutes of American Law. New Edition by Daniel A. Gleason. In Two Volumes.* Boston:Little, Brown, & Company, 1880. Two volumes. lxviii, 651; iv, 798pp. Reprint available December 1999 by The Lawbook Exchange, Ltd. LCCN 98-54288. ISBN 1-886363-80-3. Cloth. $265.

**[Cardozo, Benjamin].** *Law is Justice. Notable Opinions of Mr. Justice Cardozo.* Foreword by Robert F. Wagner. Edited by A.L. Sainer. New York: Ad Press Ltd., [1938]. xvii, 441 pp. Frontis. Reprint available September 1999 by The

Lawbook Exchange, Ltd. LCCN 99-34154. ISBN 1-58477-010-4. Cloth. $75.

**[Cherokee Laws].** *Compiled Laws of the Cherokee Nation.* Tahlequah, I.T.:National Advocate Print, 1881. 370pp. LC 98-12741. ISBN 1-886363-42-0. Reprinted 1998 by The Lawbook Exchange, Ltd. With a new introduction by Michael Weber. Cloth. $60.

**Fortescue, John.** *DeLaudibus Legum Angliae. A Treatise in Commendation of the Laws of England.* With Translation by Francis Gregor. Notes by Andrew Amos and a Life of the Author by Thomas (Fortescue) Lord Clermont. Cincinnati: Robert Clarke & Co., 1874. Reprint available September 1999 by The Lawbook Exchange, Ltd. LCCN 99-16485. ISBN 1-58477-019-8. Cloth. $65.

**[St. Germain, Christopher]. [1460-1540].** *The Doctor and Student or Dialogues Between a Doctor of Divinity and a Student in the Laws of England Containing the Grounds of Those Laws Together with Questions and Cases Concerning the Equity Thereof Revised and Corrected by William Muchall, Gent. to which are added two pieces concerning Suits in Chancery by Subpoena.* Cincinnati:Robert Clarke & Co., 1874. xiv, 401pp. Reprinted 1998 by The Lawbook Exchange, Ltd. LCCN 98-11338. ISBN 1-886363-49-8. Cloth. $65.

**Woodbine, George E.** *Four Thirteenth Century Law Tracts. A Thesis Presented to the Faculty of the Graduate Schol of Yale University in Candidacy for the Degree of Doctor of Philosophy.* New Haven: Yale University Press, 1910. vi, 183 pp. Reprint available October 1999 by The Lawbook Exchange, Ltd. LCCN 99-29294. ISBN 1-58477-007-4. Cloth. $50.

## *Legal Treatises*

**Beck, Theodric Romeyn.** *Elements of Medical Jurisprudence.* Albany: Websters and Skinners, 1823. Two volumes. xxxiv, 418; viii, [9]-471 pp. Reprinted 1997 by The Lawbook Exchange, Ltd. ISBN 1-886363-24-2. Cloth. $125.

**Freeman, A.C.** *A Treatise of the Law of Judgments. Including All Final Determinations of the Rights of Parties in Actions or Proceedings at Law or in Equity. Revised, and Greatly Enlarged by Edward W. Tuttle.* San Francisco: Bancroft-Whitney, 1925. Three volumes. 1216; 1280; 1264 pp. Reprinted 1993 by The Lawbook Exchange, Ltd. ISBN 0-9630106-6-2. Cloth. $295.

**Gilmore, Grant.** *Security Interests in Personal Property.* Boston: Little, Brown & Company, 1965. Two volumes. xxxiv, 651; xiii, 653-1508 pp. Reprinted

1999 by The Lawbook Exchange, Ltd. LCCN 99-10258. ISBN 1-886363-81-1. Cloth. $195.

**Pomeroy, John N.** *A Treatise on Equity Jurisprudence As Administered in the United States of America. Adapted for All the States and to the Union of Legal and Equitable Remedies under the Reformed Procedure.* San Francisco and New York: Bancroft-Whitney and Lawyers Cooperative, 1941. Five volumes. 914; 1134; 1063; 1104; 716 pp. Reprinted 1995 by The Lawbook Exchange, Ltd. ISBN 1-886363-05-6. Cloth. $450.

**Pothier, Robert Joseph [1699-1772].** *A Treatise on Obligations, Considered in a Moral and Legal View. Translated from the French of Pothier. Translated by Francois-Xavier Martin.* Newburn, N.C.: Martin & Ogden, 1802. Reprint available December 1999 by The Lawbook Exchange, Ltd. With a new introduction by Warren M. Billings. LC 98-38360. ISBN 1-886363-62-5. Cloth. $75.

**Sears, John H.** *Trust Estates as Business Companies. [Second Edition].* Kansas City, Mo.:Vernon Law Book Company, 1921. xx, 782 pp. [1921]. Reprinted June 1998 by The Lawbook Exchange, Ltd. LCCN 97-32423 ISBN 1-886363-41-2. Cloth. $95.

## ☙ Philosophy of Law ☙

**Fuller, Lon L.** *The Law in Quest of Itself.* Boston: Beacon Press, 1966. [vi], 150 pp. Reprint available October 1999 by The Lawbook Exchange, Ltd. LCCN 99-32863. ISBN 1-58477-016-3. Cloth. $45.

**Jhering, Rudolf Von.** *Law as a Means to an End.* Translated from the German by Isaac Husik with an Editorial Preface by Joseph H. Drake and with Introductions by Henry Lamm and W.M. Geldart. Boston: The Boston Book Company, 1913. lxi, 483 pp. Reprint available September 1999 by The Lawbook Exchange, Ltd. LCCN 99-23754. ISBN 1-58477-009-0. Cloth. $80.

**Jhering, Rudolph von.** *The Struggle for Law. Translated from the Fifth German Edition by John J. Lalor. Second Edition, with an Introduction by Albert Kocourek.* Chicago: Callaghan and Company, 1915. lii, 138 pp. Reprinted 1997 by The Lawbook Exchange, Ltd. ISBN 1-886363-25-0. Cloth. $60.

**Kelsen, Hans. [1881-1973].** *General Theory of Law and State.* Translated by Anders Wedberg. Cambridge: Harvard University Press, 1945. xxxiii, 516pp. LCCN 98-32334. ISBN 1-886363-74-9. Reprinted 1999 by The Lawbook Exchange, Ltd. Cloth. $75.

## ☙ Special Editions ☙

**Stokes, I.N. Phelps.** *The Iconography of Manhattan Island 1498-1909.* New York: Robert H. Dodd, 1915. Six volumes. Reprinted 1998 by The Lawbook Exchange, Ltd. LCCN 97-30604. ISBN 1-886363-30-7. Cloth. $750.

## ☙ U.S. Constitutional History ☙

**Bauer, Elizabeth Kelley.** *Commentaries on the Constitution 1790-1860.* New York: Columbia University Press, 1952. 400 pp. Reprinted 1999 by The Lawbook Exchange, Ltd. LCCN 98-45409. ISBN 1-886363-66-8. Cloth. $75.

**Beard, Charles A.** *The Supreme Court and the Constitution.* New York: The Macmillan Company, 1912. vii, 127 pp. Reprinted 1999 by The Lawbook Exchange, Ltd. LCCN 98-50368. ISBN 1-886363-78-1. Cloth. $45.

**Bondy, William.** *Separation of Governmental Powers in History, in Theory, and in the Constitutions.* New York: Columbia College, 1896. Reprinted 1999 by The Lawbook Exchange, Ltd. vi,[7]-185, [1] pp. LCCN 98-44994. ISBN 1-886363-65-X. Cloth. $65.

**Cooley, Thomas McIntyre.** *A Treatise on the Constitutional Limitations Which Rest Upon the Legislative Power of the States of the American Union.* [*1st edition*]. Boston: Little, Brown, and Co., 1868. xlvii, 720pp. Reprinted 1999 by The Lawbook Exchange, Ltd. LCCN 99-20589. ISBN 1-886363-92-7. Cloth. $95.

**Cooley, Thomas M.** *A Treatise on the Constitutional Limitations which Rest Upon the Legislative Power of the States of the American Union. Fifth edition.* Boston: Little, Brown, and Co., 1883. lxxxi, 886pp. Reprinted October 1998 by The Lawbook Exchange, Ltd. LCCN 98-12730. ISBN 1-886363-53-6. Cloth. $120.

**Dodd, Walter Fairleigh.** *The Revision and Amendment of State Constitutions.* Baltimore: The Johns Hopkins Press, 1910. xvii, 350 pp. Reprinted 1999 by The Lawbook Exchange, Ltd. ISBN 1-886363-73-0. Cloth. $65.

**Fisher, Sydney George.** *The Evolution of the Constitution of the United States. Showing That It Is a Development of Progressive History and Not an Isolated Document Struck Off at a Given Time or an Imitation of English or Dutch Forms of*

*Government.* Philadelphia: J.B. Lippincott, 1897. 398 pp. Reprinted 1996 by The Lawbook Exchange, Ltd. LCCN 97-41054. ISBN 1-886363-08-0. Cloth. $65.

**Flanders, Henry.** *An Exposition of the Constitution of the United States. Designed as a Manual of Instruction.* Philadelphia: E.H. Butler & Co., 1860. xii, 311 pp. Reprint available October 1999 by The Lawbook Exchange, Ltd. LCCN 99-31594. ISBN 1-58477-014-7. Cloth. $60.

**[Madison, James]. Hunt, Gaillard, Scott, James Brown.** *The Debates in The Federal Convention of 1787 Which Framed the Constitution of the United States of America.* New York: Oxford University Press, 1920. xcvii, [1], 731 pp. Reprinted 1999 by The Lawbook Exchange, Ltd. LCCN 98-51911. ISBN 1-886363-77-3. Cloth. $110.

**Minor, Raleigh C.** *Notes on the Science of Government and the Relations of the States to the United States.* [Charlottesville]: University of Virginia, 1913. x, 171 pp. Reprinted 1995 by The Lawbook Exchange,Ltd. ISBN 1-886363-09-9. Cloth. $40.

**Story, Joseph. [1779-1845].** *A Familiar Exposition of the Constitution of the United States: Containing a Brief Commentary on Every Clause, Explaining the True Nature, reasons, and Objects Thereof; Designed for the Use of School, Libraries and General Readers. With an Appendix, Containing Important Public Documents, Illustrative of the Constitution.* New York: Harper & Brothers: 1865. 372 pp. Reprinted 1999 by The Lawbook Exchange, Ltd. ISBN 1-886363-71-4. Cloth. $60.

**[Taylor, John]. [1753-1824].** *A Defence of the Measures of the Administration of Thomas Jefferson. By Curtius.* Washington: Samuel H. Smith, 1804. 136 pp. Reprinted 1999 by The Lawbook Exchange, Ltd. LCCN 99-24139. ISBN 1-886363-97-8. Cloth. $60.

**Taylor, John.** *Construction Construed and Constitutions Vindicated.* Richmond:printed by Shepherd & Pollard, 1820. iv, 344pp. Reprinted 1998 by The Lawbook Exchange, Ltd. LCCN 97-49411. ISBN 1-886363-43-9. Cloth. $65.

**Taylor, John.** *An Inquiry into the Principles and Policy of the Government of the United States.* Fredericksburg:Green and Cady, 1814. With an introduction by Roy Franklin Nichols, Yale University Press, 1950. 562pp. Reprinted 1998 by The Lawbook Exchange, Ltd. LCCN 98-11147. ISBN 1-886363-46-3. Cloth. $75.

**Tucker, St. George.** *Blackstone's Commentaries. With Notes of Reference to the Constitution and Laws, of the Federal Government of the United States, and of the*

*Commonwealth of Virginia. In Five Volumes, with an Appendix to Each volume, Containing Short Tracts upon Such Subjects As Appeared Necessary to Form a Connected View of the Laws of Virginia As a Member of the Federal Union.* Philadelphia: William Young Birch and Abraham Small, 1803. Five volumes. Reprinted 1996 by The Lawbook Exchange, Ltd. ISBN 1-886363-15-3. Cloth. $450.

**[Upshur, Abel Parker].** *A Brief Enquiry Into the True Nature and Character of Our Federal Government, being a review of Judge Story's Commentaries on the Constitution of the United States. By a Virginian.* Petersburg: Printed by Edmund and Julian C. Ruffin, 1840. 132pp. Reprinted 1998 by The Lawbook Exchange, Ltd. LCCN 97-11151. ISBN 1-886363-44-7. Cloth. $45.

**Wright, John S.** *Citizenship Sovereignty.* Chicago: Published for American Citizens, the True Maintainers of State Sovereignty, 1864. Reprinted 1998 by The Lawbook Exchange, Ltd. LCCN 98-15940 ISBN 1-886363-55-2. Cloth. $65.